Life

of

Marie-Marguerite Du Frost
de Lajemmerais, Widow d'Youville

Marie-Marguerite Du Frost de Lajemmerais, Widow d'Youville,
Foundress of the Sisters of Charity of the General Hospital of Montreal, Grey Nuns

Albertine Ferland-Angers

Mother d'Youville

First Canadian Foundress

Marie-Marguerite Du Frost de Lajemmerais, Widow d'Youville

1701-1771

Foundress of the Sisters of Charity
of the General Hospital of Montreal,
Grey Nuns

Translated
by
Richard R. Cooper

MONTREAL
Sisters of Charity of Montreal, "Grey Nuns"
2000

B
D'Youville
Fc

Table of Contents

List of Illustrations

Foreword

BIOGRAPHERS, both religious and lay have been captivated by the life of Saint Marguerite d'Youville, and since her death in 1771 many have attempted to grasp her spirituality, her social conscience, that which made her a Saint. Among the earliest were her son, Father Charles Dufrost, and a few priests of Saint Sulpice, in particular, Father Antoine Sattin. In our day, the renowned historian, Madame Albertine Ferland-Angers, a member of the Historical Society of Montreal, wrote this biography of *Mère d'Youville* in French. The book was published in 1945. At the beginning of the third millennium, I have the honour and privilege of presenting this English edition translated by Mr. Richard Cooper.

This detailed account of the life of Mother d'Youville includes many of her letters, which have never been translated into English. These letters reveal a woman who overcame not only insurmountable obstacles but also demonstrate the faithful love of a wife, a dedicated mother, a strong and committed widow, a fearless and compassionate foundress, a woman with a deep sense of justice, and an unshakeable love of Jesus Christ and the poor. Madame Marguerite-Marie du Frost de Lajemmerais, widow d'Youville, surrendered her title of nobility to stand with the voiceless, the unloved, the forgotten, the outcasts, and by her actions revealed that God is a Father who loves everyone unconditionally and without exception. To this day, she continues to inspire and invite not only the Sisters of Charity of Montreal, "Grey Nuns," and their sister Grey Nun Congregations as well as their associates, but also people from all walks of life who follow in her footsteps.

Marguerite d'Youville was beatified in 1959. Pope John XXIII recognized that she loved Jesus Christ and the poor to a heroic degree, and gave her the title: *"Mother of Universal Charity,"* thereby acknowledging that her love for others was inclusive and unconditional. On 9 December 1990, she was declared the first Canadian-born saint by Pope John Paul II. Her spirituality continues to captivate the hearts of people around the world.

We are grateful to all those who contributed to this edition, especially to Mr. Richard Cooper, who undertook the challenge of translating terminology from one era to another. His ability and experience as a translator bring to life the poignancy of the text which the reader will find enjoyable. His background in philosophy, religion, art and literature gives him a sensitivity and a way with words, enabling him to depict authentically the heart of Marguerite d'Youville, as portrayed by the author Madame Albertine Ferland-Angers.

You are invited to read this story of the history, culture and society of eighteenth century New France. It is a story about a valiant woman who made a difference. May you too, dear reader, be inspired to reach out to others in love.

Aurore Larkin s.gm.

Aurore Larkin, SGM
Superior General
Jubilee Year 2000

Preface by Cardinal Turcotte

I AM GRATEFUL to the Sisters of Charity of Montreal, "Grey Nuns" for inviting me to preface this English historical biography of Marie Marguerite d'Youville. Well-documented English biographies of the "Mother of Universal Charity" are rather scarce. The translation of this exceptional book about the first Canadian religious foundress will fill a real gap in the development of English religious history in New France. The preface to the original French edition, *Mère d'Youville, Première Fondatrice Canadienne* by Madame Albertine Ferland-Angers was written by a predecessor and remarkable pastor of this archdiocese, Archbishop Joseph Charbonneau, who spoke highly of this great historian and the quality of her book.

It also gives me great pleasure on the eve of celebrating in 2001 the three hundredth anniversary of Saint Marguerite d'Youville's birth to present this biography which will make her better known to an English population which includes historians and researchers. Those who delve into the detailed life of this pioneering servant and leader will discover a woman of action, totally confident in God's providential care. In turn, she was a mother, a widow, a religious who loved and served without distinction of race, creed, language, and colour during this crucial era of conflict and poverty in Montreal's eighteenth century. She remains for us a model of multiculturalism and ecumenism.

At the dawn of the twenty-first century with its scientific progress, there is a need to rediscover our heroes and role models. It is through their courageous work and their God-given gifts that our churches and country were built. Saint Marguerite d'Youville is a model for all walks of life. Her feminine qualities of gentleness and caring, her stamina and fortitude in the midst of turmoil and contradiction, her love of family and the poor reflect what Christ continues to tell us: "I assure you, as often as you did it for one of my least brothers and sisters, you did it to me!" (Mt 25:40). May many readers benefit from the life of this first Canadian saint!

Jean-Claude Turcotte

Jean-Claude, Cardinal Turcotte
Archdiocese of Montreal

Preface by Archbishop Charbonneau

THE TOURIST who travels along the south shore of the Saint Lawrence will see at Varennes, close to the river and facing the parish church, an elegant monument on the plinth of which can be read: "Marguerite d'Youville, Foundress and First Superior of the Sisters of Charity of the General Hospital of Montreal, called the Grey Nuns. She greatly loved Jesus Christ and the poor."

And there in a nutshell is the life of one of our heroines. It is that life which Madame Ferland-Angers is presenting to the public in this volume. We are very grateful to her; she has completed an interesting and useful work.

We know too little about the illustrious deeds of our ancestors, too little of the hidden acts of heroism that have yielded works by which society still lives and will do so more and more. In getting to know our history better, we will learn how to thank God for having sown so many noble hearts in our country and we will want to follow more closely the ideal that they have set for us.

Mother d'Youville has been justly compared to Marie de l'Incarnation and Saint Jeanne de Chantal. In her is to be found the example of virtues appropriate for every state of life.

As a young girl she turned to account the lessons of courage, honour, uprightness, and, above all, the Christian spirit that her ancestral home provided. As a boarder with the Ursulines of Quebec City, she left behind a reputation for piety and spiritual maturity well beyond her years. At the age of fifteen, she devoted herself to her widowed and impoverished mother, and through her handicrafts she guaranteed the sustenance of her brothers and sisters.

As a wife and mother she possessed the greatness of soul that breeds constant loyalty, deep devotion, and joy even in the midst of trials. As a widow she carried on simultaneously very heavy tasks for a woman already weakened by every kind of care.

In religion she found that which honour and the spirit of duty could scarcely have furnished her. She confided to God her daily problems.

As a member of the Confraternity of the Holy Family, she saw in the miseries of others an invitation to give herself; she overcame her natural repugnance and public opinion. Her charity brought slander upon her. But she cared little about the wagging of tongues. She found Jesus Christ in the poor. She remained faithful to God who was freely shaping her soul, hour by hour, for a great work.

Charity is not envious. Marguerite d'Youville desired for the people she gathered round herself her ideal of ardent charity. Little by little, the idea was taking shape of founding an Institute in which each member would promise to consecrate her time and even her life to work for the sustenance of the poor.

To a thousand other trials was added a painful illness. But Mother d'Youville's faith in Providence lifted her above everything. With joy she accepted poverty and the humiliating circumstances that often accompany it.

Is she not a model for all women who devote themselves completely to the works of charity? The grace of her manners and her gentleness attracted all classes. Ladies found her to be a wholly attentive and gracious hostess. At her touch orphans brightened up, the poor lost their shame, and prisoners succumbed to her moral influence.

Her wisdom, which presupposes in a high degree the gift of counsel, kept her calm amongst the weighty problems caused by an ill-advised policy. She bore ingratitude. She felt her heart wounded, but she manifested a loving submission to the designs of God.

Out of all the struggles, she emerged stronger in the practice of charity. "Go to the Grey Nuns," people said, "they never refuse anything."

By giving up herself completely to the divine action, Mother d'Youville succeeded in founding the Institute of the Grey Nuns to enlarge the field of charity.

Madame Ferland-Angers, in her beautiful work, depicts the various stages of the noble existence of Marguerite d'Youville. She wanted to let the facts speak for themselves. To this end, she scrutinized both private and public archives with a great care for the truth. This long work, which was pursued with intelligence and emotion, now allows us to follow Mother d'Youville step by step through the streets of Ville Marie in the unfolding of her many works of charity. The past elucidates the present.

To our congratulations and thanks, we add a wish: that many readers may profit from the apostolate of this work and may shape their souls in the image of the most charitable soul of Marguerite d'Youville; and that through their imitation of example and by their prayers, they may obtain from God the beatification of this friend of the poor.

† Joseph Charbonneau
Archbishop of Montreal
15 January 1945

Translator's Note

MADAME Albertine Ferland-Angers' *Mère d'Youville* was first published by the Librairie Beauchemin in Montreal in 1945 and reissued by the Centre Marguerite d'Youville in an only slightly modified photographic reproduction in 1977. Over the years there have been persistent requests from the English-speaking members of the Sisters of Charity, the Grey Nuns, for a translation of this work, which is the most comprehensive biography of their foundress. While there are a number of other lives of Saint Marguerite d'Youville, they are based for the most part on secondary sources. The great distinction of Madame Ferland-Angers' work is that she went directly to the archival sources, as she explains in her introduction, and indeed transcribed and reproduced a number of the primary documents. This is how first-class historical work is always done, and it is what makes a translation of Madame Ferland-Angers' book worthwhile even after more than fifty years, a time span in which most scholarly works would have long ago fallen into oblivion.

There are two main audiences for the present translation. As mentioned before, there is the large English-speaking group of Grey Nuns and their friends and supporters. But there is also the community of non-francophone scholars of Canadian history, for whom this book contains a wealth of material relating to the history of New France from the last decades of the seventeenth century through the period immediately following the British Conquest. For both these audiences, there are a number of terms that probably need to be explained. In line with the best contemporary translation practices, I have kept terms relating to forms of address, monetary units, and weights and measures in their original form. This is because it is quite misleading to pretend that these forms of expression have exact equivalents in twenty-first century English and can therefore be carried over into it without distortion. The primary task of the historian is to point out just how alien the past was; it is only afterwards that similarities can be noted. However, one also wants the reader to get through the text with relative ease and not to be distracted by what might seem to be oddities of terminology. I have, therefore, given below some brief explanations of the terms that have been left untranslated and some others that might present difficulties in understanding.

First, the terms used in eighteenth-century New France as *forms of address* are not greatly different from the contemporary forms of Monsieur, Madame, and Mademoiselle, although more frequently used are the older forms *Sieur*, *Dame*, and *Demoiselle* (often spelled *Damoiselle*), which carry more strongly the connotation that the people to whom they are applied belong to the gentry, if not to the nobility. The term *Seigneur* is used for a feudal landowner, and his particular kind of estate, a *seigneurie*, is distinctive of the kinds of great land holdings in New France. This whole feudal set-up is commonly referred to in Canadian history as the "seigneurial system."

Among the clergy the usual way of addressing a secular priest was *Monsieur*, rather than Père, or Father, as it is today. In the narrative part of the translation, I have generally used the modern term Father to avoid possible confusion. It may also be that the title Monsieur and its plural Messieurs, especially in reference to the Sulpicians, who were the Seigneurs of the Island of Montreal, connote that those to whom they were applied belonged to the First Estate.

There are a great many designations for the various *monetary units* that were in use during this period. The basic forms of money were the *livre, sol,* and *denier*. These words are derived from the Latin *libra, solidus,* and *denarius*. They correspond to the old British monetary units of pound, shilling, and pence, and were reckoned in the same way, with twelve pence (deniers) to the shilling (sol), twenty shillings to the pound (livre). The livre was in common use in Canada until the 1860's. It is always difficult to provide modern equivalents for the past value of money, though, generally speaking, during the period covered by this book the value of the livre was probably worth about $1.15 in present-day American money. A skilled workman's earnings in mid-eighteenth-century New France varied between approximately three and four livres a day.[1] The fall of New France to the British in 1759 brought about a monetary crisis, with the devaluation of French currency, as is reflected in many of Mother d'Youville's letters from that time. Another monetary term that is used quite commonly is *piastre*, which normally designates a major coin. The word is

---

1   J. W. Eccles, *Canada under Louis XIV, 1663-1701* (Toronto: McClelland and Stewart, 1964), p. 218, notes that a mason would have earned 3 livres, 10 sols a day, and a carpenter, 4 livres, 10 sols, or in mid-1960's Canadian currency, about $5.25 and $6.75.

interesting because it still survives in present-day Quebecois, usually in the form *piasse*, which refers to a dollar. Other foreign currencies are referred to in the text, for example, the *pistole* (a general term for French and foreign gold coins) and the British shilling (spelled as it would be pronounced in French *chelin*).

In the eighteenth century, particularly in New France, there was no exact equivalent of the modern banking system. Paper financial transactions were generally conducted by the use of *lettres d'échange* (bills of exchange), which could be seen as a kind of promissory note functioning somewhat as a cheque does today. Several other terms were used for paper transactions which I have generally translated as "draft notes" (*ordonnances*) or "notes" (*billets*).

The names and values of weights and measures also differed in the eighteenth century. In New France the common land measure was the *arpent*, used as an area measure equivalent to about one acre, or 3420 square metres, and as a linear measure of 190 feet, or approximately 58 metres. The arpent was used in the French-speaking areas of North America until the 1970's. Distance was measured in leagues, a variable measure, but usually about three miles, or 4.8 kilometres. The reader who is familiar with the British and American terminology for weights and measures in ounces and pounds, inches and feet will note the use in eighteenth-century French of corresponding terms, though not necessarily with exactly the same values.

There are a few other French words which have come to be commonly used in English Canada that may not be familiar to readers in other countries. For example, *fabrique* is the word used for a vestry or parish council. A *voyageur* was a canoeman employed by the merchants in Montreal to transport goods to and from the trading posts in the interior. For these and other examples the reader is referred to *The Canadian Oxford Dictionary* (1998).

In the Supporting Documents section at the end of the volume, there are a number of difficulties that the translator has had to face. Most of these texts are legal documents; and in French, as in English, there is a peculiar kind of crabbed legalese. This is particularly true of the documents drafted by the Royal Notaries. While trying to make these texts readable, I have also attempted to convey something of the flavour of the originals. In general, except where serious misunderstanding could have resulted, I have kept to the punctuation and capitalization of the originals (the latter often functions in lieu of punctuation). I have not, however, kept lower-case spelling of proper names, except in the few instances where it is used to show how a person signed his or her name. Modern spelling has been used throughout, except for proper names. In the latter case, I am continuing Madame Ferland-Angers' practice; spelling in the eighteenth century tended to be phonetic and can inform the scholar how the language was pronounced. Certain legal terms, such as "seizure *in esse*" (referring to the seizure of property but not of persons) and "arrière-fief" (land held by a vassal from an overlord who is himself a vassal), may need explication, but this can be found in any good legal dictionary or in a large English dictionary such as multi-volume *Oxford English Dictionary*.

A word should also be said about one of the commonest words in this book which may strike some readers as odd. The word "hospital" is used in its older English sense, meaning a shelter or place of refuge for those in need. It was not limited to the ill, as it is in contemporary French and English. Thus, the General Hospital of Montreal referred to in this book has nothing to do with the present-day institution with that same name.

In the Supporting Documents I encountered a few words that I could not find in any of the numerous dictionaries consulted. The context usually makes the meaning of these words clear, and I have therefore ventured a translation, but I have left the original French in square brackets. This can perhaps provide a contribution to the lexicography of North American French.

The reader will notice that there are two kinds of notes used in the text: brief footnotes are placed at the bottom of the page, while more extensive endnotes are grouped together in a section towards the end of the book. This corresponds to Madame Ferland-Angers' practice in the original version and allows the reader who does not wish to follow the more extensive scholarly details contained in the endnotes to ignore them. In this edition, footnotes have been indicated by Arabic numerals and endnotes by Roman numerals.

In translating Mother d'Youville's letters, I have been particularly indebted to translations of portions of these letters in Sister Mary Pauline Fitts' *Hands to the Needy: Marguerite d'Youville, Apostle to the Poor*.

As is the case with any translation, one owes much not only to books but also to other people for help. I should most especially like to thank the Grey Nuns of Montreal for their great assistance, particularly in pointing out the special usages of their Community. Special thanks go to Sister Jacqueline Saint-Yves, the initiator of this project, to Sister Alice Romanchuk, Sister Dorothy Cooper, Sister Marie

Bonin and Sister Estelle Mitchell as well as Sister Anne Mattappallil, Daughter of St-Paul for reading the manuscript of the translation and making many useful suggestions and corrections. For dealing with computer technicalities and for preparation of the final copy, thanks are due to Madame Monique Lamarche. The scanning and reproduction of the illustrations were skilfully handled by Monsieur Stéphane Gravel. For help with a number of technical and historical terms, thanks go to Dr. Paul Laverdure and to Monsieur Denis Lessard. As is customary to proclaim, all errors are the translator's own.

Richard R. Cooper
Montreal
February 2000

Albertine Ferland-Angers

BORN in Montreal, 15 March 1888, Madame Albertine Ferland-Angers studied with the Sisters of the Congrégation de Notre-Dame. She received a degree in literature from Laval University in 1918. In 1944 she was the first woman to be elected to the council of the Montreal Historical Society.

A diligent and patient worker she devoted five years to the present work, *Mother d'Youville: First Canadian Foundress*. For this book she won the Gold Medal of the Montreal Historical Society.

Besides being a carefully documented biography of Marguerite d'Youville, this volume also includes Mother d'Youville's extant letters, which show her to be both a wise and practical administrator and a woman filled with tenderness for her family and friends. Madame Ferland-Angers also transcribed and faithfully reproduced a number of valuable historical documents which are included at the end of this book.

Inspired by her brother, the poet Albert Ferland, Madame Ferland-Angers gave a series of lectures on Marguerite d'Youville, whom she described as a "great realizer" of visions. The admiration she felt for her can be clearly seen in her valuable historical writings.

Albertine Ferland-Angers died at the age of 84 in Sorel, Quebec, on 25 November 1972.

Rome – 3 May 1959
Blessed
Marguerite d'Youville

9 December 1990
Saint
Marguerite d'Youville

List of Abbreviations

ASGM   Archives des Sœurs Grises de Montréal
            [Archives of the Grey Nuns of Montreal]
AFND   Archives de la Fabrique de Notre-Dame de Montréal
            [Archives of the Fabrique of Notre-Dame Church,
            Montreal]
AJM   Archives Judiciaires de Montréal
            [Legal Archives of Montreal]
AV   Archives de la Paroisse de Varennes
            [Archives of the Parish of Varennes]
AAQ   Archives de l'archevêché de Québec
            [Archives of the Archdiocese of Quebec]
ASQ   Archives du séminaire de Québec
            [Archives of the Seminary of Quebec]
APQ   Archives de la province de Québec
            [Archives of the Province of Quebec –
            now Archives Nationales du Québec/National Archives
            of Quebec]
AJQ   Archives Judiciaires de Québec
            [Legal Archives of Quebec]
APC   Archives Publiques du Canada, Ottawa
            [Public Archives of Canada – now Archives Nationales
            du Canada/National Archives of Canada]
MD   Manuscrit de l'abbé Dufrost
            [Manuscript of the Abbé Dufrost]
SD   Supporting Documents
App.   Appendix
IOA   Inventaire des Œuvres d'Art de la province de Québec
            [Inventory of Works of Art of the Province of Quebec]

Introduction

IN THE GALLERY of those things that are most important to our country, there is a portrait that seemed to me in need of some restoration – that of Madame d'Youville. It is fading from our memory, and that is too bad. This thought often recurred to me when in the course of my research and discovery of documents, old registers, carefully kept letters, venerable portraits, and authentic relics there came to life before my eyes this great Canadian woman whose life is so closely bound up with the closing years of French rule in Canada. Monsignor Prohászka has written: "For me, a human being is little more than a larva until the person emerges from the cocoon woven out of thousands of threads of appearance and historical events." Contemplating this picture, in the light of the documents, was I alone able in hope and joy to trace out in these distant times the image, perhaps somewhat sketchy but always respectful of the truth, of our first Canadian foundress. The vision was beautiful; I have tried to fill in the details of the broad canvas. I can only hope that this humble work provides a glimpse of the marvellous Madame d'Youville.

In Canada, during the times when Madame d'Youville lived, the father's surname was passed on to the eldest son of the family, thus leaving the younger offspring to adopt another name. The example is well known of the seven sons of Charles Le Moyne de Longueuil, each of whom possessed a different surname. This custom has made of our Canadian annals real labyrinths for genealogists and historians. The sons of Madame d'Youville, both of whom were priests, were also known by different names. The elder, François, was known by the name d'Youville, while the younger, Charles-Madeleine, was called Dufrost, from the maiden name of his mother, Dufrost de Lajemmerais. He signed Dufrost, without a first name.

The Abbé Dufrost left a manuscript sketch of the life of his mother entitled *Memoranda towards a Life of Madame Youville, drawn mostly from the Depositions of Sisters Depeins, LaSource, Rinville, and Madame Gamelin, and another Sister.* And as though to justify his undertaking, he wrote immediately beneath the title: "Note: A number of respected people, not only among the clergy, but also among the laity, have given Madame Youville the title of valiant woman."

Since this manuscript bore no signature, it was necessary to establish its authenticity. This was done in 1884 by the experts entrusted with examining the documents destined for the Historical Commission for the Cause of Beatification and Canonization of Madame d'Youville. The following is their testimony from the *Investigative Process*, volume 1, p. 488, *Report of the Experts: Messrs. J. A. Cuoq, P. S. S., and H. A. Verreau, priest*:

> By virtue of the Commission conferred upon us by authorizing letters of His Excellency, the Bishop of Montreal, on the fourth of May in the present year of one thousand eight hundred and eighty-four, we have examined a number of documents remitted to us by Monsieur the Abbé Bonnissant, priest of Saint-Sulpice and postulator for the Cause of Beatification and Canonization of the Servant of God, Marie-Marguerite Dufrost de Lajammerais, the widow of Monsieur d'Youville.

II

We have examined two manuscript paper notebooks without signature. The first has as title: "Memoranda towards a Life of Madame Youville, etc." It consists of thirteen pages and is stamped A-B. The handwriting is neat.

The title of the second notebook is "The Life of Madame Youville etc., etc." It consists of thirty-one pages and is stamped A-C. The handwriting is careless, with numerous erasures and reference-marks that lead us to believe that it is the first draft of what would have been a considerable work had it been finished.

We first considered the external signs of age. The paper of A-B bears the watermark of an old English manufacturer. That of A-C has no watermark, but these two kinds of paper are of a texture and manufacture that are no longer sold, at least in Canada. The ink and paper have assumed the yellowish tint that is almost invariably to be found in old documents.

Secondly, we have admitted and we do state that each of these notebooks was written in its entirety by the same person without the appearance of any erasure or addition by another hand.

Comparing the two notebooks we therefore declare that they were both written in their entirety by one and the same person. We have established this identity by the shape and general appearance of the handwriting, which would be adequate proof for anyone sufficiently acquainted with manuscripts. We also identified specific traits, which we discuss below.

Thirdly, we compared both notebooks A-B and A-C with the Register of baptisms, marriages, and burials of the parish of Boucherville. The Acts in this Register from 12 May 1774 to July 1781 were almost all written and signed by Monsieur Charles Madeleine Dufrost, who was the son of the Servant of God and parish priest of Boucherville. These are legal acts that can stand as testimony in both the civil and ecclesiastical courts.

In these Acts, written down from day to day, sometimes with care and sometimes in haste, it was ascertained that the shape and general appearance of the handwriting are always the same.

Moreover, we established specific identifying traits such as the shape of the letter "r," which has a particularly marked shape in the middle of words. The same is true, though to a lesser degree, with the letters "s" and "f," especially when they are doubled. Fairly often, an acute accent mark that belongs above the letter "e" is rendered as a grave accent in words in which it is impossible that the writer could have been mistaken by a wrong pronunciation.

We have been led by both these specific and general identifying traits to establish that notebooks A-B and A-C were written by this venerable priest.

Consequently, we declare that they are authentic and whole. If it were necessary to assign an approximate date to them, the appearance of the handwriting would suggest the years 1777 to 1780.

III

The third document submitted to us was a small quarto, paper notebook consisting of vi and 181 pages and entitled "Life of the Widow, Madame Youville, Foundress and First Superior of the General Hospital." It bears no author's name, but can be attributed to Father Sattin, priest of Saint-Sulpice and chaplain of said hospital.

We compared the handwriting of this notebook and that of the numerous acts written and signed by Father Sattin in the Register of baptisms and burials of the General Hospital. The general and specific characteristics leave no doubt about the identity of the handwriting of the "Life" and that of the Register. Among the specific traits are the shape of the capital letters "F" and "T" and constant use of capital "L" in the middle of sentences. We have discovered no interpolation in this Life. We, therefore, declare it to be authentic and whole.

Signed: J. A. Cuoq, P.S.S., peritus
A. Verreau, p. Expert.

More recently, in 1937, the two Dufrost notebooks as well as several pages covering a number of different years from the Boucherville Register were photographed. After a comparative examination, other experts reached the same conclusion as Fathers Cuoq and Verreau.

The Abbé Dufrost gives the names of his informants. The following are the death dates of each of them: Madame Ignace Gamelin died 10 April 1789; Sister Rainville, 29 November 1783; Sister Despins, 6 June 1792; Sister La Source, 14 September 1778. Since Sister La Source was apparently consulted, the manuscript must be earlier than 1778. I have adopted the Abbé Dufrost as my guide and have used his work as a canvas on which to depict the contents of the present volume.

The manuscript of Father Sattin is likewise unsigned, but is dated 1828. Moreover, the fly-leaf bears in her frequently identified handwriting, the following testimony of the Reverend Mother McMullen, Superior General of the Institute: "This Life was written by the hand of our most honoured Father Sattin, Sr McM." Father Antoine Sattin, priest of Saint-Sulpice, was chaplain of the Grey Nuns from 1818 until 1836, the year of his death.

There are numerous unsigned works in Canadian writing of the period. The Abbé Etienne-Michel Faillon, priest of Saint-Sulpice and author of a number of considerable works on Canada, signed none of his books. Nor did the Abbé François Daniel, likewise a Sulpician, sign his *History of the Great French Families of Canada.* Thus, the Abbé Sattin was following a Sulpician tradition of the period.

Although I have followed the Abbé Dufrost, I have not neglected to consult the work of the erudite Father Faillon, which contains the greatest number of details and is, above all, the most carefully documented. His biography of Madame d'Youville, published by Mame in Tours in 1852, is indispensable to anyone wishing to get to know the foundress of the Grey Nuns.

Still, in spite of these estimable guides, I wished to go directly to the sources and consult the various public and private archives. I was welcomed most warmly in the public archives; it is a pleasure to acknowledge the great kindness of Major Gustave Lanctôt, Assistant Minister and Head of the Public Archives of Canada in Ottawa, and his assistants, Messrs. Norman Fee and Lucien Brault; as well as the assistance of Maître E. Z. Massicotte, LL.B., D. ès L., Head of the Legal Archives of Montreal; and of Messrs. Pierre-Georges Roy, D. ès L., and Antoine Roy, D. de l'Université de Paris, successive heads of the Archives of the Province of Quebec.

For a lay person, there were some difficulties encountered about consulting the private archives of the seminaries. Their archivists, however, found a way of removing the obstacles; and it is with a full awareness of their great courtesy, that I thank Canon J. Eugène Moreau, the Provincial Superior of Saint-Sulpice; Monsignor Paul Bernier, in 1942 Chancellor of the Metropolitan Curia of Quebec and afterwards Permanent Secretary of the Canadian Conference of Bishops in Ottawa; the Abbé Arthur Maheux, Archivist of the Seminary of Quebec, and his assistant, the Abbé Honorius Provost.

At the Grey Nuns in Montreal, the archives were fully open, and I was able to explore them in complete freedom. It is with great emotion that one handles authentic documents that the hands of holy people have previously touched. I thank very warmly the Reverend Mothers of the General Council of the Grey Nuns for having honoured me with their trust by allowing me to work in their so very well-ordered archives. I wish to assure them that if in this biography I have restrained my praise, it is not for want of enthusiasm, but rather to give rein to the eloquence of the facts contained therein. I have presented Mother d'Youville as the documents show her and as her works, supporting the documents, complete the picture. If I have quoted her so many times, it is because I believe the voice of her soul is worth more than any paraphrase.

Mother d'Youville is about to cross the threshold of the cloister and, as a noble ancestor full of captivating charm, visit us today.

Montreal, 1944

Montreal

*L*IKE a flower cast upon the waves, Montreal rises from the clear waters of the Saint Lawrence River. Mount Royal towers over the Laurentian valley, spreading a mantle of green over its gentle heights and offering on its geological shelves sheltered sites for the city and suburbs down to the irregular banks of the great river.

Montreal – city unique in your origins, one of history's mystical intersections! Even in the time of the Iroquois, you were aware of your glory. Around the solemn campfires, the standing Elders chanted your fabulous renown to the young warriors. What did you do in those distant times to merit the honour of becoming the special domain of the Virgin Mary?

In your heroic hours, you were the bulwark of the colony. A great city now, you were once only a crossroads on the fur-trade route. And, then, one dark day you had to burn your proud flags covered with fleurs de lys, but you became the city of a hundred steeples.

Rest in peace, La Dauversière, Olier, Maisonneuve, all you Gentlemen and Ladies of the Society of Notre Dame, who have revealed to us the noble secret of your generosity. It is not in vain that your apostolic project was enveloped in prayer. Montreal can count among its outstanding saintly citizens: Jeanne Le Ber, who from her birth seemed to be protected and guided by angels, and the courageous, compassionate Marguerite d'Youville who arose in a most difficult era when the very foundations of the Canadian Church were threatened.

CHAPTER 1

Varennes, Quebec

"Canada is little more than an entangled forest of all sorts of trees and plants wedged between mountains, lakes, and rivers." Memorandum of Monsieur de Catalogne to the Minister, 7 November 1712 (APC, GC, Series F, vol. 33)

U NTIL 1734 the Saint Lawrence was the main highway between Quebec City and Montreal. It was a primitive passageway running like a corridor through the forest in a virgin land that people still dreamed of making into a new France. The colonists' axes had cut gaps in the dense woods along its banks, and here and there on the horizon a steeple's silver spire mingled with the jagged, green line of conifers, thus disclosing the attempts at colonization. The life of the colonists was closely tied to this great, moving artery. The churches looked out on it, and the manor houses of the domains that stretched back into the depths of the forests gave onto it. Along the dark, rippling waters of its banks glided the treacherous Iroquois canoe, while our travellers paddled out in the open to the rhythm of cheerful Canadian songs that echoed back and forth their exuberant joy in being alive. On certain special days, government officials passed in solemn procession and the whole countryside filled with a common curiosity was on the lookout for them.

On the south bank of the Saint Lawrence about twenty miles from Montreal was the seigneury of Varennes, a grant of twenty-eight arpents of frontage by a league and a half in depth. René Gaultier de Varennes, originally from Bécon near Angers, Seigneur of Varennes and Tremblays, Officer of the Regiment of Carignan, Knight of the Order of Saint Louis, Governor of Trois Rivières for twenty years, had married Marie Boucher de Boucherville, daughter of the first Canadian to be ennobled. On 18 January 1701, their daughter, Marie-Renée de Varennes, married Christophe Du Frost de la Gesmerays, a lieutenant in the troops. Lieutenant Du Frost de la Gesmerays was entering one of the most notable Canadian families, one connected with the descendants of the oldest French nobility. He was in fact becoming the kinsman of the families of Varennes, Le Gardeur de Tilly, Marganne de la Valtrie, Sabrevois de Bleury, Hertel de Rouville, and De Muy, all names renowned in our military history. He was also becoming the brother-in-law of the famous explorer Pierre Gaultier de la Vérendrye.[1]

---

1   The younger branch of the Varennes family bore the name of La Vérendrye.

Arriving in the country as a simple Marine Guardsman (*Garde de la Marine*),[2] he fought alongside his illustrious relatives; and within this elite of brave men he still found a way of distinguishing himself, for he fairly rapidly attained the ranks of sub-lieutenant, lieutenant, and captain, the last being the highest rank attainable in the colonial troops. As the commander or adjutant of a number of expeditions, his exploits were brought to the attention of the Minister. Among other achievements, in 1697 when he was commanding the important fort of Catarakoui by his wisdom and cool-headed control he was able to outmanoeuvre the famous and dreaded Onondaga chief Chaudière Noire (Black Cauldron) at a critical moment when the Five Nations were engaged in negotiations with the Governor, Count de Frontenac. This timely success significantly increased the negotiating power of the French, much to the satisfaction of the Governor.

Lieutenant Christophe Du Frost de la Gesmerays was the son of Christophe Du Frost[3] and the Lady Marguerite de La Forest. In 1669 the Chamber established by the king for the Reform of the Nobility declared that the Du Frost de la Gesmerays were "noble and of noble descent from all antiquity and are upheld to possess the right to bear the title of Esquire, to have stamped coat of arms and escutcheon, with the privilege of a burial niche and three emblazoned tomb stones in the church of Médréac, and the right to an escutcheon in the main window behind the high altar." The coat of arms of the Du Frost family were, on a silver ground, three sable cocks' heads, crested and barbed gules; those of the La Forest family were, on a silver ground, an azure band with three silver stars.

Belonging to the elder branch of the Du Frost, Christophe was born 21 December 1661 in the Gesmerays[4] castle in the parish of Médréac in the former diocese of Saint Malo, now Rennes, the county of Ille-et-Vilaine in Brittany. The eldest son of the Du Frosts bore the title Sieur des Chapelles, the domain of the same name in Irodouër, which reverted to him by birthright. It remained for the younger sons to embrace military careers.

On 8 September 1700, three years after the Treaty of Ryswick, the Governor of New France, Monsieur de Callières, signed in Montreal a peace treaty with the chiefs of the Five Nations. In July of the following year, ambassadors from the native tribes of the West came to affix their

---

2   The *Gardes de la Marine* [Marine Guardsmen] had to be "unquestionably noble."

3   The name is pronounced Du Fro.

4   An interesting detail for Canadians is that the domain of the Gesmerays was only about ten leagues from the castle of Pontbriand in the diocese of Pleurtuit, not far from Dinard, where Bishop Du Breuil de Pontbriand, the sixth bishop of Quebec, grew up.

marks to the same treaty, thus sealing the "Great Peace of Montreal," the only one that was not broken. At last, a period of calm followed the horrors of the sixty years of the Iroquois Wars. Normal life was resumed in the country manors now that surprise Iroquois attacks were no longer feared.

By the marriage contract that was "made and done in one of the halls of the seignieurial house of Varennes, where the said Lady of Varennes dwells, in the year one thousand seven hundred and one, on the tenth day of January before midday," Marie-Renée Gaultier de Varennes brought a dowry of one plot of land extending up to the shore, adjoining the site of the church, on the seigneury of Varennes.[i] This was to become the foundation of the future home.

Even though the younger sons of noble families arrived in Canada without an inheritance, at least they brought with them the splendour of beautiful manners; and in the manor houses of the new country proper behaviour flourished. Besides, at Varennes, the rare spirit of religion dominated. This was due to the grandfather, Pierre Boucher, Sieur de Grosbois,[ii] who by his own admission had established his seigneury of Boucherville "to have in this land a place consecrated to God where people of property can live in peace and the inhabitants can dedicate themselves to God in a way distinctively their own." It was in this well-bred and openly Christian setting that the six children of the happy Lajemmerais household would be born.

The eldest daughter of this notable family, Marguerite, to whom God would grant one of his greatest blessings, that of founding a religious community in his Church, was born 15 October 1701. The following day she was carried to the baptismal font by her aunt and godmother Gaultier de Varennes who named her Marie-Marguerite.[iii] Her godfather was her uncle, Jacques-René de Varennes.

From year to year, a little boy or girl increased the size of the family until there were six, charmingly linked hand in hand – six new souls that the environment would fashion in its own image. Were not their courage, sense of honour and integrity the fruit of their education and milieu as well as their heritage? In this society in which all the leaders were military men, there was naturally a great deal of interest in the exploits of the king's troops. These were the main topic of the conversations that the children secretly overheard – these, and the latest news from France. The first ships to arrive in the spring always brought exciting news: the Dauphin had been ill, a prince had been born, the Dauphine was well, the King was at war… In the church, official prayers were said for the Dauphin, a *Te Deum* lauded the King's victories, while public festivities celebrated the birth of princes. In young hearts, loyalties took root, pride awakened. They believed themselves to be nearly of royal lineage by having come thus close to distant royalty.

On the great feast days, there was a good deal of rivalry in entertaining. At visits and receptions, the young people had not only to be good, but also to know how to curtsey and bow gracefully and to dance the minuet in imitation of the adults. Then everyday life would begin again. On some evenings at bedtime, gently caressing and rocking the little brown head snuggled in his arms, this father whom they thought to be all powerful would kneel and solemnly begin to say "Our Father, who art in heaven …" Above the fireplace and just below the crucifix, the father's sword reflected glimmers of the candle flames. The cross and the sword – these two symbols became engrained in the soul. All these various impressions contributed to the character development of these happy children. Little by little, Marguerite was developing a loyal and courageous soul that circumstances would very soon rudely jolt.

She was barely seven years old when the unexpected death of her father on 1 June 1708 plunged her mother into insurmountable financial difficulties. The salary of a captain of the troops would perhaps have been adequate for the needs of a young family, but not for establishing a fortune. Thus there began for the widow a period of insecurity, uncertain favours and the ever-present threat of poverty.[5] Nevertheless, through relations and friends, she was able to get her eldest daughter admitted to the boarding school of the Ursulines in Quebec City. This was a famous school attended by the female elite of the colony.[iv] The admissions register of the Ursulines still contains the following attestation: "9 August 1712 – Mademoiselle Marguerite Lagemerais was admitted as boarder." There she stayed for two years, making her first Communion and leaving behind a reputation for piety and spiritual maturity far beyond her years. A robust young girl, at twelve she appeared to be fifteen.[6] After she had returned to Varennes, she not only applied herself to the domestic tasks, but also, as her son assures us, it was from that time that she was seen to be making every effort through assiduous work "to earn what was necessary for her brothers and sisters to survive." How one wishes that the Abbé Dufrost had been more loquacious! What kind of work was being referred to? The sentence does not suggest something done outside the home. Most likely, it would have been one of the household arts of the time – sewing or embroidery. Indeed,

---

5   The fiefs that the king had so generously carved out of the thick Canadian forest were hardly capable of supporting a minimal existence. The case of Madame de Lajemmerais was not unique. In a letter to the Minister, Monsieur de Denonville wrote: "I am obliged to report the extreme poverty of a large number of families, all noble, who have been reduced to beggary…"

6   Cf. MD.

everything was embroidered, from slippers to gentlemen's coats as much as ladies' scarves and trimmings. It is understandable that these requirements of elegance could put bread on the table. Marguerite assumed so well her selfless role of big sister that her brothers and sisters retained throughout their lives the lively affection she had inspired in them during these diffi-cult years of childhood. For her then virtue had only one name – duty.

At the age of eighteen, Marguerite was maturing into a beautiful young woman. A rosy complexion, regular features, beautiful brown eyes that were lively and penetrating, a slender figure, and an air of nobility, all these made her breathtaking.[7] And truly, she had need of these natural charms since they were her only dowry. Fortunately, in the Canada of that time birth counted for more than fortune. We know what she had inherited from her father and mother. Also, at about that time, there was the possibility of a quite honourable marriage for Marguerite; but then her mother, after twelve years of struggling with poverty, decided to remarry. Without telling anyone, she married an Irish doctor, Timothy Sullivan, who, according to public opinion, was unqualified in several senses of the word. By the same stroke, the unfor-tunate mother destroyed the marriage plans of her eldest daughter, the fiancé's family definitely refusing to admit the Irish immigrant into their ranks. Marguerite strongly felt this humiliation, which was the first of a whole litany that the misalliance of her mother would inflict upon the entire family. Even today, for the curious investigator fer-reting in the legal annals of Montreal, there can still arise scandalous echoes of the inopportune furies of this doctor who beat up people, his wife included, on the least pretext and of the rowdy exploits for which he was often dragged before the tribunal.

In the second year of their marriage, Mr. and Mrs. Sullivan moved into a house that Madame de Varennes owned in the Rue Saint Vincent in Montreal. Soon a young Montrealer asked for the hand of Mademoiselle de Lajemmerais in marriage and was accepted. He was François d'Youville, the son of the Sieur de La Découverte.[v]

Pierre You, Sieur de La Découverte, originally from La Rochelle, had his first military experience alongside the Cavelier de La Salle in the dan-gerous expeditions that resulted in the discovery of Louisiana. These explo-rations made men: the weak perished, the soldiers of fortune became entrenched in their lack of discipline, and the bold returned from them filled with ambition. Pierre You left a simple soldier and came back an officer. The son of a mason, he reappeared a gentleman, having adopted

---

7   Cf. MD.

the name Sieur de La Découverte under the privilege accorded to discoverers by the king. After serving as a subaltern in various posts in the West, he was discharged and took up residence in Montreal. As he was enterprising and ambitious, he soon became a trusted friend of the Governor General, the Marquis de Vaudreuil, quickly made a fortune, and died at Montreal on 28 August 1718.[vi]

Marguerite thus contracted a marriage which, if it was not brilliant, was at least acceptable; for even though François d'Youville was the son a parvenu, he still possessed a fortune. According to the marriage contract, he contributed to the common estate the sum of four thousand livres, in addition to his inheritance, and he settled a jointure of six thousand livres on his future wife who, moreover, had the right to a preference legacy of a thousand livres in furniture or money in addition to her rings and jewels, as well as a bed and its fittings valued at two hundred livres. For the age, this was magnificent. On the eve of the wedding, there was a glittering gathering of friends at the house of the fiancée's mother for the signing of the contract. The Marquis de Vaudreuil presided and signed the document along with no less than thirty other distinguished witnesses. The clouds were being swept clear of Marguerite's sky, and the framework of her future was beginning to appear on her bright blue horizon.

Coat of arms of the Du Frost de la Gesmerays family

Coat of arms of the Gaultier de Varennes family

CHAPTER II

A Withered Bridal Bouquet

Supposed portrait of François-Magdeleine You d'Youville (1700-1730), husband of Madame d'Youville. Painting conserved in the Château de Ramezay, Montreal

François youville

Water-colour of Place Royale about 1842. The house where Madame d'Youville lived is indicated by an X.

B LESS, O LORD, this ring …" [vii] The wedding ring represents the mystical joining of souls; it is a ring of gold, the first link in a new relationship. In the first Church of Notre Dame, [viii] still without a façade or bell-tower, on 12 August 1722, François d'Youville, with the blessing of the Vicar General of the Diocese, placed the wedding band on the finger of Marguerite Du Frost de Lajemmerais, thus sealing their destiny.

François proudly brought to the home of his mother this beautiful young woman of real nobility who gave him a new social status in Canadian society.

Madame You de la Découverte lived at the very heart of the city on the east side of Place d'Armes, or the Market Square [now Place Royale], between Capitale and Saint Paul streets. [ix] Twice a week on this square a produce market was held, and there were large annual fairs where temporary shops were set up. The fur fairs resembled a carnival with their colourful spectacle and the lively streets crowded with the motley trappers, the picturesque bush-rangers, the Indians daubed with paint, the soldiers in white uniforms with leggings up to their knees, [x] and the merchants coming from every corner of the colony for the occasion. The voyageurs' liberality made these times of abundance that enabled the citizens to pay off all kinds of debts.

Thus Marguerite entered right away into the city's activities, an interesting change from the monotonous existence of the little fort of Varennes. She brought to the misanthropic widowhood of her mother-in-law the dash of her youth, the charm of her refinement, and her good will. She could not suspect that the old woman from Burgundy wanted nothing of these superfluities. This woman, who sued her son-in-law for the board of her own grandchild, a little girl orphaned at birth, understood only one language – that of penny pinching.

The only portrait we possess of Madame d'Youville is a funerary portrait, the work of a sculptor trying his hand at painting. It shows a woman in her seventies withered from work and hardship and struck down by apoplexy. It is far from the warm flesh, clear eye, and liveliness of a twenty year old. But let us believe her son who was not afraid to put forward the idea that she was one of the beautiful women of her time. He added that she liked good company, the pleasures of entertaining, and the elegance appropriate to her rank. These sentiments of her age and culture clashed with the most grasping passion of all – avarice, which the Great Apostle calls an idolatry.

One might want to define a young married woman as illusion on the arm of Destiny. If Marguerite had dreamed of an existence of ease based on the fortune of her fiance, she soon found out that she had moved from the constraints of poverty to those of parsimony, which presided – in the person of her mother-in-law – over her new home. These little asides sketch out an elementary feminine psychology. And it is face to face with this stingy sixty-year-old woman, in this home without gaiety or comfort, that she awaits the birth of her first child.

It is not without amazement that one reads in the baptismal entry for her first born, François-Timothée: "The father was absent." Absent … what a tragedy! It was a time of midwives and courage was the only known anaesthetic. After the throes of childbirth, not to have even the lowly reward of a tender glance, not to have the happiness of seeing the husband's pride burst forth before the first cradle! She was alone at this supreme hour of her life, alone with her maternal joy. A soon vanished joy, for her first child lived only three months. Like a quickly fading flower, four of Madame d'Youville's six children scarcely had time to smile at their mother before joining the angelic hosts. The "bitter tears" of which her son speaks perhaps sprang out of rebellion or discouragement. We may be mistaken about her intimate reactions during the sad years of her marriage, but these cradles emptying so rapidly one after the other disclose a wretched way of life.

❧

In the Lake of Two Mountains, a short distance from the island of Montreal, is Ile-aux-Tourtes, which in 1704 belonged to the seigneury of the Marquis de Vaudreuil, then Governor General of the country. On this island, the Priests of Saint-Sulpice had established a mission for the resident Nipissing Indians, and Monsieur de Vaudreuil had opened a trading post looked after by a contractor. At the beginning, from 1704 to 1718, this contractor was the Sieur de La Découverte. Pierre You de La Découverte, who strongly favoured the alcohol trade, defied all the regulations concerning it and by his keenness for gain had soon made himself odious to all honest people. His sons Philippe and François assisted their father in his trade and usually resided at his homestead at the end of the island next to the fort of Senneville. This distance from the city was congenial to their excursions into the forest in search of illegal trade. Trained to be fearless and protected by the Governor, François d'Youville was following in the steps of his father when he succeeded him as contractor in 1718. Not content with trading just with the Nipissing, he inspected the boats coming down river, thus making sure that he maintained his monopoly on the trade. The indignant city merchants protested loudly; the Governor of Montreal had eventually to report the matter to the Minister of Marine in a letter dated 15 October 1723. Monsieur de Ramezay wrote:

> About three months ago I had the honour of representing to [Monsieur de Vaudreuil] with due respect and humility that all the citizens and merchants of this country have lodged a complaint with him about the notorious business carried on by the Sieur d'Youville on Isle-aux-Tourtes by detaining there not only the resident natives, but also the Outaouais and those coming to trade in Montreal, so that the citizens and merchants find themselves deprived of doing any business, and honest people are oppressed. I have the honour of representing to you, My Lord, that before the Marquis de Vaudreuil farmed out his trade on Isle-aux-Tourtes, every year a hundred canoes came here, at least eighty of which were trading. There was a kind of fair. The merchants retailed their goods and the farmers their produce, so that everyone profited. This year only four canoes came down to Montreal. The Sieur d'Youville had detained them all at the Island, having for this purpose a sergeant and six soldiers whose job it was to inspect all the canoes coming down and constrain them to go to Isle-aux-Tourtes where only wine and spirits are traded. This he has also done in preceding years, and the merchants have complained to the Marine Council, but to no avail, since no one wrote about the situation to the Court.
>
> About the 10th of July the Nipissings who live on Isle-aux-Tourtes came to Monsieur de Vaudreuil and presented him with a necklace, by which they meant to tell him: "Father, we have come to tell you that we cannot pray to God because of Youville, who holds the trading contract for Isle-aux-Tourtes, every day we are drunk and we have drunk up all our furs, so much so that we ought to be pitied, being completely naked, without shirts or rags to cover us or ammunition to hunt with. Every morning he comes into our huts with wine and spirits and says to us, 'You have a good father, he wants you to drink his milk,' referring to Monsieur de Vaudreuil. And he always gets us drunk as long as we have furs, so that the missionary who teaches us to pray to God, finding us out of our minds, has got

angry and says that he doesn't want to teach us any more. So, we have come to give you this necklace, Father, to tell you that we want to pray to God and that if you do not drive Youville away from Isle-aux-Tourtes, we will not go there any more."[1]

Perhaps François d'Youville could thumb his nose at public opinion, but his wife, surrounded by people whose legitimate claims had been wronged, had to undergo more than one humiliation. Both her heart and her honour suffered, for this money so brutally acquired was foolishly spent on debaucheries. A poor interior to his house, a meagre table, a wife chained to the cradle, none of these things could restrain François' swaggering nature. There was no thrill of adventure in them. And Marguerite found herself being more and more neglected.

But in 1725 the wheel of fortune turned. Monsieur de Vaudreuil died, and d'Youville lost the impunity of his position. We know, however, that he continued to traffic for his business because the records of the voyageurs' pawning preserved in the registers of the royal notaries allow us to trace his activities.

Then, Madame de La Découverte was borne to her grave. At last, was Marguerite going to find herself in a better situation? Unfortunately, since her husband had slipped into indifference, loneliness came to take the place of the vanished old kill-joy. On the lonely evenings in the house on Place d'Armes, what thoughts haunted the mind of Marguerite? Rocking her last born child near the hearth, what did she see in the dancing flames – the flaring up of her dreams or the shades of her sorrows? It is a mystery … One day she will write to her nephew this impression tinged with regret: "The perfect harmony that I see between dear Josette, you, and your brother enchants me. Is there a greater happiness in life than that of a united household? Can all the wealth in the world approach it?"

Saint Francis de Sales, the chief spiritual guide for married people, writes in his metaphorical style: "There are some fruits, like the quince, which owing to the bitterness of their juice are not very useful for preserves … Likewise, women should hope that their husbands be preserved with the sugar of devotion, for a man without devotion is a cruel animal, harsh and rude."[2] If only François d'Youville had had a little of this devotion. In his portrait we see a man dressed for the evening in a velvet coat and lace ruff, with powdered hair tied at the nape of his neck with a ribbon.[3] He

---

1   Cf. APC, C 11A, vol. 45.

2   *Introduction to the Devout Life*, III, chap. 38.

3   In Canada, men wore their hair tied back in a ponytail until about 1830.

is a handsome man. Since reason has nothing to do with the enchantment of the senses, his handsome face might well have carried away the innocent heart of a young girl. What woman's love is completely free of vanity?

Freed from the maternal yoke and in possession of a rich inheritance, François played the role of the rich, young lord. He frequented the drawing-room parties to which his prodigality was the key. At that time, games of chance, and especially cards, were all the rage of the would-be rich. It appears that gambling swallowed up François' inheritance. However that may be, when at the age of thirty he succumbed to pleurisy on 4 July 1730, he died a ruined man with debts amounting to 10,812 livres. He left behind a pregnant wife and two sons, François aged six and Charles a one-year-old baby. The child born after his death did not live.

Madame d'Youville's married life was nothing if not an apprenticeship in suffering. From the beginning, mother-in-law and daughter-in-law dwelt under the same roof, two opposite upbringings and temperaments. Then came the lack of social life so bitter to a young person, the heartaches, the injustices, the devastating loss of her children, the outrages to her wifely dignity. Like a lava flow, all these frustrations engulfed her soul. Not to be overwhelmed by recriminations and to welcome with kindness her debauched husband required stronger supports than a sense of honour or a spirit of duty. She sought them in religion.

From 1727 – that is to say, before the death of her mother-in-law – she enrolled in the Confraternity of the Ladies of the Holy Family. Her heart eaten up by gall, she came to kneel in the ranks of these pious congregationists who were seeking a stable anchorage. There she heard the unhoped-for words:

Once the yoke of marriage has been taken on, it is as a couple that they get to heaven.

It is necessary to rid yourself of the rancour that is stifling you, in the furnace of love.

Have you not heard what Saint Paul says: "Wife, honour your husband"?

The Christian philosopher's stone is love.

Is there a love other than the one you know? Yes, it is the one that sees with God's eyes. It is the one that passes through God's heart and transforms into unimaginable merits the tears and heartbreaks.

Oh, Wife, do not scorn conjugal kindness; smile if it is necessary to smile in order to save the soul of your spouse.

The other name of love is self-denial.

Marguerite d'Youville understood these words. To sustain her good will and to subdue the instincts of nature, she sought a spiritual director. This man was a saint – Father Gabriel Le Pappe du Lescöat. With the help of this spiritual master she undertook the way of perfection. No doubt there were stumblings that are recorded in the Book of Life, but people saw only the heroic patience of which her son speaks: "To make matters worse, she had a husband with a very uncaring character who was no more sensitive to his wife's distress and her various infirmities than to those of someone he had never known. He often caused Madame d'Youville to shed bitter tears. Nevertheless, she was never heard to utter the least reproach to her husband, however much he deserved it, nor even to lessen her attentions and kindnesses shown to him … Such was the goodness of her heart that all the indifference and harshness of her husband to her in no way kept her from being greatly afflicted by his death." This is the portrait of a Christian wife.

Sterling silver candle-snuffers used by Marguerite d'Youville

CHAPTER III

A Resourceful Widow

T HE COMPLEXITIES of the estates of Madame de La Découverte and her son d'Youville brought the interested parties many times before the Tribunal. The official documents of these proceedings contain most interesting details that help to connect and prove facts already vaguely known. To quote again the Abbé Dufrost: "After the death of her husband, finding herself without resources, she undertook to open a small business so that she and her two children could subsist. Having found friends who would advance her some goods, she moved into a house on the Square in the lower city, a place more advantageous for retail selling." The Abbé writes a conventional account tempered, as it were, by his memories. In fact, however, he was only twenty months old when these events occurred.[1] In matters as important as this, it is better to rely upon the official documents. "Open a small business" is a euphemism. She was simply selling on commission merchandise deposited in her shop, according to the sworn declaration at the time of inventory. This means that her earnings were meagre. According to the estate inventory, François d'Youville had inherited, when his mother's property was divided, just the house where he lived on the Market Square.[2] Since Madame d'Youville renounced her husband's estate, the house was appropriated by legal lease on 31 October 1732.[3] Proof that she continued to reside there is that in 1733 the Administrative Commissioner of the estate claimed the rent from her.[4] Thus, she did not have to leave the familiar surroundings where she had lived since her marriage, although from reading the Abbé Dufrost one might get the impression that she moved.

An exact description of this house is provided by the Registration of the Seizure in esse of the Properties of the La Découverte Estate made in

1   Cf. AJM Doc. Jud. no. 966 – 4 April 1731, Requête de tutelle [Guardianship petition].

2   Cf. AJM Greffe Raimbault, fils, no. 685 – 24 April 1731, Inventaire de la Succession de sieur François d'Youville [Inventory of the Estate of Sieur François d'Youville].

3   Cf. AJM Registre des Audiences, vol. 13, p.1268 – Bail judiciaire des biens du Sieur Ladescouverte [Legal Lease of the Property of Sieur Ladescouverte].

4   Cf. AJM Registre des Audiences, vol. 14, p.168 – Lamoureux vs. Youville, 17 November 1733.

August 1732.[5] It was a two-storey stone house, thirty-one feet across the front and twenty-seven feet deep, containing two shops level with Market Square and living quarters on the second floor. The estate of Madame de La Découverte reveals that she had conducted business. It was therefore natural that Madame d'Youville would try to re-establish the clientele of her mother-in-law, people whom she in all probability knew quite well. Her customers could find displayed once again on the counters of the shop they were familiar with a variegated selection of dress-makers' supplies mingled, perhaps, with sweets. But the new purveyor of dress-makers' supplies, as well as selling merchandise, knew how to listen and to sympathize, as these family shops had been for a long time the secular confessional of the district.

The shop's door opened onto the Square teeming with the continuous flow of life. The King's Stores and the Great Barracks were there, each framing the main gate to the port where ships, small boats, and canoes were moored. To be seen also permanently set up there were the pillory, the iron collar, the wheel of torture, and the gallows. There laws and ordinances were proclaimed to the sound of the drum attracting passers-by. Madame d'Youville had only to raise her eyes to see the whole human caravan on its way.

At this time, when she was harassed by worries and besieged by perplexities, her strength and enlightenment came from prayer and a special devotion to the First Person of the Trinity, God the Father, which she developed. We know this from what she confided to the Abbé de l'Isle-Dieu in a letter of 1766. Henceforth, she showed great trust in the Eternal Father, whose merciful goodness manifests itself in his Providence. This trust, which was the fruit of her faith, shaped her soul and was evident in all her actions.

From now on, free to order her own life, she oriented it to religion. She nourished her own piety with the most excellent Christian prayer, that of the Church, whose liturgy, like manna, feeds souls according to their needs and aptitudes. Every morning, no matter what the season or the weather, she climbed the hill to the parish church to attend the Holy Sacrifice of the Mass and frequently to receive communion. During the day, as often as her duties allowed, she returned to adore the Blessed Sacrament. She participated in the spiritual life of the parish by her untiring attendance at the services on feast days and Sundays and by joining pious associations.

---

5   Cf. AJM Registre des Audiences, vol. 13, p.1245 – Enregistrement de la Saisie réelle des Biens de la Succession de défunt Sieur Ladescouverte [Registration of the Seizure in esse of the Properties of the Estate of the Deceased Sieur Ladescouverte].

She joined the Confraternity of a Happy Death and was enrolled as the twenty-eighth member inscribed on its list when it was canonically established in Montreal. In the Confraternity of the Holy Family,[xi] she was successively elected to the offices of counsellor, Lady of Charity, instructor of postulants, superior, and treasurer. Even after founding her community, she continued her activities with the Confraternity up to 1742.

The parish with its spiritual resources was a fountain flowing with graces. It was for Madame d'Youville the starting point for her mystical ascent.

Long ago the chronicler of the Hôtel-Dieu of Montreal, nostalgically recalling the early fervour of the colony, sadly confided to her Diary, "… but those happy times are long gone." Indeed, with the arrival of the Count de Frontenac, the first Governor to represent the King directly,[6] a fever of worldliness took possession of the colony. Frontenac believed that display was necessary to the regal prestige he intended to maintain in a worthy manner. Under his influence the Château Saint Louis in Quebec City became a brilliant salon, like those in France.[xii] When Monsieur de Vaudreuil, who was called the "Great Marquis" because of his love of pomp, became Governor General, he encouraged his wife, Elisabeth Joybert de Marsan, to maintain the Parisian atmosphere in the country. The Marquise, although Canadian by birth, had spent some time at the Court of Versailles; therefore, she was not at all averse to presiding in her turn over the ostentatious little court at Cap Diamant. When the "powers that be," as the heads of government were maliciously called, came to Montreal, a frenzy of pleasure seized the worldly citizens. Neither Advent nor Lent could disrupt the round of pompous receptions, balls, gaming parties, and endless dinners that often turned into drunken routs.[xiii] There were not enough dancing masters for those wishing to learn to dance; and according to one contemporary woman: "They forget religion whenever there is a chance to amuse themselves." Even the severe restrictions that forbade people in mourning to attend festivities were defied by going to them masked. After Intendant Bigot arrived in the country, in spite of the seriousness of the times, Canadian society became more and more frivolous.

Madame d'Youville belonged to the Canadian nobility, a little nobility ruled by the same code of honour, obligations, and behaviour as that of France. In Canada poverty did not mean loss of rank, but it also did not dispense one from the duties of rank. Fear of losing rank led to narrow-mindedness. The quarrels over precedence with which Quebec history is filled speak clearly enough about the worries that motivated this society

---

6   His predecessors were only agents of a business company.

jealous of its prerogatives. Moreover, there was the fanatical family spirit that took offence as a whole just as it boasted as a whole. The exceptional vocation of Madame d'Youville was going to challenge the family elan and the worldly spirit at the same time.

Adversity had led her into various and numerous spiritual paths that would all wind up in the way to perfection. To her also this way must have seemed rough and terribly narrow.

"To give oneself to God, must one love no one?"[7]

This question troubles Corneille's Polyeucte and with him all those souls who tremble in the presence of the Absolute. They want to be in the world and with God. For the womanly soul that is deeply and minutely rooted in vanity, giving up the world becomes an undescribable drama. For Madame d'Youville it was complicated by the facts of her birth, the prejudices of her environment, and the novelty of her project. Having received an interior illumination more compelling than reason, she felt a profound compassion invade her naturally generous heart. As a Lady of Charity of the Confraternity of the Holy Family she had come into contact with the wretched. Henceforth she would consecrate to them all her available time, bringing consolation, help, and encouragement to the sick, to prisoners, and to the old men in the House of Charity of the Brothers Hospitallers for whom she mended old clothes.

Pushing devotion to such unusual limits offended good taste. Worldly Montreal shrugged its shoulders and made a sulky face. Of course, it was all right to become a religious in a cloister; but to associate with poor people, was it not demeaning? A petty, gossiping, and clannish city, Montreal was going to show how brutal it could be.

---

7   Cf. Corneille, *Polyeucte*, Act I, scene i.

Clock belonging to the furniture of Madame d'Youville, preserved at the Mother House in Montreal. The face is brass with blue enamel numbers on a white enamel background.

First known signature of Marguerite d'Youville. She was sixteen years old at the time.
From the parish registers of Varennes, Quebec

CHAPTER IV

Hours That Come Not Again

T HE PROBLEM of helping the needy arose early in New France because of the adventurous life of the colonists and the Iroquois wars that quickly burdened the colony with orphans, widows and old people in need of assistance. From 1688 the Sovereign Council was obliged to set up Offices for the Poor whose function was to place the indigent sick in hospitals, orphans in apprenticeships, and generally to look after the poor. These Offices relied solely upon public charity and, for their administration, the voluntary assistance of the citizens. Their effectiveness, therefore, followed the ups and downs of public zeal or public apathy. This state of affairs could not last. Bishop de Saint-Vallier solved it in Quebec City by opening a general hospital or House of Charity. The Letters Patent which he received in 1692 authorized not only the requested foundation, but also similar institutions wherever the need for them might be felt. The Bishop, the Governor, and the Intendant were named chief administrators of all such future institutions.

In those days, a spirit of mysticism breathed upon Montreal. Jeanne Le Ber, the only daughter of Jacques Le Ber and the richest heiress in Ville Marie, had demonstrated an absolute detachment from the world since 1680 when she solemnly embraced the cloistered life. The religious communities in the enthusiasm of their youthful fervour experienced a proliferation of mysticism that was communicated to the people. It was a time of generous impulses. François Charon de la Barre, a man of action and wealthy merchant, who was won over to the devout life, resolved to dedicate his life to relieving the poor. He found two valuable associates in Jean and Pierre Le Ber, the brothers of the recluse. They were joined by Jean Fredin about whom little is known.

The goal of these associates is clearly stated in the land grant act made by Monsieur Dollier de Casson, 28 October 1688:

> Monsieur Charon and several associates, having planned to unite together to found a hospital for men in this place, and to that end create an establishment after the manner of Brothers of Charity, in so far as Providence may more fully enlighten them in the future,

and having requested of us a certain plot of about nine arpents in the vicinity of the mill of the Château, the measure of which was recently reported according to our specifications, and not yet put in writing, We, in our capacity as Bursar of the Seigneurs of this Island, with the consent of Monsieur Tronson, give the said nine arpents under the clauses and conditions notwithstanding any that the said Sieur Tronson, Superior of the Seminary of Saint-Sulpice, may be pleased to add with the agreement and consent of the parties, all aiming at in this matter only the greater glory of God. Made and done in the Seminary of Ville Marie, the Island of Montreal, under our respective signatures of Monsieur Charon and, us, François Dollier, whereby we jointly commit ourselves, the twenty-eighth day of October, one thousand six hundred and eighty-eight.

On 13 August 1691, Jean Le Ber du Chesne was killed in an ambush by an Iroquois arrow. François Charon was thus deprived by a single blow of a valuable supporter, but one who even in death provided financial support for the project. The day after the funeral his father made a gift to the future General Hospital of a farm and all its buildings in Pointe Saint-Charles of about thirty-five arpents of land "to fulfil the pious intention of the late Jean Le Ber du Chesne." The gift was received by Monsieur Guyotte, the parish priest. It was stipulated in the contract that if the plan for the General Hospital did not succeed, the revenue from the farm would be used in perpetuity for the relief of the poor of Ville Marie.

The associates Charon, Le Ber, and Fredin were possessors of real estate as a guarantee of their serious intention. They rightaway took advantage of the clause in the Letters Patent of the General Hospital in Quebec City to request permission to establish a similar House of Charity in Montreal. The chief administrators authorized it on 31 August 1692, and François Charon immediately started making the contracts that were necessary for the work of construction to begin in the coming spring.[1] Jeanne Le Ber co-operated in this pious work by lending the foundation the tidy sum of ten thousand livres.[2]

A clause in the contract for furnishing stone and lime stated that the supplier "could not during the said time [of construction] sell to other persons." Thus, the work was carried out quickly; and by the beginning of the summer of 1694, the founders moved into their house. We know this

---

1   Cf. SD, pp. 302-03.

2   Cf. AJM, Greffe Basset, 7 January 1698, confirming the loan of 23 September 1694.

because, according to the admissions register of the poor, they received the first indigent person on 1 June of that year.

The building rose outside the city walls on the site at Pointe-à-Callières granted by the Seigneurs. It was made of stone, three storeys, not including the attics, with a slate roof. It measured thirty feet wide by ninety feet long with two thirty-foot wings at the western end. Sister Morin, the chronicler of the Hôtel-Dieu, says in her history that this house "already goes beyond all the others in size of accommodation." The other "houses" were the Seminary, the Hôtel-Dieu, and the convent of the Congregation of Notre-Dame. François Charon himself in a letter to Monsieur Leschassier values the hospital and its outbuildings at "more than a hundred thousand livres."[3]

The year 1692 was a remarkable one. Besides the foundation of the first Brothers Hospitallers in the country, the year saw the installation of the Jesuits and the Récollet Fathers who were invited by the Sulpicians to share their ministry. The spiritual needs of Montreal were indeed well taken care of.

The Letters Patent of Montreal's House of Charity, dated 15 April 1694, authorize the associates to live in community. Bishop de Saint-Vallier also permitted them to live under the direction of a superior, to keep the Blessed Sacrament in the house, to have Mass said there, and to erect a small bell tower so that the bell could announce the community's exercises.[4] Nevertheless, this attempt at religious life still lacked royal approval, although it was hoped that it would be obtained through persistence and the blessed fruits of the work.

François Charon de la Barre was born in Quebec City on 9 October 1654. He was the son of Claude Charon de la Barre, merchant, and Claude Le Camus. He was thus thirty-eight years old when he founded the Brothers Hospitallers. Of an enterprising nature, he brought to his religious project the energy that had made him successful in business. There is no question about his piety; we have many proofs of it. But he remained a businessman, unaware that in the spiritual realm it is God who sets the pace. Every kind of good work attracted his beginner's zeal. The principal goal of his foundation was to provide a hospice for the poor and orphans. For the orphans, he founded a school of arts and crafts. In order to support it, he established a wholesale beer business; but to supply his brewery he

---

3   Cf. Letters of Monsieur Leschassier: Letter of François Charon to Monsieur Leschassier, Ville Marie, 15 October 1705.

4   Cf. AAQ, Entry in Register "A" of the Diocese of Quebec, 1660-1705, pp. 571-72: Letters Patent of Monsignor de Laval, 2 October 1694.

needed a windmill. This windmill would become the source of many troubles. One day, always thinking of the greater good of the colony, he thought he had found a more efficient way of regulating the fur trade in the Mississippi and Niagara posts; immediately he dispatched a memorandum to the Court. Soon he became interested in the western missions; he even sent a brother to the Tamarois.[xiv] Then it was the care of the sick in the Detroit post; and, finally, he had an idea about the good he could do by teaching boys in the country, after the manner of Marguerite Bourgeoys. He became so enthusiastic about this project that he even thought of getting rid of his poor old men by sending them to Quebec City and giving himself up completely to the education of schoolmasters.[5] Nevertheless, his numerous projects did not keep him from remembering his first goal – the foundation of an institute of Brothers. He was looking for a holy priest who would be willing to take charge of their religious education, but no one could be found to assume this heavy responsibility. He therefore sought to unite with an established society. First he thought of the Seminary in Quebec City, then of the Seminary in Montreal, and lastly of the Institute of Teaching Brothers in France. Of the last he wrote to Monsieur Leschassier, "I do not know whether these Gentlemen of the Hospital have completely decided what they should do ..." As the good will of François Charon was clear and his conduct edifying, in his own country he had the support of the authorities and the co-operation of charitable souls, but in France the Ministry was suspicious of his vacillations and the King objected to his project of a religious community. His zeal that flitted all over the place was probably the reason for the numerous defections about which he lamented so bitterly and that were in themselves so demoralizing. From 1698, Jean Fredin was considering an independent undertaking and suggested to the Abbé Mériel, a Sulpician, that they go work on converting the young Frenchmen of New England.[xv] In 1700 Jean Fredin went to France and did not return. The Abbé Philippe-Michel Boy, whom the founder had recruited to his work while staying in France, left the General Hospital shortly after arriving in Canada and asked to be received into the community of Saint-Sulpice. In the end he withdrew. Pierre Le Ber, who was an associate right from the beginning, did not wish to don the habit or take religious vows, but he remained in the Hospital until his death in 1707 and left the income from ten thousand livres to the institution.

In August 1701, François Charon and five associates adopted a uniform dress which the Constitutions describe as follows: "The Brothers'

---

5   Cf. Letter of Monsieur Leschassier to Monsieur Priat, 20 April 1700.

habits are simple and modest, a little like clergymen's cassocks. The coat, the trousers, and the hose are black, as is the rest of the habit. The professed Brothers are distinguished from the novices by a wool cross that they wear on their breasts outside the habit and which falls on the breast outside the coat. The collars and cuffs may be of batiste if it is not too expensive."

Scarcely had this innovation become known in France than the Minister wrote to the founder: "His Majesty has ordered me to write to you that he absolutely does not desire that those with whom you have set up this establishment make vows, or have statutes, or uniform habits, or be called 'Brother.' And in a word, He commands that those who are desirous of becoming a convent or community be expelled. I beg you to conform with whatever pertains to this matter that is the will of His Majesty."[6] The Minister communicated this order precluding all debate to both the Governor and the Intendant. In the autumn of 1707, Monsieur Charon went to France in the hope of having these royal ordinances modified. He seems, however, to have prejudiced his case because even more severe orders on this subject arrived by the post in 1708. To ensure conformity, Intendant Raudot was obliged to issue an ordinance making public the royal prohibitions.

> SEEING THAT the Letter written to us by My Lord the Count of Pontchartrain on the 6th of June, one thousand seven hundred and eight, in which he orders us to inform the Hospitallers of His Majesty's desire that they will no longer take vows in future and will discontinue from the present time to wear uniform habits;
> SEEING THAT also the Letters Patent granted by His Majesty on the 15th of April, one thousand six hundred and seventy [sic] four, for the establishment of a hospital in Montreal to care for poor orphaned children, the crippled, old men, and other needy persons, and registered with the Superior Council of this city on the 14th of October of the same year, we have in consequence of the above orders forbidden the said hospitallers to make vows and do declare null and void those which they may make in the future as being contrary to the desire of His Majesty and the said Letters Patent; we likewise forbid them to wear uniform habits, enjoining them from the present time to leave off the black headpiece, silk cincture, and collar, allowing them only in accord with the said Letters Patent to live in community. BE IT THAT the present Ordinance has communicated to the said hospitallers that of which they are not

---

6   Cf. APC, B vol. 29-2: Count de Pontchartrain to François Charon, 30 June 1707.

unaware. And that Sieur Daigremont, our subdelegate at Montreal, will diligently apply himself to the execution of said Ordinance. BE IT THAT the present Ordinance be registered with the Provost of Montreal so that it may be referred to as need shall arise. WE DO ORDER ... given at Quebec City this 14th of December, one thousand seven hundred and eight. Thus signed RAUDOT and further down by My Lord the Bishop

    PEUVRET.[7]

After the publication of this Ordinance, what incentive would any new applicants have to join this society that could offer no guarantee of permanence? The work of the General Hospital became a luxury for philanthropists. Indeed, according to contemporary estimates, it absorbed two hundred thousand livres of François Charon's personal fortune.

When defections had reduced his society to almost nothing, the courageous founder undertook some recruiting in France. In 1719, as he was returning to Canada with six new schoolmasters, he died unexpectedly on the 9th of July on board the king's cargo ship *Le Chameau (The Camel)* anchored off La Rochelle.

Louis Turc de Castelveyre, a native of Martigues in Provence, whom François Charon had named the executor of his will, succeeded him as director of the General Hospital. He took vows on 2 October 1722 and chose the religious name Brother Chrétien. When he was given power of attorney on 20 February 1722, the community of Hospitallers comprised eleven members including the new superior.

Brother Chrétien was more fortunate than the founder inasmuch as he succeeded in getting rules for the Brothers approved. On 8 October 1723 Bishop de Saint-Vallier endorsed them, and on 24 October 1724 he appointed Fathers Nicholas-Michel Boucher, the pastor of St. Jean, Ile d'Orléans, and François Chèze, Priest of Saint-Sulpice, as his delegates to put the Institute into canonical order and to preside at elections. Notwithstanding the royal prohibitions "on having statutes," the Brothers had definitely followed a rule before this date because from 1702, according to the records of religious professions, the founder and the Brothers made their vows "according to the Rule of Saint Augustine and the Constitutions of this House."

---

7   Cf. AJM, entry in Registre des Audiences de la Juridiction de Montréal [Register of Hearings of the Montreal Jurisdiction], 1706-1709, p. 373.

At the beginning of the Book of Rules, transcribed in a beautiful, neat hand in a square duodecimo notebook by Brother François Simonnet, called of the Cross, the official name of the Brothers is to be found: "Constitutions of the Brothers Hospitallers of the Cross and of Saint Joseph, observants of the rule of Saint Augustine." It was thus in error that "The Brothers of Saint Joseph of the Cross" was written and repeated.

After twenty-nine years the Brothers were finally constituted as a religious community with episcopal blessing, if not with royal approval. Because since 1718 the king had made an annual grant of three thousand livres to maintain six schoolmasters in the country (a condition that had to be fulfilled), the schoolmasters were a step ahead of the Hospitallers.

Thanks no doubt to his southern way of doing things, Brother Chrétien obtained a considerable amount of credit in France, both in merchandise and in cash. These loans, which were made without the knowledge of the community and which he did not have the means to repay, terrified him to such a degree that, in 1725, he fled to the Spanish Antilles in order to escape his creditors. The Abbé de l'Isle-Dieu wrote to the Minister that it was a question of "personal debts contracted above all for some mad and excessive undertakings that in no way touched the personal property of the Hospital of Montreal."[8] On the other hand, Bishop de Saint-Vallier in a letter dated 4 October 1725 let it be understood that Brother Chrétien was counting on the generosity of the Bishop of La Rochelle to cover his loans when the unexpected death of this bishop threw him into circumstances from which he could not extricate himself. The authorities brought Brother Chrétien back to Quebec in 1728 to answer to the charges of his creditors. From 28 October of that year, Bailiff Rageol notified Brother Chrétien, who had withdrawn to the Récollet Fathers of Quebec, that he was removed from the office of Superior of the Brothers Hospitallers of Montreal. His trial, presided over by Commissioner Le Verrier, was not concluded until 1735, and the Brothers Hospitallers were held accountable for the debts of their former superior contracted both in France and in Canada.[xvi]

In 1730 the King in disgust withdrew the annual grant of three thousand livres. Trials, quarrels, defections, laxness, and negligence brought about the dissolution of François Charon de la Barre's beautiful dream. In 1744 the last four Brothers, pleading their advanced age and unfitness, appealed to Bishop de Pontbriand to discharge them of the care of the General Hospital.[9] Like someone with a mortal illness whose hours are

---

8   Cf. APC, C 11 A, vol. 92, p. 226: The Abbé de L'Isle-Dieu to the Minister, 6 September 1748.
9   Cf. APC, C 11 A, vol. 82: The Bishop to the Minister, 30 October 1744.

numbered, the Institute was waning. Politics and rivalries prolonged the agony until 1747 when through a compromise a new beginning appeared in the person of a poor widow with an undaunted soul – Madame d'Youville. Where worldliness that depends upon wealth had failed, the renunciation of the gospels and pure charity would have to work miracles.

For the fifty-three years of its existence since 1694, the General Hospital had cared for sixty-five needy people divided as follows: thirty-eight enfeebled old men, sixteen former soldiers, six mentally handicapped, and five sick people. According to the Register of Investiture of Habit and Professions, eighteen Brothers took religious vows; many others merely passed through the community. The inconstancy of a great many Brothers creates the impression that not one of them remained faithful unto death. It has even been written about Pierre Le Ber that "he was the only one" to do so,[10] but this is an assertion that the registers contradict. Brother Louis Hérault, called Jerome, died after five years of his profession and Brother André De Moyres after twenty-five years in the religious life. Two of the founder's first disciples persevered up to the ends of their lives, which coincided with the end of the community: Brother Alexandre-Romain Turpin died at the age of seventy-seven, with forty-five years in the religious life, and Brother Jean Jeantôt at the age of eighty-two, with forty-six years as a religious. These two brothers had made their profession the same day as did the founder, 17 May 1702. Brother Jean Dellerme had been in the religious life for twenty-three years when the administrators turned the direction of the Hospital over to Madame d'Youville in 1747. He then went to France where he lived in retirement with his family on a pension paid by the Hospital until his death on 19 March 1772.

The mortal remains of Brothers Turpin, De Moyres, and Jeantôt were transferred to the present crypt of the Grey Nuns on Guy Street in 1871. God to whom worldly success matters little has no doubt rewarded their meritorious faithfulness in extremely difficult circumstances. They were the pillars of a house that was constantly threatening to topple over; they were workers doing a thankless task but one willed by the designs of a Provident God.

☙

We are in 1737. The two sisters of Madame d'Youville are married to rich merchants. Her two brothers, Joseph and Charles, have under-

---

10   Cf. Marie Beaupré, *Jeanne Le Ber*, p. 94.

taken the sacred ministry and are now priests, one at Sainte-Famille, Ile d'Orléans, and the other at Verchères. Christophe, the youngest son of the family, had left in the spring of 1731 with his uncle Pierre Gaultier de La Vérendrye, his four cousins and fifty volunteers for glorious adventures in the Northwest country. After having founded Fort Saint-Pierre on Lac La Pluie [Rainy Lake][xvii] he died of privations and hardships on 10 May 1736 at Fourche des Roseaux [Roseau], the first victim of this dangerous expedition.

From 1723, thanks to the influence of the Marquise de Vaudreuil, a friend of the Gaultier de Varennes family, Timothy Sullivan had become naturalized and had changed his name to the more French sounding Sieur Timothée Sylvain. Moreover, he had managed to obtain a certificate from the King allowing him to practise medicine. Where did he acquire his medical training? No document informs us,[xviii] but we know that in 1727 he underwent a professional examination before Doctor Sarrazin in Quebec City at the request of Monsieur de Beauharnois.

Thus, while Madame d'Youville was detaching herself from the world, her relatives were becoming advantageously established in it. There still remained her two sons who were getting older. The elder, François, intended to become a priest and enrolled this very year in the seminary in Quebec City. Charles, being only eight years old, attended the parish school and stayed at home with his mother. Providence put him there to become an indisputable witness to history.

The Small Catechism on Imitating the Holy Family used by members of the Confraternity exuded a strong sense of Pascal's theory of absolutism and rigourism of troubled souls of the seventeenth century. Some passages throw special light on the behaviour of Madame d'Youville who seems to have used it as her daily reading. Was she not, for example, literally following the teaching of the Small Catechism on the subject of almsgiving?

> *Question*: "But when you lack the bare necessities, how can you give to the Church and to the poor?"
>
> *Answer*: "I answer that if you do not have enough, it is because you have not given. Our Lord said: 'Give and you shall receive,' and moreover promised a hundredfold in this world to those who give of what belongs to them. Can it be that Jesus Christ would abandon those who out of love for Him follow his counsels? It is what David

in his old age said he had never yet seen. 'I have never seen,' he said, 'the righteous abandoned or children reduced to begging.' I say to you, therefore, if you have little give little, and if you have much give much; and whatever you may give, give it with a generous heart, and sowing little you will reap infinitely."[11]

How well these sentiments correspond to Madame d'Youville's enormous trust in Divine Providence. Shame therefore on calculating prudence!

Father Normant, having recognized Madame d'Youville's strong attraction to the corporal works of mercy, had no doubt that God had pre-destined her to preserve the work of the Charon Brothers. Thus, to test her zeal and her pious desires, he allowed her to receive into her home as many poor people as she could care for by her labour. Madame d'Youville began by receiving Françoise Auzon, a poor blind woman, whom she took in on 21 November 1737, the feast day that symbolizes every spiritual beginning, the Presentation of Mary in the Temple. Other examples of extreme poverty stirred her compassion and engendered in her enthusiastic projects that she could not accomplish alone.

Among her acquaintances, Madame d'Youville by a providential affinity of soul was linked in friendship with a virtuous person, Mademoiselle Thérèse Thaumur de La Source. This friend was aware of the laborious life and increasing sacrifices the resourceful widow had imposed upon herself to help the poor, while at the same time seeing to the upkeep of her two sons, which daily became more expensive because of their studies. This life of self-denial, made imperative by a singular super-natural charity, strongly appealed to the young woman. Nevertheless, when Madame d'Youville suggested that she join her in helping the poor, she remained undecided. Perhaps this new undertaking appeared rash to her. Besides, sacrifice always appears overwhelming in anticipation, and Mademoiselle de La Source no doubt experienced some hours of agonizing hesitation. The daughter of a wealthy doctor, she was pious and of sound judgement; she gauged the abyss separating the classes. It was one thing to visit the poor as a volunteer dispensing charity; it was another thing alto-gether to spend your life in their company.

While her friend wavered, Madame d'Youville sought another helper; and, in fact, found two – Mesdemoiselles Catherine Demers Dessermont

---

11   From *La Solide Devotion à la Très-Sainte Famille de Jésus, Marie et Joseph avec un catéchisme qui enseigne à pratiquer leurs vertus* [Firm Devotion to the Most Holy Family of Jesus, Mary, and Joseph, with a catechism that teaches how to practise their virtues], Paris chez Florentin Lambert, rue S. Jacques devant S. Yves, MDCLXXV [1675]. A copy is preserved in the Archives of the Seminary of Saint-Sulpice, Montreal.

and Catherine Cusson. In the meantime, Mademoiselle de La Source had finally overcome her doubts. The four innovators, meeting together, pledged themselves to the service of the poor. It was 31 December 1737. This was a simple secular association because in the colonies no one could enter into the religious state without the permission of the King upon whom the women's communities depended directly.[xix] Was Father Normant present at this daring commitment? If he was not there in person, his spirit certainly hovered by since he would have had to receive the vows that each woman made individually.

Four humble young women, heroic in their fervour, embracing a life of service and humility. This happened in secret. To all appearances, this was only a gathering of friends on New Year's Eve; but to the eyes of Heaven, it was the beginning of an unending procession of souls avid for perfection who under the sign of Charity would follow in the footsteps of Marguerite d'Youville.

According to the Abbé Dufrost, these associates of a new kind in the country only began life in common on 30 October 1738 when they moved into the Le Verrier house. Nevertheless, an authentic document proves that the nature of their association was known before that date. It is a petition addressed to the Minister and President of the Marine Council, who was in charge of colonial affairs, and is signed by twenty-eight protesters from Montreal. Because of its importance it is reproduced in its entirety.

TO MY LORD COUNT DE MAUREPAS
SECRETARY OF STATE

The Officers, Merchants, and Inhabitants of the city and government of Montreal in New France most humbly submit to Your Excellency that in the month of August, one thousand six hundred and ninety-two, Monsieur the Bishop of Quebec, Monsieur the Count de Frontenac, the Governor General of this land, and Monsieur de Champigny, the Intendant, granted permission for the establishment of a House of Charity in Montreal to take in poor orphan boys, the crippled, aged men, the sick and other needy men. For the construction of said house, the late Father Dollier, the Superior of the Seminary of Montreal, ceded a suitable piece of land to Sieur François Charon, Pierre Le Ber, and Jean Fredin, as much for themselves as for those who would join them, and to their successors, for this good work. His Majesty approved said establishment by his Letters Patent on the fifteenth of April, one thousand six hundred and ninety-four. On the establishment, the said late Sieur Charon spent about two hundred thousand livres, and the late Sieur Le Ber most of his considerable inheritance. After the death of the said late Sieur Charon, Sieur Turc, called Brother Chrétien, having become Superior, went to France where he borrowed large amounts which he then wasted through his misconduct and undertakings that were unknown to the community of Brothers Hospitallers of said Montreal, which debts resulted in the present alienation of the Brothers of the Christian Schools who were otherwise disposed to unite with the said Hospitallers, apart from the fact that the Gentlemen Clergy of the Seminary of Saint-Sulpice of said Montreal were opposed to this plan. The Superior, who is the Vicar General, not allowing them to accept further aspirants, the number of Brothers is at present diminished to five. Of these, three are elderly and the two young ones unable to attend to the schools, the care of the poor aged men, who are country people as well as invalid soldiers, and to administer the property and business affairs of said House.

These proceedings were undertaken by the said Lords Clergy of Montreal, who, it would appear, have led Monsieur Dosquet, the Bishop of Quebec and formerly one of said Clergy, to forbid the acceptance of new Brothers Hospitallers and to dispense from their vows of stability a number of them who were intimidated by the suggestion that after having spent their youth they might find themselves without a home. It appears that the said Gentlemen of the Seminary of Montreal would take possession of said House as soon as the work should cease, and this by virtue of a clause in the contract granting the piece of land of said Hospital, and following which the Superiors would replace them with some tipsy nuns [*Sœurs grises* – Grey Nuns].

This plan, My Lord, is completely contrary to the intention of the founder, to the pious purpose and will of His Majesty, and to the public welfare since this House is a refuge for poor orphan boys, aged men, both civilians and invalid soldiers, and for the education and instruction of the children of all the families of Montreal and the parishes in the country.

It is this, My Lord, that obliges the petitioners to beg Your Excellency to grant your protection to said Hospital for the support of this House, to urge the said Brothers of the Christian Schools to unite with the said Brothers Hospitallers of Montreal, and to obtain

House of Charity of the Charon Brothers; construction was begun in April 1693. This House of Charity became the General Hospital of Montreal.

Cornerstone of the Chapel of the House of Charity of the Brothers Hospitallers of the Cross and of Saint Joseph, called the Charon Brothers. The carved date 1695 agrees with the documents whereby the Brothers were only authorized to build a chapel in 1694. Unfortunately, a piece of the stone in the upper left-hand corner containing the numbers 16 has been lost. The other dates mark subsequent enlargements of the Chapel.

from His Majesty the gift of three thousand livres that was granted them during the reign of His Majesty to help maintain said Brothers in the schools, the sum of which they have been deprived of for a number of years. The said petitioners and their children will then be obligated to pray with renewed fervour for the health and prosperity of Your Excellency.

Signatures on the copy agreeing with the original: Bois Berthelot de Beaucourt, Governor; Chavoy de Noyan, Captain; De Budemont, Captain; P. Raimbault, Lieutenant General; Foucher, King's Bursar; De Vimer, Captain; Pécaudy de Contrecoeur, Capt.; D'Ailleboust de Périgny; Pothier; Lestage; R. de Couagne; Guy; Toussaint Le Cavelier; Busquet; Héry; J.-B. Forestier; Lecompte Dupré; Trutant; F.-M. de Couagne; Hertel de la Fresnière, Capt.; Le Ber de Senneville, Lieutenant; Ignace Gamelin; Prud'homme; Latour; F. Auger; Gamelin; Hervieux; Maugras.

WE, the undersigned, Dean of the Chapter of Quebec, formerly Archdeacon of the Diocese for twelve years, certify to having witnessed during our visits the great good done by the Brothers Hospitallers of Montreal, as much in their house in Montreal where we have seen a number of poor men and invalid soldiers very well cared for, as in the parishes of this Diocese by their good example, instruction, and education given to the young. The said Brothers are very useful for the public welfare and to assist in upholding good order in the parishes. Given in Quebec, this first day of November, 1738. Signed: Chartier De Lotbinière, Dean of the Chapter of Quebec.

FOR a copy compared with the originals presented by the Brothers Hospitallers of Montreal, and given to them at the same time as these presents by the Royal Notary in the Provostship in Quebec City and there residing, undersigned, in Quebec City, the second of November, one thousand seven hundred and thirty-eight.

PINGUET

GILLES HOCQUART, Knight, Councillor to the King in His Councils, Intendant of Justice, Police, and Finances in New France, we hereby CERTIFY to all to whom it may pertain that Monsieur Pinguet who has gathered together the above writings and other communications is the Royal Notary in the Provostship of Quebec

À Monseigneur
Le Comte de Maurepas
Secretaire d'État

en 1738.

Les officiers, Marchands
habitans de la Ville et Gouvernement de
Montreal En la nouvelle france
Representent tres humblement
à Vôtre Grandeur, qu'au mois
d'aoust mil six cent quatre vingt douze,
Monseigneur L'Evêque de Quebec,
Monsieur Le Comte de frontenac Gouverneur
general du païs, et monsieur de Champigny
Jntendant, auroient permis L'Etablissement
a Montreal d'une Maison de Charité
pour y retirer Les pauvres Enfans
orphelins, Estropiez, Vieillards, Jnfirmes,
Et autres Necessiteux de leur sexe; pour

Garder

Srs Grises de Montréal
Maison-Mère
Archives

Facsimile of the Petition of 2 November 1738

Construire Laditte Maison, feu Mr
Collin superieur du Seminaire de montreal
auroit Concedé aux S.rs françois, charon,
pierre Lebert et Jean fredin tant pour
Eux quepour Ceux qui Sejoindroient
á Eux, et Leurs successeurs pour ce bon ouvrag
un terrain Convenable que Sa Majesté
auroit approuvé Ledit Etablissement
par Ses Lettres patentes du Quinzieme
Avril milsix cent quatre vingt quatorze.
quepour L'Etablissement led. feu sieur
Charon a Employé Environ deux cent mille
Livres, et Le feu sieur Lebert La plus
Grande partie de Son patrimoine tres
Considerable; Qu'apres Le deced dud. feu
sieur Charon, Le sieur Turc dit freres chretiens
Setrouvant superieur passa En france.

Et fit des Empsaints de Sommes Considerables,
qu'il a dissipé par sa Mauvaise Conduite
et Entreprises à l'ynsçeu de la Communauté
des frères hospitaliers dud. Montréal
lesquelles detes Causent que les frères
des Ecoles Chrêtiennes Estant disposez
à se joindre aud. hospitaliers, s'en Eloigne
à present, outre que Messieurs Les
Ecclesiastiques du Seminaire de St.
Sulpice dud. Montréal y sont opposez.
Le Superieur qui est grand Vicaire
ne Voulant Leur permettre de prendre
des Sujets, Le Nombre des frères Estant
à present Reduit à Cinq dont trois sont
fort âgez, et Les deux Jeunes insuffisants
pas pour Vacquer aux Ecolles au point

des pauvres Vieillards, tant D'habitans

que de Soldats Invalides et a L'ad-

ministration des biens et affaires de

Lad. Maison —

Que ce procédé de la part des d. sieurs

Ecclesiastiques de montreal, qui ont selon

les apparences Induit M onss............ dosquet,

Evêque de quebec Cy Devant vû des dits

Ecclesiastiques a deffendre de recevoir

des nouveaux freres Hospitaliers, et donner

Dispence des Voeux de stabilité a plusieurs

qui étoient Intimidez par ce qui Leur

Etoit suggeré, qu'après avoir passé

leur Jeunesse ils resteroient sur le

pavé y ayant apparence que les d. fres.

du seminaire de Montreal prendroient

Possession de lad.e maison, aussitôt que
L'œuvre cesseroit, et ce Invertu d'une
clause du Contrat de Concession du terrain
dud.t Hôpital, et qu'en suite les Superieurs
y Veulent faire mettre a leur place
des Sœurs Grises.

Ce projet Monseigneur est
tout a fait Contraire a l'intention du
fondateur, au premier dessein et Volonté de
Samajesté et au bien public puisque
Cette maison est un azile pour les
pauvres Enfans orphelins, Vieillards,
tant de la Colonie que de soldat Invalides
et pour L'éducation et Instruction des
Enfans de familles de tous Ceux de Montréal
et de toutes les parroises établies dans le
pais.

C'est Monseigneur,
ce qui oblige les Representans de supplier
Vôtre Grandeur, d'accorder vôtre
protection aud hôpital pour le soutien
de cette Maison, d'engager lesd freres des
écolles Chretiennes a se joindre ausdits
freres hospitaliers de Montreal, et obtenir
de Sa Majesté la gratification
des trois mille Livres qui leur avoit
été accordée du Regne de Sa Majesté
pour aider à l'entretien desd freres
pour les écolles, de Laquelle ils sont
privez depuis Nombre d'années, et
lesdits Representans feront et leurs
Enfans obligez de redoubler leurs
voeux et prier pour la santé et

prosperité de Nôtre Grandeur.
signez a L'original

Bois Berthelot de Beaucourt G....nux
Chavoy deNoyan, Capne S. Raimbaut Lig.nat
De Budemont Capine, fouchez pxne duroy,
De Nunes Cap.ne, Lertie dela bermie Cap.ne,
Beaudy de Sontrebeur Cap.ns, Lebeu deSennevile
Lieutenaut, Daillebourt deporigny,
Ignace Gamelin, Pothiew, L'Estaige,
Prudhomme, P. deConague, Guy,
Latour, Toussaintt Le Cavelier,
f. Anger, Ousquet, Jbte forestier, hery,
Gamelin, Le Comte Dupré, hervieuf,
Tuitant, fm. deConague, Maugras,

NOUS soussigné Doyen du Chapitre de Quebec et devant archidiacré
pendant douze ans dans le Diocèze, Certifions avoir Eté témoins
dans nos visiten du grand Bien que des freres hospitaliers de Montreal
ont fait tant dans leur maison de Montreal, ou nous y avons vû
plusieurs pauvres et soldats invalides qui y Etoient tres Bien
soignez que dans les parroisses de Ce diocèse, par leurs Bons

Exemple, justruction et Education qu'ils ont donné à La
jeunesse, le que les d'freres sont très utille pour le Bien publique
et pour maintenir le Bon ordre dans les Parroisse à Quebec.
Ce 1.er 9bre 1738. signé Chartier De lotbiniere doyen du
Chapitre de Quebec.

Pour Copie Collationné aux originaux Representez par les
freres hospitaliers de Montreal, et à luy Rendu à l'jnstant avec
Ces presenté par le notaire Royal En la Prevôté de Quebec et
Residans soussigné, à Quebec le Deux novembre mil sept Cens
trente huit ___

                    Pinguet.

Gilles Hocquart Chevalier Conseiller du Roy en
Ses Conseil, jntendant de justice police, et finances En la nouvelle
France. Certifions à tous qu'il appartiendra que m.e Pinguet
qui a Collationné les Ecrits Cy dessus et les autres par le notaire
Royal En la Prevôté de Quebec, que soy En a ajouter aux actes
qu'il passe La foy En sa d' qualité, En tesmoin de quoy nous
avons signé et fait Contresigner Ces presentes par l'un de
nos secretaires, et à jcelle fait apposer le Cachet de nos
armes. fait et donné à Quebec En notre hotel le Deux novembre
mil sept Cens trente huit ___
                    Hocquart,

                    Savourneigneur
                    Vincens

City, that the Acts which he examines and signs in said capacity are authentic. In witness of which, we have signed and had counter-signed by one of our secretaries these presents and have affixed to them the seal bearing our arms. Made and done in Quebec City, in our palace, the second of November, one thousand seven hundred and thirty-eight.

HOCQUART
For My Lord
Bénard.

Two things are to be noted in this document: the dates and the name given to the women associates. They are called Grey Nuns. If they are called "nuns," it must mean that their religious consecration is already known. The adjective "grey" will require some further explanations. At the given time, they did not wear a uniform habit, but only a simple black dress without ornaments.

The above petition is only one form of opposition that Madame d'Youville would meet in carrying out her plans. The seven-headed hydra of rumour tore at the reputation of these honest young women and the most unbelievable slanders travelled from mouth to mouth. Factions became involved and each added its faggot of discord to this fiery enter-prise. Old rancours were reawakened. The shameless activities of the You d'Youvilles were recalled, including their wild ambition and their infamous trade in alcohol, which it was said the widow still secretly continued. Moreover, it was alleged that she and her companions got drunk and in their drunkenness tore each other's hair out, hence the insulting gibe of "grey" – that is, "tipsy" in French – nuns.

For many, Madame d'Youville was only a tool in the hands of the Sulpicians. Also, some said that it was they who supplied her with the fire-water that she sold to the Indians. On the other hand, the petition accused the Sulpicians of having engineered the ruin of the Brothers Hospitallers by impeding their recruitment. Yet the King's official will in regard to them had been made public by Intendant Raudot's Ordinance of 18 January 1709. According to the King's wish, the Hospitallers could only be an organization of laymen united by a common goal of pursuing charitable work. Father de Charlevoix, S. J., had foreseen their fall in 1721 when he wrote: "The Court's having forbidden them to wear a uniform habit and to take simple vows will very much impede their survival."[12] Yet the

---

12   Charlevoix, *Journal*, vol. V.

worldly people who were afraid of being impinged upon did not miss the opportunity to blame the Sulpicians for the failure of this undertaking. In a way, this was a kind of collective humiliation since it involved what was almost a common good; many charitable persons had contributed to the support of the House of Charity and, in spite of its decline, they were under the illusion that it could be revived by means of royal subsidies. These businessmen were thinking only on the temporal plane.

As for the involvement of Bishop Dosquet, he had the misfortune of arriving in the country when the Church in Canada was still troubled by dissensions that had followed the death of Bishop de Saint-Vallier. By the very fact that he was a former member of the community of Saint-Sulpice, he was suspect among certain groups. At that time more than ever before, justice was blinded by prejudice. Fortunately, for us, the Governor General, Monsieur de Beauharnois, expressed his opinion of Bishop Dosquet. On 5 November 1729, he wrote to the Minister: "The coadjutor is a holy man. He is busy setting everything in order. He is clear and precise in his decisions." The chaos that had reigned at the General Hospital of Montreal since the flight of Brother Chrétien, whose trial was under way before the Superior Council in Quebec City, was good reason for prohibiting the admission of new aspirants. Bishop Dosquet wished to prevent further complications in an already embroiled situation; therefore, as a man of clear decisions, he took drastic measures and then revealed the state of affairs to the Minister.

Some people also saw the General Hospital as a potential source of wealth that ought not to be allowed to fall into the hands of Madame d'Youville and her family clan. At the time, however, her family, finding itself associated with the humiliating venture that everyone was gossiping about, became highly indignant. Her two brothers-in-law and some cousins signed the petition to the Secretary of State. This Pilate-like gesture of hand washing deeply hurt Madame d'Youville who felt only tenderness for her relatives. They were publicly abandoning her as though she were a leper. The names at the bottom of the petition reveal the secret motives of the signatories. First, there is the name of the distrustful Governor and his favourites in office, then the names of the parish warden, a man named Guy, some vindictive merchants, and a group of relatives concerned about their prestige. It is a sad document, indeed!

In such a web of intrigues, Madame d'Youville's new project had of necessity to suffer opposition. It seems, nonetheless, that in the circumstances she was more the victim of the people she was associated with than of any personal feeling against her.

While these vile matters were muddying the waters of Montreal life, Madame d'Youville was looking for a house to shelter her work. And as with the Holy Family seeking lodging, many doors remained closed to her. Finally, the charitable Madame Soumande, daughter of Madame Le Verrier, became the owner of her mother's house. She rented it to Madame d'Youville, and the associates moved there on 30 October 1738. Madame d'Youville's biographers, from the Abbé Dufrost on, have accepted this date as that of the foundation of the Grey Nuns because it is the first mention of the life in common of the foundresses, and it is here that the dates at the bottom of the aforementioned petition take on a serious meaning. Since it is a question of the date of the foundation of the Institute, it is necessary to expand on this to some extent.

After having said that the pious plan of Madame d'Youville and Mademoiselle de La Source "remained shrouded in great secrecy until they came together in association with Catherine Demers and Catherine Cusson who for a long time had professed piety," the Abbé Dufrost continues:

> It was in 1738 that Madame d'Youville rented a house in Montreal near the Récollets. She moved into this lodging on the eve of All Saints' Day. She was accompanied by Sisters Thaumur, Demers, and Cusson. They secretly moved their few possessions there. All the money they had was about a hundred pistoles ... Scarcely had this little society moved in than the public struck out against them and actively persecuted them. Even some of Madame d'Youville's relatives were among the persecutors. On the morning following their commitment as a group when they were going to the parish service people hurled stones and insults at them.

This text is precise, but the petition disqualifies it. In the latter, the associates are called Sisters, a word evoking the idea of the common life, as well as *Grey* Nuns, which places the campaign against them before the petition and before their moving into the Le Verrier house. In fact, the petition is dated in Quebec City, 1 November 1738, the very day of their going out as a group, which was supposed to be their first outing of this sort. The drafting of the petition, collecting the signatures, and sending it to Quebec City at a time when the means of communication between the two cities were very slow clearly show that the plot had been brewing for some time.

Throughout his narrative the Abbé Dufrost condenses events and those he recounts are almost always associated with an important fact. Thus, in this case, on a holiday, the day after their move, hostile demonstrations at the time of the group's going out together must have etched the date of the association of the Sisters in connection with the Le Verrier house onto the memory of a nine-year-old child who was no doubt the terrified witness of his mother's mistreatment. It is the first date that he remembers, but it is not necessarily the date of the foundation of the Institute. Whether or not the associates lived together before 30 October 1738, it is clear from the petition that the goal of their association was known.

The Abbé Dufrost does not say anything about the secret consecration of 31 December 1737, but we have irrefutable testimonies. After the King's Letters Patent of 3 June 1753 had authorized Madame d'Youville to found a community, Bishop de Pontbriand approved the temporary rules of the Sisters at the time of his canonical visit in 1755. He then directed Father Montgolfier, the Superior of the Seminary of Saint-Sulpice and Vicar General of the Diocese of Quebec, to work out in detail the Rules in accordance with the original commitments of the Sisters. Father Montgolfier finished a first draft in 1776. Then, having corrected it and copied it by his own hand into a square duodecimo notebook, in 1781 he presented these Rules to the Sisters who formally accepted them by each affixing her signature and the date of her religious profession after the text. Now, this occurred during the lifetime of one of the foundresses, Sister Demers-Dessermont, who gave as the date of her profession 31 December 1737. A number of sisters who were contemporaries of Madame d'Youville were also still alive; among them were Sister Despins, who succeeded her as Superior, Sister Rainville, Sister Laforme, Sister Bénard-Bourjoli, all of whom were admitted into the community by the foundress.[xx] The date of 31 December 1737 is the true date on which the four co-foundresses took their vows. It is also the date inscribed in the Register of All the Professed Sisters of the Institute. Moreover, there is a note of Madame d'Youville's relating to the subject. On 17 August 1766, she wrote to her bursar in France concerning the reduction of French credit: "I cannot believe that the King will not compensate the communities of this country for the harm he has done to their interests, and especially ours to which he has given no payment at all since it came into being twenty-nine years ago." She therefore dates the beginning of the community in 1737.

Thus, if it is proved that the first four sisters vowed themselves to the service of the poor on 31 December 1737, it is clearly the date of the foundation of the Community of Grey Nuns of Montreal.

❧

The associates moved as discreetly as possible on 30 October 1738 into the Le Verrier house that had been rented by the foundress. It was a one-storey, stone house, forty-three feet across the front by twenty-six feet deep, located on Rue Notre Dame near Rue Saint Pierre.[xxi] Scarcely had Madame d'Youville entered the house than she placed in a small room, by way of dedication, a little statue of Our Lady; and kneeling with her companions, she read in a loud and firm voice an act of consecration of their work and persons to the Blessed Virgin. Women, who have founded spiritual families, casting aside family ties, have clung to the Mother of their spiritual Spouse; in the Sulpician spirit, they have gone to Jesus through Mary.

On All Saints' Day, brazen arms were rudely raised in unreasoned gestures toward the sisters as stones and jeers and gibes assaulted them. This hostile demonstration was only the distant rumbling of thunder; the storm had not yet reached its peak. To the accusation of secretly trading in alcohol was added that of licentiousness. Passing from mouth to mouth, from subordinates to superiors, the accusation moved up the ranks, finally reaching the ears of Monsieur de Beauharnois.[13] The scandal reached such proportions that one day a Récollet Father felt obliged publicly to refuse communion to the group of Sisters.

Madame d'Youville remained silent throughout the storm. Like disembodied voices echoing in the fog, slander broke through the calm of the Sisters' busy life. They had four needy people to care for and no other means of support than their own handiwork, chiefly needlework. They had, therefore, to apply themselves untiringly to their tasks.

When her activities appeared to be most indispensable to carrying out her work, a serious illness struck Madame d'Youville. For some time she had felt sharp pains in her knee. During the winter of 1738, a large inflammation produced sores. The King's Surgeon Major in Montreal, Sieur Joseph Benoît, was summoned. Finding two sores, one on each side of the knee, he made a single incision to join them, thus hoping no doubt to clear up more quickly this site of infection. Nevertheless, in spite of all his care, the illness not only persisted, but spread. After several months, another physician whose name we do not know undertook to cure the sores with medicinal herbs; but neither did he obtain any improvement. When God wishes to test his servants, he has innumerable mysteries of disease and medical science at his disposal. After the death of Doctor Sarrazin, the country no longer had any brilliant healers, if we are to believe Mother

---

13   Cf. *Histoire du Monastère des Ursulines des Trois-Rivières* [History of the Ursuline Convent of Trois Rivières], vol. 1, p. 264.

Duplessis de Sainte Hélène, a nun of the Hôtel-Dieu in Quebec City. On 16 October 1734, she related the death of Doctor Michel Sarrazin to Madame Hecquet in France and concluded by saying: "We are left at the mercy of a few surgeons who do not know anything except treating wounds. We are desperately in need of a physician."ˣˣⁱⁱ

At that time surgeons were not necessarily physicians as they are today. They were originally barbers and remained so up to a certain point, doing blood-letting and applying cauteries. As for their skills, they were able to acquire them easily with a little practice under an experienced master. The recruitment of the year 1738 brought to Canada an Austrian surgeon, Sieur Ferdinand Feltz, who settled first in Quebec City where he married Ursule Aubert on 4 November 1741. The ministerial correspondence indicates that he remained there at least until the summer of 1742. Monsieur de Beauharnois had recommended him to the Minister for the post of Surgeon Major to the troops in Quebec City. The Minister responded on 17 April 1742 that he had already named Sieur Briant of Rochefort to this post when Monsieur de Beauharnois' letter had arrived "recommending Sieur Feltz who has been filling the functions of the office since the death of Sieur Berthier."[14] In fact, the dispatches from the Marine Council of 28 March 1742 announced the nomination of Ferdinand Feltz to the post of Surgeon Major of the King's Troops at Montreal.[15] The Surgeon Michel Berthier had died on 5 September 1740.[16] Feltz who was already practising at the Hôtel-Dieu, according to the correspondence of Sister Duplessis de l'Enfant-Jésus,[17] extended his care from that time to the king's troops. The ships of the spring of 1742 having brought the news of his appointment to the post in Montreal, he must have settled there during the summer. A solid reputation preceded him. Perhaps, Madame d'Youville thought that this stranger possessed the secret of her cure, for she committed herself to his care. Doctor Feltz "employed extreme remedies that caused her intense suffering."[18] He then began a treatment using live toads. Two or three toads were applied to the sores, which they would lick and thus infuse the sores with their supposedly curative venom. At a short distance, the scratching of their little feet could be heard until it was realized that their feet should be wrapped. As her companions testified, the sick woman suffered without

---

14   Cf. APC, series B, vol. 74, fol. 46: The President of the Marine Council to Monsieur de Beauharnois.

15   Cf. ibid., folio 18: The same to Messrs. Beauharnois and Hocquart.

16   Cf. *BRH*, vol. XX, p. 209: "Nécrologie de l'église Notre-Dame de Québec" [Necrology of Notre Dame Church, Quebec City].

17   Cf. *Nova Francia*, vol. V, no. 1, p. 360.

18   Cf. MD.

complaint for the four weeks that this repulsive and ultimately unsuccessful torture lasted. The illness continued for seven years and then "she found herself suddenly cured without human aid," according to her biographer.

Both surgery and medicine tried to conquer this stubborn illness. Exactly what was it? Doctor Gabriel Nadeau,[xxiii] in his article "Un Cas de Bufothérapie sous le Régime français" [A Case of Toad Therapy under French Rule], tries to determine what the mysterious illness of Madame d'Youville was. Among a number of possible diagnoses, he suggests the four following: a malignant tumour of the knee, menopausal monarthritis, tubercular arthritis, and chilblains, of which the Abbé Dufrost speaks.

The application of live toads indicates that Feltz had diagnosed an ulcerated cancer because this was one of the treatments used in such cases. Time revealed that he was mistaken about the nature of the illness. The possibility of tubercular arthritis can also be eliminated. Madame d'Youville does not seem to have suffered from any bacillary infection. She died of paralysis at the age of seventy. The Abbé Dufrost's suggestion of chilblains would be possible if it is supposed that the chilblains had resulted in gangrene, but gangrene does not disappear spontaneously. Given the age of the patient, the course of the disease, and its automatic remission, it is probable that it was a case of menopausal monarthritis aggravated by inappropriate treatments. Still, the presence of the sores creates a serious objection to this diagnosis, although they may be plausibly explained. Whatever the illness may have been in origin, the treatments certainly aggravated it. As for its duration of seven years during which Madame d'Youville was obliged to keep to her room, she affirms this in her first will dated 8 October 1757 drafted by the notary Danré de Blanzy.[19]

During this time, even if Madame d'Youville was following the counsels of human prudence, she was not forgetful of petitioning Heaven. She increased the number of novenas, confident that Father Le Pappe du Lescoät would obtain healing for her. Once she hoped to obtain healing through the intercession of Bishop de Lauberivière who died at the age of twenty-nine, a victim of his charity towards the infected passengers on the ship *Le Rubis* that was bringing him to his Canadian flock. To this end, she went to Quebec City by barge and, in spite of her suffering, struggled through a novena in the crypt of the Church of Notre Dame de Québec where the remains of the young bishop reposed. God's time, however, had not yet arrived.

Although suffering had almost incapacitated her, she did not lessen her direction of her house and even strove to expand it. In the summer of

---

19   Cf. SD, p. 324.

The Seminary of Saint-Sulpice in Montreal as it appeared during Mother d'Youville's lifetime

Monsieur Louis Normand de Faradon (1681-1759),
Priest and Superior of the Seminary of Saint-Sulpice in Montreal

1739, she was sheltering ten poor people and in the month of July she opened her mother's heart to a seventeen-year-old orphan girl from Boucherville, Mademoiselle Thérèse Lemoine-Despins. A boarder at first, she later joined the community, and on the foundress's death became superior.

While sickness tormented Madame d'Youville's body, other kinds of anguish gripped her heart. The domestic misfortunes of her mother were now a matter of public notoriety; the violence of Doctor Sylvain, her mother's second husband, knew no bounds. He would fly off the handle at anything and harangue people regardless of who or where they were. Having insulted Sieur Guiton de Monrepos, the King's Counsellor and Lieutenant General for Civil and Criminal Affairs in Montreal, he became the cause of an endless and bitter altercation involving the honour of both parties.

Jacques-Joseph Guiton de Monrepos, a proud man filled with a sense of his own importance, had become unbearably conceited. As the King's Lieutenant General, he assumed it was his right to use such pompous expressions as "my people," "my countrymen," "my secretary," etc.[20] People of wit smiled about it, but he had few friends. It goes without saying that such a man would demand legal reparation for the insult received from Sylvain. The case came before Maître Adhémar who was sitting in the judge's seat for the occasion. The prosecution having obtained a warrant for the arrest of the accused, the bailiff and his assistant, who while previously exercising their functions in a like case had been beaten and wounded by Sylvain so that they had to be confined to their beds for three weeks, obtained from the judge authorization to request assistance from the garrison. They therefore went to the Guard's Corps barracks where they found Monsieur de Varennes in command of the Guard and asked him for a detachment of eight soldiers under a sergeant for the execution of the warrant.

Infantry Captain Jacques-René Gaultier de Varennes, who had previously been dragged into court by the same Sylvain for having defended his sister against her husband's brutalities, was so imbued with family spirit that he felt it was his duty to defend the husband against other parties. Orders required a note signed by the judge when the court of justice asked for assistance, but no note when it was demanded by the Lieutenant General. Since the bailiffs had no judge's note and, on the other hand, since the writ issued at the request of the Lieutenant General was not from his

---

20   Cf. APC, C 11 A, vol. 79, p. 352: Intendant Hocquart to the Minister, 1 October 1743.

office, Monsieur de Varennes, using uncertainty as an excuse, refused to lend assistance without a note from the Governor. The latter, brought up to date by Maître Adhémar, gave his verbal authorization; but while the bailiffs were going from Pontius Pilate to Herod, Doctor Sylvain, having been warned, slipped away, so that the bailiffs were unable to execute the warrant. Guiton de Monrepos, frustrated, filed a complaint with the Superior Council of Quebec. Monsieur de Beaucours, the Governor of Montreal, for his part, complained about the military men who had given depositions in favour of Monsieur de Varennes, for he saw this as a criticism of his management. In consequence of this conflict between the civil and military authorities, the city was flooded with anonymous satirical and risqué poems and songs.[21] People either gloated or flew into a rage, depending upon whose side they were on.

Nevertheless, following the inquest, Monsieur de Beauharnois ordered the imprisonment of Monsieur de Varennes. The matter was duly reported to the Minister who, due to the gravity of the alleged breach, referred it to the King. Wanting at all costs to maintain discipline in the colony, the King dismissed Monsieur de Varennes[22] without possibility of appeal, in spite of the pleadings of persons in high position who favoured his case. Thus, notwithstanding his valiant military exploits and his many years of service, Monsieur de Varennes saw his career destroyed because of his instinctive, blind family spirit.

Like a stone thrown into a stream, the insult given to Guiton de Monrepos enclosed the whole family in its expanding circles. None of this bothersome fuss surrounding her name was likely to help Madame d'Youville. In the meantime, her tender heart had felt other pains besides that of seeing her godfather disgraced. It was then that Father Normant fell ill and she also had the sorrow of closing in death the eyes of her first spiritual daughter Sister Cusson, in her final journey to God.

Louis Normant de Faradon was Superior of the Priests of Saint-Sulpice in New France and Vicar General of the Diocese of Quebec. In spite of these duties, he wanted to see to the spiritual formation of Madame d'Youville's association. He composed a rule which while incorporating the essentials of the monastic life, adapted it as needed to the sisters' life of service to the poor. The associates' day began at four o'clock in the morning with silent prayer, followed by attending Mass at the parish church. Then pious readings, examination of conscience, and recitation of the rosary and

---

21   Cf. APC, C 11 A, vol. 81, fol. 427: Hocquart to the Minister, 10 October 1744.
22   Cf. APC, Series B, vol. 78, fol. 22 1/2: 24 March 1744.

the little office of the Holy Name and Coronation of Mary interspersed the day's work and kept the sisters' souls turned towards things spiritual.

On the evening they moved into the Le Verrier house, Father Normant had come to confirm the settling in of the associates, to give them a short exhortation, and to bless them. He was concerned about the details of their life and, being aware of their poverty, with charming kindness he alleviated it with little gifts – pins, needles, writing paper,[23] scissors, rosaries, etc. He oversaw their interests and guided the foundress through her time of turmoil. Fatherly, wise, a holy man, and influential, he alone was able to dispel the plots that surrounded the community. Unfortunately, he was struck down by an illness that progressed so rapidly that all hope was lost for his life. At that moment, his death would have had inestimable consequences. As disturbed water brings to the surface what lies hidden in its depths, so the anguish of Madame d'Youville revealed her great inner strength, her profound trust in God the Father. Her vow was a challenge of faith and a pledge of external worship. She promised to have a picture painted in France depicting the Eternal Father, a considerable expense at that time. She also promised to light a candle before the Blessed Sacrament every year on the main feast day of the Sulpicians, the Presentation of Mary in the Temple. Every 21st of November Montrealers can see the votive offering of Mother d'Youville burning in Notre Dame Church, while the painting of the Eternal Father still hangs in the community room of the Mother House in Montreal.

God restored the health of Father Normant, but in exchange gathered to himself the youngest of the group, Sister Catherine Cusson, who had been suffering from progressive tuberculosis for some months. She left the fervent cenacle in the Le Verrier house for heaven on 20 February 1741 at the age of only thirty-two after four years of exemplary religious life. But even if the good God wanted to test his servant, it was not His will to extinguish her work through lack of strong recruits; He therefore found a replacement for the young deceased woman. Six months after her death the foundress joyfully admitted into the community on the feast of the Exaltation of the Holy Cross the robust young woman Catherine de Rainville who was only thirty years old. In September 1744 Thérèse Lasserre-Laforme joined the small group, increasing the number of associates to five.

---

23   These imported articles were costly. For example, a folder of pins cost three livres and a quire of writing paper one livre, ten sols.

Fire! The cry so feared by Montrealers woke Madame d'Youville during a winter's night in 1745. The interior of her house was in flames. They only had time to throw on a few clothes and rush out; most of them were barefoot. Madame d'Youville with no stockings wore one good shoe and one old, worn-out slipper. Huddled together in the snow and shivering – on the 31st of January – the disaster victims wept and moaned, believing now that Madame d'Youville was homeless she would abandon them. In the general confusion, a mentally retarded woman whom they had forced to come outside, remembering her precious wooden shoes, leapt quickly as a deer back into the house to collect them and there met her death, to the great sorrow of Madame d'Youville. The public, running to the spectacle, far from feeling compassion for the misfortune of the foundress saw in it the hand of God bringing down her ambitions. Evil people quickly make God an accomplice to their own wicked desires. The detractors of the foundress even cynically used her misfortune to try to prove their accusations: "You see," they said, "these purple flames? That's the alcohol that was destined for the Indians burning."[24]

Madame d'Youville also saw the hand of God in this accident, but the hand was beckoning her closer to Him. She used this test as a stepping-stone to virtue. Detached, she wished always to remain thus. "We have had too much comfort," she told her Sisters, "perhaps too much attachment to worldly things. Hereafter, we shall live more in common and in greater poverty." And forthwith, on 2 February, she signed an act of renunciation, drafted by Father Normant, that has subsequently been known as the Original Commitment.

> We, the undersigned, for the greater glory of God, the salvation of our souls and the relief of the poor, wishing sincerely to leave the world and to renounce everything that we possess in order to consecrate ourselves to the service of the destitute, united by the bonds of charity (without any intention on our part of forming a new community), in order to live and die together, so that this union may be firm and lasting, unanimously we have agreed and of our own free will we have promised the following:
>
> 1. Henceforth, to live together for the rest of our days in perfect union and charity under the direction of those who will be given to us, in the practice and faithful observance of the rule which will be

---

24   Cf. MD.

prescribed for us; in complete submission and obedience to the one among us who will be charged with the government of the house; and in entire poverty and renunciation, putting in common from now on everything that we possess and everything that we shall possess in the future, without keeping for ourselves the ownership of it or the right to dispose of it, making by this act a pure, simple and irrevocable gift to the poor, which no one among us nor among our relatives may claim after our death for any reason whatsoever, except landed property, however, if there be any of it, which they can dispose of freely.

2. Unreservedly to consecrate our time, our days, our work, indeed our lives, to labour, the product thereof to be put in common to provide subsistence for the poor and for ourselves.

3. To receive, feed and shelter as many poor as we can take care of by ourselves or by the alms of the faithful.

4. All persons who will be received in the association will bring with them everything that they have: linen, clothes, furniture and money, all to be put in common, nothing excepted or retained; renouncing every right of ownership or withdrawal by a voluntary and irrevocable gift which they make to Jesus Christ. And if they have any income or annuities, they will be included and put into the common fund. All landed property will be excepted, as said above, which they can dispose of at death.

5. If any one of those who will have been received into the society is obliged to leave it for good reasons, she will not claim anything that she may have brought to it, having freely surrendered it and made gift of it to the poor; but she will be satisfied with what others may have the charity to give her.

6. If, in the course of time, there are no persons capable of maintaining this good work, or if, for some other reason, it is not wise to continue it, the undersigned wish and intend that all property, moveable and immoveable, will be put into the hands of the Superior of the Seminary of Montreal, to be used according to his discretion in good works, and especially for the relief of the poor, transferring to him every right of ownership, making to him a gift of it, in their name as well as in that of the poor, to whom everything belongs, declaring anew that such is their intention.

This act of union having now been read and reread, we do approve it and with the help of God's grace we obligate ourselves with all our hearts to fulfil its terms.

Made at Montreal in the presence of the undersigned, 2 February 1745.

> M. Lajemmerais veuve Youville
> Catherine Demers
> Marie-Louise Thaumur[25]

Jointly signed by the first three associates and incorporated into the Constitution of 1781, this contract of complete detachment has since been signed by every sister on the day of her religious profession and forms the basis of the Institute of the Grey Nuns.

Several days after the fire, a wealthy businessman, Monsieur Fonblanche offered the unfortunate foundress a house, free of charge, that he owned on Saint Paul Street west of the Market Square.[26] Some friends[xxiv] – thank God she had some – and several other charitable souls lent beds and other necessary furnishings, and Madame d'Youville was again able to reunite her poor who had been scattered hither and yon. Everyone must have been quite crowded since the house measured only twenty-three feet by thirty, but at least it was a shelter. But how were people going to be fed during this state of total upheaval? The priests of the Seminary, with their usual generosity, took charge of feeding everyone; and they did this for almost six months, that is, during the time the poor spent in the house of Monsieur Fonblanche.

In the summer, Madame d'Youville concluded a verbal contract to rent for three years[27] the house of Dominique Janson-Lapalme on Notre Dame Street across from the Récollet Fathers. The year had not yet ended, however, when the landlord, going back on his word, wanted the house returned. A more important person, the Governor, desired to have it. On 16 July 1746, the tenant was ordered to vacate the premises. The summons was issued in the name of the wife of Governor Du Bois Berthelot de Beaucours, Gabrielle-Françoise Aubert, who held the power of attorney for Dominique Janson-Lapalme. The landlord hid under the disguise of legal proceedings thus allowing the overbearing Governor to conduct the affair. Madame d'Youville protested and asked for at least three months to find other lodgings, but the Governor took the case to court. The case was heard by Lieutenant General Guiton de Monrepos and Maître Adhémar, who

---

25   Translation quoted with modifications from Estelle Mitchell, S. G. M., *The Spiritual Portrait of Saint Marguerite d'Youville 1701-1771*, trans. Sister Joanna Kerwin and Sister Antoinette Bezaire (N.P.: N.Pub., 1993; originally published 1977), pp. 132-34 [Translator's note].

26   Cf. APQ, Oath and Enumeration of Montreal in 1731 by Messire Louis Normant, p. 55.

27   Cf. MD.

was standing in for the absent King's Procurator.[xxv] The following is the conclusion of the judgement that was rendered:

> WE, having heard the parties, together with Maître Adhémar for the absent King's Procurator, seeing that the summons made to the said Defendant the 16th of July last, together with the power of attorney and letters sent from the said Lapalme, which were duly read and tabled, have declared the said notice to tenant good and valid for the 15th of the present month of August, the completion date of their verbal lease; we, therefore, do command and order the said Lady Defendant to vacate the premises on the said date, having made any repairs for which the tenant is liable and left the place clean; if not, and as a result of not having done so, we order that the furniture found on the premises be sent to auction, and we command the Lady Defendant by these presents that whatever may befall in case of an appeal implemented in the form of a retainer *non cossion* [sic], by whatever summons and without prejudice in giving warning to her, she present herself before us in the accustomed manner. WE DO ORDER AND COMMAND, etc.
>
> Guiton Monrepos
> Danré de Blanzy

How familiar these names are: Guiton de Monrepos, Adhémar, Du Bois Berthelot de Beaucours. Are they not those of 1743? Was not de Beaucours's at the bottom of the 1738 petition? Is this a coincidence or despicable harassment?

No one better than the evicted woman knew the scarcity of houses for rent in Montreal – and just ten days to find one. She might as well already be out on the street. The nastiness of these proceedings, however, aroused the indignation of a noble soul who having no house to rent, gave up her own. Madame de La Corne by a gracious gesture turned over to the poor her house on the north-west corner of Saint Paul and Saint Claude Streets and retired to her country estate.[xxvi] Obviously, this gracious hospitality could only be temporary, so Madame d'Youville was once again in search of a dwelling. Before the end of the year, she was able to rent a rather large stone house on the Church Square that belonged to Monsieur D'Ailleboust de Cuisy.[xxvii] Her household now consisted of eighteen people.

In spite of its apparently precarious status and the austere life lived by its members who had completely given up the life of ease, this young community was nevertheless attracting new candidates. Thus, in this memorable year of 1746, Sisters Véronneau, Bénard-Bourjoli, and Arelle joined the ranks of the servants of the poor.

These recruits, like a pledge of hope or a balm from heaven, soothed the wounded soul of the foundress. Her courage, as we have seen, knew no obstacles, but so many disappointments, frustrations, and worries took their toll on her health already weakened by seven years of sufferings. Furthermore, scarcely had they moved than a serious illness struck her. Days of agonizing worry followed for the little community that had been wounded to the heart, for they loved her as a mother. Even through her sternness there always shone the charm of her goodness arising from a sensitive and generous heart filled with divine love.

At the very moment Madame d'Youville was struggling for her life, the government authorities, who were in a quandary, decided to confer provisionally upon her the administration of Montreal's General Hospital. Empowered by her trust in the Eternal Father and deaf to the pleadings of reason which assailed her, with her eyes fixed beyond human horizons, she accepted.

Braid and profession cross of Mother d'Youville on the book, *Les saintes voies de la croix* (The Holy Ways of the Cross), written by Monsignor Henri-Marie Boudon.

Note: the personal mark of Mother d'Youville "at the General Hospital of Montreal P+"

CHAPTER V

A Hospital Administrator

I N A JUDGEMENT given on 22 April 1735, the Superior Council of Quebec, after examining the claims held in France against the General Hospital, held it responsible for the debts incurred by its former Superior, Brother Chrétien. The claims amounted to 24,940 livres, 13 sols, 9 deniers, in addition to the legal fees, which added another 587 livres, 11 sols. In Canada the debts of the Brothers Hospitallers were 12,471 livres, 15 sols, 3 deniers. The General Hospital of Montreal was thus 38,000 livres in debt.

Even though the claims had been officially recognized, they had not been settled. In April 1744, the Minister was putting pressure on the administrators of the colony to find a solution for the Hospital because the creditors were getting irritated at the administrative postponements. This is quite understandable since they had been waiting since 1735! According to Monsieur de Lamarche, who held the power of attorney for the Hospitallers, several creditors "had found themselves reduced to extreme need," and several others had lost everything through the failure of the Superior Council to settle this affair.[xxviii] Hence the general discontent.

When Bishop de Pontbriand arrived in the country in the summer of 1741, one of his first matters of concern was this complicated business. The following year he suggested to the Minister that the General Hospital and the Hôtel-Dieu of Montreal be merged. The administrative costs would be reduced, and the country would be relieved of a religious community. Nothing could have pleased the Court more, and the idea was most congenial to the Minister. Nonetheless, the debts posed a severe obstacle not only to this solution but to many others also. Thus, the Minister concluded his letter of the spring of 1743 to the administrators with this direction: "Whatever proposal you have to make as a result of this examination, it will be necessary to establish the true situation of the temporal affairs of the General Hospital, for on that position must be based all the decisions to be taken."[1]

---

1   APC, series B, vol. 76.

In November 1746 the Bishop, being better informed on the affairs of the country than he was when he had been there for only a year, wrote to the Minister: "We still have reached no settlement for the Charon Brothers. Messieurs the Governor General and the Intendant have been very busy. These Brothers, except for the oldest, write to me incessantly that they are not able to carry on, that they are in no condition to care for the poor, that all their properties are falling apart from lack of repairs. It is absolutely necessary to make some kind of provision for them. Indeed, I would have already done so by installing Madame d'Youville there with the five ladies she has gathered round herself in Montreal and who are performing many useful works, but I was awaiting your orders this year."[2]

Events hastened the administrators' decision. On 30 June 1747 Brother André De Moyres died, and on 9 August Brother Alexandre Turpin, who was seventy-seven years old, went to his eternal reward. There remained Brother Jean Jeantôt, an old man of seventy-nine, and Brother Joseph Dellerme, who was in his sixties. There were only four residents in the Hospital, of whom the oldest was eighty-eight and the youngest seventy-three. These patriarchs were vegetating in a pitiful state in several rooms that they occupied on the ground floor. Through broken windows on the upper floors, gusts of rain were damaging the woodwork, causing mould to accumulate. The outbuildings were also collapsing and the grounds lay waste. It was to these ruins, both human and material, that the Ordinance of 27 August 1747 entrusted this work to the keeping of Madame d'Youville.

Possessing the keys to this huge, dilapidated building was not everything; it had to be made habitable. The cleaning took eighteen work days from five in the morning until the evening Angelus[xxix] at a cost of 831 livres, 10 sols just for the cleaning women. As for the repairs, the following is an excerpted list from the report of the specialists[xxx]:

> Repair the main door of the church which is ruined and falling to pieces.
>
> Install steps to the entrance door of said Hospital.
>
> Remove completely the stone flooring in the hall of the poor, replaster the latter all around inside and all the window casements.
>
> The dormitories and rooms on the first floor are badly damaged. The partition walls, passages, window casements, and beams need to be completely replastered.

---

2   APC, C 11 A, vol. 86, fol. 143 – 10 November 1746.

The corridor and its window casements on the second floor need to be roughcast and completely replastered as well as the dormitories, rooms, window casements, and the hall from top to bottom.

Completely redo seventy large window frames, eight others, and eight partition doors.

Reroof fifteen dormers.

Two hundred feet of paving stones are required.

One thousand two hundred and twenty-six window panes are required. [It should be said that these were only seven by eight inches and that thirty-two of them were needed per window.]

The inventory is pitiable. The linen had been reduced to a few rags, the table and kitchen utensils to a small number of chipped, dented, and perforated pieces, the furniture dirty and mostly rickety. The most frequently recurring word in this report is "old." Madame d'Youville was hardly surprised by the specialists' findings; she was familiar with the poverty of the Hospital since she had often gone there to mend the rags of the old men. But after her various vagaries of fortune, these long corridors and large rooms lined with windows must have seemed like Paradise.

On 7 October, the time for taking possession of the property had finally arrived. Madame d'Youville, still too weak to walk, rode across the city on a cart on which a mattress had been placed. Leaving the Church Square, she descended Saint François Xavier Street, crossed the Market Square, and exited the city through the Port Gate, which obliquely faced the Hospital located on the Plains of Saint Anne. On this occasion, her spirit of poverty exposed her to ridicule, but this spirit rose far above these prickings of pride. To her, being a servant to the poor was not merely a label, but a stringent reality with its own humiliating situations.

According to her commission as Director, Madame d'Youville was obliged to keep the registers. Her manuscript daybook still exists. On the first page, we read:

The year 1747, the first of September, I received the Letters Patent from Messieurs the Bishop, the General, and the Intendant to administer the property of the General Hospital and to care for the poor there, along with my associates, who are
Marie Louise Lasource, age 39
Marie Catherine Dessermont, age 49
Catherine Rinville, age 37, admitted 14 September 1741
Térèse Laforme, age 34, admitted 23 September 1744

Agathe Véronneau, age about 40, who is not yet a member of the society, admitted 10 February 1746

Marguerite Térèse Despins, age 28, a boarder for 9 years.

We found in said Hospital four poor men

Jean Barrier, age 88

Louis Lemagre, age 80

Louis Moro, age 74

Pierre LeBeuffe, age 73.

We brought along Françoise Oson [Auzon], the wife of Pierre LeBeuffe, she has been blind for fourteen years and has been with us since 21 November 1737.

Marie Morin, Widow Tomas, a paralytic about 90 years old, admitted 20 April 1747

Marie Joseph Bourjoli, age 23, admitted 12 July 1741

Antoinette Arelle, age 26, admitted 2 November 1741

Marie Joseph Latreilye, age 34, admitted 28 August 1743

Térèse Lagarde, age 15, admitted 25 April 1742

Angélique Brindamour, age 6, admitted 25 July 1747

Marie Louise de Bralye, age 16, paying 120 livres for board, admitted 14 September 1747.

The annual income of the General Hospital, which had originally been 2,113 livres, had declined to 786 livres and in any case was still under seizure by the creditors. The farm at Pointe Saint-Charles yielded an income of six hundred minots of wheat, half of which went to the farmer. The farm in Chambly yielded three hundred on the same terms. Besides the paltry income from the lands, Madame d'Youville could only count on her own industry; but her noble daring born out of her trust in Divine Providence never wavered.

After the heads of government had authorized the repairs that had been declared urgent by the specialists, Madame d'Youville negotiated the loans necessary for carrying them out. Soon two halls were ready to receive residents, one for men and one for women. Her sense of organization, her vigilance and her economy, along with the ceaseless work of the associates in a short time restored order and comfort to the Hospital. Some ladies of social standing, filled with admiration for the courage and capability of the Director, expressed their desire to live in this peaceful setting as boarders; and from 1748 Madame d'Youville could count on this source of income.

In the summer of this same year, the successor of the wise Intendant Hocquart arrived in Quebec City. He, François Bigot, was a close relative of Marshal d'Estrées. Intoxicated with his newly acquired powers, he could

Façade of the General Hospital showing the additions made by the Grey Nuns. Note between the enclosing wall and the main gate to the Chapel the houses for the insane built in 1802 and demolished in 1844. The houses that Mother d'Youville had built were in the garden behind the main building.

The original habit of the Sisters of Charity of the General Hospital of Montreal, called the Grey Nuns. Designed by the Mother Foundress, it underwent no modifications until the 1960s.

only talk about improvements and expansions and whetted appetites for his beautiful projects. Madame Bégon, the Canadian Madame de Sévigné and as witty as her French counterpart, before having met the Intendant reported the hearsay: "Nothing could be more magnificent in everything than this Intendant, and we never cease hearing about it." In January 1749, he visited Montreal. After having recounted the worldly social whirl resulting from his visit, the same letter writer describes his departure. "He left this morning, followed, I believe, by a thousand sledges. It was a caravan as never seen before, for conveyances were needed for all his mirrors and knickknacks. Had Monsieur Hocquart seen that, I think he would have died of grief."[3] Undoubtedly, Bigot loved pomp; but in bringing along his silverware and household furnishings, perhaps he wanted to dazzle the Canadians in order to put pressure on them later.

Shortly after she had moved into the Hospital, an important social work was suggested to Madame d'Youville. Since 1744, Father Antoine Déat, the parish priest, had been advocating to obtain from the authorities a place of refuge for prostitutes. Familiar with the virtue of Madame d'Youville, he made new requests to Monsieur Hocquart and received permission for her to undertake this work of rehabilitation. As a result, Madame d'Youville had twelve rooms prepared in the attic to receive these young women who had been condemned by the courts of summary jurisdiction.[xxxi] This area received the name of Jericho, alluding to the famous high walls of that city, because a similar establishment in the past had been given this name. The good priest was not satisfied merely to initiate this project; he also contributed financially, assuming a large part of the cost of feeding the young women in Jericho until Intendant Bigot added it to the list of the King's expenses.

Madame d'Youville's graceful manners and gentleness drew all classes to her. Ladies found in her an attentive and affable hostess. In her presence, orphans blossomed and the poor lost their shame. The women prisoners also benefitted from her moral influence. Madame Bégon, the bantering letter writer, bears trustworthy witness to this. On 8 January 1749, she wrote to her son-in-law, the Sieur de Villebois: "Today, dear son, we saw Madame Bouat who, as I related to you, has been at the Charon Brothers with Madame d'Youville since Saint Martin's tide. It's entertaining to see her. She does nothing but preach and proclaim the pleasure of living there in retirement from the world. She assured us of the conversion of four ladies who had been sent to Jericho; she visits them from time to time. All

3   Cf. APQ, *Rapp. 1935* [Report 1935] – Letters of Madame Bégon, p. 43: 2 March 1749.

that Madame Bouat fears is that the soldiers may want to rescue these ladies from captivity, but I do not think for all that that they would want to do anything so out of place."[4] Madame Bégon was mistaken. For one day a soldier, who was probably drunk, arrived at the Hospital pistol in hand and loudly announced that he would strike down Madame d'Youville if she refused to free his mistress. The doorkeeper, terrified, ran to warn the Director so she could hide; but the latter, instead, went resolutely to the door and firmly ordered this firebrand to leave immediately without further trouble. The calm and dignity of Madame d'Youville so disconcerted the unhappy man that he turned on his heels and fled without replying.

According to Madame Bégon, not only did Madame d'Youville have a moderating influence on a worldly woman like Madame Bouat, to the point of giving her a taste for devotion, but she also succeeded in helping four public sinners to repent. This zeal so vexed the libertines that they could not keep quiet about it, and they found a ready ear in Bigot. On the pretext that Madame d'Youville had overstepped her rights by cutting the prisoners' hair, he wrote to her:

> Madame:
>
> I have been informed that Jericho is beginning to cause abuses which might have considerable consequences in the future if I do not establish order there.
>
> And what has most surprised me is that you have taken it on yourself to cut the hair of the women who have been sent there, even of one among them who was confined there unexpectedly. If I had not as much consideration for you as I have, I would have you prosecuted for having acted so indiscreetly. I am glad to inform you, if you do not know it, that it is the business of a superior court to impose such a shameful penalty.
>
> To prevent similar abuses, I expressly forbid you to take in any girl or woman at this Jericho except by my order, which I shall send you in writing when I consider it expedient to confine any of them; and maintenance will be furnished at the King's expense. I trust that you will not fall again into the fault that you have committed; otherwise I shall effectively remedy the situation.
>
> The judge will be keeping an eye on how they are being treated in order to report to me; and he will likewise let me know of girls leading a dissolute life in the city whom I shall order to be trans-

---

4   Cf. APQ, *Rapp. 1935* [Report 1935] – Letters of Madame Bégon, p. 25: 8 January 1749.

ferred from the prisons to Jericho if I deem it appropriate. Monsieur Varin will do the same for the country girls.

I think, Madame, that I have written enough on this matter; and I hope that no other complaint about this establishment will be brought to me in the future.

I am with respect,

> Madame
> Your very humble and most obedient servant
> BIGOT[5]

Can you hear the whip cracking? Such is the law, full of zeal but restrictive. Since these girls were a source of trouble and an expense on the Director's meagre budget, only the salvation of their souls could commit her to keeping them. Resources being irregular, the feeding of thirty poor people, the staff, and then these girls became a nagging problem. Once again, the priests of the Seminary lent a hand by taking up collections for the General Hospital. Father Pierre Navetier, P. S. S., took up one in the city and suburbs that produced an abundant manna of foodstuffs, various goods, and coins. Father Joseph Hourdé, P. S. S., also, travelled through the parishes of Laprairie, Longueuil, Varennes, and Verchères. There too the almsgiving was generous. The greatest comfort that Madame d'Youville received from these collections, however, was to find out that the populace had recovered from the hasty prejudices spread about by gossipmongers.

We have seen the foundress at work, and we know her virtue. Henceforth, we shall eagerly await to see whether perchance she will need champions on her behalf.

---

5   Cf. ASGM, original letter, signed and dated 17 August 1750. [Translation, in part, from Sister Mary Pauline Fitts, *Hands to the Needy*, p. 147. *Translator's Note.*]

CHAPTER VI

Abraham's Sacrifice

*T*HE DIRECTOR'S commission for the General Hospital[1] contained the conventional phrase "at the good pleasure of His Majesty." As always, the heads of government were committed to having their choices ratified. It is easy to understand that nothing less than this assurance was required to persuade Madame d'Youville to undertake the reconstruction of this ruin. In the meantime, she had to submit her proposals for acquitting the debts. A letter from Bishop de Pontbriand, dated 8 September 1748, corroborates this undertaking. He wrote to her concerning this: "I am going to begin a memorandum to show the Minister that no better means could be found to consolidate this house than to place it in your hands."[2] In equally laudatory terms, he recommended the foundress to his vicar general in Paris in a letter dated the same month. On 22 February 1749, in a letter to the Secretary of State, Monsieur Rouillé, the Abbé de l'Isle-Dieu wrote:

> I shall report later on the proposals made on this subject by the Lady, the Widow Youville, who is at present the administrator of the Hospital of Montreal. Monsieur the Bishop of Quebec speaks to me of her in the following terms: "She is," says this Prelate, "a person of rare merit, and I think that this Hospital would prosper in her capable hands; I highly recommend this good work to you." It would appear, therefore, that Monsieur the Bishop of Quebec would like this Lady to remain in charge of the temporal administration of the Hospital of Montreal perhaps because, in addition to the merit he recognizes in this Lady, he is partial to the proposals made by the Lady Youville and of which I shall give an account in the excerpts from her letters and memoranda which she has sent me on this subject. Besides, Monsieur the Bishop of Quebec thinks that the care and administration of the Hospital of Montreal will be best and

---

1   Cf. SD, pp. 305-07.
2   Cf. ASGM, autograph letter, signed and dated 8 September 1748.

most advantageously entrusted to women rather than men since both men and women will be received and looked after there.[3]

A little further in the same report, the Abbé de l'Isle-Dieu refers to Madame d'Youville's proposals and says:

> It is this Widow Youville whom Monsieur the Bishop of Quebec so greatly praised to me in his last letters. It appears that he wishes that she remain in charge of the Hospital of Montreal, both as Superior and Administrator. She also seems to be desirous to do this, which is truly praiseworthy for it appears to be only for the good and advantage of the Hospital of Montreal that she is requesting the supervision and direction.
>
> I have the honour of drawing your attention to excerpts from the letters of Monsieur the Bishop of Quebec in which he expresses the Lady d'Youville's merits and abilities that give him reason to favour her. Clearly, he knows her piety, zeal, ability, and intelligence; but the last is a new reason which, added to the first, may be of a great advantage to the Hospital of Montreal and enable it to become completely debt free.
>
> The Lady d'Youville gave me to understand and afterwards told me clearly in her letters that if the Court were willing to confer upon her Letters Patent for the little community of Daughters of Piety that she organized for the service of the poor and the care of the sick, she is certain of finding 8,000 livres which she will send me as soon as possible to acquit the debts of the Hospital; but whether this money comes from her or from various persons that piety has united for this good work, she adds that it will only happen if they are established and set in place by Letters Patent.
>
> She suggests that the Court's opposition to establishing new religious communities is not relevant because one which no longer exists would be suppressed to form another that will be much more useful for:
>
> She will add education to relief of the poor and the care of women as well as men, thus bringing relief for both.
>
> This new little Community will dedicate itself not only to the education of young girls, but also receive women who have led

---

3   Cf. ASQ, Jacques Viger, *Ma Saberdache* [My Sabretache], vol. A, p. 154.

dissolute lives, without prejudice to the care of the sick poor either in time or care given.

These are apparently the factors that decided Monsieur the Bishop of Quebec to give preference to the Lady Widow Youville.

> I am with respect, Your Excellency …
> At Paris, this 22nd of February, 1749[4]

As can be seen, Madame d'Youville did not delay presenting her proposals. By October 1747, she had sent to the Abbé de l'Isle-Dieu along with the letter mentioned above, a copy of her commission as Director with a power of attorney for managing in France the financial affairs of the Hospital.

The Bishop, the Governor, the Marquis de Beauharnois, and the Intendant, Gilles Hocquart, were all most favourably disposed towards Madame d'Youville, and the future looked bright. But who can predict the future? Three years later the situation was not the same. In 1750 the Intendant of New France was François Bigot who, unlike his predecessor, had not toiled over this thorny business and whose administrative qualities were motivated by greed and who, moreover, was preoccupied with making a fortune very quickly. On his first sojourn in Montreal, in 1749, he visited the General Hospital and showed his satisfaction with what he found there. Still, if his bristling letter to Madame d'Youville on the subject of Jericho can be seen as a barometer of his feelings, by 1750 they had changed from warm to frigid.

The Minister had approved the provisional nomination of Madame d'Youville as administrator of the General Hospital. He had nonetheless added: "Whatever may be the success of this arrangement, I have to inform you that His Majesty is in nowise disposed to consent to anything that might lead to the formation of a new community of young women in the colony. There are already all too many."[5] The religious communities were the Minister's nightmare. Every year there were appeals for gifts from one or another of them. In view of the Court's firm opposition to increasing religious communities, Bishop de Pontbriand probably believed that Madame d'Youville's society would collapse under the same prohibitions as that of François

---

4   Cf. ASQ, Jacques Viger, *Ma Saberdache* [My Sabretache], vol. A, p. 165. The original copy, made in Paris by the Abbé Holmes and brought to Canada in 1837, is preserved in the Archives of the Seminary of Quebec.

5   Cf. APC, series B, vol. 87: the Minister to Messsieurs de La Galissionnière and Hocquart, 12 February 1748.

Charon and end up the same way. Why, then, should not his General Hospital of Quebec City profit from the break up? He therefore proposed to the new governor and to Bigot the merger of the Hospital of Montreal with that of Quebec City. Monsieur de La Jonquière, who had no inkling of the intricacies of this matter, was easily won over to the Bishop's view. The annual joint letter of the Intendant and the Governor for 1749 declares: "We should have thought that there was no other alternative regarding the General Hospital of Montreal than to merge it with the Hôtel-Dieu of this city; but on the objections made by the Bishop that it would be more profitable to merge it with the General Hospital of Quebec City, since we deemed it necessary that the mentally handicapped, incurables, and elderly of the colony be therein received, we agree with him that this latter merger would be more useful and fitting for several reasons …"[6] One of the reasons invoked was that the Hospital of Quebec City being poor, the funds that the Hospital of Montreal would bring to it would help to relieve its financial straits.

The Minister approved the merger on condition that a hospice be left in Montreal that would be served by two or three nuns from the General Hospital in Quebec City. But his response to the Bishop was ambiguous because he added: "if the General Hospital of Quebec is not deemed adequate for all the invalids of the colony."[7] The administrators seized this condition as a pretext to decree the suppression of the General Hospital of Montreal. Consequently, on 15 October 1750, they issued an ordinance which annulled the provisional agreement made with Madame d'Youville in 1747. By this ordinance all the moveable and immoveable property of the Montreal General Hospital was amalgamated to that of Quebec, and it authorized the nuns in Quebec City to sell the hospital buildings with all their surrounding houses and even such furniture as would be deemed of too little value to be moved to Quebec City. The ordinance added that if any parties should have representations to make in regard to this sale, they should lodge an appeal with Monsieur Bigot within three months.[8] What an extraordinary proceeding – to begin selling the property and then to allow an appeal against the sale! The Abbé de L'Isle-Dieu wrote as much to the Bishop: "It seems to me, My Lord, that in the country

---

6   Cf. APC, C 11 A, vol. 93, fol. 25: Messieurs de La Jonquière and Bigot to the Minister, 1 October 1749.

7   Cf. APC, B vol. 91, fol. 216: Rouillé to the Bishop of Quebec, 14 June 1750.

8   Cf. SD.

where you are, people are over-hasty and begin executing projects without having scrutinized them. This is – or so it seems to me – like hanging someone provisionally and then initiating his trial."[9]

The slippery Bigot, foreseeing the protests of the citizens, only proclaimed the ordinance when the last ship had left Quebec for France. Montrealers could petition to their heart's content, but nothing would arrive from the Court for the next six months. Confronted with an accomplished fact and finally rid of this bothersome problem, surely the Court would uphold the administrators' decision. Thus reasoned Bigot, but he overlooked the rights of the Sulpicians. He was forgetting, or was unaware of, the influence at Court of their Superior, Father Cousturier[10]; and he, who would trample on any obstacle that got in his way, was underestimating the King's sense of justice and religion.

At the Hospital in Montreal, life went on as usual from day to day. Not having the means to stock up on supplies, Madame d'Youville herself would go to the market to buy food, like any housekeeper. On 23 November 1750, as she was passing through the Port Gate, she heard the rolling of drums which preceded the publication of an ordinance. How astonished she must have been to hear the town crier proclaim first her name and then her destitution. There on the Square she received publicly this undeserved blow. The ordinance was dated 15 October; no one had had the decency to notify her personally about it before it was proclaimed throughout the city. Had it not been for her chance presence at the market, the whole city would have known about it before she did. This conjunction of events at least allowed her time to prepare her associates for the heavy blow when the bailiff finally came to read the ordinance to them. When he arrived, she did not remonstrate in any way; she listened to him with her usual calm and supernatural resignation. She would be completely poor; and scorn, which is the worst suffering of poverty, would be her lot.

Father Normant, in informing his bishop, has passed on to history the sentiments of the populace about this event. He wrote:

> The ordinance has caused a great stir here not only by the drums announcing it, but also by the murmurings, slanders, and calumnies that it has occasioned. Everyone was so shocked by it that without restraint and without regard for the laws of charity, they have

9   Cf. APQ, *Rapp. 1936* [Report, 1936]: *Lettres et Mémoires de l'Abbé de L'Isle-Dieu* [Letters and Memoranda of the Abbé de L'Isle-Dieu], p. 319, Letter of 2 June 1751.

10   He signed his name Cousturier with an "s".

exploded with resentment against both Your Excellency and Monsieur Bigot, whom they assume to be the authors, with the exception of Monsieur the Governor General, to whom they assign no part in this business which they believe to be contrary to his sentiments. I have been and still am very distressed to see such blameworthy excesses, God offended, and the trust and respect that are owed to Your Excellency altered and diminished. In my opinion, it is a very poor way to defend a good cause.

Here, My Lord, is more or less and insofar as I have been able to ascertain it what is being said about the matter. I can only repeat the reasons the public is giving, without adding my own or approving of their excesses. First, they are attacking the motivation of the ordinance, they think that it is neither the glory of God nor the relief of the poor that has been envisaged by it, but rather for reasons of patronage, partiality, inclination and human considerations, the Hospital of Quebec City has been favoured. What has given rise to these false judgements are the false reports and complaints that the other communities in Quebec City have unwisely made and communicated to several people in this city about the special benefits Your Excellency and Monsieur Bigot have shown to that hospital without, or so they maintain, regard for the needs of the others who in a spirit of jealousy have spoken thus.

They regard this merger as unjust inasmuch as it deprives the poor of this municipality of an acquired and very legitimate right to the goods that are being disposed of in favour of outsiders, and also inasmuch as it is directly contrary to the intention of the founders who had in view to establish this hospital only for the poor of this municipality.

They maintain that this merger is absolutely null in its form since the interested parties were not all summoned or heard, the merger having been concluded without previous information or report that might have proved its necessity or usefulness. On the contrary, it seems that it was kept secret until the means of communication with France had departed and that it was only published when there was no longer any means of recourse to His Majesty, which is contrary to the rules.

They are also amazed how Monsieur Bigot, who is the pursuant party, has appropriated to himself alone the knowledge of this matter, the qualities of judge and plaintiff being incompatible according to the laws. Moreover, it is being said that Monsieur the Intendant has already supplied on a number of occasions, and is still supplying, grounds for a just and legitimate challenge to his being a judge in this matter since he has publicly revealed his intentions and affirmatively announced the destruction of this good work, which in any other case would be grounds for a challenge. But in this case, a new kind of jurisprudence is being followed, which is giving rise to murmurings. Some people have deceived themselves, nonetheless, in believing that they will be denied neither the time nor the means of making their most humble petitions to His Majesty, and that when they are able to inform the Court about it, the merger will not take effect.[11]

Father Normant also drafted a petition addressed to the Minister, with copies in the form of an appeal sent to the Bishop, the Governor General, and the Intendant. This petition was signed by twenty-four citizens with the Governor of Montreal, Monsieur de Longueuil, at their head. After demonstrating that the merger of the General Hospital of Montreal with that of Quebec City was null and void, the petition quotes a clause from the Letters Patent that stipulated: "said establishment will be in perpetuity and unable to be changed, either in place or into any other pious work; … that it shall be in perpetuity for sheltering and relief of the poor of Montreal in accordance with the intention of the founders."

For their part, Madame d'Youville and her associates presented a petition containing the same arguments with the addition of the following unconditional offer:

They offer to liquidate the debts of Brother Chrétien in France within three years, to come to terms with his creditors for the remission the latter have proposed, and to pay as soon as they possibly can the debts he contracted in Canada. In exchange, they are asking to replace the Brothers Hospitallers, to enjoy all the rights, benefits, and privileges stipulated in the latter's Letters Patent, which will remain in their respect the same for the establishment and administration of said Hospital; in consequence thereof, they commit themselves to give an annual account of the income of said Hospital and of the alms distributed to the poor; and, later, if for some unforeseen reasons, His Majesty should be pleased to rescind the administration of said Hospital from the suppliants, they shall be reimbursed for any improvements, repairs, and repayments that they have made out of their own funds and shall be accredited any sums they will have paid to the creditors.

---

11   Cf. ASGM, autograph draft by Monsieur Normant.

In January Madame d'Youville was courageous enough to take these documents herself to Quebec City. She was received coldly by the Bishop and the Intendant who refused to support her petitions.[12] Monsieur de la Jonquière, who did not have any biases, was, on the contrary, struck by the justice of these pleas and promised his mediation. His letter to the Minister of 19 October 1751 displays a brave candour: "Although I had the honour of writing to you jointly with His Excellency the Bishop and Monsieur Bigot on the subject of the merger of the General Hospital of Montreal with that of Quebec City, nevertheless I cannot excuse myself from the honour of sending you the attached petitions that were made by all the Estates of Montreal to the Bishop, Monsieur Bigot, and myself on the strict necessity of allowing this Hospital to remain. You will see, My Lord, the arguments made in this petition, which must be addressed directly to you. Monsieur Bigot maintains his previous view to which I myself had adhered, not having foreseen the wrong that this merger would do to the poor of Montreal."[13]

At the beginning of 1751, Madame d'Youville had presented her accounts to Bigot for his approval. Using various pretexts, he refused to give it. There ensued a real duel through correspondence between guile and honesty. Bigot hedged, evaded, and was underhanded. Madame d'Youville retorted masterfully with reason and moderation. The struggle of this humble woman against official despotism spontaneously brings to mind the promise of the Psalmist: "You shall tread upon the asp and the viper: you shall trample down the lion and the dragon" without harm if the Lord is with you. The Intendant retorted in his letter of 5 February 1751:

> Madame
>
> I am responding to the letter which you gave me the honour of writing to me on the 10th of January last.
>
> I have examined the accounts that you have sent of the income and expenditures of the General Hospital of Montreal for the years 1749 and 1750, as well as those of 1748 which you had previously remitted. From these it appears that the expenditures exceed the receipts by 10,486 livres, 17 sols, 10 deniers. I have noted that the receipts from the house, excluding the income from the lands, just about balance the expenditures of the house for food and maintenance of the poor, but the maintenance cost of the land at Pointe

---

12   Cf. MD.

13   Cf. APC, C 11 A, vol. 97, fol. 123: Monsieur de La Jonquière to the Minister, 19 October 1751.

Saint-Charles and Chambly is double the income they produced, which greatly surprised me.

Please, I implore you, Madame, note that the ordinance of the Bishop and Messieurs de Beauharnois and Hocquart of 27 August 1747 established you only as director of this Hospital for the care of the poor in residence and the property belonging to it, and it even authorizes you to receive the revenues of said property to feed and support said poor and to have essential repairs made to the building, but it does not allow you to incur expenses for these poor in excess of the revenues.

When you noticed, Madame, that the revenues would not be sufficient for supporting the number of infirm people whom you received and that the lands were incurring more expenses than profits, you ought to have advised these Gentlemen, by asking them to authorize you to exceed the expenditures, which they would have allowed you to do had they approved your request; otherwise, they would have decided either to diminish the number of poor people or allow you to transfer some funds in order to be able to support them. Since you have not taken these precautions, and since it is not within my power either to dispose of or transfer the funds of this Hospital, except for debts ordered and approved previously by the directors, I will in no way accept the claims that you allege to have on these funds and the General Hospital of Quebec will in nowise, for the same reason, be obliged to pay them.

Moreover, according to the Rules of this Hospital, firstly, only twelve poor people can be admitted, excepting that the number can be increased in proportion to an increase in the revenues of the community. When you arrived at the Hospital, there were only fourteen or fifteen of whom some had a small income. Until then, no women had been admitted; and you ought not to have increased the number of men, nor indeed received fifteen or sixteen women, for whom you set up a new hall, without having been formally authorized to do so. For this second reason, which is not necessary, the first being sufficient, the expenses incurred in increasing the number of the poor men and women cannot be allocated to the funds of this Hospital.

You request me to notify the nuns of the General Hospital of Quebec to ensure that the fields of Pointe Saint-Charles and Chambly are sown. Since this Hospital will only take possession of these lands in the month of July next, it seems to me only just that you should take charge of sowing the fields in the spring; and I know too well your zeal and charity towards the poor not to hope that you would in any way refuse them your care in this regard, all the more so since, as appears from your last accounts, the seed for the sowing have already been put aside and thus there will not be any reimbursement for this work.

Besides, you will recall that when you came into possession of this Hospital, you enjoyed the harvest sown by the Charon Brothers; and as you will be leaving it at just about the same time as you entered, it would be appropriate if you were to leave the fields, with respect to their cultivation, as you found them.

I also count on you, Madame, and greatly implore you for the sake of these poor people to have the goodness to hire another farmer for Pointe Saint-Charles if the one who is there at present does not wish to remain.

Brother Joseph, the last remaining of the Charon Brothers, having to be maintained by the community, a pension of 500 livres was set aside for him in the inventory of this Hospital's property; and in case he should not remain in the Hospital, this amount was reduced by his consent to 300 livres per year. You paid him the first year which ended in the month of September 1749. You must, Madame, begin to pay this pension in preference to the feeding and maintenance of the poor, since the support of this Brother is assured and privileged against the first revenues of the funds of this Hospital. I therefore implore you to pay him for the year ending September last.

I am with respect ... [14]

Madame d'Youville replied:

Sir

I received the letter which you gave me the honour of writing and which surprised me the more so since it seemed completely contrary both to the ordinance that provisionally established me as director of this General Hospital and to what you yourself gave me the honour of telling me when I presented to you the sad state of this poor house; all of its real estate, buildings, and barns were in ruins and required immediate and extensive repairs. Please remember, Sir, that you engaged me to maintain everything in good condition and to repair whatever needed to be repaired. The Bishop and Monsieur the General have given me the same order. It is thus, Sir, through your consent and that of these Gentlemen that I have laboured for the

---

14   Cf. ASGM, original letter, signed and dated, Quebec City, 5 February 1751.

good of the poor. It is true that I did not take your orders in writing, but your word is just as good, and I trusted it, Sir, as I ought to do by the respect that I owe you and the knowledge I have of your integrity. I acted in consequence. It seems to me that I am right and that you cannot, either in the face of God or man, refuse to allocate to me the said expenses or to reimburse me the amounts I have spent. I borrowed them and I owe them. Besides, Sir, when I had the honour to submit my accounts at the end of the first year of my management, the expenditures exceeded the income by 3,377 livres, 2 sols, 9 deniers. You did not appear to disapprove of this or to be dissatisfied with it. Had I exceeded my powers and acted against your will and the welfare of the poor, it would have been natural to let me know it and to forbid me from continuing to have the said repairs done. But to the contrary, Sir, you exhorted me to continue them because, in fact, you recognized their necessity. Thus, it is not on my own that I acted, Sir, but in full view and with your knowledge and approval.

I would add further, Sir, that it is even by your orders since in establishing me as Director of said Hospital, you ordered me to keep a register of income and expenditures so as to be able to render my accounts; and in the same way, you authorized me to make the more urgent repairs that would be so assessed by experts appointed for this purpose in the presence of the King's Procurator. That was done; the specialists made their reports of necessary and urgent repairs. Those that I had done, Sir, were included therein and were deemed necessary by the said specialists; they were done under authority and in conformity with your orders. You cannot therefore in good conscience refuse to pay me for them since I have in no way exceeded my powers and I have had done only a small part of the repairs deemed necessary and indispensable by the reports that you yourself had drawn up. Sir, when it is necessary to restore farms that have fallen into ruin, to acquire the necessary furnishings for them, to buy ploughs, ploughshares, carts, harnesses, and everything that is needed for the cultivation of the land, fences, ditches, roofs, floors, walls, and hundreds of other indispensable things, the expense becomes necessarily large; and had I through negligence left the houses and barns to fall into ruin and abandoned the cultivation of the fields, you would have held me accountable. I have acted, Sir, for the best, without any personal interest and only for the good of the poor; if I do not have the consolation of having satisfied you, it is not out of ill will but through lack of ability.

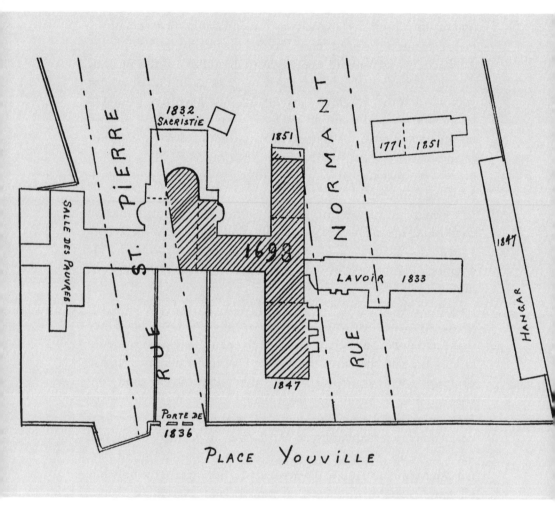

Place Youville
From the Archives of the Grey Nuns of Montreal. The shaded part shows the walls left standing in 1945.

The west wing of the former General Hospital of Montreal as it could be seen in 1945, abutting Rue Normant on the south side of Place Youville

The General Hospital and Mother House of the Grey Nuns at Pointe-à-Callières, today Place d'Youville, seen from the garden side. The position of the chimneys allows us to identify what remains of the building.

This photograph shows the walls of the former edifice as they existed in 1945. The location of the chimneys corresponds exactly to that shown in the view from the garden. The transverse section that joins the west wing on Rue Normant to the wall of the chapel is intact, except for the roof that has been partially modified. The section joining the two wings has been preserved, as can be seen from the roof gable with its chimney.

This photograph shows part of the building constructed by the Charon Brothers in 1693 as it looked in 1945 from Rue Normant. After the fire of 18 May 1765, Mother d'Youville wrote to Madame de Ligneris: "… we are bold enough to be trying to recover a corner of our house whose walls are still in good condition" (10 June 1765). In another letter she mentions the "wing" that the poor will soon be moving into. The walls built by the Charon Brothers were not therefore destroyed by this fire. In 1843 Monsieur Jacques Viger, the archaeologist and historian, affirmed in his *Ma Saberdache* [My Sabretache], Notebook "E," that the walls of 1693 were then still standing; and we know that they have not been destroyed since. The cross marks the room of Marguerite d'Youville, in which she died 23 December 1771.

You seem to blame me, Sir, for having taken in more poor people than the house can support, the number of which is fixed at twelve. I never knew that the number of the poor had been fixed at twelve and I do not think that there is any act that indicates it; but even if that should be so, Sir, I should not be guilty because I was authorized to establish a place for women and to take in, lodge, and feed those women whom I already had in my care. You yourself, Sir, paid them the honour and charity of visiting them, and you appeared to be satisfied and to approve of this good work. You also saw for yourself, Sir, by the minute examination of my accounts as you paid me the honour of pointing out, that this excess expenditure was not for feeding and caring for the poor. As you yourself say, Sir, the income from the house, not to mention the revenue from the lands, just about balances the expenditures made by the house for the feeding and care of the poor. It is therefore exactly and only for the repairs and the maintenance of the real estate that this excess expenditure was incurred. The real estate has thus been improved or, at least, preserved at its initial value; whereas without the repairs, it would have fallen into ruin and become unproductive and a sheer loss. It seems just, Sir, that the said real estate value corresponds to the said expenditure for its profit and preservation. You are too fair not to yield to reasons that are so just.

You show me the honour, Sir, of remarking that when I took charge there were twelve poor people in the Hospital, of whom the majority had a small income. I assure you, Sir, that there were only four and only one of those had a small income. They had great difficulty in surviving there; but since I have come, the number has surpassed thirty and they have had what is necessary, not from the revenues of the lands but through God's Providence and our labours. When I arrived, I did not find that the fields had been sown or a single furrow of fallow land been ploughed; it is I who had this done as well as the seed sown. Thus, Sir, I am bound only to leave things as I found them. The farmer, besides, wants to leave and I have no one to replace him; and even should I find someone, I do not believe I have sufficient authority to transfer the lease to him.

I await, Sir, your goodness in receiving and signing my accounts. They have been done with all the honesty of which I am capable.

I have the honour of being …[15]

---

15   Cf. ASGM, autograph draft, signed and dated 16 February 1751.

Madame d'Youville knew the domineering Bigot too well to hope to win her case solely on the grounds of her rights. She therefore turned to her Bishop, who was likewise one of the chief administrators. She was counting on his spirit of fairness to obtain justice. Unfortunately, her trust only revealed his coolness, as can be seen from the following letter:

> Madame
>
> I have the honour of informing you that I did not take up the accounts that you have rendered and that I left to other powers the care of examining them.
>
> I doubt that by the ruling made during the time of Monsieur Hocquart you were authorized to make the repairs without an order, much less to borrow. It had never been foreseen that you would put the house into debt. The transfer of funds was absolutely forbidden.
>
> You have received many poor people, your charity is admirable, but I fear that you will only be told that you were not obliged to do so.
>
> You received sown fields; I doubt that you will be allowed to leave them in any other state.
>
> I believe that this whole affair will be brought before His Majesty, who has ordered the merger with the General Hospital of Quebec City. I hope that he will see what difficulties have been occasioned by his decision.
>
> When the merger has been accomplished or when some other conclusion to this matter will have occurred, I shall take care of what pertains to my ministry.
>
> I am with great respect ...[16]

Disapproval lingers under the correct phraseology. It was a bitter disillusionment! Her legitimate protector was evading responsibility. Moreover, he seemed to echo the Intendant on the subject of the fields. Had he at least looked into the facts, he would have found out that they had not been sown at the time of the transfer to the foundress in 1747.

His passion about points of honour, underlain by a hundred other political reasons, forbade Bigot from admitting that he might have been mistaken. Thus, his reply of 15 March 1751 to Madame d'Youville is merely a repetition of his letter of 5 February. In addition, he directs her to turn over the lands to the farmer hired by the nuns of Quebec City. Madame d'Youville replied:

---

16   Cf. ASGM, autograph letter, signed and dated 4 February 1751.

Sir,

In conformity with your orders, I have turned over to the bearer of the power of attorney of the nuns of the General Hospital of Quebec City in the presence of Messieurs Foucher and Danré, in accordance with the report they have prepared, the houses and lands of Pointe Saint-Charles and Chambly together with the animals and moveable property so that they can be evaluated. You will see, Sir, from the account which will be rendered to you how part of the money that I was obliged to borrow was used to provide the said lands with everything that was necessary to cultivate them and that had been completely lacking. In accordance with your instructions and by your orders, Sir, the agent of these ladies has been pleased to accept the additions I made to them and has given me assurances, which I trust, of your willingness to pay me fully for all that I have advanced. I never doubted or feared, Sir, that you might have had any intention of keeping the full sum without reimbursing me, thus obliging me to remit everything that was in excess of the first inventory delivered to me and which I purchased with money which you at first contested but which you now see how necessary it was to borrow and how rightfully it was used. My accounts, Sir, are complete with the details of the full sum. In my capacity as Director, with which you honoured me, I made these purchases for the said lands and it is right that whatever remains and the advances I made for them be reimbursed to me in their entirety. I have always acted, Sir, with all possible integrity and honesty, without any personal interest or politics, of which I know some people wrongfully accuse me. I hope, Sir, that for your part, you will do me justice. All the expenses that I incurred were necessary and the number of people hired for the fences, ditches, and other needs were by no means useless but added to the profit of the lands. Had you disapproved of this expense about which I had the honour to inform you in rendering my accounts at the end of the first year of my management and of which I was already aware, I would not have continued with them; but you said nothing to me nor did you limit my powers in this matter. On the contrary, you encouraged me to continue, which I did by your word and in virtue of the ordinance that made me Director of this Hospital.

You have done me the honour of remarking that you have not examined my accounts, and that if you have not settled them, it is because I did not ask you to do so. It would seem, Sir, that simply sending my accounts would signify clearly enough that it is only for the reason of having them examined and settled that I had the honour of presenting them to you without making an express request, which I nonetheless believe I did in the letter sent with them.

I have just read, Sir, in your last ordinance that you are allowing the sale of the building, courtyard, and gardens of this Hospital; but in your letter that I received a few days ago, you formally remark that you do not have the right to transfer property funds. I find it difficult to reconcile the one with the other, and I am inclined to believe that this is only a pretext that you are using to defer reimbursing the advances I have made. Since the building and gardens are no less property funds than the lands on which they are situated, I am given to hope that you will have the goodness to procure for me the means of paying my debts.

The agent of these ladies has asked to receive the lands of the tannery of Côte des Neiges and of the Baronnerie. I was inclined to turn over to him the first two, but Messieurs Fouché and Danré said that he had no orders for that. I hope, Sir, that you will have the goodness to leave me the lands of the Baronnerie to help me with the expenses that I have been obliged to incur for the poor since last October. The land is only good for pasturing animals. That of Pointe Saint-Charles provides more than enough pasturage.

As for the pension of the Brother whom you honour me by mentioning, on All Saints' Day for each of the past two years I gave to Monsieur de Lalanne one hundred and fifty livres, to the Reverend Father Saint-Pé one hundred and fifty livres, and I sent to the Bishop one hundred and fifty livres, for which I have the receipts. A hundred and some odd livres are left over which I do not believe myself obliged to pay, Sir, since it is owing to me and I have nothing for him or for the poor.

I have the honour of being …[17]

If Madame d'Youville seems to be repeating the same arguments, it is because her opponents keep repeating their inaccuracies. On 16 March, Bishop de Pontbriand repeats what he has already written; but this time the mask is slipping rather pitiably.

---

17   Cf. ASGM, autograph draft, signed and dated 12 April 1751.

Madame

I seem to recall having told you this past autumn that some difficulty might perhaps arise about what you believe to be owed you and even that objections might be made to the large number of associates and poor for whom you care.

You quote the writ that established you as Director in 1747, but it seems to me from reading it that it is only a question of repairs to the building you are at present occupying. However that may be, I think that some people have made up their minds that you did not really borrow and that the expenses were covered by the alms that you have been given. If you were to present these loans as incurred in your capacity as Director perhaps they would cause less difficulty. I say perhaps because I am in nowise interfering in this business. I have been obliged for various reasons to consent to the decreed merger. I am with much respect ...[18]

Madame d'Youville's reply is a moving cry of wounded pride.

Your Excellency

I am sincere, upright, and incapable of any evasion or reservation that might disguise the truth or give it another meaning. My Lord, I truly borrowed 9,550 livres for the good and renewal of the lands of this Hospital; I owe them and I have no other resources to pay them except the reimbursement which I expect from Your Excellency and the other gentlemen. What I am telling you, My Lord, is the pure truth and I would not tell the least lie for all the wealth in the world. In this matter, I have only sought the renewal of this Hospital and its properties; and I never had in view in incurring these expenses creating any kind of situation that would put anyone under obligation to me through lack of ability to reimburse me, as some people are thinking and saying. That kind of person, My Lord, is not who I am. I can assure Your Excellency that that never occurred to me; but what has committed me to this course, in spite of myself and my inclinations, is the multitude of necessary repairs that, following one upon another and demanding prompt attention, have obliged me, indeed as a matter of conscience, to have them done lest being responsible for this work before God, I should let things perish. That is the sole cause of all these expenditures,

---

18   Cf. ASGM, autograph letter, signed and dated 16 March 1751.

which I believed to be necessary and which, in fact, were. It is neither my companions nor the number of the poor that have brought about these debts, as Monsieur Bigot admits; alms and our work have provided for them. I beseech you, My Lord, that I be reimbursed for these advances. I have left everything on the premises even though I purchased it with my own money. There has even been an increase in the number of cattle. They have kept everything without restricting themselves to what was reported on the first inventory. Since they are enjoying the profit, they ought to pay me the price. Nothing would be more just.

I have the honour of being with very deep respect ...[19]

Bishop de Pontbriand replied rather drily:

I believe everything you have the honour of telling me; and in consequence, you can take all legal measures to obtain what is your due. Surely, the religious of the General Hospital of Quebec City will not bring the matter to trial. The King will probably resolve all these difficulties; you will be in a position to assert your rights and to present once again your previous submissions. I hope that everything will succeed. I am with much respect ...[20]

As the Bishop said, "the King will resolve," but in the meantime the lands had legally passed into other hands. The Hospital's furniture was being moved to Quebec City, beginning with the most valuable item, the church's pulpit in remarkably carved woodwork, one of the most beautiful in the country. In this Hospital that had been renovated by her care, Madame d'Youville spent her days coming and going under the ghostly shadows of her noble dreams. What would the future hold? The Bishop's brevity allowed no room for possible assumptions. This was indeed defeat.

When the Holy Scriptures call God a "fire," this is not a purely rhetorical figure. God acts in souls in the way fire does, destroying and purifying. As when ground has been cleared of trees and fire is set in the stumps to reach the roots, so God sets the souls of his servants afire to destroy every human attachment. Before the flame of love can spring up bright and clear of the smoke of pride, the souls of the saints have to pass through the mystical purification of suffering. This supernaturalization of the soul, this

---

19   Cf. ASGM, autograph draft, signed and dated 12 April 1751.
20   Cf. ASGM, autograph letter, signed and dated 26 April 1751.

annihilation of self-will, in a word, this sanctification, does not occur in a single day or without trials and hardships.

Madame d'Youville had proved her administrative abilities, her industriousness, her rare courage. Her success ought to have brought some recognition. Instead, she was being ruined. During the moving of the furniture and the reports that tore away from her strip by strip the fruit of her labours and during the correspondence laden with unjust reprimands, subterfuges, and suspicions, are we not to think that the demons of pride, doubt, and discouragement did not suggest to her thousands of rebellious thoughts? She has not shared with us the heart-rending pain, the secret agony, which she must have had to endure, since she was only human: she showed only an admirable submission to the designs of God, a submission which reflected even more brightly her purity of intention.

The arrival of the spring dispatches took the wind out of Bigot's sails. They contained nothing relating to the ordinance of October 1750 according to which Madame d'Youville had to vacate the Hospital by the 1st of July.xxxii He thus thought it more prudent to play for time.

> Madame
>   I had thought that we would receive by the first ship the Court's ratification of the Merger that we have made between the General Hospital of Montreal and that of Quebec City. As we have not had any news, you may remain in the house you are occupying until we have heard something. I am only making this proposal to you inasmuch as it may be helpful to you. Please be so good as to reply to me, so that in case you should not accept this offer, the General Hospital of Quebec City can make arrangements for when you will have to leave the house.
>   I am with respect …[21]

Bigot rightly suspected that something was afoot. In Paris certain influences were impeding his plans. Father Cousturier, the Superior of Saint-Sulpice and the true and legitimate Seigneur of Montreal, was asserting his rights and, in support of them, presenting to the Court the conditional proposals of Madame d'Youville to acquit the debts of the Hospital. It should be recalled that when the free land grant was made to François Charon with a view to the establishment of a house of charity, Father Tronson had inserted a clause precisely to keep in Montreal this house of charity. The contract stipulated that if at some future date the establish-

---

21   Cf. ASGM, original letter, signed and dated, Quebec City, 19 June 1751.

ment were to cease to exist, the land with all its buildings should revert by right to the Seminary unless the Hospitallers were to pay the cash value of the land. The foreseen case had arrived. The Brothers being unable to buy back the land, the Hospital had thus since 1747 belonged by right to the Seminary; and Bigot, even in his position as Intendant, could not sell the property of someone else.

The Abbé de l'Isle-Dieu,[xxxiii] with his consummate experience in these matters, saw from the beginning the obstacles to the merger; and no doubt unaware of the change of opinion of the Bishop after his letter of 1748, began to get ready to make his representations to the Minister. In his letter of 4 April 1750 he tells Bishop de Pontbriand about the steps he has taken: "… I can assure you, Excellency, while I am dealing with this matter of the merger, that I have omitted nothing to demonstrate not only its uselessness and the danger for the Hospital of Quebec City that will result from it, but also the impossibility of achieving it in accordance with the provisions of the establishment of the Hospital of Montreal and those of its first endowment."[22]

For his part, the Minister informed the administrators that they had gone beyond their powers. He wrote to them:

Gentlemen,

I have received the letter that you took the trouble to write to me on the 16th of October last, along with the ordinance that you and Monsieur the Bishop of Quebec have issued to merge the General Hospital of Montreal with that of Quebec City. When I suggested this merger as a way of dealing with the affairs of the Hospital of Montreal, I still intended that there would remain in Montreal a kind of Hospice that would be served by nuns sent from the General Hospital of Quebec City. It is only, in fact, on this condition, that a merger would be able to occur … Would you please defer the execution of your ordinance for the sale of the establishment until further orders from His Majesty. I must, indeed, point out to you that your ordinance would not be sufficient for a transfer of this kind, which cannot be done without the express authorization of the King and, indeed, without certain formalities that I shall explain to you if and when the occasion should arise.[23]

---

22   Cf. APQ, *Rapp. 1936* [Report of 1936], p. 296 – Lettres et Mémoires de l'Abbé de L'Isle-Dieu [Letters and Memoranda of the Abbé de L'Isle-Dieu].

23   Cf. APC, Series B, vol. 93, fol. 116; also Series F 3, vol. 14, fol. 20: The Minister to Messieurs de La Jonquière and Bigot, 2 July 1751.

Thus, the ordinance for the merger had to be revoked. The administrators found a way of doing this while safeguarding their own reputation. In the following ordinance, which they issued 14 December 1751, they skilfully invoked the authorization of the Secretary of State which they had, but which previously had always been interpreted according to their own wishes:

> SEEING THAT our Ruling of 15 October 1750 whereby in consequence of Letters from Monsieur de Rouillé, Minister and Secretary of State of the Marine, We would have merged with the General Hospital of Quebec City all the properties pertaining to the General Hospital of Montreal, of which Madame Youville and her companions then held the administration by virtue of a Ruling of 27 August 1747, And on the representations that the said Madame Youville has since made to the Court, the Latter notes that its intention is to suspend the said merger until it issues a new order.
>
> In consequence of which, And Seeing that the said General Hospital of Quebec City is resigned in this regard,
>
> WE ORDER that the said Madame Youville and her companions from this present and until a new order will resume possession of all the properties pertaining to the General Hospital of Montreal, of which she shall continue to have the direction and administration, in accordance with the said ruling of 27 August 1747. WE likewise ORDER that the Sieur Foucher, Procurator of the King in the jurisdiction of Montreal, whom we have instructed to make an inventory of the said properties, will have returned to the said Madame Youville by whomsoever it shall pertain the lands, animals, utensils, etc. contained in the said inventory and of which the said General Hospital of Quebec City had been in possession by virtue of the said merger, and BE IT that the present Ruling be read and proclaimed everywhere where there shall be need. MADE AND DONE at Quebec City, the 14th of December, 1751.[24]

In the letter to Madame d'Youville that accompanied the ordinance of 14 December 1751, the administrators stated: "At present, Madame, it is a matter of your letting us know the means you have at your disposal for acquitting this house. We shall examine them and report them to the Minister." Consequently, Madame d'Youville set out her assets in the following memorandum:

---

24   Cf. ASGM, collated copy signed by Bigot.

Our Lords, pursuant to your letter of 14 December 1751, we are sending the present memorandum whereby it will be easy for you to inform My Lord the Minister of the reality of the proposals that we have made to acquit the debts of the General Hospital, of the assets that we have in order to do so, and, lastly, of the precautions that appear necessary to be taken to provide for this establishment.

From the inventory that you had made in 1747, you have seen that what is owing in Paris is about twenty-five thousand livres,

item 25,000

To Monsieur l'Estage in Montreal there are owing five thousand livres, not including interest,

item 5,000

To the heirs of Monsieur D'Amour, seven thousand livres, not including interest,

item 7,000

You have seen, Our Lords, from the accounts that Madame Youville has rendered to you each year of her administration that a sum of more than ten thousand livres is owed to her,

item 10,000

This inventory also reveals how run-down this house had been and how much in need of urgent repairs. Thus there are forty-seven thousand livres in principal that this house owes. It possesses only lands that cost more than they produce because they are not cultivated. What is more sure is an income from the Hôtel de Ville of seven hundred and eighty-six livres that the creditors in Paris have claimed until now.

The repairs are mounting and it is also necessary to pay a pension to a former Brother of the house that previously had been paid at the rate of three hundred livres but which we hope, Our Lords, you will modify in view of the poverty of said Hospital and since it is in the process of doing something. All the property is perishing, yet we hope to restore this house, and here are our prospects.

We have been fairly well assured that creditors in Paris to whom was owed in 1747 about twenty-five thousand livres will grant a total remission in return for a sum of eight thousand livres and the arrears on the income from the Hôtel de Ville of Paris. The Bishop knew about this from the time he was still in Paris. The Abbé de

The farm house at Pointe Saint-Charles, restored by Mother d'Youville and demolished in 1931 after having been partially burnt.

The former Notre Dame Church, situated perpendicular to Notre Dame Street. The façade and the square tower were built between 1723 and 1725, but the bell tower was not added until 1777. Thus, Mother d'Youville would have known it without the bell tower. In front of the church was the public well. On the right, one can see the present Notre Dame Church, facing onto Notre Dame Street, which was opened to worship in 1829.

l'Isle-Dieu, his Vicar General, has given us the same hope, not to say certainty. We shall ask him to speak to Monsieur the Minister. Now, we know definitely that Father Cousturier, Superior of the Seminaries of Saint-Sulpice, has on hand the sum of eight thousand livres to pay the creditors should it please His Majesty to put us in charge of the care of this house. This is a fact of which Father Cousturier will inform the Minister and which is otherwise impossible for us to commit to in this country. Thus, there are twenty-five thousand livres that have been acquitted.

Father Bouffandeau, a priest of the Seminary of Montreal, has bequeathed about six thousand livres to this Hospital if we are placed in charge of it, a condition so essential that if it is not fulfilled, the gift will go instead to the Hôtel-Dieu.

Lastly, Madame Youville and her companions, if they are placed in charge of this house, wish to renounce the ten thousand livres that are owed to them according to the accounts that they have had the honour of presenting to you. By joining together these three resources: in Paris there will be eight thousand livres that will acquit the debt of twenty-five thousand livres, we shall remit the ten thousand livres that are owed to us, and we will have the gift of Father Bouffandeau. In total, forty thousand livres will have been acquitted.

Thus, there will remain only six thousand livres, with some arrears, to be paid. Providence, our labours, and the good will of several people who await what His Majesty may decide are the other resources on which we count to pay completely the debts, to have the repairs done, and even to make some useful improvements.

Our Lords, we have had in all these proposals no other intention than to maintain an establishment useful to the government of Montreal, but it seems to us necessary for fulfilling this intention, that it please His Majesty to declare that this Hospital, formerly administered by the Charon Brothers be henceforth administered by secular persons who will not have to instruct the young and who will receive in the said Hospital infirm people, elderly men and women, who will succeed to all the rights and privileges granted to the said Brothers; that this change, which is basically more to our advantage, will in nowise be a reason for former donors and benefactors to withdraw their gifts on the grounds that the direction of the house has passed into other hands; and, in a word, that the Letters Patent of one thousand six hundred and ninety-four and of one thousand six hundred and ninety-nine will be retained entirely in favour of the secular persons who will take charge of this Hospital.

If later, for reasons unforeseen, it should please the King to make new arrangements, either by dissolving this house completely or placing it under the direction of women or men religious, we ask that in this case we be reimbursed for the amount of eighteen thousand livres that we have sacrificed to re-establish this house, and this in such a way that the last one among us to die may be able to claim the said reimbursement to dispose according to her will or following any agreements that we shall make together.

Moreover, if this change should occur only after our death, those who succeed us in the same employ and administration shall in nowise preserve this same right unless we grant it to them; but rather they will be granted an annuity as the case may require, but which is estimated at present at about two hundred livres at least, it not seeming right that after all their labours they should be sent away without assistance. If by our labours we re-establish the above-said house, we shall have the same pension.

There are still several rules that need to be laid down regarding the number of women who can be associates; on exceptional cases and the reasons for which they can be dismissed; on whether persons who leave of their own free will the service of the poor ought to have the right to request a pension. It will still be necessary to rule on innumerable temporal and spiritual matters. We shall conform insofar as possible to what has already been decreed for the Charon Brothers; and you, Our Lords, as heads of this Hospital will be able to make the most helpful rulings as circumstances shall arise. This 19th of June, 1752.

> M.M. Lajemmerais, Widow Youville
> Marie Louise Thaumur, Catherine Demers,
> Catherine Rinville, Theraise Laser,
> Agathe Veronneau, Marie Antoinette Relle,
> Marie Joseph Benard[25]

The Abbé de l'Isle-Dieu, at the request of the Minister, provided memoranda, statements of the debts,[26] and plans first developed in a series of collaborative studies with Monsieur the Abbé Cousturier and the Marquis de

---

25   Cf. ASGM, autograph draft with the signatures of the associates.
26   Cf. APC, C 11 A, vol. 92, fols. 226-49: The Abbé de L'Isle-Dieu to the Minister.

La Galissonière, who was in charge of this business.[27] At last, on 17 April 1752, he had the satisfaction of writing to his Bishop:

> The merger of the Hospital of Montreal has finally been abandoned as a result, I believe, of the representations that I so strongly pressed and on my offers to have the debts in Paris audited and settled, it being understood that a party will be found to underwrite the money for the creditors, but only that portion of their claim resulting from the interest, minus the principal, for paying cash.
>
> In order to conclude this matter, first of all as firmly as may be, an order of Council of State will be issued that will confirm the commission given to Madame d'Youville and her companions, after which the Court will not be able to delay granting Letters Patent, because without these, Madame d'Youville and her companions, not forming a legal community and still being secular and thus able to bequeath their possessions to their natural heirs, this would put Madame d'Youville's heirs in the position of laying claim once again against the Hospital the amounts that she would have appeared to have paid to settle the debts of this house ... I consulted about this with the Abbé Couturier and he seemed to be satisfied. He is my only guide ...
>
> Monsieur the Abbé Couturier has informed me, Your Excellency, that the authors and promoters of the merger by taking the law into their own hands had already begun to execute it by removing a certain number of furnishings that it is now a matter of returning and restoring to the Hospital of Montreal. I therefore immediately had the honour of writing to Monsieur Rouillé to apply for an order to have the furnishings that had been removed returned to the Hospital of Montreal. I do not doubt that his orders on this matter will be executed. I am informing you about this, Your Excellency, lest anyone should keep this a secret from you, for it is usually easier to take than to give.[28]

On 12 May 1752, the King in Council revoked the ordinance of October 1750 and ordered the administrators to make a contract with Madame d'Youville to determine the type of administration of the General Hospital

---

27   Cf. APQ, *Rapp. 1936* [Report of 1936]: Lettres et Mémoires de l'Abbé de L'Isle-Dieu [Letters and Memoranda of the Abbé de L'Isle-Dieu], pp. 319, 327, 366.

28   Cf. APQ, *Rapp. 1936* [Report of 1936]: Lettres et Mémoires de l'Abbé de L'Isle-Dieu [Letters and Memoranda of the Abbé de L'Isle-Dieu], pp. 326, 327.

of Montreal. The conventions decided upon by the parties were inspired by Madame d'Youville's memorandum and were made public by an ordinance of 28 September 1752.[29] There was no mention, however, of the reimbursement of the 18,000 livres she was claiming in case of retrocession, and the number of associates was still limited to twelve. Madame d'Youville turned to the Abbé de l'Isle-Dieu, who wrote to the bishop on 3 March 1753:

> I have consulted with Father Couturier about the matter of the Hospital of Montreal. We read the contract that you sent along with Madame d'Youville's power of attorney and the letters in which she speaks about 1) the fixing of the number of members at twelve and 2) that the temporal powers are interfering rather too much in the details of the governance, not of the Hospital, but of her little community, which she is convinced, Your Excellency, pertain only to you …
>
> As for how this matter has ended for Madame d'Youville and her companions, I believe that they will have to be satisfied, the more so because as regards the 18,000 livres not mentioned in the contract, it will be much more difficult for the Court to add anything, as it always has a tendency to diminish rather than to increase.[30]

On 1 April 1753, he reassured the Bishop about the Letters Patent:

> You can, Your Excellency, remain calm about the business of the Hospital of Montreal. The Minister himself has taken charge of preparing the Letters Patent in accord with the contract enacted in Quebec City between my lords the administrative heads and Madame Youville the widow. Father Couturier and I have made several observations that are also included which do not make any alterations to the respective conventions but which – between you and me – make some of the articles a little clearer than they were. Nothing has been said in regard to your authority with respect to the governance and inner running of the community that is in the process of being formed. Only a simple observation has been made

---

29   Cf. ASGM, collated copy; also published in *Edits et Ordonnances des Intendants de la Nouvelle-France* [Edicts and Ordinances of the Intendants of New France], vol. II, p. 407.

30   Cf. APQ, *Rapp. 1936* [Report of 1936]: Lettres et Mémoires de l'Abbé de L'Isle-Dieu [Letters and Memoranda of the Abbé de L'Isle-Dieu], p. 366.

on the appointment of special councillors, which can be left to the discretion of the superior. [31]

Finally, the Vicar General wrote to his Bishop on 31 May 1753:

> I was informed yesterday by the Court that the Letters Patent for the Hospital of Montreal have been drawn up and sent to the Council. All that remains at present is the formality of recording them, which is being held up by the recess of the Parlement …[32]

The Letters Patent arrived in Quebec City in the autumn. They were dated 3 June 1753 and bore the signature of the King and the Secretary of State, Rouillé. They were registered with the Superior Council of Quebec on 1 October 1753.

Innumerable details and formalities, as well as the slowness of the mail between the two continents, prolonged the settlement of the debts until 1756. The untiring Abbé de l'Isle-Dieu nevertheless concluded this business to the great satisfaction of the creditors who had once believed that they had lost their capital.

Like a gentle wind from the south promising the softness of spring, the following letter from her Bishop came as an unhoped-for balm to Madame d'Youville:

> Madame
>   You are too just to doubt the feelings of affection and respect that I take pride in having for you. What a consolation it is to me that your project for the establishment of the General Hospital has been confirmed! Now that things are settled, we shall be able to think seriously about organizing matters. For this year, I shall be occupied with the Ursuline Sisters.
>   I have the honour of being with much respect, Madame …[33]

If, in the midst of political turmoil, Bishop de Pontbriand had caused Madame d'Youville much grief, he fundamentally had always esteemed her. He still thought in 1753 as he did in 1748 that she was "a person of rare merit"; and out of the nobility of his soul, he wanted to reassure her of it.

---

31   Cf. APQ, ibid., p.386.
32   Cf. APQ, ibid., p.409.
33   Cf. ASGM, autograph letter, signed and dated 15 January 1753.

As for Madame d'Youville, for two years in scandal-mongering Montreal, she had been wounded by the malicious glances of her opponents. For two years, her soul tormented and scourged by distrust, she thought herself truly ruined. For her, the sacrifice was accomplished. But God, as when he stopped Abraham's uplifted arm at the last minute, redirected minds towards justice; and Madame d'Youville, having recovered her means of doing good, followed her upwards path.

The key to the room of Marguerite d'Youville

CHAPTER VII

The Rainbow

To each person the manifestation
of the Spirit is given for the common good.
(I Corinthians 12:7)

THE COMPLEX political strategies had ended in an unforeseen result: the royal sanction of a new religious community, and moreover the first indigenous one. It was in Montreal and the foundress was a Montrealer.

As when the sands of a dune reflect the sun after the wind has shaped them into little hills and valleys, so all the pettinesses, jealousies, and fawnings, all the moral smut, like so many grains of dark sand, had made the qualities of Madame d'Youville shine even more brightly. She came out of these troubles a much stronger person. Furthermore, opposition had given her practice in the art of politics, which is difficult for an ordinary woman. She had discovered at her own cost how paralysing political meddling can be. Henceforth it was a question of ensuring freedom and continuity by channelling duty according to royal statutes. Also, by taking advantage of the impasse in which the Court found itself, she found it possible to envisage a way of amortizing the General Hospital's debts: she would supply the money if she was granted letters patent. Indeed, she would get these letters patent, but at the price of forty thousand livres that would have otherwise gone to the poor of Montreal.

Having achieved success, Madame d'Youville humbly anchored herself in her chosen rank among the poor. The authorities wanted to insert a clause into the Letters Patent that would separate the property of the nuns from that of the poor, in accordance with the practice of other religious communities in Quebec. Madame d'Youville vigorously opposed this. She wanted to prevent among her sisters any spirit of ownership, this insidious virus of greed. According to the act of renunciation signed in 1745, the sisters and the poor formed one close-knit family; and the foundress was thinking only of making this bond much closer. "Being married to the poor as members of Jesus Christ our Spouse, all our possessions must be held in common," she wrote on this matter.

It was necessary to make everything new – habit, customs, Rules. It is in the constitution of her Institute that one can see her organizational mind and her practical sense, these virtues of a prosaic temperament that she inherited from her well-balanced military and governing ancestors. Completely imbued with the special character of her Institute, her originality was rivalled only by her humility. In designing the religious habit, she did not forget that the sisters would have to devote themselves to all sorts of labour to support the poor. Therefore, Madame d'Youville rejected the monastic veil, however traditional and lovely it might be, and replaced it with a simple black bonnet. The sisters had once derogatorily been called "grey" (tipsy); but insult is a jewel to the eyes of faith. She therefore chose the colour greyish-beige for the dress. Without veil, wimple, or headband and with a wide-pleated dress in the Norman style, a camlet dress that was not even an ascetic frock, her habit differed radically from all others. But did it matter? Her way toward God was unique; she would wear this habit without wincing. Too bad if vanity suffered. Since then, this grey religious dress, a reminder of humiliations assumed, has been so nobly worn in the vanguard that it has become in America a symbol of heroism.[xxxiv] From the monastic habit she kept, however, the crucifix, but even here she added her personal touch. Her silver crucifix would bear a heart in relief representing the Sacred Heart of Jesus, the Source of all charity and King and Heart of all hearts. At the suggestion of Father Normant, she added to the ends of the crossbars a heraldic fleur de lys to commemorate the king of France who had just constituted the Institute as a legal body. Unique with these additions, this crucifix is truly remarkable. The first twelve, worn by the administrators, were cast in France. The Mother House in Montreal preserves four of these original crucifixes, priceless souvenirs of the first architects of this foundational endeavour.

In 1755, Bishop de Pontbriand on a pastoral journey to Montreal made a canonical visit to the new Institute. For eighteen years of common life, the Rule of the associated sisters consisted only of the three loose leaves of counsels drafted by Father Normant; their fervour supplied all the rest. The bishop approved these original commitments, countersigned the three foundational sheets, upheld Madame d'Youville as Superior, and approved the habit she had designed. The charge he issued on 15 June before leaving Montreal is practically a laudatory brief and must have especially comforted the foundress.[1]

Legally and canonically constituted as a religious body, the Sisters henceforth would wear their habit; but Madame d'Youville, wanting to associate Father Normant in this happy congregational event, delayed the vesting ceremony until 25 August, feast day of Saint Louis, and patron of her revered spiritual guide. Thus, on the morning of his saint's day, within the intimate confines of the convent, Father Normant blessed the approved habit and distributed it to the eleven professed administrators in a cere-

---

1   SD, pp. 319-21.

mony he had drafted and which is still in use. Saint Louis' was a feast day of obligation; the people of Montreal saw the Sisters for the first time at Mass dressed in this strange habit. The citizens were at their doors; but this time, unlike 1738, a current of friendliness ran through their hearts. The injustices of Intendant Bigot to the foundress had rallied everyone's sympathy towards the foundress.

Bishop de Pontbriand seemed to have experienced some apprehension about the habit because he asked about the public reaction to it in a letter addressed for the first time to "Madame d'Youville, Superior of the Ladies of Charity": "I do not know how the public will have taken your uniform. You were already performing the duties of ladies of charity, and I know that they approve of this name."[2] The public approved of it but continued to call them the Grey Nuns. Having been able to keep them, they appreciated them all the more; and this name, purged of all its venom, took on an air of possessive pride. People became attached to this new kind of religious closely associated with their daily activities and not hidden away in a cloister. This sympathy demonstrated itself when Madame d'Youville undertook to build a wall around the hospital. The people made of this undertaking a corvée in the Canadian style with some supplying materials, others labour, some cartage, others monetary donations.

The General Hospital raised its bold silhouette at Pointe-à-Callières outside the city walls as a challenge to marauders and hostile Indians. Madame d'Youville had long wished for the decent protection of a surrounding wall, especially since she built in the garden in 1750 four wooden cabins for the mentally ill. Difficulties did not discourage her. If she was enterprising, she never was rash and always knew to wait for the right moment. In the spring of 1754 she decided to erect this wall, which the King's specialists had recommended in 1747. So as not to put herself in debt, she resolved upon doing the work piecemeal and on a daily basis. This would allow her to stop or continue the work according to her means. As an economy she had the lime prepared on site, and to save on labour costs the Sisters worked as masons carrying stones in their aprons and mortar in buckets. Thanks to these measures and to the voluntary assistance of the citizens, a stone wall twelve feet high and 3,600 feet around was erected for the modest sum of 10,715 livres, 12 sols. On 3 June 1756, Paul Jourdain Labrosse, clerk of the chief surveyor, gave the certificate of alignment[3] and the great work was finished.

---

2   Cf. ASGM, autograph letter of 22 September 1755.

3   In conformity with the Ordinance of Intendant Hocquart of 19 August 1732. Cf. *Edits & ordonnances des Intendants* [Edicts and Ordinances of the Intendants], vol. II, p. 351.

In 1755 an epidemic of smallpox broke out in the Indian missions around Montreal and reached the city. There were so many victims that the Hôtel-Dieu could not accommodate them. Madame d'Youville, whom every kind of suffering moved, transformed her hospice as quickly as possible into a hospital, for even though the house was called a general hospital, it was only an alms-house in the present sense of the word. It was thus to help the contagious that the Grey Nuns began their nursing service. Not being bound by rules of enclosure, they gave nursing care in the homes of the sick who could not be brought to the hospital. Bishop de Pontbriand had only praise for this wonderful zeal which he, as administrator of the hospital, was asked to approve.

Once set on the path of caring for the sick, the charity of Madame d'Youville could not turn back. At that time, the colony was galvanized by the military triumphs of the troops, but after the *Te Deums* had been sung the Intendant needed to solve the pressing problem of finding hospital space for the wounded. In 1756 Bigot turned to Madame d'Youville whose patriotism equalled her compassion. She accepted as a new form of dedication the care of the wounded and sick soldiers and prisoners of war. But as always, the dealings of Bigot were deceptive. These soldiers had to be provided for at government expense. Nevertheless, the Intendant covered their meat ration only and paid a quarter below the going price for it. Furthermore, he paid in paper drafts which could only be converted into coins much later. Madame d'Youville reported Bigot's trickery in a letter to the Abbé de l'Isle-Dieu about collecting on these bills of exchange: "After having been treated harshly here, it has happened again. Monsieur Bigot never paid the true value of the rations ... The Hospital has lost on bread, peas, small provisions, drinks, and domestic labour ..." In 1756 alone, the maintenance of the English Hall, named after its chief occupants, cost Madame d'Youville 18,000 francs, 3 sols, of which she got back only a very small part. As a businesswoman she kept her accounts, but deficits put no brakes on her zeal. Her charity was completely devoid of chauvinism. Having made real monetary sacrifices for the enemies of her country, she did not feel herself free of obligation to them. She found ways of helping them, for once they were cured, the majority of these Englishmen found themselves destitute. Before the tribunal of history her account books stand as irrefutable witnesses. There are recorded the facts that she employed twenty-one Englishmen on her farm at Pointe Saint-Charles, another at the Chambly farm, still another as a mason, and six as orderlies in the Hospital itself. The last greatly helped the nursing sisters who understood only a few words of English.

In addition to the increasing number of the needy, the sick and several foundlings whom Madame d'Youville had taken in since 1754 filled the huge house to overflowing. Madame d'Youville then thought about doubling the building's capacity by adding a wing. The need was so clear that the administrative authorities of the Hospital approved her project. Bishop de Pontbriand wrote to her about this matter on 7 January 1758: "Madame, I admire your trust in Divine Providence. I have recognized this in many evident ways since I have had the honour of knowing you."

Without an assured income, how was Madame d'Youville to meet her financial obligations, feed the poor who required at least 1800 minots of wheat per year, and in addition begin new construction work? Her secret was economizing, prudence, and hard work. It should be noted that although she accepted gifts with gratitude, she never asked for them; she relied on her industry alone. Her skilfulness and obligingness became so well known that people came to her in all sorts of straits. It was said, "Go to the Grey Nuns; they never refuse anything." In fact, she never refused a task provided it was honest. In her community, she had subordinated ascetic mortifications to hard and undiscriminating work. In this she was wonderfully supported by her sisters who followed her faithfully along all the rough paths where she led them. If their perseverance witnesses eloquently to her moral influence, it likewise witnesses to their virtue. The Abbé Dufrost says that his mother had the gift of making herself loved and feared at one and the same time. This presupposes a happy blend of firmness and moderation – the gifts of real leaders. In her these natural gifts were reinforced by humility and the love of God, the sources from which sprang a joyful obedience. A measure of the affection in which she was held both inside and outside of the convent was the custom begun in 1758 of giving her a birthday bouquet.[xxxv] The cost of this bouquet rose from ninety francs in the first year to a hundred and fifty francs in the third. These gifts, which were strictly personal, show how her popularity was growing. And here again it is the account book that bears witness. How fascinating it is to read the account book! The pen that was aligning the numbers was tracing unbeknowst to her a veritable moral portrait. What order, economy, labours, cleverness, and wise administration are revealed there! Madame d'Youville put everything to profitable use. She rented the lofts to the king's storekeeper. She also rented out an ice house and two small houses on the Hospital grounds. She had a watch set on the animals she allowed to be pastured on her land in the Baronnie. She undertook carting and bought leaf tobacco so that her old men could prepare it for sale at a profit. She also sold sand, stone, and lime.[4] The farm products likewise contributed to the budget: eggs, chickens, ducks, butter, lard, feathers, animal skins, cereals, cattle, wood – everything is minutely inscribed in the account book, and each penny helped to swell the receipts at the end of the year. If a resident in the Hospital had a skill, she employed him in so far as he was capable. Thus, the Hospital soon had its tailor, shoemaker, and baker, as well as the occasional mason. According to an ordinance of 1721, widows inherited their husband's pew in the parish church; she profited from hers until her death. From her first year as manager of the Hospital, she had admitted gentlewomen as boarders; she also took in sick priests. And since, above all, she sought the welfare of souls, she began from July 1754 to receive retreatants, thus beginning the work of private retreats.

Father Claude Poncin, one of the priests at the Seminary, who had a lively interest in Madame d'Youville's work, taught the Sisters to make hosts, altar candles, and tubular copper candlesticks with an internal spring mechanism, which were still unknown in the country, to replace candles that were then difficult to obtain. Having imported the necessary tools for these tasks from Europe, he donated them to the Hospital and thus ensured it a future source of revenue.

The Sisters also made church linen; and as they excelled in this kind of work, several parishes entrusted the upkeep of their altar linen to them.

From 1744 Madame d'Youville had been doing sewing for the king's stores; but after 1754, the storekeeper, finding that he was profiting from this, increased his orders.[xxxvi] For the King, she made military uniforms, officers' braiding, decorative fringes, fish nets, campaign tents, and innumerable other things for the use of the army. For the merchants who outfitted traders in the wilderness, she made many objects for trading and above all embroidered ornaments for the Indian chiefs. Before the departure of the *voyageurs* (that is, those who travelled into these remote areas), it was not unusual to see the Sisters' community room filled with rolls of braid, printed calico, glazed and woollen cloth, and so on and so forth. It was then that the true spirit of unity that ruled the house could be seen. The poor, the boarding ladies, and the sisters were all plying their needles side by side until late at night to fill the merchants' orders. The total receipts from these various kinds of work rose from fifteen thousand livres to twenty thousand and finally to thirty-one thousand livres per year under French rule.

---

4   Messieurs Jodoin and Vincent in their *Histoire de Longueuil* [History of Longueuil] (1889) say that there is a tradition in Longueuil that the first boat to travel between Montreal and Longueuil was started and kept in service for a number of years by Madame d'Youville. This initiative reveals a business sense rare among women at that time, but I have not been able to find any document that supports the oral tradition of the old people of Longueuil.

As the head of this humming hive of activity, the Superior set the example of assiduous work and selflessness by taking as her own the most arduous tasks. One day as she was making candles, a messy task if there ever was one, a Sister all in a tizzy came to alert her that they could see Monsieur the Intendant approaching. Was not Madame d'Youville going to tidy herself in order to receive him? "I had not at all expected the visit of Monsieur the Intendant," she replied, "he will therefore excuse me and be willing to see me as I am. None of this will keep him from speaking to me." She always scrupulously observed social conventions, but the unexpected arrival of the Intendant from Quebec City provided her with a chance to practise humility. This recalls an event in the life of Saint Bonaventura. When the envoys from Pope Gregory X arrived at the monastery of Mugello to present the cardinal's hat to the saint, he was busy washing the dishes even though he was Minister General of the Order. He declined to interrupt his task, saying: "Let us first complete the duties of our station; then there will be time to take up heavier burdens." By the simplicity of her manners and her deep humility, our foundress here draws close to the great Franciscan saint, so true is it that at a certain level of virtue the saints resemble one another in spite of the differences in their talents and temperaments.

If Madame d'Youville used all her wits to make money, it was only to satisfy her insatiable charity, for she gave numerous proofs of her complete detachment. One among others is that at a time when ready cash was scarce, she paid the Indians two hundred francs to ransom an Englishman whom they had captured and were getting ready to torture to death. During the war, the French as well as the English sent out scouting parties that always included some Indian allies. On many occasions, the General Hospital, situated as it was between the woods of Pointe Saint-Charles and the city walls, was the focus of lively skirmishes. Many Englishmen caught between the walls and the river fled into the Hospital enclosure, risking imprisonment rather than falling into the hands of the Indians. To understand their fear it is sufficient to read the reports of the army scribes about the unheard-of cruelties of the Indians. After their victories in war, it was not unusual to see Indians wearing as trophies human hearts suspended from their necks and hands and bloody scalps hanging from their belts.[5] With complete Christian impartiality, Madame d'Youville hid both French and English fugitives in the church cellars and fed them surreptitiously until the time was right for their escape.

5   Cf. *Mémoires de M. de La Pause* [Memoranda of M. de La Pause], *Rapport de l'Archiviste de la Province de Québec pour 1931-1932* [Report of the Archivist of the Province of Quebec for 1931-1932].

One day as she was sewing a tent[xxxvii] in the community room, an English soldier burst in. From his distraught expression she understood that he was being chased. Lifting the large and heavy material of the tent, she signalled to him to hide himself beneath it. She had barely finished arranging the folds over him when an Indian brandishing a tomahawk appeared. Completely calm, Madame d'Youville pointed a finger at a half-open door at the other end of the room. The Indian, believing he was on the trail of his victim, ran into the corridor that led outside. There is no doubt about it that Madame d'Youville had just saved her house, for when Montreal was under siege in 1760 this soldier, whose name was Southworth,[xxxviii] prevented the destruction of the Hospital. The English general, seeing this tall building outside the city walls, feared a trick on the part of the French and ordered his artillery to fire their cannons at it. At that moment, the soldier whom Madame d'Youville had saved came to tell his commander what had happened. The general sent some officers to scout out the situation. Madame d'Youville, whose innate courtesy had been further refined by the teachings of the Church ("Render therefore to all persons their dues ... honour, to whom honour"[6]), received the investigators with so much civility that they had no doubts about the neutrality of this oasis of charity.

❧

The admirable dynamism of Madame d'Youville undermined her strong constitution so that she fell ill in the autumn of 1757. The onslaught of the illness was so serious that she felt compelled to set out her last will and testament.[7] She recovered from the illness, but the testament remains and allows posterity to see clearly what her feelings were in those years. It gives the diapason of the soul, and the key note is gratitude, with its harmonics of humility and justice. In this document, the foundress leaves all her possessions to her co-workers, her faithful, courageous, and dear sisters. Without rhetoric, it is a sincere thanks from the heart. Madame d'Youville said little in her life, but how eloquent were her works!

In 1747, during the darkest hours for her foundation, when she was wasting away in her room, devoured by worry as much as by illness, her son François received Holy Orders in Quebec City. And as God gently lightened the burden of his servant, in 1752, even while she believed her work to be disintegrating after Bigot's ruinous edict, her son Charles was ordained. A summary of the payments made by Madame d'Youville to the

---

6   Romans 13:7.
7   Cf. SD, p. 324.

seminary in Quebec City for the board of her sons between 1737 and 1752 shows that they were not educated free of charge, even if they benefited for some time from partial bursaries from the foundation. The ordination of her younger son freed Madame d'Youville from duties as guardian; her maternal task had come to an end. These two distinguished priests clearly revealed the upbringing she had given them in spite of her cares as a needy widow. Beyond doubt, her mother's heart trembled with joy before God at this crowning of her rightful maternal ambitions. In September 1748, Bishop de Pontbriand wrote her about the Abbé François d'Youville: "I intend to send your son to Lavaltrie where he will be under the eyes of the Priests of Saint-Sulpice and of yourself, and he can but profit from following your advice." On the part of so reticent a bishop, this was indeed a compliment.

While the foundress was devoting herself to her work, the sands in the hourglass were running out for some members of her family. In 1750, her older brother, the Abbé Charles de Lajemmerais, who was parish priest of Verchères, died. He was followed by Monsieur de Varennes, her uncle and godfather. In 1758, the death of her mother, preceded by that of Monsieur Sylvain, brought Madame d'Youville into her inheritance. Since the amortizing of the debts of the General Hospital by the Abbé de l'Isle-Dieu in 1756 had brought Madame d'Youville the income from the Hôtel de Ville in Paris that had been frozen for more than twenty years, her financial situation had improved considerably. She was scarcely back on her feet after her serious illness when she resumed her project of enlarging the Hospital. In the meantime, Father Montgolfier had worked out a plan that would place the chapel in the centre of the building with a proposed wing matching the old one. With the approval of her bishop, Madame d'Youville had had the work started; but just as the stonework was rising above the ground, everything had to be stopped. War had been declared between France and England.

In this unforgettable year of 1759, a more personal trial struck the heart of Madame d'Youville and her community. On 18 June, Father Normant died. Louis Normant de Faradon, a priest of the Society of Saint-Sulpice, had been Superior of the Seminary of Ville Marie since 1732 and the spiritual director of Madame d'Youville since the death of Father du Lescoät in 1733. He had witnessed the action of grace in the soul of the young widow, had welcomed her first aspirations towards a life of perfection, and discerned her remarkable attraction to the works of corporal mercy. For twenty-two years he had inspired in the little community a deep Sulpician spirituality that was liturgically centred and unshakeably Roman. He had inculcated a thoroughly Sulpician devotion to the Pope, a spirit of poverty, humility, and a discreet zeal that still today characterizes the Grey Nuns. The foundress would not have been able to find a surer guide than this man of great prudence and eminent virtue. He knew well all the important people in the colony as well as all the social and political rivalries and internal workings of the administration. He was Madame d'Youville's advocate to Father Cousturier who had considerable influence at the French Court. Without doubt, God gave Madame d'Youville the special grace of being a foundress, indomitable courage, and the endowment of a rare business genius, but one wonders whether she would have been so richly rewarded with success without the help of the Society of Saint-Sulpice. Certainly, the Grey Nuns' founder is Madame d'Youville, but is not the rock on which she founded Saint-Sulpice?[xxxix] During her lifetime, at every fearful occurrence, a Sulpician came to the rescue. First there was Father du Lescoät who providentially pointed the foundress in the direction of her vocation; then, Father Normant, the experienced guide possessing untiring concern; later, there were Fathers Navetier, Hourdé, and Déat, agents of Providence to the poor. There was Father Bouffandeau who shifted the balance in favour of the King's saving the Hospital by providing the lacking six thousand francs. Then there was Father Montgolfier who elaborated the Constitutions of the Institute. Later came Father Thavenet, the tenacious bursar who rescued the money engulfed in the tragic upheaval of 1760. But in the end, they would all have to be remembered: these humble chaplains who were, as occasion required, teachers of plain chant, instructors to the sisters in the crafts of candle making, printing, bookbinding, gilding, and so on and so forth. In a burst of gratitude Madame d'Youville wrote: "Never will this house forget its benefactors!" Never is forever. Forever, as long as there are Grey Nuns, certain traditional feast days and prayers will echo before the Eternal Father the foundress's gratitude to the Society of Saint-Sulpice – as is only just.

CHAPTER VIII

The Cross Shines Forth

*T*HE YEAR 1759 was the horrific year in the history of Canada. It was a year of alarms and confusion as well as hope. The army crowned with the victories of Monongahela, Chouagen, and Fort Carillon (Ticonderoga) seemed invincible to the population. The generals alone foresaw the inevitable hour when bravery would have to bow before the crushing manpower of the enemy. For two years the people in the countryside had been fighting; there had been no harvests. In Montreal there was no bread, rations were reduced to two ounces per day, misery was everywhere and extreme.

Seeing the serious peril of conquest by a Protestant country, Bishop de Pontbriand administered in his cathedral the sacrament of Confirmation to more than twelve hundred people, even to infants at the breast.[1] He gave detailed instructions and extraordinary powers to his priests who were authorized to say Mass in cabins without lights or servers as the missionaries did. This holy pastor, in his remarkable charges, exhorted his flock to penitence, prescribed public prayers, public penance, and processions, not only in the parishes, but also in the forts and camps.

The time was serious and anxiety was pervasive. For Madame d'Youville the anguish was tormenting because her younger son, the Abbé Dufrost, was at the heart of the danger as he was then parish priest of Saint Joseph's in Pointe de Lévy.[xl] Indeed, he was the only parish priest taken prisoner. The bad news descended like a rain of arrows, wounding his mother's heart. Subject to supernatural grace though it was, it was still a mother's heart filled with unrelenting dread for months on end. On 30 June 1759, Brigadier Monckton attacked Pointe de Lévy, occupied the town and turned the church into a hospital. As the English fleet was approaching Quebec City, the governor had ordered the inhabitants of the parishes downstream to hide in the woods. It was then that the Abbé Dufrost accompanied his flock inland. On 24 July he was taken prisoner with 287 parishioners; all were taken on board the

---

1   The Abbé Auguste Gosselin, *L'Église du Canada* [The Church in Canada], part III, chap. XXXIV, p. 478.

English frigates anchored across from the camp at Pointe de Lévy. The Abbé Dufrost appears to have been kept in captivity until the surrender of Quebec because from 18 June until 2 October no entries were made in the registers of the parish of Saint Joseph, including the parochial duties at Saint Henri de Lauzon. In contrast, from October 1759 until January 1760 there are sixty-eight entries in the registers, all signed by Father Dufrost. In February a detachment of the English army was billeted in the rectory. At that time, the Abbé Dufrost, his freedom hampered, suspected of extreme patriotism and thus fearing a second imprisonment – since the Jesuits had just been driven out of Quebec City for the same reason – thought it more prudent to absent himself for awhile. Helped by some of his parishioners and carrying his most valuable papers, he succeeded in escaping the occupied territory and reaching Montreal where the French flag still flew. There he was reunited with his bishop who, having entrusted the conquered part of his diocese to his Vicar General, Father Jean-Olivier Briand, had taken refuge in Montreal so as to be able to continue to rule the French part of the diocese. Bishop de Pontbriand's biographer gives an interesting detail about the bishop's choice of a place of residence: "In Montreal, it was the Grey Nuns who took care of the holy bishop; and it was at their house, at the beginning, that he went to lodge before asking for accommodation at the Sulpicians'." I have not been able to locate the document that the Abbé Gosselin relies upon here; but in any case his reputation as a historian inclines one to accept his statement, which is much to the honour of Madame d'Youville.

At the beginning of the siege of Quebec, the seminarians were sent back to their families except for the finishing students who moved to Montreal to continue their studies accompanied by the two directors, Fathers Pressart and Gravé. Father Gravé developed the habit of celebrating his daily Mass at the Grey Nuns', and from 27 September 1759 to 9 September 1761 he signed most of the burial entries in the General Hospital's register. This shows how attentive were his relations with Madame d'Youville. Later, he would render her a homage full of praise.

In the midst of the turmoil, the wise foundress was trying to ensure the future of her Institute, so unshakeable was her trust in Divine Providence. The Letters Patent allowed for only twelve administrators, a number that was already insufficient. In order to circumvent these restrictions that had become disastrous, Madame d'Youville proposed to the bishop that more women be admitted as postulants or novices and that they remain on probation for an indeterminate time. There would be no change in the statute, for as vacancies gradually opened on the administrative council they would be filled.[2] In this way, in 1759 six postulants and four novices joined the community. After the surrender of Quebec and the imminent threat of a change in rule, Father Montgolfier, the Vicar General for the region of Montreal, authorized the profession of the three novices, which brought the community up to fifteen professed sisters.

The shortage of food in the Hospital exercised the directress's ingenuity. As the supply of flour was nearly out, Madame d'Youville suggested to her sisters that they eat only corn for breakfast and collation so that the poor could have bread longer; but in the end the bread was also gone. Without bread and with no means of getting any during general famine, the sisters were visibly aided by Divine Providence. One day to their great surprise they found in their refectory "several quarter pounds of fine cornflour."[3] They were unable to find out where it came from or how it had been left there. Given the particular arrangement of the rooms and the number of people always about, it would have been practically impossible to bring these barrels of flour into the Hospital, and especially into the sisters' refectory, without being seen by workers. Yet, when enquiries were made, it could not be discovered who gave this gift or how it came about that the barrels were there. Those people surrounding the foundress considered this help to be miraculous, and especially when later unexplained happenings rewarded her unerring trust in Divine Providence.

Father Normant had obtained from Pope Benedict XIV a brief, dated 5 May 1749, establishing in perpetuity a Confraternity of the Sacred Heart, endowed with many indulgences, at the Grey Nuns' General Hospital. From that day, Madame d'Youville had dreamed of adding to the church a chapel dedicated specifically to the Sacred Heart. At the beginning of 1760, amid the general disarray, she, like a true devotee to the Heart of Jesus, had a chapel constructed in the right transept of the church by "her men" assisted by the sisters. This would rally the congregation and the people around the Sacred Heart of Jesus. And as in her devotion the Father and the Son were only one God, she consecrated the chapel in the left transept to the Eternal Father, the object of her special devotion. Since 1731 Madame d'Youville had been registered in the Confraternity of the Sacred Heart at the Ursulines in Quebec City, which explains why her name does not appear in the register of the Montreal Confraternity.

On 8 September 1760, Montreal fell and the whole colony along the Saint Lawrence was split from France. Over these French people the Union

---

2   Cf. ASGM, autograph letter of Madame d'Youville, dated 24 May 1758.

3   Cf. MD.

Jack would henceforth fly. In religious institutions, the worst fears troubled people's minds. Would they live? Would they be dispossessed, exiled, or tolerated? Bishop de Pontbriand, who had died the preceding 8th of June,[xli] had foreseen the catastrophe and had left clear instructions. To his Vicar General in Quebec City, Father Briand, he laid down the following line of conduct: "We must in no way be involved with anything that concerns the temporal; the spiritual alone must occupy us."[4] Of the Superior of the Hôtel-Dieu in Quebec City, he required a more perfect attitude of mind: "I am convinced that you will comport yourself in a manner that will not occasion any reproach from him [Governor Murray]. The king of England is now by conquest the sovereign of Quebec, and we owe him all the sentiments of which the Apostle Paul speaks ... I wish you all great joy, great courage, and great patience. You will have all that if you truly convince yourselves that your situation comes from God and that we must lovingly submit to it. I well know that the first movements are rebellious, but reflection will soon inspire the sentiments of that holy man Job."[5] Madame d'Youville entered fully into the spirit of her holy bishop. She, a Frenchwoman to the core, showed perfect civility to the conquerors. Much has been conjectured about the feelings of the *Canadiens* in regard to the change in allegiance; hers, however, are clear as they are disclosed in her personal correspondence. After the Treaty of Paris, which ended all hopes, she wrote to Father Villard: "We were surprised as we lived under the illusion that France would not abandon us, but we were mistaken in our expectations. God willed it thus, and blessed be His Holy Name." Yet, the exodus of the *Canadiens* constantly kept open the wound in her sensitive heart: "All the good citizens," she wrote, "are leaving the country. One is filled with sorrow to see relatives, friends, and benefactors leaving, never to be seen again. Nothing is sadder. Every day, new sacrifices ..." In 1765 she wrote to Madame de Ligneris: "I am more and more delighted that you are in France, and I would like to see my whole family there. The tenderness in which I hold them will never allow me to keep them here." In September 1770, referring to the fall in French credit, she confided to Monsieur Feltz: "Our good king of France will retain everything in the end. I would not regret it if we could return to him, as some people would sometimes have us believe." After ten years of keeping a correct attitude, out of her heart escapes this soft and pathetic sigh: "Our good king." But is it surprising? What do ten years of life weigh in the balance against the noble French blood that flowed in her veins, against a whole

---

4   Cf. Letter of 16 February 1760.
5   Cf. Letter of 13 November 1759.

upbringing in fierce loyalty? Such slips of the pen reveal her secret heart-breaks and point to the loftiness of her virtue. The flesh may tremble, but virtue always triumphs with Madame d'Youville.

More than anything else, Carleton's restrictions on religious communities threatened her. Truly, ruin was close on her heels. Her worry is communicated in her letters: "How shall we get along, how shall we live with the English? … We can scarcely keep ourselves alive. Money is extremely scarce and there are no means of earning it …" Was she then going to decrease her charity? On the contrary, she extended it to a work that demanded not only devotion but ready cash – the care of abandoned children.

Under French rule illegitimate children were supported by the government and were supervised by a midwife who put them out to nurse and after they were eighteen months old placed them with families that were given grants for this purpose.[6] This system resulted in revolting abuses. It even happened that the wet-nurses sold the little outcasts to the Indians. When Madame d'Youville was asked to make known her projects before the granting of the Letters Patent, she proposed the following to the authorities: "Should the Court approve that we remain here, and should it be so disposed as to support us in the good that God has inspired us to do, we shall take foundlings into our care. There is so much misery here through neglect that out of twenty children baptized only two or three are properly brought up. We still see eighteen-year-olds who do not know the first principles of their religion. I know of some who at the age of twenty-three have not made their first communion."[7] The Court did not authorize any new works; and, officially, Madame d'Youville had to leave these unfortunates to their sad fate. Nevertheless, between 1754 and 1760 she took in seventeen of them at her own expense. Under the new regime, since there was no law for the care of abandoned children, they were frequently found along country roads, at crossroads, and in rivers, like the two who one day floated down the little river that ran by the Hospital. Once going into the city, she saw another half buried and one winter morning yet another stabbed in the throat and frozen in the ice. At once she resolved to henceforth take in all the abandoned children. The future was uncertain, financial help from France doubtful, and there was less and less work; but what did it matter? She would give these souls back to God, at least through bap-

---

6   Cf. P.-G. Roy, *Inventaire des Ordonnances des Intendants de la Nouvelle-France* [List of the Ordinances of the Intendants of New France], vol. 2: 203 – Hocquart, Ordinance of 9 June 1736.

7   Cf. ASGM, autograph manuscript.

tism. True zeal does not attend to the objections of human prudence; its boldness wells up out of an unshakeable faith that hears only the cries of the afflicted. Father Montgolfier could only approve such dedication and a work that was so useful to society and to the greater glory of religion. He even thought that it would be best to remove those infants who had been weaned from the wet-nurses and to leave the others with them in exchange for an agreed-upon fee. This decision was approved by General Thomas Gage, the Governor of Montreal, who himself wished to contribute to the work by allocating to it all fines incurred by violations of the law. But since the present rule was only military and the succeeding civil government did not share General Gage's views on this matter, Madame d'Youville received in total from this source only 288 francs.

God, however, responded to heroism with a miracle. One day when Madame d'Youville had only one piastre left in her pocket, a wet-nurse arrived claiming exactly this amount as immediately owing to her. Madame d'Youville did not hesitate to surrender her last coin. But putting her hand in her pocket, what was her surprise at drawing out a handful of coins! Instinctively, she put her other hand in her other pocket and pulled out as much. Then lifting her eyes to heaven and joining her hands, she exclaimed, "Oh, my God, I am a wretched creature!" This was an outburst of emotion, a stammering of humility, thankfulness, and love. A number of saints have uttered such mysterious and apparently contradictory exclamations. At the miraculous draught of fishes, did not Saint Peter cry out: "Depart from me, for I am a sinful man, O Lord."[8] According to Pascal, "miracles are a flash of lightning" – indeed, a flash of lightning to shake up our materialistic complacency. What is the inexplicable multiplication of Madame d'Youville's single coin if not the confirmation of her heroic virtue?

From 1760 to 1761, Madame d'Youville took in forty-seven abandoned children, and by the time of her death eleven years later, in 1771, she had received 318. She had paid the wet-nurses 9,300 francs, not including the baby clothes, medicine, etc. The last letter in her letter book is addressed to the colony's governor, Sir Guy Carleton, whom she is soliciting on behalf of these privileged guests in her house, the abandoned children.

In the midst of the general upheaval, Madame d'Youville was struggling through a real financial jungle. At the cession of the colony, the French Treasury owed Montreal's General Hospital 120,799 livres. While

---

8   St. Luke 5:8.

The altar stone from the Château de La Gesmeray, Médréac, Brittany, France, where the father of Mother d'Youville was born. The parishioners of Médréac gave it to the Community of Montreal in 1896. Today, the magnificent sanctuary of the chapel of the Institute founded by his daughter echoes across the centuries the chapel of the Château.

Sanctuary of the chapel of the Mother House of the Grey Nuns in Montreal. The paintings on either side of the high altar represent the Finding and the Exaltation of the Holy Cross, the principal feasts of the Institute.

the Court was investigating the embezzlements of Intendant Bigot and his supernumeraries, the value of bills of exchange remained undetermined, which resulted in a depreciation of French currency in Canada. To a correspondent in France she wrote in 1763 about her brother-in-law, Ignace Gamelin[xlii]: "The little property they have ... and [the] bills of exchange that would not get one hundred livres to the thousand." As the value of French currency depended upon chance, and relations between the two countries were difficult, a correspondence ensued that was tedious, slow, and frustratingly uncertain. In 1763 Madame d'Youville wrote to Father Cousturier: "You inform me that you have our bills of exchange of which I have had no news since 1760." In the same year she wrote to another correspondent: "We still do not know anything about the fate of the bills of exchange from '59 ..." – "We do not know whether we have a bursar or who he is ..." In short, every ship brought contradictory rumours. – "We have also heard that the papers in this country, even though they have been registered here, will not be paid." To all these troubles she applied her usual remedy: "I leave everything up to Providence, my trust is in it, everything will work out as God wills."

When at last the long-awaited judgement came to complete the ruin of the Canadian subjects, the General Hospital suffered more than others because a good part of its expenses represented advances for food, medicine, and so forth for the soldiers. For these, Madame d'Youville had had to borrow at interest. By the king's decision, the bills of exchange were reduced by half, while orders to pay, paper money, and receipts for supplies and rations were reduced by a quarter. After cuts, which represented for the Hospital 79,811 livres, the initial invoice of 120,799 livres was worth only 40,987 livres, 15 sols, 11 deniers. By an edict of November 1767, the king decreed that all bills payable to the king would be converted into bonds paying an annual interest of four and a half per cent. But in January 1770, by a judgement in council, the king ordered that the interest paid by his Estates would no longer be four and a half but two and a half per cent. Hence the Hospital's bonds, which initially returned 1,132 livres, 7 sols, 7 deniers, from that date yielded only 699 livres in interest annually. The 120,000 livres had vanished like snow in the sun. Faced with this fiasco, Madame d'Youville had only words of forgiveness for the Court: "It has done us a great wrong, may God forgive it."

❧

Holiness is a surpassing of oneself, a spiritualization of one's being, and it is only by the touchstone of trials that the soul achieves stability. So that the soul can reach this state of unshakeable resolve, God does not cease to test its faith. In the present as in the past, God asks the soul: "Do you love me more than anything? More than reputation or friendship, more than riches, more than health, more even than the good that you can do?" And if the answer is yes, then inevitably saints are in the process of being created.

In 1765 Madame d'Youville had once again to say yes out of her generosity. In May another disaster struck. In less than two hours a fire reduced to nothing eighteen years of work. The fire started in the city at the corner of Notre Dame and Saint François Xavier Streets.[9] Since they were outside the city walls, Madame d'Youville believed that they were safe, but a strong wind quickly carried the flames in their direction. In relating the accident, she repeated to all her correspondents her belief that "We would have been able to save much had we imagined that we would burn …" – "If I had only been able to convince myself that the fire would reach us …" – "I was scarcely able to convince myself that God would not preserve this house which, as you know, was an asylum for the outcast. With this in view, I did not hasten to safeguard it, but even sent into the city those among us who were able to help …" She proposed, God disposed. At a single stroke, her faith lifted her up again to rest serenely with God. Surrounded by her pitiable family of the underprivileged, she made this request surpassing human nature: "Kneeling, we are going to recite the *Te Deum* to thank God for the cross that he has just sent us." At the conclusion of the hymn of thanksgiving, rising she prophesied in a voice full of assurance: "My children, be of good courage, henceforth this house will not burn again." The prediction has proved true up to the present time. Even after assessing the extent of her losses, her submission to God's plans did not falter, as her letters demonstrate: "The fire has cast us into great poverty, but God has his plans and I adore them." – "God has allowed this to happen. Blessed be his holy Name." – "… but what can we do but adore the designs of His Providence and submit to His holy will, as indeed we have tried as best as we are able to do."

Yet, night was coming on and one hundred and eighteen people in her care were without shelter.[10] After having consulted with her sisters, she decided that they would move into the house and barns of the farm at Pointe Saint-Charles. In the meantime, however, Father Montgolfier had asked the religious of the Hôtel-Dieu to take in the disaster victims from the General Hospital. In spite of her desire not to be a burden to anyone, Madame d'Youville submitted obediently to her superior and went to the

---

9   Cf. Appendix IV. The letter of 10 June 1765 to Madame de Ligneris contains some interesting details about this fire.

10   See SD for the names of these people, pp. 322-23.

Hôtel-Dieu. She was welcomed there with great sympathy and the sisters, who were themselves extremely poor, received the sorely tried Sisters at their humble table for many months. Several days after the disaster, some of the men took up residence in the Hospital's brewery, which had been spared from the flames, and others moved to the farm at Pointe Saint-Charles so as to make the rooms at the Hôtel-Dieu less crowded. The Seminary once again assumed most of the cost of feeding the poor. The citizens and the sisters of the Congregation of Notre Dame also showed their sympathy through generous gifts of provisions. A few days after the fire, a cask of wine two-thirds full was found in the cellar of the Hospital. When it was tasted the wine proved to be excellent. It was served to the poor until the bursar seeing that it was running out alerted Madame d'Youville that only a thin stream no wider than a straw was flowing. "Keep drawing, my Sister," she replied, "do not tire from drawing." And enough wine came out to meet the needs of the poor for two and a half months.

According to a detailed, notarized memorandum of 5 June 1765, the General Hospital's losses amounted to 91,045 livres, 10 sols. Furnishings, clothing, shoes, provisions had all been destroyed. Even now, the catastrophe seems overwhelming, in addition to the decline in the value of French money and at a time when even the country itself lay in ruins. Madame d'Youville did not conceal the extent of her misfortunes. Asking for the prayers of the Abbé de l'Isle-Dieu, she wrote: "Pray, dear Father, that God will give me the strength to bear patiently all these crosses and to make a holy use of them. Here all at once we have lost King, country, possessions, and, worse yet, we are in fear that our holy religion will be obliterated." With Madame de Ligneris she shared her plans: " …We are bold enough to try to recover a corner of our house where the walls are still quite sound." To another correspondent she revealed her reason: "… all hope to see us rebuild. We have begun and will try to continue, in the hope that Providence, which has always sustained us, will continue to do so." She was sixty-four years old, but her courage was up to the task: she would rebuild her Hospital.

The fire destroyed a quarter of the city and left two hundred and fifteen families homeless. The misfortune so affected the new city that in London public collections were taken up for the Montreal disaster victims.[11] Madame d'Youville received a large portion of this aid and her gratitude was far from silent. "I have been most fortunate in what we have received from these funds: we have had in three instalments almost 20,000

---

11 Cf. "The Case of The Canadians of Montreal distressed by Fire" [English original], Montreal, May 1765.

livres, but it takes so much for such large buildings." – "… to have endured a fire that submerged us in debts and of which we would never be free without the charity we have received from the collections made in London which have considerably lightened our burden." – "Had we not been relieved by the charitable donations from London, as indeed we were, having had in three years close to 18,000 livres, we would never have been able to revive ourselves after our fire." In total, she received 19,407 livres in proceeds from the London collections.

In her misfortune Madame d'Youville received, among other things, a touching example of devotion from the Indian converts. She had always welcomed them and cared for them with kindness, especially during the smallpox epidemic of 1755. They took advantage of the present situation to show her their gratitude by making a generous contribution. For her benefit they disposed of some of their most treasured possessions – silver brooches, porcelain beads, knives, woollen blankets, gloves, deerskin moccasins, cloth, cotton, sugar, and so forth, as well as coins. The Indians of the Lake of Two Mountains gave a total of 360 livres, 2 sols, while those of Sault Saint Louis gave 101 livres, 6 sols.

These gifts and charitable offerings accumulated over a period of three years, but immediately following the fire Madame d'Youville found herself completely destitute. The Seminary of Saint-Sulpice furnished her with emergency funds. Father Montgolfier himself advanced fifteen thousand livres to begin reconstruction of the house and to supply the strict necessities for her settling in. On 19 September 1765 she wrote to Father Cousturier, the Superior of the Society of Saint-Sulpice, in Paris: "I have the honour of paying you my most humble respects and of asking you that if you obtain anything from the Hospital's bill of exchange for 7,620 livres that you are holding, that you keep it. This will be the beginning of the repayment of the advances that Father Montgolfier gave me to rebuild our house…" She then notified her agent in Paris: "We were greatly assisted by the Priests of Saint-Sulpice. I gave them our bill of exchange for 7,620 livres that Monsieur Cousturier is holding for us in payment for some of the money they have advanced us."

In a charge dated 21 May 1765 from Boucherville, Father Etienne Marchard, the Vicar General of the diocese, the see being vacant, enumerated the consequences of the fire and said about the Hospital:

> [There was] a General Hospital, the former asylum where the poor, the sick, incurables, enfeebled old people without resources or support, illegitimate children, and mentally ill men and women found a secure retreat and were untiringly cared for by the lady adminis-

trator of this house and those of her community; in a state of wretchedness they found a place of consolation that made them forget their previous misery … For this cause, we are allowing a general collection to be made in all the parishes of the Montreal region … We are likewise allowing for the same reason work on Sundays and feast days after attendance at Holy Mass and with the consent of the police officers.[12]

Thanks to these special privileges and the general co-operation of the people, the men's section of the Hospital was opened by the following 23 September. The old men accompanied by two sisters moved in. The community was able to return to their conventual rooms on 5 December, and the poor women were back in the Hospital for Christmas 1765. Thus this extensive fire did not cause too long a break in the exercise of Madame d'Youville's charity. Seven months after the blaze the last of the General Hospital's disaster victims left the Hôtel-Dieu, and not eighteen months as Sister Morin no doubt inadvertently wrote in her *Annales de L'Hôtel-Dieu* [Annals of the Hôtel-Dieu].

The Hospital had been rebuilt, but how bare it was inside! Madame d'Youville reveals a little of what it must have been like when she writes: "… these bills would give us great pleasure here, and even more if they could be converted into cloth." – "[We were given] 1,000 livres in draft orders that had not been registered here; we traded them in at 15% to buy straw mattresses and shirts for the poor." To the Abbé de l'Isle-Dieu she did not conceal her troubles. Speaking of their return to the Hospital, she writes: "It will be very difficult there, but we shall be home. We shall lack no end of means for doing penance, but we have need of them. We shall try to profit from it." After her house had burned in 1745, she had said: "We have been a little too comfortable … from now on we shall live more poorly." Twenty years later her reaction to the trial was the same; she still made of it a stepping stone to virtue. The valiant sisters would have ample time to practise mortification, for the reconstruction of the Hospital was not completed until 1767.

The Treaty of Paris allowed the Canadians who wished to return to France eighteen months to sell their property. After this time, the unsold posses-

---

12   *Mandements, Lettres pastorales et circulaires des évêques de Québec* [Charges, Pastoral Letters, and Encyclicals of the Bishops of Quebec], 6 vols., published by Monsignor H. Têtu and the Abbé C. O. Gagnon (Quebec, 1887-1900), vol. 2, p. 180.

sions would become the property of the British crown. This clause of the treaty triggered a lowering of real estate value in Canada which the new arrivals knew how to take advantage of.

At the General Hospital the slowdown in work following the Conquest became alarming. Madame d'Youville constantly felt that a way had to be found to overcome it. She was looking for a solution. One of her boarders, Mademoiselle Marie-Anne de Lanoue, offered Madame d'Youville her seigneury of Châteauguay, which was completely undeveloped but held potential for the future. As the daughter of a landowner, Madame d'Youville thought that she could see a way out of difficulties by possessing exploitable land. It was a time of bargains, but her means of payment were not amenable to the sellers, most of whom were in a hurry to leave and required more ready cash than Madame d'Youville possessed. The seigneury of Châteauguay, located on Lake Saint-Louis, presented a number of advantages of which Madame d'Youville was well aware since she had been leasing it since 1751. She therefore started negotiations for the property.

The seigneury of Châteauguay, consisting of two leagues of frontage on Lake Saint-Louis and three leagues deep into the land, along with the eight islands of Iles-de-la-Paix, had been granted by Count Frontenac on 29 September 1673 to the Sieur Charles Le Moyne de Longueuil. The latter sold it on 6 August 1706 to his first cousin, Zacharie Robutel, Sieur de Lanoue. The seigneury passed by inheritance to Lanoue's children, Joachim and Marie-Anne de Lanoue. On 25 August 1764 Joachim Robutel de Lanoue made over all his rights to his sister Marie-Anne, and Madame d'Youville received the property by subrogation on payment of eight thousand livres: "The seller acknowledges having received from Marie-Marguerite de Lajemmerais, Widow Youville, the sum of 2000 livres and the remaining 6000 livres by a bill of exchange drawn by the said Widow Youville on the amount held by Monsieur the Abbé de L'Isle-Dieu in France." Moreover, Madame d'Youville had to acquit an obligation of 7122 livres to the heirs de Francheville and Charly and to pay an annuity of 900 livres to Mademoiselle de Lanoue.

The following spring, the fire of 18 May made of this undertaking a heavy burden to bear. Nevertheless, Madame d'Youville, a woman of principle, signed the bill of sale on 8 June: "Madame d'Youville states that the present purchase is made through the reinvestment of funds acquired from the sale she has made to the Sieur Deaudegan of a fief and land held by commoners possessed by the poor of said General Hospital in the Seigneury of Chambly, in conformity with permission granted by His Excellency, the Honourable James Murray, Governor of the Province of

Quebec." The Chambly property yielded a negligible return, while the lit-igation of the seven co-landlords created innumerable difficulties for the tenants. Thus, Madame d'Youville had sought authorization, as stipulated in the Letters Patent, to get rid of it. When Bishop Briand returned to Canada, she brought him up to date on these transactions in a letter which also helps us to understand them.[13]

The seigneury of Châteauguay was bordered on the north by the Saint Lawrence River, on the south by the seigneury of Ville Chauve or Beauharnois, on the east by the seigneury of Sault Saint Louis (the Indian reserve of Caughnawaga), and on the west by the Rivière du Loup, now the Châteauguay River. The manor house had been built on Saint Bernard Island, an area of 690 arpents. It was a low wooden structure measuring twenty feet by fifty feet with a stable, a stone barn with loopholes, and a small windmill. Surrounding it were about a hundred arpents of cultivated land. A small mound on the island permitted a panoramic view of the country round about. From there could be surveyed the meanderings of the Rivière du Loup, the Saint Lawrence and its surroundings, and farther away part of Beauharnois, Ile Perrot, Pointe Claire, and in the background Mount Royal. It was the close presence of the Iroquois of Sault Saint Louis that had impeded the development of the seigneury. Father de Charlevoix reported an ambush on the island in 1690, and the burial records of Lachine contain the names of a number of soldiers and colonists in Châteauguay who fell victim to the Indians. Even in Madame d'Youville's time some Indians were still taking scalps. The *Mémoires des anciennes Soeurs de l'Hôpital-général* [Memoirs of the Senior Sisters of the General Hospital] recount an adventure that is at once terrifying and amusing. One day one of the sisters was coming home across a field when she felt herself being followed. She was grabbed by an Indian who hastily pulled off her bonnet. Seeing her shaven head, however, he gave an exclamation of sur-prise and fled in disdain. This recalls how the Cavelier de La Salle bewil-dered the Indians by throwing his wig at them. In 1854 excavations on the island's hillock uncovered eighteen skulls, a large number of human bones, and a whole skeleton. Arrows and stone axes found at the same site lead one to conjecture about whom these bones may have belonged to. Were they those of Indian braves or of equally brave white settlers?

Beginning in 1765, the landowner opened her farming record book. This parchment-covered notebook in which Madame d'Youville made all the entries in her own hand forms part of the treasure she has left to pos-

---

13   Cf. ASGM, Letters of Madame d'Youville, to Bishop Briand, 26 September 1766.

terity. It exhibits the same methodical mind as can be found in the account books of the General Hospital.

In 1766 Madame d'Youville hired the surveyor Jean-Baptiste Perrot to map out the seigneury. She was also projecting several improvements. The tenants had difficulty getting to the ordinary little mill, which had been built by Charles Le Moyne de Longueuil in 1687, in order to grind their grain. Having explored her domain, Madame d'Youville decided to build another, larger, water-driven mill at the northern watershed of the Rivière du Loup, about a league from the manor. To make sure that there was enough water power, she had a 200 foot long canal dug and built a dam of about 400 feet. The new mill was 70 feet high and 36 feet wide. In its construction, Madame d'Youville used all the salvageable materials she could from the General Hospital's old mill as well as the millstone. When in 1839 the mill on the Rivière du Loup had to be demolished, one of the most competent businessmen of the time, Mr. William Burry, observed that Madame d'Youville had chosen the best site on the river for a mill, and he built the new mill in the same place.

Madame d'Youville also had a bakery constructed and rebuilt the barn and the stable. She had several arpents of land ploughed and sown, and she planted an orchard on a slope of the hill. To pay for this work she had to draw on her own inheritance as well as that of Sister Lemoine-Despins. Still, all of this was exhausting labour, and at her advanced age her health suffered from it. At all times of the year, notwithstanding the weather, she travelled from Châteauguay to Montreal first by jolting cart to Lachine and then by canoe on the rough waters of Lake Saint-Louis. Every year on Saint Martin's day, when rents were due, she was at her country manor to greet her tenants. As the landlady, she held all legal rights over her domain, but she only exercised her ardent zeal in teaching the rudiments of religion to the numerous children of her tenant farmers. Like a spring welling up from within, Madame d'Youville's supernatural spirit spread through all her actions. Just as one is admiring the businesswoman in her, the saint solely preoccupied with the welfare of souls springs up. Etienne Duranceau, who died at Châteauguay on 25 December 1857 at the age of ninety-four, unconsciously confirmed the tradition of Madame d'Youville as a catechist. One day in 1850, Mother Deschamps, having given a catechism lesson to the children of Pointe de Châteauguay under the trees, was distributing slices of bread and butter to the children as a reward for their paying attention. Monsieur Duranceau, who by chance was passing by and saw all these children surrounding the sister, recalled a previous event. He told Mother Deschamps: "I also learned my catechism here. That was a long time ago. It was Mother d'Youville who taught us the catechism, and she like you rewarded us when we had been good." In order to be certain about the memories of this octogenarian, Mother Deschamps asked him several questions. "How tall was Madame d'Youville and what was her colouring?" – "She was tall, fairly dark, with a rosy complexion." – "And her eyes, what colour were they?" – "As for that, I wouldn't be able to tell you." This response convinced Mother Deschamps of Etienne Duranceau's sincerity, and she decided to record his testimony. To perpetuate the memory of Mother d'Youville as a catechist, in 1884 the Grey Nuns opened a free elementary school in Châteauguay on the common across from the manor. This school is at present under the Catholic School Commission.

Through her wonderful energy and know-how, Madame d'Youville transformed this uncultivated island into a beautiful domain whose produce still nourishes the poor. This oasis of peace, Saint Bernard Island, has become a retreat milieu for the sisters. It is in these delightful surroundings, before this horizon that recalls a past that fulfilled its promises and a future that extends endlessly the procession of Grey Nuns, that these apostolic workers come to re-gather their strength, thanks to the foresight of their foundress.

The tower of the ordinary little mill from 1687 is kept in good repair and is still standing. It is now an oratory and on its dome is a life-size statue of Saint Joseph. Since 1896 the hillock has been a cemetery. There in splendid isolation the rows of small white marble tombstones mark the graves of the deceased sisters.

But among the daughters of Mother Youville the poor are never far away from the sisters. On this island of retreat, from July 1932, when the sisters donated a large site of land with a beautiful sandy beach to the Charity for Handicapped Children, there was a holiday camp.

The spirit of Mother d'Youville has always continued to support and sustain her Institute.

CHAPTER IX

The Finished Canvas

FROM 1739 Mademoiselle Thérèse Lemoine-Despins had been living at the General Hospital as a boarder. Although she had witnessed the hard work and poverty of the sisters, she nevertheless decided in 1753 to become a Grey Nun, as Mother d'Youville had predicted she would. Yet, she found it odd that in this canonically constituted community there was no novice director. Mother d'Youville assured her that the day she entered there would be one. Mademoiselle Despins did not notice the ambiguity in the reply and was astonished to find herself nominated as novice director on her entry into the community. Fourteen years of training in the way of life, example, and counsels of the foundress had made her a perfect disciple. The novitiate now had a head, but Mother d'Youville still remained the true director of the community's spirituality. After Bishop de Pontbriand had canonically confirmed her as Superior, the sisters spontaneously gave her the title of Mother, even though they had always considered her to be their spiritual mother and held her in the greatest affection. In fact, it was her personal charm that had drawn so many women of good will to her work and kept them happy and united. In the memoirs of each of her senior sisters, one finds the same note of warm intimacy: "We so much enjoyed gathering round her, and we savoured every sort of satisfaction listening to her discourse in our midst." Crouched around their Mother, they formed a happy family circle. Love is a great teacher; indeed, it is the only teacher who makes a difference. Out of the foundress's heart an overabundance of her spirituality poured out on her daughters. At times serious and at other times playful, these outpourings bonded the sisters' hearts together in a perfect union that was the wonder of the public. It was during one of these carefree family hours that Mother d'Youville made one of her remarkable predictions. Looking over the group of sisters at her feet, she singled out Sister Thérèse-Geneviève Coutlée and said in a voice full of confidence: "She will live the longest and will survive all of you." This prophecy came true, for of all of Mother d'Youville's Sisters it was Sister Coutlée who died last. Mother d'Youville made this prediction in April 1766, and Sister Coutlée died on 17 July 1821.

As a leader of souls on the way of renunciation, Mother d'Youville always remembered that "the entrance into piety is a challenge."[1] She knew how difficult it is to change mental attitudes and how much courage is required to uncover the faults that conceal themselves beneath seemingly innocent displays of virtue. And she did this with all gentleness and solicitude. She encouraged cheerfulness among her daughters as a safety-valve and she interspersed days of relaxation to compensate for unexpected, burdensome tasks. Then they would take brief holidays in the country at the Pointe Saint-Charles farm where fresh air, sun, and frolicking about renewed their energies.

Yet, Mother d'Youville's gentleness contained no weakness and she knew how to be strict when it was necessary. One day she unexpectedly entered a room where several sisters were engaged in heated words while they worked. As soon as she appeared the chattering stopped. When asked what was going on, one of the sisters admitted to having made some barbed comments to a companion. Since Mother d'Youville esteemed sisterly charity above all else, she ordered the guilty woman to kiss the feet of all the other sisters present. The sister had to do this right away in spite of the supplications of her companions who wanted to spare her this humiliation.

On another occasion, Mother d'Youville showed great severity in regard to obedience. She encouraged acts of dedication, but her prudent judgement made her reprove excesses that could endanger health. She thus forbade the sisters to carry heavy burdens alone; when necessary, they should ask for help. Now it happened that one of the novices, Sister Céloron, was busy with the laundry and thought that she could carry a heavy tub full of wet washing. She collapsed from an internal rupture and died several days later in spite of all the care that was lavished upon her. This novice had reached the end of her novitiate; she could therefore be professed as a sister before her death. Mother d'Youville, however, was determined to punish her act of disobedience in a striking manner; and despite the sorrow she felt at this sad conclusion, she refused to let Sister Céloron pronounce her vows in full solemnity. There is, nonetheless, a tradition that she pronounced them privately, but her name does not appear in the Register of Professed Sisters of the Institute. By this severe punishment Mother d'Youville risked offending one of her boarders, the novice's mother, Madame Céloron de Blainville, and in consequence setting off scandalmongering in the worldly salons. The foundress, however, held the

---

1   Pascal, fragment 498.

maintenance of discipline in the community to be above her personal popularity. Fortunately, there were no bad results. On the contrary, through grace the mother gained the desire to take her daughter's place and asked for admission to the community. Catherine Eurry de La Pérelle, the widow of Pierre-Joseph de Céloron, Sieur de Blainville, Knight of Saint Louis, was forty-seven years old at the time. Mother d'Youville found that she possessed "an uncommon virtue." She pronounced her vows on 3 July 1771 and was the last nun professed by Mother d'Youville. By coincidence, they both were widows.

This was not the only occasion on which Mother d'Youville exercised control over her feelings, for her sense of justice was stronger than her natural inclination towards gentleness. Her elder son, the Abbé François d'Youville, when he became priest of the parish of Saint Ours in 1759, wanted to replace the mission chapel, which was falling down, with a proper parish church. To this end, Mother d'Youville lent him nine thousand livres of the General Hospital's funds with his promise to pay it back as soon as possible. Years went by, but the Abbé D'Youville did not think about paying back the loan. He maintained that his mother, having given so much to the poor, could indeed help him in his turn to perform a pious work. Furthermore, he thought that his mother owed him something since his mother had neither accounted for nor had he received anything from the inheritances of his father and his maternal grandparents. When his mother presented her bill, he persisted in his claims. After the burning of the Hospital in 1765, Mother d'Youville, finding herself in extreme need, sought the help of Father Montgolfier, the Vicar General of the diocese, to get her son to pay back the loan. The affair was submitted to the arbitration of three disinterested persons chosen by the Abbé d'Youville himself. Nevertheless, the judgement went against him. He emphatically refused to accept it, and this time his poor mother appealed to the bishop.[2] Bishop Briand, having examined the matter, wrote a sharp reprimand to the hotheaded priest. Mother d'Youville was charged with delivering the letter, but she delayed doing so because in the meanwhile her son had broken his arm. She did not have the satisfaction of seeing this money returned to the coffers of the poor before her death; her son repaid it only after 1773. She also shed the bitter tears that mothers expend on their children; her son's unkindness added to her already heavy heart. Still, she exerted as much tenacity in defending the funds of the poor from her son's abuse of trust as she did against official encroachments.

---

2   Cf. Letter to Bishop Briand, 1769.

As a widow Mother d'Youville followed the counsels of the Apostle and divided her time between her children and the poor. It is possible that she modelled her life on the valiant woman of Holy Scripture, so much is she like her. Moreover, the comparison to the valiant woman of the Book of Proverbs was the first homage that her contemporaries paid her.

Being of a magnanimous heart, Mother d'Youville could never set barriers to her generosity. Her whole life was passed under the tension of one constraint or another. First, there was extreme poverty, then the avarice of her mother-in-law, later the greed of Bigot, and finally unexpected disasters. None of this lessened her noble dreams, but it did make their realization especially difficult. In spite of her poverty, the habits of the *grande dame* persisted in her. Thus, after she had fairly paid her employees, she did not forget small tips, which her account books betray; and she also observed the custom of giving them gifts on New Year's Day. One year she sent a lynx muff to the Abbé de l'Isle-Dieu's servant. The Abbé de l'Isle-Dieu on another occasion, having discovered an error in the accounts of the late Monsieur Nicolas de Paris to the detriment of the Hospital, was worried about it, as were Monsieur de Paris' heirs. Mother d'Youville wrote to him: "The dear departed did his best to serve us, and we would be most ungrateful if we were to bother his family. No, Sir, assure them to the contrary, and if it is agreeable with you, we will hold him acquitted before God and man and pray for the repose of his soul." And the letter contained an official discharge from liability.

Among Mother d'Youville's business letters there are concealed, like sweet-scented sachets, several personal letters. How human she is in them! To a forgetful daughter she wrote about an aged mother: "For four years she has drunk only water, and this is very hard for someone who never lacked for wine or the treats that a person of age ought to have." Of a father, she asked: "Has Lisette grown up and is she as beautiful as ever?" To Madame de Ligneris: "You have lost your beautiful gown; it was in a trunk in which there were a number of good things." And this happy one: "All our Sisters greet you with untold friendship, and especially Despins who is coming with open arms to tell me not to forget her ..." Then there was the tenderness of a surrogate grandmother: "I cannot close without telling you about Benac. He is too handsome. He is a big, well-built, beautiful boy and not at all naughty for having been spoiled. He often speaks of his Uncle and Aunt Figuery." Louis Porlier Benac was four years old at the time and her niece Josette was his godmother. In other letters the deep feelings of Mother d'Youville find full expression. At the moment of her niece's final departure for France, she wrote to her nephew: "You are looking upon our dear Josette, but we have lost her forever. It has been several days since I

Marguerite d'Youville on her bier. Painted by Philippe Liébert,
it is the sole authentic portrait of the Saint in existence.

Stained-glass window in Notre Dame Church in Montreal. In the centre is Mother d'Youville. On each side are figures representing the works of her Institute: abandoned children, the poor, the sick, the blind, orphans, and old people.

have seen them, nor do I wish to go until I know she has left. I do not have enough courage to say goodbye to her … I am closing because my eyes are blinded by tears." To Monsieur Héry she wrote: "As I did not have the courage to bid you farewell and to thank you at your leaving, I am today accomplishing this duty …" After four years of being apart, she declared to Dr. Feltz: "I admit to you that your absence and that of your Wife weigh upon me daily."

Her letters are filled with her spirit of thankfulness. To one correspondent she wrote: "Tomorrow Mass will be said for the healing of your leg. I am confident that it is healed at present, but with God nothing is ever lost." To a benefactor: "This house will never forget your generosity. It is inscribed in so many of our records that those who come after us will know the good you have done for us. Everyday we commend you and your family to the Eternal Father." To another: "I shall never forget the friends from whom I have received so many kindnesses and benefits." Her letters to the Abbé de l'Isle-Dieu are variations on the theme of gratitude. The following excerpt can stand for all the others: "We owe you so much that we shall never be able to repay you unless we as members of Jesus Christ can delve into the riches of His treasury to repay those who have shown us their charity, and you chief among them. Your charity is of a worth that can only be repaid in this divine currency. My Sisters and I often implore Our Divine Saviour and His Divine Father, who has been the object of my devotion for nearly forty years, that He will preserve you for a number of years to come and at the last will reward you with eternal glory." Thus, hearts always inclined to the good can only grow better by losing themselves in God.

Mother d'Youville managed simultaneously all sorts of activities. She directed her house, lands, and building plans, which were almost always in progress. The Hospital's precarious finances kept her continually on her toes. How many hours she must have spent drafting long, irksome letters that had to be copied in duplicate and often in triplicate to disentangle the years and years of so many financial complications caused by the changes in agents and the disappointing royal ordinances. The Abbé de l'Isle-Dieu, being of a highly methodical mind, gave her the following excellent recommendation: "Returning to Madame Lajammerais, she seems to me a good person who is thoroughly committed to and relentlessly pursues her task …"[3] If she had money troubles, they were certainly not due to lack of foresight. She invested her funds in France where the returns were more

---

3   Cf. the Abbé de L'Isle-Dieu to Bishop de Pontbriand, February 1759.

profitable and where she could buy at a better price and avoid local monopolies. Other people better informed than she could not have foreseen the catastrophic outcome of 1760. War was a kind of endemic plague between France and England, and people thought that the present one like all the others would end in a treaty restoring the status quo.

After 1760 the situation of Catholics in Quebec was extremely serious, aggravated as it was by the scarcity of priests. Mother d'Youville saw the dangers clearly, but instead of wasting time in lamentations, she went about doing what she could to remedy the situation. She pressed on and minded her money. To Madame de Ligneris she wrote: "My respects ... to Monsieur the Abbé de Joncaire to whom I wish a little more courage to come to the succour of his native land." To Monsieur Héry: "I hope that in several years you will be sending Charles back to us to give spiritual succour to his native land." In spite of uncertainty about French credit she contributed to support a young seminarian[xliii] who was finishing his theological studies in France.

In the turmoil of the times misery increased. In 1769 Mother d'Youville wrote to her bishop: "There is a great deal of good we could do if we had anything. Every day poor people come who are truly in need. We do not have any more room to accommodate them, and it is with a heavy heart that I turn them away, but I have to do so ... God in his goodness will have to be content with my good will." All kinds of wretched people had already experienced her "good will," for she had welcomed poor old people, the blind, the incurables, the mentally ill,[xliv] abandoned children, fallen women, people with contagious diseases, sick soldiers and prisoners. She indeed had a very heavy heart not to be able to receive more of them.

The closer a soul comes to God, the more it shines with an ever-growing charity. Mother d'Youville's zeal was far-reaching, it knew no bounds, it only knew hindrances that her intelligence overcame through courage. In her numerous undertakings, after having done all that was prudently possible, she surrendered whatever was left over in risks to Providence as a proof of faith. This extreme trust compelled God, as it were, to respond abundantly. How much humility and wonder then poured into the soul of our foundress. "Providence is wonderful," she wrote, "it has means we cannot understand to relieve those who trust in it, it provides for everything, in it is my trust." – "On the verge of lacking, and yet we lack no more, at least not for the necessities. I marvel each day at Divine Providence that is willing to use such poor subjects to do a little good." – "Blessed be God! Divine Providence provides for everything. All my trust is in It." – "[God] has shown so much goodness and mercy to us that I make bold to believe that our desires will be granted."

In this new community of servants of the poor that Mother d'Youville established, the dominant virtue seems to have been mortification. Their frugality was ascetic. It will be remembered that in 1758 they went without bread for months so as to stretch the flour supply for the poor. This hardship reached heroic levels when the sisters' usual breakfast consisted of only bread and water on four days out of seven; the other three days barley replaced bread. Yet, after the fire of 1765, owing to the excessive amount of work the sisters had to do, they had barley every day. Mother d'Youville never bought fish for the sisters; on days of abstinence they ate only vegetables.

As they were continually busy with the poor, the sisters did not have time to knit stockings. They therefore wound strips of cloth around their legs in place of stockings. Their pocket handkerchiefs were only strips of leftover material from the cotton cloth that the merchant outfitters sent them to fill their orders. It is from this practice that the custom developed among the Sisters of using coloured handkerchiefs.

At the entry to each hall for the poor there was a covered jar of water with a drinking cup for the use of everyone. When Mother d'Youville visited the halls she used to take several sips of water from the common cup. Was she thus trying to remove any tendency towards disgust? How would we know how much her inherited noble sensibility suffered from constant contact with the poor? The Canadian nobles were the prouder the poorer they were, and their conceit is well known. Considering her family upbringing and the mentality of her culture, her choice in life is particularly admirable. She practised mortification relentlessly as the breeding ground of religious virtues, especially the spirit of religious poverty that people in the secular world have so much difficulty understanding. A religious is seen, as Saint Paul says, "as having nothing, and possessing all things."[4] Nothing is owned individually; all the necessities are held in common. This is not poverty over which a person has no control, but a chosen poverty, a poverty of spirit. Hence these little denials that ceaselessly check the desire to possess something as one's own, these tiny severances that prick like a thorn in the flesh but allow detachment to come into daily life, and thus the heart freed from every bond can more easily turn to God. The whole teaching of Saint John of the Cross has been epitomized in the saying: "To love is to divest oneself for the sake of God of everything that is not God." *Every* thing includes things spiritual as well as things temporal. Is not Mother d'Youville's complete surrender to the will of God as mani-

---

4   II Corinthians 6:10.

fested in Providence a perfect example of spiritual poverty? What external sacrifice can equal the sacrifice of one's own will? The whole of Mother d'Youville's spiritual life focuses upon her surrender to the will of God. Surrender is the bass note that, as in a fugue, runs throughout her life. Surrender is the atmosphere in which her soul basked.

As a perfect model of a Sister of Charity, our foundress knew how to reconcile ordinary tasks with the mystical work of inner adoration. On her business trips to Châteauguay and the farm at Pointe Saint-Charles, if there was a break, she immediately turned inward to prayer. The Abbé Dufrost, who was acquainted with consciences through hearing confessions, could not refrain from remarking that "her devotion was solid and without affectation, having nothing austere or eccentric about it ... She sought God with all the sincerity of her soul and approached Him with true, childlike trust." This is the same mental balance that one finds in her no matter from what perspective she is viewed. Simplicity, trust, love – are these not Faith, Hope, and Charity in all their purity?

Pascal speaks of the "eyes of the heart that see wisdom." It is indeed with the eyes of the heart that Mother d'Youville, without theological training, intuited the ineffable Fatherhood of God in the exercise of his Providence. As a scientist sees the unseen by means of a microscope, so Mother d'Youville through the prism of an extraordinary grace was able to apprehend the depths of the goodness of God the Father. Her devotion, nourished by the liturgy, is none other than that of the Church, for the Church always has its eyes and heart lifted up to God the Father. "*Credo in unum Deum Patrem* ... I believe in One God, the Father ..." And turning towards the Holy Spirit, "Grant us to know the Father ... *Per te sciamus da Patrem.*"[5] When the Church rises up to sing in joy the dazzling hymn *Te Deum*, it is the Father first and foremost who is addressed: "*Te aeternum Patrem* ... Thee, the Father everlasting ... *Patrem immensae majestatis* ... The Father of an infinite Majesty ..." The Father is the very source of the Love that the Word came to reveal to us: "I have made known thy name to them."[6] "When you pray, say: Father ..."[7] "God is charity."[8] Mother d'Youville, who was predestined to be God's visible Providence to the poor, was gifted with a spark of the Eternal Father's mercy, mercy beyond expression which gave her an understanding of the poor person. Out of her naturally generous heart, God willed to make a means for distributing his love.

---

5   Cf. *Veni Creator Spiritus.*

6   St. John 17:26.

7   St. Luke 11:2.

8   I John 4:8.

Thus, her remarkable devotion to God the Father would be her special grace as a foundress. In order to leave to her successors this spirit of filial surrender whence comes every virtue fitting to their state in life, Mother d'Youville prescribed the daily recitation of the Litanies of the Eternal Father that Father Pierre Huet de Lavalinière – again, a Sulpician – had composed at her special request. When a Grey Nun has learned these litanies, she has a theological compendium of the truths of our faith that she can use in place of any other pious text. All orthodox belief is unfurled in these fervent aspirations:

> Our Father, Who art in heaven,
> Hear the voice of Thy children on earth …
>
> Father, Thou Who art without beginning, but the beginning
> of all that is …
> Father, Whom Thy Son hath revealed,
> Increase in us the gift of faith …
>
> Father, from Whom cometh all fatherhood,
> Multiply our works of charity and make them fertile …

Father … Father … Father … is there any other word that can better teach brotherhood to human beings? Is it any wonder that from these expressions of charity the Grey Nun imbibes an infinite gentleness towards the poor person, the invalid, the sick person, and the unbeliever? They are all brothers and sisters. And here we can grasp in its essence the psychology of Mother d'Youville. Furthermore, when a postulant is clothed in the holy habit of the Institute, she gives her adherence to the principal devotion of the community by reciting the following act of consecration that forms part of the ceremony of vesting: "Eternal Father, we consecrate ourselves to You, and we give ourselves to the Blessed Virgin, your beloved Daughter and our true Mother, so that we may practise through Her and with Her, the Obedience and Charity that must reign among your children."

In the spirit of its foundress, the Institute of the Grey Nuns honours God the Eternal Father in a special way. The Constitutions of 1851 state: "In order to conform to the wish of their Venerable Foundress and to abide by her dispositions, the Sisters of Charity will have a special devotion to the Eternal Father and will often beseech him for an abundant participation in the spirit of his Holy Fatherhood, which contains all the feelings by which they should be moved in regard to the poor, the sick, and other needy people."

The convent chapel of the Mother House has an altar devoted to the Eternal Father. On the Carrara marble frieze of this rich altar are the first words of the Lord's Prayer: *Pater noster qui es in coelis* … Our Father, who art in heaven. The central arch of the altar base bears the inscription: *Benedictus Deus Pater D. N. Jesus Christi Pater Misericordiam* … Blessed be the God and Father of Our Lord Jesus Christ, the Father of Mercies. On the panels on each side of the place of exposition of the Blessed Sacrament are the phrases: "Be perfect as your Father in heaven is perfect" and "Be merciful as your Father in heaven is merciful." And on the panel in the niche behind the place of exposition is depicted the creating hand of the Eternal Father. The altar first erected by Mother d'Youville in 1760 has thus been fittingly replaced.

On the wall in the foundress's room[xlv] was an engraving depicting the Holy Family with the Eternal Father hovering over the group, his hands outstretched in blessing. Here is the essential core of Mother d'Youville's devotions. Saint Joseph, the venerated image of the hidden Eternal Father, in his quiet watchfulness logically had to inspire an ardent devotion in this servant of the Eternal Father. In the autumn of 1771 she wrote to her agent in Paris: "Let me know how much it would cost to get a picture of Saint Joseph in a gilded frame … feet high by … feet wide. The Holy Child Jesus would be caressing Saint Joseph, who would have his workbench and carpenter's tools. A cross would be above his figure." Unfortunately, the good Mother died before receiving the painting she had ordered showing so much originality.

It was in her own home that Mother d'Youville had received her first poor person, the blind woman Françoise Auzon. But before letting her enter, she waited for the feast of the Presentation of Mary in the Temple. This act clearly indicates her chosen allegiance, but it is only at the installation in the first house dedicated specifically to her work that she placed her foundation under Mary's protection by reading in a loud voice an act of consecration. The little statue of Our Lady of Providence was the memento of this formal dedication, and it was miraculously preserved from destruction in the fire of 1765. It was made of brass and set on a brass base. In the intense heat of the burning building, the base melted, but the figure of Our Lady was found intact in the ruins, even though it was narrower than the base and was only five inches tall. Was not the survival of this little statue, made precious through emotional attachments, a sign from heaven and a pledge of hope and blessings? This cherished relic presides today over all the major events of the Institute. Formed by a Sulpician – that is to say, a Marian – spirituality, Mother d'Youville lived the spirituality of Mary and joyfully observed all her feasts, not one of which, by tradition, is allowed to pass unnoticed at the Institute.

Nevertheless, the Institute's solemn, holiday feasts are the two feasts of the Cross of Our Lord – the Finding and Exaltation of the Holy Cross. The solemn celebration of these feasts goes back to the time of the Charon Brothers. According to their constitutions, these Brothers were called the "Brothers Hospitallers of the Cross and Saint Joseph." They, therefore, honoured the Cross in a special way and their chapel was dedicated to it. The cross as the consolation of the afflicted was such an appropriate symbol for her work that Mother d'Youville could not have chosen one better; she merely increased this devotion. Each morning she and her sisters greeted the Cross with a fervent outburst:

> *O crux ave spes unica!*
> *Mundi salus et gloria,*
> *Piis adauge gratiam*
> *Reisque dele crimina.*

> O Cross, our one reliance, hail!
> So may thy power with us avail
> To give new virtue to the saint,
> And pardon to the penitent.[9]

For more than two centuries the Grey Nuns have daily recited this verse from the hymn *Vexilla regis*; it has become a custom.

The chapel of the Mother House is dedicated to the Holy Cross and many indulgences have been attached to it. Just those of interest to the general public may be mentioned here. On 30 May 1852, His Holiness Pius IX granted in perpetuity a full plenary indulgence, under the usual conditions, to all the faithful who visited the Mother House of the Grey Nuns of Montreal on 3 May and 14 September. This convent chapel thus shared its spiritual riches with all the friends of the community in a wide gesture of religious hospitality.

In 1771 Mother d'Youville had reached her seventieth year, the perfect length of life according to Dante. It was a life of difficulties, but nonetheless a triumphant life. In the springtime, in the space of a night, the under-

---

9   English translation by John Mason Neale [Translator's note].

growth bursts into bloom. It looks likes a spontaneous outburst of life because yesterday everything was bare. But this is only an appearance, for from under the humus, indeed from under the ground, the buds are drawing on their roots and only awaiting a ray of warm sunshine to burst forth. Mother d'Youville's Institute, likewise, was only awaiting the precise time in the divine plan to flower in everyone's sight. The foundress could close her eyes forever, the great tree had been firmly planted. She had spent her days defending it against opposition, ruin, instability, and sterility. She had come to the final stage.

On 9 December a first attack of paralysis alerted the community. Sister Martel, the famous nurse from the Hôtel-Dieu, left her cloister to combat the terrible sickness of the venerable foundress, but although she gained a short remission, she could not prevent a relapse on 13 December. The following day, the sick woman received the Holy Viaticum and Extreme Unction. Then she dictated her last will and testament to the notary in so far as her material possessions were concerned. To her spiritual daughters she left the testament of life in the numerous pages on which this great soul had inscribed a model of the highest sanctity. Yet, seeing them in tears around her bed, she spoke to them as in the past from the fullness of her heart:

> "My dear Sisters, be constantly faithful to the duties of the state that you have embraced. Walk always in the path of regularity, obedience, and mortification. But above all, let the most perfect union reign among you."

These sacred words have become maxims of life in the Institute.

From 14 December "she seemed a little less listless."[10] They began to hope that the fatal hour, as sometimes happens, would loosen its grip on the sick woman. On the afternoon of 23 December, her niece, Madame Porlier Benac, came to visit her and offered to sit with her that night. "Oh, I shall not be here any longer this night," replied Mother d'Youville in a very clear and fully confident voice. Since on that day, as for several days past, there had been nothing alarming about her condition, this reply greatly surprised the Sisters. But, in fact, about 8:30 that same evening a rapid stroke freed the holy soul of the foundress.[11]

---

10   Letter from Sister Despins to Monsieur Feltz, 9 September 1772.

11   Sister Despins wrote: "About 8:30 in the evening she was stricken by an apoplexy; but it was so quick that she died in my arms in less than five or six minutes." The details of Mother d'Youville's death are contained in the letters of Mother Despins to Madame de Ligneris, 13 August 1772; to Monsieur Héry, 9 September 1772; and to Monsieur Feltz, 9 September 1772.

At that moment, Monsieur Jean Delisle de Lacailleterie was walking beside the city walls in the direction of Pointe-à-Callières when he all at once saw in the sky above the General Hospital a regularly shaped, luminous cross. According to his obituary in *Le Spectateur* [The Spectator] of 15 March 1814, he was a naturalist recognized throughout Canada and, moreover, "a respectable man who united to the social virtues a profound and extensive knowledge, who held a distinguished position among men of letters, and who, lastly, delighted in the study of nature and cultivated it with success." The luminous cross stayed long enough over the Hospital for Monsieur Delisle to summon a friend to see it. It was so bright that the inhabitants of the suburb Saint Laurent saw it also. Saint Laurent was a fair distance away and outside the city walls. Monsieur Delisle so little suspected the supernatural origin of the cross that he saw it as an omen of misfortune. "Oh, what cross will these poor Grey Nuns again have to bear?" he exclaimed. The next day when the news of the foundess's death had spread throughout the city, the astonishing phenomenon of the luminous cross, confirmed by a number of eyewitnesses, was the topic of every conversation. The sisters, enclosed in their convent, had not seen this strange manifestation. Monsieur Delisle related the details of it to them, and when he died on 11 March 1814 he affirmed that it was a miraculous event.

After Mother d'Youville's death, her face, which the illness had greatly altered, resumed its colour and its former features. Her relatives and the Sisters could not bear to let go this dear face that death's cold hand had spared. They therefore thought of having her picture painted. On several occasions during her life, she had been asked to sit for her portrait, but her humility had always made her decline. "If they absolutely want my portrait, they can have it done after my death," she replied on every occasion. Now that death had respected her venerated features, the Sisters out of filial piety believed that the time had come to fulfil their rightful desire. A painter was therefore sought. But when he got there, the face of the deceased had changed so rapidly that he was scarcely able to get a resemblance. The single portrait of Mother d'Youville to come down to posterity is thus quite imperfect and, according to her contemporaries, does not do justice to the original. The closed eyes preserve the mystery of the soul that will no longer animate the face. It is a complete eclipse of personality, the triumph of humility. If charm is the reflection of an inner beauty, Mother d'Youville's soul must have communicated an untranslatable beauty to her whole person. As for the physical aspect, the Abbé Dufrost has described it: "She had so many positive physical qualities that it suffices to say that she was one of the beautiful women of the age. She was a light brunette, with lots of colour, lively and expressive eyes, and completely regular facial features. She was quite tall and had a totally gracious air about her."

On 26 December, Mother d'Youville's mortal remains were buried in the crypt of the Hospital's church after a solemn service celebrated by Father Montgolfier surrounded by numerous clergy and attended by a great number of citizens. The voice of the people was already placing the foundress in the ranks of the beatified. The following letter from the Abbé François Gravé,[xlvi] the Vicar General of the diocese and Superior of the Seminary of Quebec, summarizes the general opinion. He was writing to Mother Despins:

> You are familiar with my attachment to Madame d'Youville, and thus you can infer what sadness her death has caused me. If I were able to console myself, I would try to console you. This loss is great and it is difficult to recover from it. Or rather, it is irrecoverable. She merits so many tears! Yet, I believe that even in this we should praise God that he has taken her from us only to reward her merits and so that she may act as a patron on our behalf. I also praise him that he allowed her enough time on earth to perfect the work that he inspired in her. This would not have been accomplished had he taken her fifteen or twenty years ago. This worthy teacher, this much-loved mother, whose merit was so much above the average, was a new Chantal. I am not afraid to make the comparison. Reading the life of the latter, one has only in a thousand instances to change the name in order to recall Madame d'Youville. May she before the throne of God have for me the same goodness of heart she had during her life! But, alas, now that she knows me better, perhaps she likes me less.

In Châteauguay there was a young man whom Mother d'Youville had previously taken in who was employed to work on the farm. It was ordinarily he who drove the foundress on her trips to the Châteauguay manor. On 24 December, early in the morning, he was distributing feed to the animals and using a rather liberal hand to do so. Suddenly, he heard the voice of Mother d'Youville saying, "My son, mind the fodder!" Not seeing her in the barn, he thought that she had arrived the previous evening unknown to him, and he looked for her as soon as he got back to the manor house. She was nowhere to be found. Very puzzled and quite sure that he had heard her voice which he knew so well, he reported her words. When they learned of Mother d'Youville's death, this reminder about economizing was engraved on everyone's mind. "My son, mind the fodder" has now become a kind of allegorical figure of speech among the Grey Nuns.

Monument in honour of Marguerite d'Youville, erected in Varennes, Quebec, beside the river, on land that was formerly the property of her father and where she spent her childhood.

Stained-glass window of Mother d'Youville in the parish church of Charny, Lévis, Quebec.
The view of the lower half of the window is blocked by the rood screen.

On 11 March 1846, Mother d'Youville's grandniece, Madame Stubinger, died at the Grey Nuns' in Saint Hyacinthe. Another prediction of Madame d'Youville's was thus realized. The following account was given by Madame Stubinger:

> My cousin Sabrevois de Bleury and I, Marie-Charlotte de Labroquerie, along with my mother, were leaving the Grey Nuns' after visiting Mother d'Youville, when my great-aunt lightly tapped my cousin on the shoulder and said to him, "You will die a priest, my little man." Turning to me, she said, "You, my little girl, will die at the Grey Nuns'."

Charlotte de Labroquerie married Jean-Georges Stubinger in 1787. Widowed and living in Boucherville, she had her home destroyed by the fire of 1843 that consumed most of the houses in the village and the church. Being in her seventies, she sought refuge in a convent and ended up retiring to the Hôtel-Dieu of the Grey Nuns in Saint Hyacinthe. It was then that Mother d'Youville's prediction came back to her and she signed the declaration quoted above. Her cousin, Jean-François Sabrevois de Bleury, was ordained priest in Quebec City on 20 March 1790. He died 23 September 1802 as parish priest of Saint Charles de Lachenaie and was buried there.[xlvii]

After the burning of the Hospital in 1765, Mother d'Youville expressed her confidence that the house would never burn again. On any number of occasions afterwards it could have burned through carelessness or accident. Yet, it has been preserved up to the present day. Out of the hundreds of occasions when fire was avoided in an extraordinary way, the following two are noteworthy examples.

On Holy Thursday, 9 April 1849, the nuns sent for oil for the lamps and lanterns that decorated the altar of repose. This altar of repose was pyramid shaped and covered with pine and artificial flowers. Whether through carelessness or misunderstanding, the merchant delivered oil of turpentine instead of oil. The sisters filled the lamps and lanterns and began to light them, but as soon as the wicks were lighted they went out. After several vain attempts, the sisters sent to ask the merchant for an explanation. The latter, knowing the inflammable qualities of turpentine, was horrified to think of the conflagration that might have occurred if Mother d'Youville had not been watching over her house from heaven.

After a political uprising the Canadian Parliament building was burned on 25 April 1849. The rooms of the Legislative Assembly were separated from the General Hospital by only the width of a street. A strong wind was blowing the flames towards the Hospital and already the window casements had begun to catch fire. When the firemen tried to direct streams of water onto the building, they found that the rioters had cut the leather fire hoses. In the midst of the growing peril the sisters said to one another, "We shall not burn, our Mother d'Youville has promised us." The resident poor had the same confidence. When they tried to carry an old, invalid man out of the house, he did not wish to go, convinced that Mother d'Youville would save her Hospital. This confidence was not misplaced, for at the moment when all seemed to be lost, the wind suddenly changed to the completely opposite direction and the Hospital was saved.

The Abbé Auguste Gosselin opens chapter XIX of his *Histoire de l'Eglise de Canada* [History of the Church in Canada], Part III, with the following homage to Mother d'Youville:

> We have evoked at the end of the preceding chapter the great figure of Marie de l'Incarnation, and now arising before us in her time is the venerable Mother d'Youville, this other Mother de l'Incarnation, the emulator of the first by her virtue, courage, unshakeable trust in Providence, and above all by constancy throughout the trials of a tumultuous career.

"The valiant woman of the Holy Scriptures," "a new Chantal," "another Marie de l'Incarnation" – so many mirrors of sanctity boldly held up to Mother d'Youville. And truly she was not unworthy of being reflected in them.

Saint Paul assures us that those "whom [God] justifed, them he also glorified."[12] God has glorified Mother d'Youville. He has glorified her in her predictions, all of which have been fulfilled. He has glorified her in her fruitful Institute. Among the great figures who make up the glory of the Church in Canada stands Mother d'Youville suffused with an especially important light as the first Canadian-born foundress. In the Laurentian valley, in the City of Mary, God set this height of holiness, Marguerite d'Youville. Towards her, all Canadians can lift their eyes in hope, for her humble mysticism, which leads to the summits of Charity, passes along the paths of everyday life. Her whole life is summed up in her epitaph:

She greatly loved Jesus Christ and the poor.

---

12   Romans 8:30.

The monogram of Mary used on the convent gates of the Grey Nuns. The one shown here is brass and dates from the time of Mother d'Youville. It was retrieved from the rubble left by the fire of 1765.

Appendices

Appendix I

Charge of Bishop Ignace Bourget, 23 December 1849

IGNACE BOURGET, by the grace of God and with the blessing of the Apostolic Holy See, Bishop of Montreal, etc., etc.

To all whom these presents shall come, Salvation and blessing in OUR LORD.

Seeing that the permission granted by us on the fifth of this month for the exhumation of the body of the Reverend Mother Marie-Marguerite de Lajemmerais, the Widow d'Youville, foundress and first superior of the General Hospital of this city, so that it may be laid and preserved in a more fitting place, which permission was approved by His Honour Monsieur Rolland, the Chief of Police of Montreal, on the twentieth of the same month;

Seeing also that from the report of our dear Brothers, Fathers Faillon and Bonnissant, priests and directors of the Seminary of Saint-Sulpice, dated the twenty-second of this month and approved by us this day, it appears that the body which we have permitted to be exhumed is truly that of said foundress;

Seeing yet again that the petition made to us by the said Sisters of Charity, administrators of this Hospital, to have transported and respectfully preserved in a reliquary prepared for this purpose the precious remains of their foundress, to which petition we have already done justice, as appears from our above-mentioned act of approval concerning the authenticity of the body found and recognized to be that of the said foundress;

We came ourselves this day to the church of said General Hospital to proceed with this pious ceremony in accordance with the ceremonial approved by us yesterday.

In this place, after having celebrated a pontifical service in the presence of the said body, re-clothed in a wax mask and the special habit of this Institute, to commemorate the seventy-eighth anniversary of her death, we transported the body and placed it in the reliquary prepared for it, offering the prayers of the Church and assisted by Father Billaudèle, one of our Vicars General and Superior of the Seminary of Saint-Sulpice of this city; by Fathers Faillon and Guitter, Directors of said Seminary of Saint-Sulpice in Paris; by Father Bonnissant, the confessor of this community; by Fathers

Barbarin, Toupin, and Chalbos, priests of the said Seminary; by Father Pinsoneault, priest of the bishop's palace; by the Reverend Fathers Havequez and Larcher, Jesuits; and by a number of the clergy of the Greater Seminary and of the brothers of the Society of Jesus and those of the Christian Schools; and in the presence of the whole community and the assembled poor, we closed and sealed with our seal the reliquary so that nothing can be removed from said body nor any thing foreign be introduced. We leave to God, who has promised to exalt the humble, the concern to glorify his servant; and to the Holy Apostolic See the exclusive right of examining and judging the facts that may pertain to the glory of this pious foundress. We only ask of this faithful servant of the Lord, if, as we hope, by the divine goodness she is in heaven, to allow us to experience her worthiness in the presence of God by obtaining for us the grace to guide in her spirit and by her rules the daughters whom she has committed to our care. She has seen us at her feet with her cherished flock, presenting to her with confidence our special needs and those of all the diocese. May she deign to send down help with that gentle charity that always characterized her great heart.

We would very much have liked to do something that would express all the gratitude that the pastors and faithful of this diocese owe her for all the generous sacrifices she made for the glory of her GOD and the relief of the poor. But being unable to do it suitably, we would ask her to accept the labours, however slight they may be, that each has undertaken to show his or her good will on this occasion.

Given at the General Hospital of Montreal, the twenty-third of December, one thousand eight hundred and forty-nine, under our signature and seal and countersigned by our Secretary.

† Ig., Bishop of Montreal.

For the Bishop, J.-O. Paré, Canon, Secretary.

Appendix II

List of the Legal Proceedings of Madame d'Youville

Request of Mme Widow de Youville, 4 April 1731: Guardianship – Judicial Documents No. 966.

Guardianship, 5 April 1731: Madame d'Youville, the person appearing, was named guardian of her minor children, and Jean-François Malhiot surrogate guardian (Judicial Documents No. 967).

Vessières vs. Widow Youville, 4 July 1732: The court ordains that the interested parties be assembled to decide whether Mme d'Youville, the person appearing, will accept the inheritance of her husband (Register 13, p. 1165).

Vessières vs. Widow Youville, 11 July 1732: Mme d'Youville, the person appearing, renounces the inheritance of her late husband, and Jean-Baptiste Neveu is named trustee of the estate of François d'Youville (Judicial Documents, Trustees, No. 1083).

Inventory of the Properties of the Estate of Sieur Youville de Ladescouverte, 24 April 1731 (Register of the Notary Raimbault the Younger, No. 685).

Closure of Inventory, 7 May 1731: Judicial Documents – Raimbault.

Vessières vs. Ladescouverte, 4 July 1732: Vessières demands that Philippe You de Ladescouverte recognize a note in the amount of 1041 livres, 16 shillings, dated 9 June 1730, for merchandise supplied to his mother, the deceased Madeleine Just (Register 13: p. 1165).

Bondy vs. Ladescouverte - Widow Youville, 4 July 1732: Bondy demands that Philippe You de Ladescouverte recognize a note in the amount of 702 livres, 7 sols for merchandise supplied to his mother, the deceased Madeleine Just. Philippe Ladescouverte demands that Madame d'Youville be responsible for half the sum by virtue of her being the widow of François d'Youville, heir of his mother, Madeleine Just (Register 13: p. 1165).

Vessières vs. Ladescouverte, 5 September 1732: Verdict of Discharge of Debt by Auction (Register 13: p. 1230).

Registration of the Seizure *in esse* of the Properties of the Estate of the deceased Sieur Ladescouverte, 16 August 1732 (Register 13: p. 1245).

Ladescouverte vs. Widow Youville, 26 September 1732: Philippe Ladescouverte requests that Mme d'Youville be required to pay half the note of 4,000 livres. Mme d'Youville is present (Register 13: p. 1264).

Vessières vs. Ladescouverte, 10 March 1732: Sale by Bailiff Decoste of the Properties of the Estate of the late Dame Ladescouverte (Register 13: p. 52).

Widow Youville vs. Cerry d'Argenteuil, 20 January 1733: Mme d'Youville, represented by Sieur Sylvain, lays claim to the hay taken by the defendant from her land on Ile Jésus (Register 13: p. 1371).

Lamoureux vs. Widow Youville, 17 November 1733: Sieur St-Germain Lamoureux, the trustee appointed by the court for the Properties of the late Ladescouverte, lays claim to the sum of 181 livres for one year's rent on the house on the Market Square that was conceded to her by the judgement of 31 October 1732; Mme d'Youville, appearing, replied that she did not think that she had to deliver the money to the claimant before the judgement ordering thus should be rendered, and that in the meantime the pledge of Sieur Ignace Gamelin would suffice as surety for the payment (Register 14: p. 168).

Vessières vs. Ladescouverte, 8 June 1735: Special session to decide the allotment and distribution of the money arising from the sale of the properties of the Ladescouverte Estate. Mme d'Youville was present (Register 15, p. 266).

Widow Youville vs. Edeline, 26 March 1737: Again pertaining to the hay previously removed from the land of Mme d'Youville on Ile Jésus. Mme d'Youville appearing (Register 16, p. 160).

Cerry d'Argenteuil vs. Widow Youville, 28 February 1735: Judgement directing the litigants to write and to show, within the limits allowed by the Ordinance, before Nicolas Lanouiller, Councillor, in the case of Philippe d'Ailleboust de Cerry, appealing the verdict of the jurisdiction of Montreal of 9 March 1733, and Demoiselle Marie-Marguerite Dufros de La Gemmeraye, the widow of Sieur Youville de Ladescouverte (*Délibérations du Conseil Supérieur de la Nouvelle France* [Deliberations of the Superior Council of New France], vol. 13: p. 79).

Widow Youville vs. Charon, 16 April 1737: Claim on a debt of 82 livres, 6 sols, 3 deniers, owed by Pierre Charon. Mme d'Youville present (Register 16: p. 318).

Sylvain vs. Widow Youville, 28 January 1738: Sieur Sylvain alleges that Mme d'Youville, represented in court by Danré de Blanzy, abducted his slave by night (Register 17: p. 298).

Sylvain vs. Widow Youville, 4 February 1738: Summons of Sieurs Gamelin and Lescuyer concerning the alleged abduction of the slave by Mme d'Youville, who was represented in court by Danré de Blanzy (Register 17: p. 308).

Widow Youville vs. Cerry d'Argenteuil, 22 May 1739: Appointment of experts on the matter of the hay, and judgement by default in favour of Mme d'Youville, appearing (Register 18: p. 483).

Widow Youville vs. Demoiselle Jallot, 2 October 1739: Claim on the amount of 71 livres, 14 sols owed by Demoiselle Angélique Jallot. Sieur Prud'homme cited. Mme d'Youville was represented in court by Demoiselle Louise Thaumur (Register 19: p. 130).

Gugnière vs. Widow Youville, 16 February 1740: Gugnière, trustee of the Levasseur estate, laid claim to the sum of 1189 livres, 9 sols. Mme d'Youville had undertaken a bill of exchange in order to help the said late Levasseur. The court recognized her innocence and Gugnière's case was dismissed. Mme d'Youville appeared on her own behalf (Register 19: p. 208).

Widow Youville vs. Major, 26 February 1740: Judgement by default in favour of Mme d'Youville, appearing (Register 19: p. 225).

Widow Youville vs. Widow Omier, 11 March 1740: Judgement by default in favour of Mme d'Youville, appearing (Register 19: p. 234).

Widow Youville vs. Lasonde, 15 March 1740: Judgement by default in favour of Mme d'Youville, appearing, against Lasonde, tenant farmer of M. Lafresnière (Register 19: p. 236).

Widow Youville vs. Widow Lespérance, 15 March 1740: Judgement by default in favour of Mme d'Youville, appearing (Register 19: p. 239).

Widow Youville vs. Major, 10 June 1740: The defendant is sentenced to pay 7 livres, 4 sols, and court costs of 3 livres, 1 sol. Mme d'Youville appearing (Register 19, p. 300).

Widow Youville vs. Lasonde, 19 July 1740: Lasonde is found guilty by default a second time. Mme d'Youville appearing (Register 19: p. 318).

Jehanne vs. Widow Youville, 27 August 1742: Pierre Jehanne, official trustee of the Levasseur estate, claims the sum of 1061 livres, 19 sols, 8 deniers. The case is dismissed. Mme d'Youville appearing (Register 21: p. 188).

Beaucours vs. Widow Youville, 22 July 1746: Entered by Dame Gabrielle-Françoise Auber, wife of Messire Josué Boisberthelot de Beaucours, Governor of this city. Notice to vacate the house in which she lives no later than 13 August next. Mme Youville appearing (Register 24: p. 7).

Beaucours vs. Widow Youville, 5 August 1746: Mme d'Youville, appearing, requests a delay of three months in order to find another dwelling. The Court refuses and orders that she vacate the premises by 15 August, the present month, under penalty of being evicted (Register 24: p. 14).

Widow Youville vs. Widow Roland, 12 March 1751: Mme Youville in the name of and as administrator of the General Hospital, appearing. Dame Roland is sentenced to pay 14 livres, 15 sols in payment of balance owing (Register 25: p. 137).

Chevalier vs. Réaume - Widow Youville, 12 January 1753: Mme d'Youville intervening and appearing in said lawsuit. (Register 25: p. 436).

Widow Youville vs. Chevalier, 21 September 1753: Mme d'Youville, appearing, lays claim to the payment of a bond owed by the Chevalier estate. The Court orders Réaume to remit the money to Mme d'Youville (Register 25: p. 563).

Widow Youville vs. Chevalier - Gamelin, 26 September 1753: Ignace Gamelin stands surety for Mme d'Youville (Register 28A: p. 14).

Widow Youville vs. Charon, 4 March 1755: Judgement by default in favour of Mme d'Youville, not appearing but represented by François Masson (Register 26: p. 211).

Charbonnier vs. Widow Youville, 13 May 1754: Sieur Jacques Charbonnier, in the name of and as heir of the late Sieur François Charon, owner and founder of the General Hospital of Montreal, desires that all the moveable and immoveable property in this country as well as in Old France of the said estate be seized to guarantee his inheritance. Mme d'Youville appearing in her capacity as Administrator of the General Hospital. In view of the judgement of the Superior Council of this country of 24 November 1721, the action is dismissed (Register 26: p. 51).

Widow d'Youville vs. Charon, 8 April 1755: Mme d'Youville, appearing, lays claim to 72 livres, 3 sols in payment of balance owing (Register 26: p. 232).

Widow Youville vs. Piver, 11 June 1755: Louis Piver, guardian of the minor children of Pierre Charon. Mme d'Youville is represented by Bailiff Robert. The verdict rendered on 16 April 1737 against the estate is declared enforceable (Register 26: p. 272).

Widow Youville vs. Larivière, 14 October 1755: Judgement by default in favour of Mme d'Youville, not appearing but represented by Bailiff Robert (Register 28A: p. 11).

Widow Youville vs. Larivière, 7 November 1755: René La Rivière is ordered to pay 63 livres, 13 sols on the balance of the account to Mme d'Youville, not appearing but represented by Bailiff Robert (Register 28A: p. 23).

Widow Youville vs. Widow Jassemin, 2 December 1755: Judgement by default in favour of Mme d'Youville, not appearing but represented by Bailiff Robert (Register 28A: p. 61).

Widow Youville vs. Lacroix 2 December 1755: Judgement by default in favour of Mme d'Youville, not appearing but represented by Bailiff Robert (Register 28A: p. 61).

Widow Youville vs. Couvret, 2 December 1755: Judgement by default in favour of Mme d'Youville, not appearing but represented by Bailiff Robert (Register 28A: p. 61).

30 January 1756: Copy of the three above-cited cases (Register 28A: p. 62).

Widow Youville vs. Morel, 19 March 1756: Judgement by default in favour of Mme d'Youville, not appearing but represented by Bailiff Robert (Register 28A: p. 27).

Ducharme vs. Lanoue - Widow Youville, 29 May 1756: Demoiselle Lanoue had a raft of wood seized that said Ducharme is alleged to have had cut on her lands at Châteauguay. Mme d'Youville is cited (Register 28A: p. 111).

Ducharme vs. Lanoue - Widow Youville, 4 June 1756: The same case returns to court but is postponed to the following Friday.

Ducharme vs. Lanoue - Widow Youville, 11 June 1756: The provisional verdict is rendered definitive and the lady defendants are ordered to pay 12 livres in damages and interest and court costs of 14 livres, 12 sols (Register 28A: p. 115).

Charbonnier vs. Drouin vs. Widow Youville, 10 October 1756: The seizure of the properties of the Poor of the General Hospital of Montreal is declared null and replevin. Mme d'Youville appearing (Register 28A: p. 170).

Deguire vs. Widow Youville, 23 January 1759: Pierre Deguire lays claim for masonry work done; Mme d'Youville as Administrator of the General Hospital, and appearing, retorts by presenting the accounts for supplies and payments already made. The claimant is ordered to pay Mme d'Youville 86 livres, five sols, six deniers, as well as the court costs of the present action (Register 28B: p. 97).

Stamp for official documents, France, eighteenth century

Stamp for official documents, France, eighteenth century

Appendix III

Localities Bearing the Name d'Youville
in honour of Mother d'Youville

Montreal:

Place d'Youville: a square formed by McGill, Saint Paul, and Saint Pierre Streets and Place d'Youville, located on land formerly occupied by the General Hospital where Mother d'Youville lived and worked.

Rue d'Youville: from 101 Rue Saint Pierre going west to 72 rue des Soeurs Grises (Grey Nuns).

Quartier Youville in which is located the entire parish of Saint Alphonse d'Youville. In the past this neighbourhood formed a distinct municipality with the name Village d'Youville. It has since been incorporated into greater Montreal.

The Youville Shops: one of the large garages of the Montreal Tramways Company was called the Youville Garage.

Lymans Pharmaceutical Company Limited gave the name Youville to a finger-stall it manufactured: The Youville Finger Protector.

Varennes:

Rue d'Youville: one of the village's streets.

Between the ramparts of the Saint Lawrence River and the provincial highway that passes through the village of Varennes is a little square to the right of the Church Square. This land in the past was part of the land owned by Mother d'Youville's father. A monument has been erected there with a statue of Mother d'Youville. The statue was carved by Nicolas Petrucci and is of reconstituted marble; the shaft is of granite from the Stanstead quarries and the base of stone from Deschambault.

Quebec City:

Place d'Youville: a square formed by Rues Saint Jean, des Glacis, d'Aiguillon, and d'Youville. On this square is located the Palais Montcalm, a municipal building containing a concert hall, a swimming pool, a cinema, etc.

Nicolet:

Avenue Youville: the avenue leading to the Hôtel-Dieu of the Grey Nuns.

Hull:
Rue Youville.

Beauharnois :
Rue d'Youville. Also the name of one of the city's neighbourhoods.

Saint Hyacinthe:
Place Youville: a triangular plaza located at the intersection of Rues Dessaules
    and de l'Hôtel-Dieu and the Montreal-Quebec City highway that passes
    through the city.

Abitibi:
Lac d'Youville in the county of Trécesson, Province of Quebec. The name was
    given to this lake in 1912 by the Geographical Commission of Canada.

Sudbury, Ontario:
Youville Street; Youville Court.

Winnipeg, Manitoba:
Youville Street: North from Carrière Avenue to the Seine River.

Mission d'Youville:
Diocese of Hearst, Cochrane County, Ontario. The mission and then the
    parish bore the name d'Youville, which the Post Office in Ottawa prom-
    ised to reserve as the official name of the local post office.

Charny, Quebec:
In the parish church dedicated to Our Lady of Help is a window depicting
    Mother d'Youville. The fabrique installed this window in 1932 at the
    request of the parish priest, Father Omer Poirier, "with the aim of making
    better known this holy foundress" in whom the priest had a great trust. It
    should be noted that there are no Grey Nuns in the parish.

Notre Dame de la Salette, Papineau County, Quebec:
At the instigation of their parish priest, the farmers in this parish put their fields
    under the patronage of a saint of their choice. Monsieur Télesphore
    Larocque placed his under the protection of Mother d'Youville.

Appendix IV

Letters of Madame d'Youville

The following letters, together with those reproduced in the text of the present volume, constitute the known correspondence of Mother d'Youville. They are autograph letters in a steady script, somewhat laboured but without flourishes. The spelling of proper names has been retained in order to document pronunciation. The sentences of Madame d'Youville often become lapidary under the strength of her conviction that "with God nothing is lost." In the letters that deal with legal matters each item is treated with clarity and with a gentle firmness that presupposes great self-control. The beautifully simple friendly letters are imbued with the wisdom of a profoundly spiritual mind. The elevated tone and honesty of judgement are remarkable in all of them. The collection as a whole is highly important for the detailed history of Montreal.

My Lord

I am sincere, upright, and incapable of any evasion or reservation that might disguise the truth or give it another meaning. My Lord, I truly borrowed 9,550 livres for the good and renewal of the lands of this Hospital; I owe them and I have no other resources to pay them except for the reimbursement which I expect from Your Excellency and the other gentlemen. What I am telling you, My Lord, is the pure truth and I would not tell the least lie for all the wealth in the world. In this matter, I have only sought the renewal of this Hospital and its properties …

I have the honour of being with very deep respect your very, very humble and most obedient servant,

Widow Youville

This 12th of April 1751

Facsimile of letter to Bishop de Pontbriand of 12 April 1751, beginning of letter and closing salutation.

1762, 16 September. To Father Couturier by Monsieur Benoist.

I had the honour of receiving your [letter] conveyed by Father Mongolfier, whose arrival has filled with joy all those in this country by whom he is most loved and respected, and our community in particular. I am not at all worried about the bills of exchange pertaining to our hospital that you have in safe keeping; I am convinced that you will take all possible care of them.

I have the honour of being …

1762, 16 September. Monsieur Figuery by his wife (Etienne-Guillaume de Figuiéry).

You are looking upon our dear Josette, but we have lost her forever. It has been several days since I have seen them, nor do I wish to go until she has left. I have not enough courage to say good-by to her. I shall do my best to console her father, her mother, and her brothers and sisters when she will no longer be here. I fear that this departure will cause a great change in her father and mother. I am closing because my eyes are blinded by tears.

I have the honour of being …

1763, 26 July. To Father Couturier.

Sir, I have the honour of presenting you with our most humble greetings and of assuring you of our heartfelt gratitude for all your acts of kindness. The situation in which we find ourselves makes us daily aware of how much we are indebted to your charity in the person of your priests. It is not our house alone, but the whole colony that finds itself in need of your acts of continued kindness. I received your letter in 1761, at which time I had the honour of replying. Since then I have received nothing further. I await this blessing with deepest respect.

M …

1763, 26 July. Monsieur Goguette.

Sir, each year I have had the honour of writing to you, and I also have received your letters, with the exception of this year. Perhaps, however, they will arrive by the vessels that we are expecting. We have been given hope that the goods purchased in France will be sent to us. I trust that you will be so kind as to send what you have that belongs to us. We still do not know anything about the fate of the bills of exchange from '59; perhaps we shall learn something about them from the last ships. I rest entirely upon your care for these small matters of business.

I have the honour of being …

1763, 23 July. Monsieur Débarrasse[1] par Monsieur.

I received one of your letters in November 1762 in the envelope from Monsieur the Abbé de L'Isle-Dieu. You mentioned a letter for Madame de Louche which she has not received. She had a letter from you on your arrival in Calais and since, like me, nothing further. You mentioned the death of your uncle. I feel your pain greatly, knowing how closely you were attached to him. I pray to God for the repose of his soul.

Let us hear your news and those of your dear daughters. It is the only consolation that we have, since France has abandoned us, to have news of our friends.

I wrote you on the 16th of August, 1762, by Madame de Noyelle. I informed you that I had the honour of your receipt for the shipment of 25 quintals of cod. In fact, we received only 16 quintals. You therefore owe us 9. At 5 piastres a quintal, that makes 45 piastres that I would ask you to remit to Monsieur Mongolfier, who is travelling in France, or to …

I embrace my dear little girls and am with respect …

1763, 22 July. Father Villard, priest.

Sir, I had the honour of writing to you on the 16th of August, 1762, by Madame de Noyelle, who was leaving this country. I sent you the letters of Monsieur the Abbé de L'Isle-Dieu and a power of attorney with the name left blank. I beseeched you to fill it in as you saw fit and to have the kindness to take under your care the business affairs of this hospital. I had learnt that Monsieur de Paris was dead and that Monsieur the Abbé de L'Isle-Dieu was gravely ill. I have since received three letters from him to which I am replying and am including this present one in his packet. As he says, he is very old and quite infirm, and I fear that he may be in no condition to continue his charitable care for us. I hope, sir, that you will not refuse us your care. I shall ask it of you with entreaties and importunities should it be necessary. All my sisters implore you likewise, and they assure you of their most humble

---

1   André Débarras, Visitor of the King's Domains, married Louise de Louche.

respects and commend themselves to your prayers and offerings of the Holy Sacrifice of the Mass.

I have the honour …

1763, 5 August. To Father Villard by Father Mongolfier, and later by Monsieur Dufix (1763, 4 October).

Sir, I received your letter dated the 26th of February, 1763, for which I humbly thank you. I never thought but that you would take responsibility for our business affairs as you tell me you have done. Since you have a complete understanding of them and in case the power of attorney is found to be missing, would you please suggest another and instruct him so that he can conduct the business successfully. I wrote to Monsieur Savary asking him to communicate to you everything with respect to this Hospital, so that, in case of death, there should be someone to take over our interests and who could provide the necessary information to the new bursar. Like you, I believe that Monsieur l'Abbé de L'Isle-Dieu will keep him abreast of our business. Should anything be lacking, he will see Monsieur Mongolfier, the bearer of this letter, who also has another one from the other month. He has left for Quebec, but the circumstance with which this letter deals depends upon his being there. He knows about everything that relates to us and has a new power of attorney for selling in case of need.

We were surprised as we lived under the illusion that France would not abandon us, but we were mistaken in our expectations. God willed it thus; and blessed be His Holy Name! If we are as free to practise our religion, and to do all the good that we find to do, as we have been since we fell under English domination, we shall not have to complain about spiritual matters, but in temporal affairs there will be more suffering. People cannot earn their living under them as they did under the French, but I hope that Divine Providence will supply their need. All our Sisters assure you of their most humble respects and commend themselves to your prayers and offerings of the Holy Sacrifice of the Mass.

I have the honour of being, with a most …

1763, 5 August. Monsieur Savary, Bursar, by Father Mongolfier, by Monsieur Dufix (1763, October 4).

Sir, I have learned from Monsieur Villard that you are willing to undertake the business affairs of this Hospital. Monsieur the Abbé de L'Isle-Dieu tells me of a new authorized agent for the power of attorney, but does not mention his name. I believe that he will inform you about everything that relates to us. I would like him to show you my letters. I am asking him to receive our accounts. I believe that there is an error to our disadvantage in that of 1761 and 1762. In his letter of the 27th of February, 1763, he reminds me of some bills of exchange which he tells me were paid the year before. It may very well be I who am mistaken. Do not mention it to him if he does not say anything about it to you, as you can judge whether or not it might hurt him. He has rendered us too many services for us to cross him in anything. Should anything not be clear to you, see Monsieur Mongolfier, a priest of the Seminary of Saint Sulpice, who is our superior, knows our business, and can enlighten you. Ask me whatever you need if what I have told you is not sufficiently clear. If something untoward should happen to Monsieur de L'Isle-Dieu, I beseech you to communicate the state of our affairs to Monsieur Villard, Director of the Seminary of Foreign Missions, in the hope that he will not refuse to concern himself with us and our house should the occasion arise.

I have the honour of being with respect …

1763, August 5. Father Couturier by Father Mongolfier; 1763, 4 October, by Monsieur Dufix.

After finishing my letter, I have just received one from you which you had the kindness to write to me the 6th of March, 1763, and in which you inform me that you have our bills of exchange of which I have had no news since 1760. I am not at all worried about your looking after them, since I am convinced that whatever fate may befall them, good or bad, does not depend upon you.

I have the honour of being with very deep respect …

1763, 5 August. Monsieur Débarasse by Father Mongolfier.

Sir, after giving Monsieur Montgolfier the letter I wrote to deliver to you since he was going down to Quebec City to go to France, I received yours of 17 February 1763. In my first one you will find another letter from Madame de Louche. I have sent that of Monsieur Cressé but fear that he may not get it in time. I have written to Dufrost who is presently at Pointe Lévy to get the two baptismal certificates of your young ladies and to give them to Father Montgolfier. I have also acquitted the tasks you gave me for Messieurs Deschambault, Gamelin, Bedard, and Lafond. I have not yet seen Monsieur Lagottery. I shall ask him for the 80 livres that you are giving to Madame de Louche who has great need of it for her upkeep and that of her young lady. I am only able to give them food and you know better than anyone what they have. If I can find money here for the 45 piastres you owe me, I shall draw a bill of exchange on you, and if not you can remit them to Father Montgolfier, as I have already mentioned to you.

Ten thousand kisses to my dear little girls,

I have the honour …

I wrote to him on the 4th of October by Monsieur Duffix, addressed to Monsieur Débarasse the Elder, Place de Digne, in Provence.

1763, 5 August. Monsieur Figuery by Father Mongolfier.

Sir, I was honoured to receive your letter of 24 February 1763 in duplicate. I wish I had something good to tell you in reply; but, on the contrary, poor Gamelin, the goodness of whose heart you know, is deeply troubled at not having any money to give to Josette so that she can come to you. I can assure you, however, it would be beyond them to find 100 livres. I am constantly amazed at how they have been able to survive these past three years without any business. You know that it has been 8 or 9 years since they have had any. The little property they have is in merchandise bought in France and in bills of exchange that would not get one hundred livres to the thousand here. As you know, they have seven children to support. They cannot be placed anywhere and they are now grown up and thus cost more than when they were little. Let us hope, my dear nephew, that Providence that always attends to the needs of those who serve it will set everything in motion either here or where you are to provide your dear wife with what she needs to be reunited with you. I am going to pray to God and have our whole community pray for help in this matter.

All our Sisters gratefully remember you and assure you of their good regards, especially Sister Despins and Rainville.

I have the honour of being most respectfully …

1763, 5 August. To Father Mongolfier in Quebec City, by Monsieur Viger.

Sir, here is a new burden I am giving you with all these letters addressed to you. At least, they provide me with the opportunity to assure you of my most humble regards and to express my gratitude for your goodness to all at our house and especially to me. My son arrived just as you were embarking and waited until he was leaving to tell me that he was going to abide by your decision but that I would have to wait for my payment. Neither he nor the fabrique were in any condition to make payments at present, and I fear they will not be able to do so soon.

All our Sisters and Ladies take the liberty of assuring you of their most humble regards. All together we are offering our unworthy prayers to the Lord for your safe-keeping, success, and speedy return.

I have the honour …

1763, 2 September. Monsieur the Abbé de L'Isle-Dieu.

Would you be so good as to ask and receive from Monsieur the Abbé Viet the shares and coupons pertaining to the attached note. More than 4,800 livres are due to our Hospital. Would you be so good as to keep the surplus and to let me know how much it accrues.

I have the honour of being …
Monsieur Savarie, 2 September 1763.

1763, 12 September. Father Mongolfier in Quebec City, by Monsieur Jorien.

Sir, forgive me for importuning you again. You paid me the honour of saying before your departure that you would speak to these gentlemen and that you would let me know if we could confer the habit on our postulants who are ready to become auxiliary sisters, and also to receive several others who have presented themselves. As I have had no reply, I fear that you may have forgotten me. Father, you can remind Monsieur Briand that the Bishop left a document with us signed by himself and Monsieur Briand, his secretary, and sealed with his coat of arms on the 15th of June 1755 in which he allows us to receive three more girls than the twelve permitted. The three will not have the rights of the twelve while the latter are still alive, and we will not confer the habit on them until after one year of novitiate. Sister Dulude would already have been received this way. I trust, Father, that you will exert all your efforts to obtain this permission and to give it to us yourself. More than anyone you know our need; you also know that among the twelve only half are worth anything.

On the account of Monsieur Delorme, he still owes the Hospital 4,800 livres for Mademoiselle Guy. He gave me his note in this amount and two others to draw on Monsieur the Abbé Viet in order for him to remit to Monsieur the Abbé de L'Isle-Dieu the shares and coupons of the India Company that he got from the estate of Monsieur Saint-Paul. I have sent them in duplicate to Monsieur de L'Isle-Dieu. I have addressed these letters to Monsieur Gravé, asking him to remit one of them to you and to send the other by another ship. These days we are getting some new boarders: Madame St Blain and her unmarried daughter, and Madame de Ligneris who will be coming in a month. She is placing her two unmarried daughters with the Sisters of Laprairie. She is doing her inventory and then will have an auction so as to go to France next year.

1763, 4 October. To Father Mongolfier by Monsieur Dufix.

I had the honour of yours dated 19 September from Quebec City. I thank you, Father, for the trouble you have taken in replying to me, and I accept what you have said on the subject of our novices and postulants. Like so many others, they eagerly await your return. Your long, involuntary stay in Quebec City makes one fear that the rest of your journey may be likewise prolonged. As for myself, I shall be consoled if you are able to succeed and to come back in perfect health.

Mademoiselle Janotte St Nozard is leaving for Quebec City to die. As you know, her sister is remaining here.

Madame Volant from Laprairie begged me to receive her in the ward so as to be treated by Monsieur Felz. She is remaining as a boarder; she seems to take her perfection to heart. One hopes that she will persevere in this vocation better than she has in all the others.

All our Sisters ask you to accept their most humble regards.

I am most respectfully …

1763, November. Monsieur de Murez (The Honourable James Murray).

I have just learned that the King in renewed recognition of your merit has appointed you Governor General of this colony. I beseech you, Sir, to accept my compliments and the assurance of my most profound respect. Allow me to ask you to be so good as to take the Hospital that I serve under your protection. This is a blessing that one asks of you who has the honour of being with great respect,

Sir,
Your most humble and obedient servant,
M. Lajemmerais, Widow Youville,
Director of the General Hospital.

1763, 29 December. To Monsieur Gage (General Thomas Gage).

Sir, allow me to anticipate by a couple of days the New Year and assure you of my most humble regards and those of my Sisters. We offer all our unworthy prayers to the Lord for the preservation of your health and the fulfilment of all your desires, as well as for Madame your wife and your whole family who are most dear to us and whom we hold in everlasting memory.

I have the honour of being with deepest respect.

Forgive me, Sir, the liberty I have taken in transmitting this letter to you by Father Mongolfier.

1764, 2 [January]. Father Mongolfier.

Sir, I have the honour of sending you my most humble regards at the beginning of this New Year and of assuring you that we do not miss a day in offering our unworthy prayers to the Lord to bless your work and to bring you back to perfect health. We hope to hear your news sometime during this month, as do your priests. None of them is sick. Father Yzambert was admitted here on the 20th of August and died on the 14th of December at four o'clock in the morning. He was taken to the Chapel of the Seminary at eleven o'clock, at four o'clock a Libera was sung in the Parish Church, and he was taken to the riverbank where Monsieur the Parish Priest of Longueuil received him to transport him there as he had requested in his will. In the will he left the Hospital 3,500 livres in draft notes and 1,100 livres in bills of exchange from '59 and his clock. Perhaps, this is not a great deal, but as you yourself said, he did not live here for a long time.

We have also received 1,200 livres in draft notes from Monsieur Lartide,[2] the surgeon, in gratitude for our having taken on the elderly man Cory, his guest.

Allow, Father, all my Sisters to assure you of their most humble regards and that they, as do I, commend themselves to your prayers and Masses.

A great deal of property is going to be sold and, it looks as though, at a great bargain. Had we received payment for our notes, and if we were sure that we would be allowed to purchase here and if you were sure about it also, we would have been able to profit from this situation. Some proposals have already been made to us, but I have replied that we could not conclude anything until you have returned.

On the 7th of this month, my sister Gamelin is marrying her daughter Lacroix to Monsieur Porlier the Elder; and Madame de Beaujeu, her older daughter to Monsieur St Georges Dupré and the other daughter to Monsieur Charly.

---

2   Jacques Lartigue, father of the future Bishop, Jean-Jacques Lartigue, first bishop of Montreal from 1836 until his death, 19 April 1840.

1764, 10 September. To Monsieur Goguette in LaRochelle, copy by LeGay, sent 15 October.

Sir, after the letter I wrote last year, I had the honour of receiving yours dated 10 March. You give me news of Monsieur de Lanoue, who you say is at Tours, as indeed he was. He arrived here at the beginning of September and is leaving again for France. Could you please remit to him the 2,962 livres, 7 sols on the bills of exchange that I sent you in 1759. One of them is for 1,693 livres for me, one for 999 livres for Mademoiselle Lanoue, and another for 500 livres for Mademoiselle LeGardeur, although it is I who sent them all to you. All together, they amount to 3,192 livres, if I am not mistaken. Monsieur Lanoue still has to be paid 229 livres, 13 sols, which I would ask you to make allowance for when you know their fate. In 1759 you indicated that you owed me a balance of 1,121 livres, 11 sols, 10 deniers; and in 1761 that I lost the equivalent of 100 livres on a bale of merchandise going to Monsieur Despins, and that the remainder is in your store. I had the honour of indicating to you last year that you could dispose of it as you wished, if it could not be returned to us. I rely completely on your honesty in this matter and approve whatever you decide to do, convinced as I am that you will do your best for the sake of the poor. I have not received any of your letters this year. No doubt, it will be as it was last year and I shall get them after the ships have left.

I have the honour …

I am asking Monsieur Denis Goguette to give Monsieur de Lanoue, Officer of Canada, two thousand nine hundred and sixty-two livres in bills of exchange from 1759, of which I am making allowance for the one I gave him in October 1759. May he be pleased to oblige his most humble servant.

1764, 16 September. To Monsieur de L'Isle-Dieu, by Monsieur Benoit.

Sir, at the same time I had the honour of receiving one of your letters dated 12 February from Monsieur Ménard together with another dated 20 April from Father Mongolfier. You will find attached a receipt for the accounts of the heirs of Monsieur de Paris and one of the extra pay that you have remitted to these priests. If it is not enough, Monsieur Savarie will be able to give you something since it is contained in the power of attorney I sent him last year. Sir, I have given all the attention of which I am capable to your letter and to that of Monsieur Gendron. I have already had the honour of indicating to you to pay what he is asking; I believe that he is not the sort of man who would ask for what is not his due. This, however, will not be for this year since the notaries here cannot give me anything without the documents. I believe you have them all, obtained from Monsieur Lamarche. He is asking for a contract form for next year. I think that I can ask for that since I have not touched a penny of my dowry of 6,000 livres during the 34 years I have been a widow. If we still had Monsieur Danré who is now in Paris and who was a notary here, I should not be having any of this bother, for he was well-informed on all these affairs. It will be necessary to wait until next year, when you will be so good as to send me a form. I have also received, Sir, the certificate for 450 livres in interest of 22 July 1758 to the profit of the General Hospital of Montreal, as well as the declaration that you have made of the bills of exchange and papers that we have amounting to 106,624 livres, 5 sols, and the bill of exchange that is held by Monsieur the Abbé Couturier for 7,620 livres, 10 sols. Doubtless, that for 9,700 livres drawn in 1759 has been recovered and can be added to these amounts. Sir, I am asking you to pay first Monsieur Lanoue the 6,000 livres for which I gave him a bill of exchange payable at the same time as that of the Hospital. If it is not possible for these payments to be made this year, could we not, Sir, obtain on your credit 7 or 8 thousand livres of which 6 would go to Monsieur Lanoue and the remainder to us who are in very great need?

You still appear to be worried about the former accounts of Monsieur de Paris, especially the note on the India Company. All of that is old business. We hold him acquitted of everything and approve all that he did.

All our Sisters join with me in earnestly beseeching you to withdraw from the money that we have with Monsieur Savarie the 133 livres, 18 sols, 10 deniers that you put there out of your own money to reimburse what you thought was an error. The dear departed did his best to serve us, and we would be most ungrateful if we were to bother his family. No, Sir, assure them to the contrary, and if it is agreeable with you, we will hold him acquitted before God and man and pray for the repose of his soul.

I am most surprised that Madame Péan has not paid the bill of exchange drawn on her for 1,050 livres in settlement for her aunt, Madame Laronde, since she has her own money and this sum is due to the Hospital for her aunt's board and funeral arrangements. She had no need to wait for her husband to be let out of prison to find this amount. The deceased said that she had 21 thousand livres to hand and lots of bills of exchange.

Allow me, Sir, to repeat here my thanks for your goodness and the zeal with which you attend to our affairs. All the thanks that my Sisters and I can give you are our unworthy prayers that we offer to the Lord for your safekeeping and growth in holiness.

I have the honour …

I hold Monsieur the Abbé de L'Isle-Dieu acquitted of two grants of 500 livres each given by the Court to the religious communities of this country. One is remitted to the heirs of Monsieur Jacque de Paris, and the other to Monsieur Savarie, at Montreal, this 16th of August 1764.

M. M. Lajemmerais.

In the copy to Monsieur Savarie, I tell him of the power of attorney of Mademoiselle St Michel, of the draft notes of Father Yzambert and of the bill of exchange from the same for which Lefaivre is responsible, and of 1,200 livres in draft notes from one of the poor.

I hold the heirs of Monsieur Nicolas de Paris acquitted of all the accounts that he had with the General Hospital of Montreal and approve the account they have rendered of both receipts and expenditures to Monsieur the Abbé de L'Isle-Dieu in Paris, 16 April 1764. At Montreal, this 16th of September 1764.

M. M. Lajemmerais, Widow Youville.

1764, 16 September. Father Villard, by Monsieur Benoit, copy by Monsieur Legay, sent 15 October.

I had the honour of receiving yours from Father Mongolfier whom it has pleased the Lord to return to us in good health to the great satisfaction of all the French, most of whom were afraid they would never see him again. Our Priests who are going to France will tell you the rest. For a long time, Sir, I have been closely acquainted with the goodness of Monsieur the Abbé de L'Isle-Dieu towards our community. I can also assure you that I and all my Sisters are deeply grateful to him in ways that will be long remembered. We are very glad, Sir, that you have been appointed to replace him. Please allow me to express my most humble thanks to you for getting Monsieur Savarie as our bursar. Your familiarity with him is enough for us to place all our trust in him. All our Sisters assure you of their most humble respect. They commend themselves to your prayers and Masses; we have greater need of them than ever. We find ourselves separated from our relatives, friends, and bene-factors; all the good citizens are leaving and we are left in a place where we hardly know anyone any longer. No doubt, this is as God wills, and it is necessary to submit to His holy Will.

I have the honour of being with very deep respect …

1764, 16 September. To Monsieur Débarasse, by Monsieur Benoit.

Sir, I received from Father Mongolfier your letter dated 2 April. I discovered after the bill of exchange had been sent that I had drawn 33 livres, 55 sols more than was needed. But it is done – we will make up the surplus in prayers. Tomorrow Mass will be said for the healing of your leg. I am confident that it is healed at present, but with God nothing is ever lost, so it will be for some future needs. How shall we get along, how shall we live with the English? Up until now they have done neither good nor ill to us. We scarcely keep ourselves alive. Money is extremely scarce and there are no means of earning it. Those people do not provide any work at all, and their King even less. The worst is that this poor country is isolated. All the good citizens are leaving the country. One is filled with sorrow to see relatives, friends, and benefactors leaving, never to be seen again. Nothing is sadder. Every day, new sacrifices are to be made. Like you, we are waiting for the decree that will establish the payments for our papers, which should allow us a little more leeway and put us in a position to help a larger number of those in need. My children are doing well; they are still in the same parishes. All our Sisters ask me to give you their compliments. Kiss your dear little girls for me. I shall not tell you anything of Madame de Louche and Angélique because they themselves are writing to you. They have kissed I do not know how many times the letters from your little girls and showered them with their tears. They asked me if they could keep your letter as a blessing from above.

I have the honour …

1764, September. Monsieur Savarie, by Monsieur Benoit.

I had the honour of receiving your two letters and your two accounts of 12 April 1764. You will find attached a signed and approved copy of your accounts. Before I received your letter, I had drawn on you a bill of exchange for 2,000 livres, and then your letter informed me of the balance of 1,369 livres, 17 sols, 10 deniers. Nevertheless, since you will have collected the interest before my bill of exchange arrives, you will be able to honour it. Besides, Monsieur Benoit, an officier of this country who is moving to France, is the bearer of it and he has told me not to worry at all, that he will wait until the money is there. Monsieur the Abbé Viet indicates to me that he gave you four shares and four coupons, but you mention only the shares. That would appear to put him in a difficult position, but you can work it out with him. He is satisfied that the person to whom they belong owes the Hospital 4,800 livres, but he has to pay the surplus. Should these payments be insufficient or any risks involved, I cannot be responsible: such are our agreements. When you have paid the 2,000 livres to Monsieur Benoit, pay the Brother's pension. I would also appreciate it, Sir, if you could give 40 livres to the wife of Claude Bologreille to whom you gave 60 livres last year in assistance. Her husband, who has been a domestic servant here for almost three years and who had continuously worked for one of my sisters since his arrival in this country, plans to come back to her next year.

I thank you greatly, Sir, for having accepted my power of attorney when you are responsible for the business of so many communities; this one, however, is totally for the poor and you will have double merit, you will share in their prayers and those of all our Sisters, who beg me to express their gratitude to you for being willing to render them this service.

Monsieur the Abbé de L'Isle-Dieu has asked me for a discharge from obligation for the heirs of Monsieur de Paris and for himself. I believe that you are authorized by my power of attorney to give him everything that is necessary for this. If what I have sent is not sufficient, give him whatever he wants.

1764, 14 October. To Madame Mercier.

Madame, as you are aware, your Mother has been in this Hospital for ten years. This is why, Madame, you will not find it ill on my part if I describe her rather sad situation to you. She has no linen; for more than ten years she has not been able to buy a washcloth for herself. She owes here 1,800 livres for her board, yet her expenses are very modest. For four years she has drunk only water, and this is very hard for someone who never lacked for wine or the treats that a person of her age ought to have. Her resources amount only to a title-deed worth 4,000 livres and 150 livres in interest on her dowry. As you can see, she does not have enough to provide for her needs, honour her debts, and pay her board. Here she pays only 700 livres a year. Board is 1,000 livres because everything is extremely expensive in this country. If she wants to have a bottle of wine, it costs 30 sols, and similarly for the rest. For these reasons, Madame, I join with her in beseeching you to transfer your part of the dowry, which in any case you would not be able to receive on her death since it would have to go the King of England. Be assured, Madame, that I have told you nothing but the truth and that I should be sorry to impose on you for anything.

I have the hon. …

Madame Ligneris (née Marie-Thérèse Migeon de la Gauchetière)

I am making use of Benac to convey our news to you. The whole community and the others in the house are still suffering from your departure. I, especially, shall not be happy until I have learned of your arrival in France and how you have settled in. I hope that you will give me this satisfaction as soon as you are able to do so. We are offering all our unworthy prayers to the Lord that it may please him to keep you in complete health, as well as Monsieur Lanoue and our two dear little girls. Mademoiselle Lanoue will not be writing this time. Since your departure, she has lost a quantity of bad blood from her head and face, which is very distressing for her. I wish I could report to you that Nanon is here, but it was judged better to receive her only when she can no longer stay where she is. Father Mongolfier told me to take pains to find out whether she has any needs, so that they could be provided for. I hope that everything will have been settled by the spring and that she will be able to come. I shall do my best to make that happen.

1764, 15 October. Monsieur Héry par Benac (Joseph Porlier, called Benac).

Sir, as I did not have the courage to bid you farewell and to thank you at your leaving, I am today accomplishing this duty not only for myself, but for our whole community which will never forget your kindnesses and acts of charity. We offer our unworthy prayers to the Lord for your preservation and that of your whole family and the success of your undertakings. Dare I lead myself to believe that you will give us your news, and that I shall be able to hear from you, how you are getting on and where you are living? I ask for the continuance of your friendship as well as that of Madame Héry and of your daughter to whom I extend my regards.

I have the honour …

My dear niece (Josette Gamelin, wife of Etienne-Guillaume de Figuiéry).

Let us not speak of leaving and farewell. Let us say rather that you arrived in good health and that you are with your dear husband. Let us think now only of how we can work so that we shall be reunited in Paradise where we shall never again be separated. All our Sisters greet you with untold friendship, and especially Despins who is coming with open arms to tell me not to forget her. Likewise, our Ladies wish to be remembered, St-Michel first and, above all the others, your Aunt Maugras. We hope that you will let us know your news. They said here that you had to leave on the 10th. On that day there was a north-east wind and since then a mild south-west wind and the most beautiful weather in the world. We rejoice in it and hope that by now you are out of the River.

My compliments to your dear husband, whom I hold, as I do you, in utmost affection.

Your aunt,
Widow Youville.

1765, 1st of March. To Monsieur the Abbé de L'Isle-Dieu, by Monsieur Conbelle.

I had the honour of writing to you on 16 September 1764 by Monsieur Benoit, an officer of this country who has left forever, and I sent a copy with Monsieur Legay who plans to return. I hope that you will convey your news through this channel. Yet, even if they have reached their destination, we have not got any news of what is happening.

We have seen a decree of the King of France that says that he will pay the bills of exchange of '55, '56, '57, and '58 in their entirety, those of '59 at half loss, and the other papers at three-quarters. That is a great deal to lose and to lose in so many ways and not to know when the total will be reimbursed. That is what we do not know. I hope you will let us know where we stand in all these business transactions. You can see how great our need is by the bills of exchange that I have drawn on you without knowing whether you will have the wherewithal to pay them, and I shall have still more debts to pay this year. We have also heard that the papers in this country, even though they have been registered here, will not be paid. I mentioned to you last year that I had received in October 1763 from Father Yzambert, who died here, papers for 3,500 livres, and from a poor person 1,200 livres, and since then 400 or 500 livres in alms, and some 500 livres in certificates, all of which have been registered with the notary or the General. I leave everything up to Providence, my trust is in it, everything will work out as God wills.

The gentleman who is bearing this letter is going to Paris. I anticipate the goodness of your reply from there.

I have the honour …
All our Sisters assure you of their very …

1765, 9 June. To Father de L'Isle-Dieu. From 22 July, by Monsieur Courthiau.

Sir, we have learned of the decision on Canadian money by the King of France, who will pay the bills of exchange at half loss and the draft notes at three-quarters, and for which he will give coupons that will yield four per cent interest. Please, Sir, could you obtain, through your credit, from the Minister a cash payment of 9 to 10,000 livres to help us rebuild our house which it pleased God to take from us by fire on the 18th of May at two o'clock in the afternoon. The fire started in a house in the city about ten arpents from us and we are more than two arpents outside the city, but the wind that was blowing in our direction was so strong that in less than two hours more than 100 houses in the city were destroyed by the fire. If only I had been able to convince myself that the fire would reach us, we could have saved much; most of what we succeeded in getting out was beneath the wind and got burnt where it stood. I think that we have been left with a twelfth of what we had. The Ladies of the Hôtel-Dieu have given us shelter, and not only us but also our poor people and our lady boarders, all of whom have lost a great deal. The charity of the faithful is providing food for us, especially the Priests of the Seminary of Saint-Sulpice, who all hope to see us rebuild. We have begun and will try to continue, in the hope that Providence that has always sustained us will continue to do so. I rely greatly upon your kindnesses which are never exhausted but, on the contrary, ever increase. After God, my trust is in you. It is enough for you only to know of our wants to busy yourself immediately with relieving them. I beg of you to let me hear from you as quickly as possible. It is now the 22nd of July, and we …

1765, 10 June. Madame de Lignery.

We have had no news of you except from Monsieur Héry and Madame Figuery, who say that everyone arrived perfectly well, with an account of your sad crossing. But what has become of Madame Lignery? What role has she been playing? We have not heard anything. I met Monsieur Macailye[3] several days ago and he told me he had no news of you and that Nanette[4] was about to give birth. She is at Madame Herbin's,[5] where she has gone for her lying-in. He has been living in Laprairie since the end of March in Dumay's house that he bought for 2,000 livres. He is a judge in that district. He has put up for sale his house in the city and his lands at Saint Michel and Châteauguay. The misfortune that befell us has confirmed him in his plan never again to have a house in the city. This misfortune is, that on the 18th of May at two thirty a fire started in the store-room of Monsieur Leveston [Levingston] from some cinders that had been left there. This house belonged to the Spinsters Giasson. The fire spread from the lower storey to the house of Laprery, which did not burn, then it caught the house of Décary on the corner at the Charon gate, as it is called, and from there spread to Monsieur Charles Rhéaume's and on the other side from the St-Onge house to that of Monsieur Ranger. On that side, there was only a single row of houses; but on the other, all those that extended up to the ramparts. The wind was frightful and blowing in our direction. In no time at all we were burnt to ashes, like all the houses in Pointe-à-Callières and those behind our garden, so that in all this vast area there remained only our brewery and our mill. All of us – Sisters, boarders, and poor people – are now at the Hôtel-Dieu in the Royal Hall; and we are bold enough to try to recover a corner of our house where the walls are still quite sound. We would have been able to save much had we imagined that we would burn. The distance inclined us to hope that we would be spared. In total, 111 houses were burned and 143 households lost. All our Ladies have lost a notable amount. Madame Lobinois and Mademoiselle Le Gardeur are lamenting the most, although they have not lost more than the others. Poor Monsieur Lamonodier, the churchwarden on duty, was going to go through the Sulpicians' garden to get what he could from the church, when on entering the alley that led there, he was struck by beams falling from Monsieur Dufère's little house. He lived fully conscious for eleven hours. Poor Labrosse, the sister of Monsieur Lacoste, was burned on their doorstep. Several people have been left crippled. At least 20 barrels of gunpowder blew up during this fire; and the night Madame l'Espérance's vaults burst, five blew up one after the other. We thought our last hour had arrived, and I regard it as an act of Heaven that the whole city did not perish.

---

3   Francis Mackay, he and his brother Samuel belonged to the 60th Regiment of General Wolfe.
4   Her goddaughter, Marie-Anne de Ligneris, wife of Francis Mackay and daughter of the addressee.
5   Born Marie-Anne Boucher de Niverville, her daughter Louise married Samuel Mackay.

Since this misfortune, I have received a letter from Madame de Joncaire,[6] along with six minots of wheat and one minot of hulled barley. I sent her her draft notes this winter. She is doing well. Gabrielle is with her. Her boy has gone permanently to England. The rest has been sown.

You have lost your beautiful gown; it was in a trunk in which were a number of good things. It was carried out of the house, but was burnt at the door along with more than twenty other trunks. We have found some burnt money that I will clean and sell so that you shall not have lost everything. François Lamarche, whom you knew, was killed two days after the fire by a chimney falling on him. He was crushed and lay dead on the ground. He had not yet paid the interest on his deeds; I think I shall have to resort to his brother.

My compliments to my friend[7] and to dear Thérèse and Ursule. We hear that Marchand and Lagirardière are at Cayennes. I pray God to preserve them and grant them health. If you see Monsieur and Madame d'Hauterive[8] and Monsieur de Joncaire, please give them my best regards. Please let us hear from all of you. Awaiting the blessing of hearing from you, I am with best regards …

1765, 11 June. To Monsieur de Murez (General James Murray).

I have the honour of paying you my most humble respects and of thanking you for the rations you have given me. I urgently request your continued kindness. We offer all our unworthy prayers to the Lord for the preservation of your health and that He will grant you every kind of prosperity.

I have the honour of being with deep respect …

1765, 15 June. Monsieur Héry.

I had the honour of receiving your letter of the 17th of February, which filled me with joy to receive news of you directly. We had not heard anything until the 27th of April, when Gamelin received one of your letters and one from Madame de Figuery. I was at his house when Carignan brought your letter, which he could not read for the tears that were choking him and all the company likewise, so happy were we to learn of your safe arrival. That is all we desired, having nothing other left to hope for than our reunion in Eternity.

---

6   Born Madeleine Le Gay de Beaulieu, wife of Louis-Thomas de Joncaire. She lived at Repentigny.
7   Constant-François-Daniel de Ligneris.
8   Born Marie-Thérèse de Joncaire, she married Philippe-Antoine d'Hauterive in 1749.

I am grateful to you for once again paying Catherine's board.[9] It has been quite awhile that you have provided for her through your great generosity. She is doing well. She lost a large part of her wardrobe in our fire which was quite upsetting to her but since she has seen that she will be remaining with us, she has been consoled. I shall not give you the details of this misfortune since I believe Gamelin has already done so. I will only tell you that we are working to rebuild the house and one end of the wing so that we shall be able to move into it by winter. We shall be quite crowded there for there were 119 of us left homeless and all have remained except for my sister Maugras, Madame Mouchette the mother, Mademoiselle Forestier, and Mademoiselle St-Michel, who are all planning to return as soon as we move in. We are in the Royal Hall at the Hôtel-Dieu, with our boarders downstairs, our poor women upstairs, and part of the men in the hall for the sick and the other part at Pointe Saint-Charles and in the brewery. This year we have started to get a great deal of work, and I hope that Providence will find the means for us to rebuild.

I was scarcely able to convince myself that God would not preserve this house which, as you know, was an asylum for the outcast. With this idea, I did not hasten to safeguard it, but even sent into the city those among us who were able to help. And they did not return until the house was already beginning to burn. We were not able to save an eighth of what we had. God allowed this to happen. Blessed be His Holy Name. Most of what we have is from the Church.

Please give my best regards to Madame Héry and to all your dear family from all our Sisters as well as from me. We remember you in our humble prayers. We are all very happy with Catherine, who wishes to send her greetings to all of you.

I have the honour of being with deep respect …

1765, 15 June. Monsieur Goguet, by Monsieur Lemoyne 18 September.

I received your letter of the 8th of February telling me that you have not remitted the bills of exchange to Monsieur de Lanoue, as I had asked you to do. No doubt, you will have seen him since then. As I had the honour of mentioning to you, there will remain 229 livres, 13 sols, which I would ask you to be so kind as to add to what you had in stock in 1759. You mention that you have credited me with 1,121 livres, 11 sols, 10 deniers, and you tell me that in 1761 you had sent in the ship *Lamilis* in a large trunk for Monsieur Lemoyne a hundred and some livres and that the rest was in stock. Sir, would you please sell these goods and send me the money. We are in extreme need, God having allowed the fire in the city to reach us and leave 120 people homeless. Some people from this country will give you the

---

9   Catherine Guillette.

details of this misfortune. Were we under another rule, these bills would give us great pleasure here, and even more if they could be converted into cloth; but all this only depends on what you are able to do. When I know what you are going to get, I will draw up a bill of exchange for you.

I have the honour …

A favourable occasion has arisen. Monsieur Lemoyne Despins is willing to take responsibility for everything. Please be so good as to remit it to him. He will give you a release form.

1765, 22 July. Monsieur Savarie, by Monsieur Courthiau.

Sir, you will no doubt have heard of the misfortune that befell us on the 18th of May. It was God's will to visit us through a fire that took away not only our buildings, but almost all of our furniture, clothing, linen, and beds. Nevertheless, we are trying to rebuild. In this event, we should be gratified to know how the King of France is dealing with the payment of our papers. If favourably, we should be able to borrow to help us rebuild; if not, we shall limit ourselves to a very few things so as not to run into debt. But knowing nothing, we are in the saddest of all possible conditions. We have received no letters from you nor any from Monsieur de L'Isle-Dieu, and I fear you may have entrusted them to Monsieur Briand who will be coming perhaps this winter or perhaps next year. I would kindly ask you, Sir, if this letter reaches you, to reply to me as soon as possible. I ask this favour from you with the honour of being with very deep respect …

1765, 26 August. Monsieur Héry.

I had the honour of writing to you on the 15th of June. I do not know whether my letter reached you. I received yours of the 17th of February, for which I am most grateful. You give me your news and those of all your family to whom I am most deeply attached. I thank God for having brought you to a safe harbour and I pray that he will shower you with His blessings.

Enclosed is the power of attorney for a man who was at our place six days before our fire and all of whose linen and clothing were burned. He gave us 1,000 livres in draft notes that had not been registered; we traded them at 15 per cent to buy straw mattresses and shirts for the poor. He ought to have quite a lot of property in France; he wishes to make good use of it. I am sending you his papers. Could you please find out what he possesses and act on it or start the proceedings to do so. Whoever executes his papers will be paid directly from the property, if there is any.

A thousand greetings to Madame Héry and your dear family. Our Sisters send you their best regards. Catherine is doing wonderfully; she comes every day to see if I am writing to you so that she can send her greetings.

I have the honour …

1765, 28 August. Madame de Ligneris (Madame the Widow François-Marie Marchand de Ligneris).

I had the honour of writing to you on the 10th of June. I do not know whether that letter has reached you yet. I received one of yours dated the 12th of January that filled me with great delight to find out that you are settled and happy in a community. You have not yet seen anything beautiful; but when you are in Paris you will tell us what is beautiful and what is most beautiful. Even then, I believe that the peacefulness of your community will enchant you more than whatever you shall see. You cannot suspect, I think, the pleasure I had from seeing you here with your family; but still I am more and more delighted that you are in France; I would like to see my whole family there. The tenderness in which I hold them would never allow me to keep them here. I am not going to talk about the sad misfortune that befell us; I said enough about it in my first letter. I hope that we shall be able to return home in October when half the house will have been rebuilt. Mademoiselle Lanoue is doing well and sends you a thousand greetings. Enclosed is a letter for Monsieur her brother. In the fire she lost her mattress, her trundle bed, her straw mattress, and her bed curtains.

Monsieur Robutel should not be surprised by Monsieur de L'Isle-Dieu's letter. I have told him any number of times that we do not have any money in France, that there are only the bills of exchange for '57, '58, and '59, and I have therefore given him a bill of exchange to draw on these papers. The first of them ought to have been paid; but as they have not, he can only get the money at that due date. He will be able to draw on the interest if the King pays us and at the same rate that the King shall pay. I am writing to Monsieur de L'Isle-Dieu about this. No doubt Monsieur Goguette will require a commission on these bills of exchange if that is paid in the transaction. I beg you to give him and my friend my compliments. I kiss Thérèse and Ursule.

I have the honour …

1765, 28 August. Monsieur the Abbé de L'Isle-Dieu.

I had the honour of writing to you on the 9th of June and the 22nd of July, telling you of our misfortunes. I have nothing further to add. This letter is to let you know that I have drawn a bill of exchange on you for 1,500 livres that I received from Madame Charly to whom I had given 1,650 livres, and this will greatly assist us with our needs. I did this with trepidation, fearing that you may not have the money if Madame Péan has not paid and that you may not have got anything for our papers. Necessity made me lay aside these considerations. I imagine that you will have the charity to advance the sums, as you have done in the past, and reimburse yourself from the interest. Monsieur de Lanoue has sent me the letter you wrote to him with respect to the bill of exchange for 6,000 livres that I gave him to collect from the first money that the papers which you hold on behalf of the Hospital will yield. I pointed out to him that he must have known about this, as I explained it to him many times. If, as is said here, the King is paying interest on this money at four per cent, I ask you, Sir, to pay him the 6,000 livres and the principal when they will have been paid. If he wants these coupons at what they are said to yield, he can have them at the amount if you think it is just.

I hope that we shall have restored one end of our house and that we shall be able to move in there in November. It will be very difficult there, but we shall be home. We shall lack no end of means for doing penance, but we shall have need of them. We shall try to benefit from it.

All our Sisters make bold to offer you their most humble respects.

I have the honour …

1765, 18 September. Monsieur Savarie, by Monsieur Lemoyne, with a copy sent with someone.

I had the honour of writing you on the 22nd of July when I spoke briefly about our misfortunes and of my desire to hear your news. On the 26th of March, I received a letter from you dated the 15th of September giving the account of your receipts and expenditures. I am returning it to you allowed and approved. I learn from your letter how the French Court has treated our papers; it is very harsh and does a great wrong to the poorest of the poor of this country. We acquired those papers through much pain and hard work. With respect to the bills of exchange and the list and returns on the draft notes, of these we received nearly a third in alms. This is a new "fire" for our poor and for us. Blessed be God, we must bear his cross. Truly, he has given us many crosses in this sad country.

I am sending you by Monsieur Lemoyne-Despins the draft notes and documents that I have and a bill of exchange for 320 livres, all of which have been registered anew. Of these, I am sending you the list of draft notes amounting to 52,994 livres and the list of documents amounting to 2,113 livres, 10 sols, 0 deniers. If you foresee, Sir, that they would yield more to the subjects of the King of England than they would in France, you would do me a great service to cash them wherever they will yield the most. I have altered nothing since my first list, and you will find them as they are there stated.

Mademoiselle Gourville de St-Michel has received no news from you about her power of attorney and thinks that it may have got lost. Thus, she gave a new one to Monsieur Deschambault who may, however, not have had time to attend to it. She would be greatly obliged to you if you would procure it.

I should so much like, Sir, to be able adequately to express my gratitude for your kindnesses and attention, but I can do no better than offer my unworthy prayers to the Lord that He may shower His blessings upon you.

I have the honour ...

1765, 18 September. Monsieur the Abbé de L'Isle-Dieu, by Monsieur Lemoyne.

I had the honour of writing to you on the 9th of June, the 22nd of July, and the 28th of August. In the last letter I notified you that I had drawn a bill of exchange on you for 1,500 livres for Madame Charly. The only letter I have received from you was that of the 8th of May which only tells me about my children's business affairs. I sent to them so that they could see how to make up their minds; it is too late for them to get there this year. You promise me something concerning this by Monsieur Legay who has not yet arrived; we have had no news about it. I received a letter from Monsieur Savarie dated the 26th of March informing me of the reduction on our bills of exchange and of the little hope we can have for our other papers. After having been treated harshly here, it has happened again. Monsieur Bigot never paid the true value of the rations: when beef was 30 sols, 30 sols were paid for rations and during the final months when beef was 3 livres, 10 sols, 4 deniers, we were paid 3 livres, 10 sols. The Hospital has lost on bread, peas, small provisions, drinks, and domestic labour. And for the kind of work that we have been doing for more than twenty years they have not increased the payment even though the King paid twice the amount to the storekeeper. The surplus was used to pay the employees' wages. The merchant outfitters always paid us more than the King. Monsieur Savarie is asking me for draft notes; I am sending them by Monsieur Lemoine-Despins, along with the lists; and I am asking him as well as you, Sir, that if you find out that the subjects of the King of England are being paid more than those of France that you would try to get the best yield on the notes.

Pray, dear Father, that God will give me the strength to bear patiently all these crosses and to make a holy use of them. Here all at once we have lost King, country, possessions, and, worse yet, we are in fear that our holy religion will be obliterated.

I mentioned to you that I can only pay Monsieur de Lanoue when the bills of exchange have been redeemed and since we do not know their fate, I am asking you to give him the interest on these 6,000 livres at the rate at which the King is paying us and when you have received the money to give him the principal.

I see from my account that Monsieur Couturier's bill of exchange for 7,260 livres had not been remitted to you but that you have received the one for 9,700 livres.

Monsieur Savarie does not mention Madame Péan's bill of exchange, hence I assume that it has not been paid.

All our Sisters assure you of their most humble respect. They are filled with gratitude for your kindnesses. All together, we offer our unworthy prayers to the Lord for your preservation.

I have the honour of being …

1765, 18 September. Father Villard, by Monsieur Lemoyne.

I had the honour of receiving your letter of the 28th of March. I am much obliged for the care you have taken in replying. I have also heard from Monsieur de L'Isle-Dieu who makes me fear that we shall lose him. He is constantly telling me about his great age and his infirmities. I think he has been affected by our misfortunes. I did not give him all the details of our fire. If you think it is necessary for him to know them, Monsieur Lemoyne-Despins, the bearer of these letters and our draft notes, will be better able to inform you than anyone.

I received a letter from Monsieur Savarie and his accounts, which are very well done. His trouble must not go unpaid. I ask you, Sir, to see to it. I approve of whatever you will have the kindness to do for him. I forgot to mention this to Monsieur de L'Isle-Dieu; please tell him.

All our Sisters assure you of their most humble respects. They and I both ask for your prayers and Masses.

I have the honour of being …

1765, 19 September. Monsieur Couturier, by Monsieur Lemoyne-Despins.

Sir, I have the honour of paying you my most humble respects and of asking you that if you obtain anything from our Hospital's bill of exchange for 7,620 livres that you are holding, that you keep it. This will be the beginning of the repayment of the advances that Father Montgolfier[10] gave me to rebuild our house, which was destroyed in the fire that occurred in this city on the 18th of May, the details of which you will have heard from people from this country who have gone to France. It has reduced us to great poverty, but God has His plans. I adore them and ask for your prayers and those of your Priests.

I have the honour …

---

10   Abbé Etienne Montgolfier, Priest of Saint-Sulpice, Vicar General of the Diocese of Quebec.

1765, 5 November. Monsieur de L'Isle-Dieu, by Monsieur Grande [William Grant].

Sir, only at the end of October did I receive your letter through Monsieur Legay. It came by way of York, which greatly retarded its arrival. I had the honour of writing you a first letter by way of Monsieur Cainbelle [Campbell] on the 1st of March, then a second letter on the 9th of June addressed to Monsieur Villard, a third by Monsieur Courtiot, a French merchant returning home, a fourth on the 28th of August borne by I know not whom, and a fifth letter by Monsieur Lemoyne on the 18th of September. I shall not repeat here what I had the honour of telling you, in hopes that you will have received at least one of the letters. I cannot keep from beseeching you to redouble your entreaties to move the Court to pity our sad fate. It could pay us more than the others without creating any envy and that would give us a little cash. I can assure you that we are in great need. We are indebted more than 10,000 livres for rebuilding a corner of our house and providing ourselves with the mere necessities.

I have written to Monsieur Daine, the executor of Madame Laronde's will,[11] who also gave me the bill of exchange on Madame Péan, asking him to please pay me. Sir, I am sending you a discharge as you dictated it to me in your letter. I did not realize that Monsieur de Paris owed me 500 livres from the first grant, even though the Bishop had told me that they had been set aside for me and you added the same at the end of your letter of 18 October 1760. Having finished writing my letter and re-reading the one I received from the Bishop of Quebec in which he indicates to me the destination of the 5,000 livres set aside for the relief of the poor communities of the diocese, it appears to me that he employed you in this for 500 livres. Please check this and if such is the case, I shall add the said 500 livres to your power of attorney funds. During all this time, I heard nothing about it, which made me think it was for others, especially since Monsieur de Paris entered as expenditures all the bills of exchange that I drew on you. Moreover, please use the discharge as seems fit to you, approving everything you judge fitting to do.

I cannot express my gratitude enough and that of my Sisters for all your kindnesses that I cannot stop telling people about and marvelling over. I hope and pray that God will reward you abundantly for your kindnesses. I ask this blessing of him and also that of your believing me to be with deepest respect …

1765, November. Monsieur Dainé, by Monsieur Grande [Grant].

I believe that you will have found out that Madame Péan has not yet paid the bill of exchange for 1,050 livres that you gave me for what Madame Laronde owes

---

11　　Born Louise Chartier de Lotbinière, widow of Louis Denys, Sieur de La Ronde.

our Hospital. I hope, Sir, that you will be so kind as to have this amount remitted to Monsieur the Abbé de L'Isle-Dieu at the Seminary for Foreign Missions who is responsible for the bill of exchange. You will be doing me a great service. We have suffered a fire that has left us in great want.

I have the honour …

Please give your Wife and Daughters my best regards.

To Monsieur Saint-Ange Charli.

Sir, I have the honour of writing to you to convey my respects and to let you know that I bought the seigneury of Châteauguay some time before a fire in the city burned our house and other buildings. This fire was considerable, although we little expected it to get to us seeing how far we were from it. You can judge the straits in which this accident has left us. In consequence, we are not able to pay you what the seigneury owes you. I dare to believe that you will have the goodness to wait for a few years and, indeed, that you will have the charity to remit part of the arrears on the interest.

I have the honour of being with respect,
Sir …

1765, 5 November. Monsieur St-Sauveur, by Monsieur Grande [Grant].

I and our whole community are most grateful to you for remembering us and for offering us your services, which, convinced of your sincerity, we shall remember and make use of should the occasion arise. We do not fail to offer our humble prayers to the Lord for your preservation and for that of your dear family who, I learn with joy, have arrived safely. I pray God to shower His blessings upon you.

You will have heard of the sad fire here that it pleased God to bring upon us, but what can we do but adore the designs of His Providence and submit to His holy will, as indeed we have tried as best as we are able to do. By going into debt, we have repaired a corner of our house where our poor men now are. Our lady boarders and we will be going there at the end of the month. Madame Lahaie was with her nephew, Father Curotte, with all her belongings, or she would have lost everything as we did.

Many assurances of our respect to Monsieur Fonblanche and to Madame your Wife.

I have the honour …

1766, 17 August. Monsieur Savarie, by Monsieur Feltz.

Sir, I had the honour of receiving your letter dated the 18th of April in which you inform me that you received from Monsieur Lemoyne our papers and draft notes and of how they were dealt with, as well as our lists of supplies, rations, and accounts of work. I cannot bring myself to believe that the King will not compensate the communities of this country for the harm he has done to their interests and especially ours to which he has given no payment since it came into being 29 years ago. We always had the work for the King's stores, and especially for the 12 years that the storekeepers noticed the profit that the King was getting from having us work; and we were paid no more in 1760 than we were in 1728 [?], even somewhat less. As for the rations, Monsieur Bigot was always tightfisted and never wanted to pay us what was fitting. When beef was selling at 4 livres a pound, he finally consented to give us 3 livres, 10 sols, and the Hospital had to make up the rest. You can see, Sir, how we were treated: to have borrowed money on which we had to pay interest and to have to wait for our payments from 1757.

You will find enclosed, as you requested, our settled account, along with my baptismal certificate, a notarized act, and a power of attorney. I hope everything will be all right since these things are very expensive under the English. Their signature costs 16 livres for each document; the six cost me 96 livres. As for the notaries and other Frenchmen, they do not cost anything; they show great kindness to the hospitals, and especially to this one. I hope that you will be able to get the nine thousand livres due from the bank and will use 6,000 livres to pay Monsieur Lanoue. This is the money from France that I promised him. It is true that I could only pay him when the bills of exchange we had in France were paid and that, nevertheless, I would pay him the interest on it if the King paid us. As he would pay it, thus, Sir, will you pay him for one year if he requires it? He indeed sold his seigneury for more than it was worth, but since his departure there have been better ones for sale, and for a better price. He has a bill of exchange for 6,000 livres for Monsieur de Lanoue, and for 2,500 livres, in triplicate, for Monsieur Feltz, the Surgeon General of this country, who is going to France and to whom I have given a bill of exchange for this amount. The remaining five hundred livres and the 1,307 livres, 5 sols, 7 deniers that you say are still owed me will pay the bills of exchange for 1,675 livres for Madame Dartignie. You will be left with 450 livres if you get the interest on the 900 livres and the 786 livres, 14 sols in interest from the Hôtel de Ville in Paris. You can use these sums to pay a year's interest to Monsieur de Lanoue and a year's pension to Brother Joseph Dellerme.

I have also given Monsieur Feltz a bill of exchange for 1,000 livres payable during the course of the year 1767 and another for 1,000 livres payable during the course of the year 1768.

No, Sir, I do not disapprove; on the contrary, I approve very strongly that you charged 100 livres to my account for your work and the care you have taken. I do not find that this is too much.

As you note, I have drawn all my bills of exchange on you. I am very much obliged to you for what you have done concerning the accident that has befallen us. After much work and care, we moved back into a corner of our house in December – all the residents of this Hospital: the community, the poor men and women, the foundlings, and all our young and older lady boarders. We were greatly assisted by the Priests of Saint-Sulpice. I gave them a bill of exchange for 7,620 livres that Monsieur Couturier is holding for us in payment for some of the money they advanced us.

The credit vouchers of Rondard, the carpenter, Ménard, the chandler, and Rainville, the tailor, belong to the Hospital and not to me.

You will be receiving from Sieur Bisquet Lefebvre coupons in the amount of 1,176 livres in bills of exchange from 1759 that he received from Father Izambert, the parish priest of Longueuil who died in this Hospital and who gave this sum.

If it is passed on to you, you will be receiving I do not know how much from Mademoiselle St-Michel for Madame Duplessis-Fabert, and again I do not know how much from Monsieur Benoit for Madame Lobinois. I have not yet arranged any of this.

You should have found in the papers Monsieur de L'Isle-Dieu sent to you a deed on the Hôtel de Ville bought by the grandfather and grandmother of my children from Messieurs de Saint-Ours. Last year he asked me for a number of papers that I sent to Monsieur Lamarche and then to Monsieur de L'Isle-Dieu. In 1753, he pointed out to me that all that was necessary for me to collect the 1,800 livres in arrears was my children's power of attorney, which I sent to him. He returned it to me last year and asked for additional papers that it would be almost impossible to get now or, if they could be secured, they would cost almost the sum of 110 livres in interest on which the arrears are owed. Monsieur Gendron will be able to bring you up to date on this business, as well as Monsieur Danré de Blanzy who was our notary here. There are so many difficulties! If there is any hope of collecting anything, I shall send you next year whatever papers may be absolutely necessary.

I have the honour …

In this same letter I asked that the 786 livres, 14 sols in interest that we hold on the Hôtel de Ville in Paris be reinvested if we are reimbursed the funds.

Sir, if Madame Péan has not yet paid the bill of exchange for 1,050 livres drawn on her in 1761 by Monsieur Daine from Madame Laronde's property, for which he was the executor, please present to her the bill that I am sending to you, and if she wishes to remit coupons for this amount, please take them. If she has paid, burn this bill. It seems to me only right that she should pay the interest on this money. Please act on this as you deem best.

1766, 20 August. Madame Péan (born Angélique Des Méloizes), by Monsieur Feltz.

I have learned from Monsieur Daine that you can only pay the bill of exchange that he drew on you for one thousand and fifty livres for the board and funeral expenses of Madame Laronde in coupons in the amount that the King has issued for bills of exchange. Please be so kind, Madame, as to remit the equivalent amount in coupons to Monsieur Savarie at the Seminary for Foreign Missions, who is the bursar for our Hospital. Madame Laronde told me any number of times that she had money deposited in France and that the Hospital would not suffer for the advances made to her. Nevertheless, six years[12] have passed since we advanced her everything in coin, a type of money very scarce in this country, and in spite of its scarcity I was obliged to pay fifteen francs per pound for the wax for her burial. I implore you, Madame, to bring this business to a conclusion. We are more than ever in need. You would be obliging most kindly her who has the honour of being with deep respect …

1766, 20 August. Monsieur and Madame Figuery, by Monsieur Feltz [Captain Etienne-Guillaume de Figuiéry].

I had the honour of receiving your letter dated 3 January, which gave me at least as much pleasure as mine did you. The perfect harmony that I see between dear Josette, you, and your dear brother enchants me. Is there a greater happiness in life than that of a united household? Can all the wealth in the world approach it? I thank God for the blessing He has given you and pray unceasingly that He will continue and increase it. You must not think that there will not be some crosses to bear. They are necessary to get to heaven; but, united as you three are, you will be strong enough to bear them and greatly benefit from them.

Please convey my respects to Monsieur St-Martin.

I have the honour …

All our Sisters send you their best regards, and especially Despins and Rainville.

---

12   Madame de La Ronde died 24 March 1761.

My Dear Niece [Josette Gamelin, wife of Etienne-Guillaume de Figuiéry].

I received two of your letters, the first from September 1765 and the second from 3 January 1766. I know your goodheartedness too well to doubt for a moment how you suffered along with us in our misfortune, but it is over and we must put it behind us. I shall do nothing to stand in the way of your family's leaving; but to tell you the truth, if that happens I do not think that it will be any time soon. Their absence will have to be the cross you bear for several years. It is possible that in the end you will all be reunited. You will learn from their letter that Monsieur and Madame Feltz are leaving, and Madame Sermonville and Mademoiselle St-Michel with them, the first to rejoin her husband and the other to keep her pension of 150 livres from the King in hopes of finding a refuge with her cousin, Monsieur de Noraie, in Rochefort. She asks me to convey many greetings to you and to assure Monsieur de Figuéry of her respect. To replace them, we are getting dear Charlotte Mayotte and Mademoiselle Vitré. For some time Madame Duplessis and her unmarried daughter have been with us. Mademoiselle Frédéric is marrying Monsieur de Courtemanche, who is staying here.

Farewell, dear niece. I do not forget you before God, nor those who are close to you, and I hope that we will be reunited in a blessed eternity.

> Your aunt,
> Widow Youville.

I cannot tell you how much joy fills this community when we receive your news. Everyone sends you innumerable good wishes – and chief among them, Despins, your grandmother, LaSource, and Sister Rainville. I cannot close without telling you about Benac.[13] He is too handsome. He is a big, well-built, beautiful boy and not at all naughty for having been spoiled. He often speaks of his Uncle and Aunt Figuery.

1766, 20 August. Monsieur Héry, by Monsieur Feltz.

Sir, I had the honour of receiving your March letter. The fate of the power of attorney was as I thought it would be. It is not necessary to send me the priest's certificate. I believe completely what you say and that is enough for me. Our whole community assures you, as well as Madame Héry and all your family, of their respect. We are all very happy with the establishment of Mademoiselle Charlotte and of her sister Héry, who is in the kind of community she wanted. She is ever remembered at the Hôtel-Dieu. There is great hope that our communities will survive.

---

13   Louis Porlier Benac, Josette's godson, who was then four years old.

Our Bishop has allowed the profession of a novice at the General Hospital; the elder Mademoiselle Douville has entered the Hôtel-Dieu; Mademoiselle Louchette will be entering here at the beginning of September, as well as a Lefebvre from Longueuil and a Cherrier. Things appear to be going very well for our religion. Many young people are beginning to take up their studies again. Let us hope that God will pour out his blessings on this poor country; I commend it to your prayers and to those of all you know. Monsieur St-Hubert was ordained and received into the Seminary of Quebec City; Monsieur Désery and Maugras, so we hear, into that of Montreal. I hope that in several years you will be sending Charles to us to give spiritual succour to his native land. Poor Catherine has been quite sick for a week, although she is out of danger. She sends many greetings to you all.

I have the honour …

I paid your respects to the Priests of the Seminary and to the Sisters, all of whom are very grateful for them. My respects to Monsieur and Madame Lechelle; I do not forget them in my unworthy prayers.

1766, 20 August. To Madame de Lignery, by Monsieur Feltz.

I received three of your letters, dated 24 October 1765, 29 January 1766, and 20 March 1766. Each gave me as much pleasure as the others and, I must say, to the whole community, the Sisters and the lady boarders who were happy to hear your news. I passed on the letter you sent me for Madame Joncaire who is in remarkably good health. She has sent back Madame Mercier's letter to her mother. She promises a number of powers of attorney and other papers, but nothing has arrived. I fear she will die wanting to go to France. You will see Monsieur and Madame Feltz with Madame Sermonville who is bearing my letter and who will give you all the news from here and from our country. St-Michel is leaving with them so as not to lose her pension. You will have the pleasure of seeing Madame Macaye[14] who has left with Monsieur de Murray.[15] Her husband arrived and left after a short time with her. According to what his brother tells me, he is planning to send his wife to spend the winter with you and then to go get her to return to this country. He has not sold his house, and it is said that he is on the way to making his fortune.

Madame de Bienville thanks you for the news of her son, and she asks you to let her know when you have any for he does not write.

Mademoiselle Philie is doing well. It seems very likely that she will be joining us this autumn. Your recommendation is more than enough for me to try to soften

14   The addressee's daughter.
15   James Murray, Governor General of the Province of Quebec.

her fate. She will be able to go with us in spirit to France whenever she wishes. We now have a Bishop. It seems very likely that religion will continue and be maintained in this country. A large number of young men have presented themselves for the priesthood since His Excellency arrived. He has had a nun professed at the General Hospital. The elder spinster Douville has entered here. Josette Louchette and several others will be entering next month. You mention that the Abbé Joncaire has decided to come here. He has not yet arrived and he himself does not say he is coming. I think that he made this resolution before God but the courage failed him when the time came to carry it out.

I shall be happy to hear from Monsieur Lemoyne news of my associate. He has not yet arrived, he is going by way of New York and is expected next month. Always let me know the news of your family who remain most dear to me. Madame Sermonville will tell you all the news from our country; therefore, I am not writing it down.

I shall send you next year the 100 livres I owe you, the 100 livres of burnt money that I sold for you, and I shall try to sell the rest and add it to these amounts.

Monsieur Chabert[16] seems to be doing very well in his business. He has quite a large trade and is very happy with his business. Madame de Joncaire has sent me two letters for you. I am giving one of them to Madame Sermonville and the other to Monsieur de Longueuil.

My sons remember you very fondly. They assure you of their respect and do not forget you in their prayers. They are still in the same parishes.

All our Sisters assure you of their respects, as do all our lady boarders and especially Mademoiselle de Lanoue who asks that you to give her greetings to her brother – she is very heavy hearted that he has not replied to her letter. She has suffered much this winter from a sciatic gout. I hope that Monsieur de Lanoue will be paid this winter if our powers of attorney finally prove to have some validity. My respects to Monsieur and Madame d'Hauterive if you see them and to Monsieur the Abbé de Joncaire to whom I wish a little more courage to come to the succour of his native land. I kiss Thérèse and Ursule and am with deep respect,

Madame …

1766, 21 August. Monsieur Couturier, by Mademoiselle St-Michel.

I had the honour of your letter from March. I have no doubt about what you have done in relation to the loss we suffered in the fire. I am also convinced, Sir, that you took all necessary measures to make the most of our bill of exchange, but what

---

16   Daniel de Joncaire, Sieur de Chabert et de Clausone, married in 1752 Marguerite Rocbert de La Morandière.

can one do? The King is master and nothing can be said about what he has done. It is quite certain that we acquired it legitimately and that it must not be confused with those that were not so acquired. I shall abide by whatever you do. Father Mongolfier told me that he would arrange everything; therefore, I am not worried. He has done and is still doing for us more than I would have dared to ask him.

I commend myself to your prayers and Masses.

I have the honour …

1766, 22 August. Monsieur Goguette [Goguet], by Monsieur Feltz.

Sir, I received the two letters that you paid me the honour of writing to me on the 25th of March. From them I learn that you have remitted to Monsieur Lemoyne the few effects and bills of exchange which you were holding for our Hospital. I thank you for this. When he arrives, I shall know what there is.

I have the honour …

1766, 22 August. Father Villard, by Monsieur Feltz.

I learn from Monsieur Boirette that you have become Superior and are ill. I feel for you as much for the one as for the other.

I pray the Lord that He will help and sustain you in both. I commend myself to your prayers and Masses, and I ask you not to lose sight of the small business affairs of our community about which I am giving the details to Monsieur Savarie.

I have the honour …

1766, 22 August. Monsieur the Abbé de L'Isle-Dieu, by Mademoiselle St-Michel.

Sir, I had the misfortune to lose your letter that I received by way of Monsieur Briand. I cannot recall what you paid me the honour of mentioning except something about our last accounts and that you thought you owed me something. Please, Sir, do not say any more about that; and if the receipt you have is not sufficient, get Monsieur Savary to give you one more. I am sending him some new powers of attorney. If I knew how it should be done, I would send it to you, although I think I have already sent you two of them. How, Father, can you worry about a mistake of 4 or 5 hundred livres that may not even exist when you have rendered us services that cannot be repaid and that we and those who come after us must never forget. You are always telling me that you are approaching your eternal home. Consequently, this whole community and I especially offer up our prayers, although I hope the Good Lord will still preserve you for a number of years.

I have the honour …

1766, 26 September. Bishop Briand in Quebec City.

I am taking the liberty of sending you the deed for the seigneury of Châteauguay that the Hospital purchased in 1765, the agreements for which were made in 1764. I am asking you, my Lord, to present it to Monsieur Mills to try to get a remission of the sales levy or if that is not possible, to give us some time to pay it. I had obtained permission from Monsieur de Murray and Monsieur Marchand, the Vicar General, to sell the property that the poor had in Chambly in order to use it for a more profitable property. I then sold part of it to Monsieur Dodego [Dondegan] for 10,500 livres – 1,500 livres in cash and a title deed for 9,000 livres comprising a half-league by a league deep of the seigneury. To possess this land litigation will be necessary with the Seigneur and the seven co-seigneurs for the boundaries. I also sold a plot six arpents wide and almost sixty deep that could not support the farmer. There is still one left that has, I believe, an area of 1,000 arpents on which there is a barn in poor condition. Of this land, I do not know what to have done about the boundary ditches and the fences with the neighbour. For it, I am being offered 10,000 livres – part in cash, of which I have great need – and the rest in title deed. I await your permission to conclude this business if you find that it is acceptable.

I have the honour …

1768 [sic], 12 October. Reply to Monsieur the Abbé de L'Isle-Dieu's letter of 9 June, by Father de Joncaire.

Very dear Father, I received your letter of the 9th of June from which I learn that Monsieur de Lanoue is urgently requesting his payment from you. I hope that Monsieur Savarie will have received my letters of the 17th of August in which I ask him to pay him in full and a year's interest if he requires it. As you will see from the bill of exchange that I gave him and that he will present to you, he has no right to challenge it since I promised him only the bills of exchange that you were holding or the interest based on what the King will pay when he reimburses the funds. But I shall be happy if Monsieur Savarie has the wherewithal to pay him and that this business can be concluded.

I have no doubt whatsoever, my very dear Father, about the care you have taken to obtain from the King an indemnity for the losses we have had on our papers. It is very just, as I have mentioned to you many times and as I am repeating again to Monsieur Savarie. We owe you so much that we shall never be able to repay you unless we as members of Jesus Christ can delve into the riches of His treasury to repay those who have shown us their charity, and you chief among them. Your charity is of a worth that can only be repaid in this divine currency. My Sisters and I often implore Our Divine Saviour and His Divine Father, who has been the object of my devotion for nearly forty years, that He will preserve you for a number of years to come and at the last will reward you with eternal glory.

I have the honour …

Sir and very dear Father, if Monsieur Savarie needs our letters patent, he can find them at Versailles where the originals must be.

1767, 28 August by Monsieur Courtemanche and 17 October by another bearer.

Father de L'Isle-Dieu, I have not had the honour of receiving your letters. I learn from the letter I received from Father Villard dated the 14th of March that Monsieur Savarie died on the 27th of January. I am deeply moved by his death. Father Villard points out that the blank power of attorney that I sent last year in duplicate can be used by filling in the name of whomever I judge appropriate. Would you please, Sir, give me the pleasure of filling in someone you think would be good. I rely completely on your choice and on what you will have the kindness to do in regard to all that concerns our community. I cannot tell you how grateful I am for all the good services that you have rendered us. I hope that at some time business will make it necessary for me to go to France so that I can thank you fully and in person. Until then I offer up thanks to God who takes into account all the services rendered to the poor. I pray to him and ask others to pray that He will grant you everything you desire in this life and in the life to come.

All our Sisters take the liberty of offering you their most humble respects and of commending themselves to your prayers and Masses.

I have the honour …

1767, 30 August. Father Villard by Monsieur Courtemanche, and 17 October by another bearer.

Sir, I received your letter of 14th March in which you mention the death of M. Savarie on the 27th of January. I greatly mourn the loss of this gentleman both to your seminary and to our house, of which he took such great care. I thank you, Sir, for your care in giving me this news and for your kindness in claiming our papers. You ask me to send a power of attorney, but Monsieur Boisvet tells me on your behalf that Monsieur Savarie's heirs gave you my power of attorney of 1 July 1766 along with my notarized act and baptismal certificate. He says that since the power of attorney was blank there is no need to send a new one; it will be sufficient to fill in the name of whoever I judge may best serve our business interests in France. I am asking Monsieur de L'Isle-Dieu to be so kind as to make this choice; but in case he can no longer do it, I ask you, Sir, to render us this service. You know the honourable people over there while I know nothing about it.

I have learned from those to whom I gave bills of exchange that they have been cashed, which relieves me greatly. Monsieur Savarie rendered us this service before his death. Monsieur Feltz still has one for 1,000 livres payable in January 1768. The need in which I find myself has necessitated my drawing bills of exchange for 1,000 and 1,200 livres. I shall draw them on Monsieur de L'Isle-Dieu and postdate them by a month. In case he is no longer with us, would you be so good, Sir, as to cash them through the new bursar.

A bill of exchange postdated by two weeks to Madame D'Artigny for 600 livres; one for 115 livres postdated by a month to Monsieur Jean Antoine Dubois, shoemaker, at Master Camber's shoe shop, Rue Croix Baraiguin, Toulouse.

In August 1767, I wrote to Monsieur and Madame Sermonville in reply to Mademoiselle St-Michel, and to Madame Lignery asking what Monsieur Lanoue has received from Monsieur Goguette and what he still needs to receive.

A friendly letter to Monsieur and Madame Figuery.

To Monsieur Feltz in Paris.

To Madame Nouchette in Brussels.

To Monsieur Héry in La Rochelle – all conveyed by Monsieur Courtemanche, 30 August 1767.

On 17 October 1767, a reply to Father Couturier, Superior of Saint-Sulpice, in Paris, and on the same day I gave Father Mongolfier a receipt in duplicate for a bill of exchange for 7,620 livres reduced to …

1768, 25 August. To Monsieur the Abbé de L'Isle-Dieu,
by Mademoiselle Lefebvre.

I hope that this finds you in good health and that I shall again next year have the satisfaction of hearing your news, not from yourself, since it is two years that I have been deprived of that, but from Father Villard and our dear Bishop as well as Father Mongolfier. We have not had any news this year, though we daily hope for it. God grant that it arrive! We do not know whether we have a bursar or who he is, but I rely upon your usual goodness and wait with patience for you to let us know.

All my Sisters assure you of their most humble respect and commend themselves to your prayers and Masses. All together, we offer our unworthy prayers to the Lord for your preservation.

I have the honour …

1768, 25 August. To Father Villard, by Mademoiselle Lefebvre,
and 6 October, by I know not whom.

Sir, we still have had no news from France. I should think that you will have been so good as to appoint a bursar for us. I greatly need to know what state our business affairs are in in France. If we have anything, we are greatly in need of using it, but I dare not do anything until I have had some news. Nevertheless, I have drawn a bill of exchange for 753 livres, 16 sols on Monsieur de L'Isle-Dieu made out to Monsieur Ignace Gamelin and have indicated that if he is no longer with us, it should be presented to you for payment. I rely upon your charitable care and am with very deep respect …

Monsieur …

On the 7th of October, I am adding Monsieur Héry's bill of exchange for 1,000 livres and an account of what Monsieur Savarie was holding for us.

1768, 25 August. To Monsieur Feltz, by Mademoiselle Lefebvre
[Ferdinand de Feltz, surgeon].

Sir, we have not yet received your news, nor has anyone had any word from France. I only know that it was you who wrote to La Jemmerais and Monsieur Héry and to Gamelin and me, which we received in May. Since then not a ship has arrived from Europe except one that sank at Ile Rouge. Only two men were lost who, it is said, died from the cold. From the 10th of May until the 18th of July we had almost continual heavy rains. We thought that everything would be lost, but thanks to Divine Providence there is some fairly good wheat, but lots of blighted, no peas, beans, or oats, and few apples, melons, and pumpkins. We shall have to go without that this year, but we shall have bread and meat, because there is hay.

How is Madame Feltz?[17] Is she as unhappy at not seeing her friends as they are at not seeing her? All our Sisters assure her of their most humble respects, and especially Despins and I. The whole community is constantly praying for you and Madame. They are all as you left them, right up to Sister Arelle. I had the sorrow of seeing my sister Maugras[18] die on the 22nd of March after two weeks of illness and nearly constant agony, without losing either speech or consciousness. My consolation is that her death was prepared for. Poor Gamelin worries me. He is declining rapidly; he has grown so thin since my sister's death that he is hardly recognizable. We are very happy with Landriau; he has quite a large practice owing to his wisdom and prudence. There have been many sudden deaths this year. Father Chambon was the last, on the 20th of this month, Monsieur de Couagne last winter, and a number of others.

I thank you for the offer you made me with regard to Ile Saint Paul. All I have to pay for it are the papers we have in France about which I have had no news. Monsieur Héry tells me that the Crown is legally drawing up perpetual title deeds at four per cent interest. If that is agreeable to you, we could see what we could do about it in February. I believe that it will only be auctioned then. If you have the chance to inform me about what is happening at Foreign Missions with respect to us, you would be doing me a great service.

I have the honour …

25 August. Monsieur Héry, by Mademoiselle Lefebvre, and by I know not whom, 4 October.

Sir, I had the honour of your letter dated 20 March 1768. I cannot express to you the delight I have on receiving your letters telling me your news and that of your wife who is so dear to me. I beg you, Sir, to continue to give me this satisfaction and to assure Madame Héry that I as well as the whole community never forget her in our prayers. You with her and your whole family can thus share the assurance of all our respects.

It pleased the Lord to visit us in calling to Himself my sister Maugras (23 March 1768). I commend her to your prayers. My consolation is that she had a most edifying death. Poor Gamelin has been very rapidly declining for the past six months and I very much fear that he will not survive the winter.

---

17   Born Cécile Gosselin, the surgeon's second wife, married 1757.
18   Marie-Clémence, widow of Pierre Gamelin-Maugras.

Sell the recognizance that you have for the account of Sieur Baptiste Laforme, to whom we owe a like sum; what you have in interest will also be his; and as you let me know, next year he will be able to draw a bill of exchange on us.

I received a letter from Monsieur Huard dated the 28th of May 1767 and another dated the 29 of March 1768. I am waiting for letters from Paris in order to reply to him. If our affairs there are in order, I will draw a bill of exchange for everything that is owing to the Charly heirs on the seigneury of Châteauguay; if not, I shall try at least to pay the interest on the deed and part of the arrears. He had sent his power of attorney to poor Chenneville who died at the end of March. Also, on the 19th of that month, we lost by sudden death Monsieur Chambon, aged 60 years, 5 months. He completely entered his second childhood more than a year ago. Monsieur René de Couagne also died a sudden death in February, also Marien Dulude and a number of others whom I cannot recall at the moment.

I am writing at the same time a reply to Monsieur Débarasse on 27 August 1768; to Madame Lignery, 27 August 1768; to Mademoiselle St-Michel, 27 August 1768; early to Madame Sermonville, 27 August 1768. On the 8th of October, to Monsieur Héry, Monsieur Feltz, Monsieur Huard, and Father Villard.

THE ACCOUNT OF MONSIEUR SAVARIE received in the year 1766, sent to Father Villard, 4 October 1768.

He drew 9,000 livres on the City of Paris for a deed; it should have been reimbursed to us by the bank. I had asked Monsieur Savarie to give 6,000 livres to Monsieur Lanoue and 2,500 livres to Monsieur Feltz. I know that that has been paid. He indicated to me that he hoped to collect the interest for that year,

yielding the sum of . . . . 450 livres			
Remainder . . . . 500 livres			
He indicates that there remains to him at the			
closing of the account he is sending me. . . . . 1,307 livres	5 sols	7 deniers	
The interest from the Hôtel de Ville . . . . . 786 livres	14 sols		
A recognizance of 1,000 livres on the India Company . . 50 livres			
3 other coupons on the same Company,			
yielding 120 livres in interest . . . . . 120 livres			
For interest on all our bills of exchange, documents,			
and draft notes . . . . . 1,492 livres	18 sols	5 deniers	
To be drawn in 1767 . . . . . 4,206 livres	18 sols		
To be drawn in 1768 . . . . . 2,449 livres	12 sols	5 deniers	
6,656 livres	**10 sols**	**5 deniers**	

Whereupon to draw in 1766 to pay in
1767 to Monsieur Feltz . . . . . 1,000 livres
To Monsieur Savarie for his trouble and care 100

To Madame D'Artigny, that of 1,675
In 1767 for the same 600
To Dubois the shoemaker 115
To Monsieur Feltz........................... 1,000
                                          _____
                                           4,490 livres

Besides, interest on 9,000 livres .... 2,166 livres   10 sols   5 deniers
Remainder 500
                                          _____
                                           2,666 livres   **10 sols**   **5 deniers**

To have drawn in 1768 for Mademoiselle Noyelle ... 753 livres   16 sols
For Monsieur Héry 1,000
2 years' pension to the Brother................. 600
                                          _____
                                           2,353 livres   **16 sols**

                              Balance **312 livres**   **14 sols**   **5 deniers**

In 1765 I sent a bill of exchange that Monsieur Savarie told me Monsieur de Larochette had informed him would have to wait until something was decided about the Canadian papers being held by subjects of the King of England. There is also a bill of exchange of 1,050 livres drawn on Madame Péan by Monsieur Daine, the executor of Madame Laronde's will, which Monsieur de L'Isle-Dieu tells me will have to be contested since Madame Péan refused to acquit it.

1768, 17 October. Monsieur de L'Isle-Dieu, by the last ships.

Sir and very dear Father, I learn from Father Villard's letter of the 24th of March 1768, which I received on the 8th of October, that you have chosen Monsieur Maury as our bursar. He is an honest and worthy man who is known to a number of people in this country. This is again proof of your kindness to us and of our gratitude to you. I am sending this note to thank you and to ask you to continue that of which we have great need, for our affairs are not going well: to have lost what we lost in France and to have endured a fire that plunged us into debts of which we would never be free without the charity we have received from the collections made in London, which have somewhat lightened our burden. Providence is wonderful, it has means we cannot understand to relieve those who trust in it, it provides for everything, in it is my trust.

All my Sisters offer you their most humble respects and commend themselves to your prayers and offerings of the Holy Sacrifice of the Mass.

I have the honour ...

1768, 17 October. Monsieur Maury.

I have learned with real pleasure that you have agreed to take on the responsibility of our business affairs, and I am more than delighted to be assured by upright people in this country that they could not have fallen into better hands. We are under an obligation to Monsieur de L'Isle-Dieu who has always taken care to choose everything that would be best for us. I have not had the consolation of receiving any letters from him this year, nor from you. I was hoping for one, but it may be that it got lost. On the 8th of this month, I received one from Father Villard who related to me what I have just said. I wrote to them both on the 25th of August and then to Father Villard on the 6th of October, wherein I sent him an account of what we had with Monsieur Savarie, of which a copy is enclosed.

Knowing nothing about a bursar, I drew two bills of exchange on Monsieur de L'Isle-Dieu together amounting to 1,753 livres, 16 sols.

I have the honour of being respectfully …

1769.

Your Excellency, I received your letter and the one your wrote to my son. I have not sent him the latter, in the first place because of an accident that befell him on the 2nd of February. In showing out a visitor, he fell at his door and broke his left arm at four finger breadths from the shoulder. He has enough with this misfortune for the present. I got this news on Saturday and left Sunday to go see him. I found he was doing well enough – no fever and no swelling. I came back Thursday and promised to send him someone to look after him. Mademoiselle Legardeur went with one of our Sisters and they are still there.

Secondly, it seems to me that Your Excellency may have forgotten the account that I gave him of this affair; and it may be necessary for You to familiarize yourself with it before the letter is transmitted to him. When he undertook to build his church, he asked me to advance to him and to his fabrique what would be needed. I promised to help him all I could out of that which belonged to the poor since I myself have nothing. When all was finished, I told him that I did not think that either he or his fabrique were in a situation to be able to pay and that he had only to ask for the credit he needed and to conclude and sign the accounts. He told me yes but did not do it. Much later he wrote to me and informed me that he had sent his papers to Father Mongolfier and for me to approve that he arrange these accounts. He told me that I had not given him an account of the inheritance from his father nor of that from his grandmother. I took my inventory, my papers, and all my accounts to the Seminary; and Father Mongolfier after having examined everything, informed him that his father had left nothing and that I am his grandmother's heir and that he could lay claim to nothing of this inheritance until after my death. He was not happy with this decision. He asked that Monsieur Ignace Gamelin and Monsieur Héry bring this business to a conclusion and that he would abide by whatever they decided. When that was accomplished, he no longer wanted to have anything to do with it. Still, I have more to complain about than he does. On this reckoning, my son owes three thousand one hundred and forty-one livres, 11 sols, 4 deniers in cash money, and on that of the fabrique one thousand five hundred and seventy livres for supplies delivered in 1757 and four thousand eight hundred and forty-five, 7 sols, 6 deniers in draft notes. There are many things that ought to be said that would take too long to write.

I have the honour of being with a …

1769, in the month of July, by a ship which is supposed to depart on the 20th, to Monsieur the Abbé de L'Isle-Dieu.

Sir, I received yours on the 15th of November when there was no longer an occasion to reply. It was dated the 12th of April. I truly do not know, most dear Father, what words to use to express my gratitude. You have taken your kindnesses to a level at which there is no comparison. God alone can recompense such care. He indeed will be your recompense, and I pray to him every day, along with all our Sisters who, like me, offer you their most humble thanks.

The best news that I could hear this year is that God has preserved you, as Father Villard tells me in his letter of the 16th of April. I had hoped to have a letter from you and from Monsieur Maury by Monsieur Berthelotte, who had promised to ask you for one, but he arrived at the end of May bearing nothing for me.

Father Mongolfier gave me a most glowing testimony of Monsieur Maury, but the choice you made for us is more than sufficient to convince me that he is all we could desire. I pray to the Lord that He will preserve him for many years and that we shall not have the misfortune of losing him as quickly as we have the others. He has rendered me a most precise and well-ordered account of what he received from the heirs of Monsieur Savarie.

I fear that Monsieur Maury may receive my letter too late to draw up the contracts for the recognizances that remain for our community; but I imagine that since that was your counsel, you will have followed it and it is done. I should hardly hope to imagine that there might be some indemnity from the Court. They say it is very hard. It has done us a great wrong, may God forgive it.

I am very happy that you have remitted the 120 livres in errors to the heirs of poor Monsieur de Paris, but I should like you to forget about the 500 livres you speak of and, I believe, have spoken of several times before. I have already written to Madame Péan about the bill of exchange for 1,050 livres drawn on her that was paid in hard cash to Madame Laronde. She has not replied. She has a daughter who is a nun in France and I am going to write to her so that this business can be brought to a conclusion.

As for the previous contract relating to me, Monsieur Maury will be so good as to work on it. I had sent all the necessary documents to Monsieur de Paris. I should think his heirs would have passed them on to Monsieur Savarie unless they were lost. Monsieur Maury will no doubt have found them among the others.

All of this is a great deal of trouble for you at your age, most dear Father. Still, may the Lord grant you health like that of a lady boarder here, the widow of Monsieur Robino de Portneuf, who is more than 81 years old and who fasts and abstains on all the prescribed days and who works like us for the welfare of the poor although she pays her own board. She is charming in both her great piety and in her good humour. Every day I wish and pray to the Lord that He will give you like health.

All our Sisters assure you of their most humble respects and commend themselves always to your prayers and Masses.

I have the honour of being …

1769, 9 July. To Madame La Ronde-St-Elzéar, Religious of the General Hospital in Quebec City, at present at the Hôtel-Dieu of Loche.

Madame, as you know, Monsieur Daine gave me a bill of exchange in the amount of 1,050 livres drawn on Madame Péan that is owing to our Hospital for the illness and funeral expenses of your dear mother. Please be informed by the present, if you have not already been notified, that this bill of exchange has not been acquitted, and this has caused us a great deal of inconvenience. I implore you, Madame, to see to having us paid, if not by Madame Péan, then by someone else. You would be rendering us a very great service for we are in extreme need. If you would be so good as to remit everything that is owing to us on this bill of exchange to Monsieur Maury, lawyer in the Parlement of Paris and business agent of the Grand Seminaire of Saint-Sulpice, Rue Pot de Fer, Paris, or to his office at the Grand Seminaire of Saint-Sulpice. I have had the honour of writing to Madame Péan beseeching her to pay me this money. She has not given me the honour of replying. I implore you, Madame, to attend to this matter. It is a blessing that she asks of you who has the honour of being with very deep respect …

1769, 8 July. Monsieur Maury.

Sir, I received the account that you sent of the documents and articles you received from the heirs of Monsieur Savarie. I could not notify you that I received it since it arrived in November when there was no further opportunity to reply. I had the honour of writing to you in October having learned from Father Villard that you wished to take responsibility for our business affairs. I hoped to have your letters by early spring. Monsieur Berthelotte promised me to ask you for them, but he arrived at the end of May without anything for me. I fear that you may be confused by our coupons and afraid to draw contracts on them, although that is what would be most helpful to us for we have already lost nearly half of what we could get for them. I am still hoping for a letter from you and from Monsieur de L'Isle-Dieu. When I know what we have, I shall draw some bills of exchange on you. If I have not had a letter from you, I shall still draw them for I am in need.

I wrote two years ago to Madame Péan concerning the bill of exchange for 1,050 livres that she owes. She has not replied. I have written to the daughter of the lady for whom this debt was incurred. I was told that she is at the Hôtel Dieu in Loche. Could you find out from Monsieur the Abbé de la Corne where she is and pass on my letter to her so that she can persuade Madame Péan to pay. If you have already done this, please burn my letter.

I am also sending you a letter for Monsieur Goguette in La Rochelle. Would you please send it to him as soon as possible. It is so that he can remit the recognizances that he has for us amounting to 499 livres, 10 sols that derive from a bill of exchange of 1757 for 999 livres, 10 sols drawn in the name of Mademoiselle Lanoue. I expected her to remit it to her brother, but I see from our accounts that she has not done so.

I am also sending a letter from Madame the Widow Lobinois to Monsieur Benoit, formerly a captain in this country, who owes her 1,550 livres in coupons and interest for one or two years, an amount that he owes the Hospital and that she will make over to us. This is all that I have for you for the present.

I have the honour of being with very deep respect …

1769, 8 July. To Monsieur Goguet.

Sir, I see from an account rendered to me of the business affairs in Paris of our Hospital that Monsieur Lanoue was paid the bill of exchange that I drew on you and that, consequently, the bill of exchange for 999 livres drawn in the name of Mademoiselle Lanoue is still being held by you. You remitted to Monsieur Lemoine the yield of the bill of exchange for 1,693 livres in the name of Monsieur Ménard and of the bill of exchange of 500 livres in the name of Mademoiselle Legardeur. I am happy with that and expect that you gave the third to Monsieur de Lanoue, to whom I gave one drawn on you for a larger amount. What constituted this mistake is that Mademoiselle de Lanoue kept and endorsed these bills of exchange "Amount received from us" rather than "Amount received from the bills of Madame Youville." I hope that this is a mistake and that you will be good enough to correct it. I am sending you the fourth letter that is left with me and the one that you wrote in 176? [sic] to notify receipt by Mademoiselle Lanoue. I am sorry to disturb you about this after the pains you have taken over the purchases that you have made free of charge for this Hospital and for which I owe you all imaginable thanks. I implore you to be convinced of this and to believe me to be with very deep respect.

I forgot to ask if you have the shares or money and interest from this bill of exchange. Would you be so good as to remit them to Monsieur Maury, lawyer in the Parlement of Paris and business agent for the Grand Seminaire of Saint-Sulpice, Rue Pot de Fer, Paris.

1769, 20 September. To Monsieur Maury.

Sir, I had the honour of receiving at the beginning of August your letter dated the 13th of March 1769. I also received the account which you enclosed with it wherein I see that I owe you one thousand nine hundred and eighty-one livres, eight sols, six deniers. I am not going to worry about this since you have told me, but I fear that the King may not have paid the interest on the recognizances of 1768 and 1769, which would put me very much in arrears because before hearing from you I gave a bill of exchange for two thousand livres to Father Montgolfier. He, however, promised me to wait until you had the funds to pay it.

I had the honour of writing to you on the 8th of July and I sent you a letter for Monsieur Goguet, the treasurer in France, at La Rochelle. In case you have not received my previous letter, I shall repeat that I sent one for Madame St-Elzéar, the daughter of Madame Laronde. Monsieur the Abbé Lacorne will give you her address. I imagine, however, from what you have written me that you will have no need of that. Madame Péan will yield to your just pursuit.

Monsieur Benoit informs me that following the orders of Madame Lobinois he has remitted what he had from her, without saying to whom, how much or when. If it was to you, no doubt it was after your letter was written. Please let me know about this in your next letter. Would you also be so kind as to let me know whether I should send our accounts or the copy approved and signed by the Community to you as I did to Monsieur Savary. I do not see anywhere that you have charged anything for your honoraria. Please do so; that will in nowise lessen my gratitude for your care. I pray the Lord to give you long life and perfect health.

Monsieur the Abbé de L'Isle-Dieu tells me that he owes you 265 livres. If he gives them to you, please give him a receipt, as he expects it.

I have the honour …

On the 18th of September, I replied in duplicate to Monsieur Héry and at the same time sent a single letter to Monsieur and Madame Figuery. On the 21st, I likewise sent single letters to Madame Sermonville, Madame Ligneris, and Monsieur Feltz.

1769, 21 September. Monsieur the Abbé de L'Isle-Dieu.

Sir and very dear Father, I had the honour of receiving your letter dated the 22nd of March. It was again filled with all your care and kindness, for which I thank you. That is all I can do in return for your so great and so often repeated services.

I had the honour of writing to you on the 20th of July. I hope that you got that letter. In it I told you that those who know Monsieur Maury gave him a very good recommendation and that your choice of him inclines me to think that everything will be for the best. I have told him that I expect him to be paid and that he should charge what he thinks appropriate. If he is hesitant to do so, be kind enough to fix an amount that you think appropriate. I should be most grateful to you for that.

Since you absolutely insist upon paying the 500 livres by giving to Monsieur Maury the remaining 265 livres, he will give you a receipt, as you like.

All my Sisters assure you of their most humble respects. They commend themselves to your holy prayers, as do I who am most respectfully yours.

I commend to your prayers one of our Sisters, who is 42 years old, and a novice (Sister Bonnet) who is ready to make her profession in her twentieth year.

1769, 22 September. To His Excellency, the Bishop of Quebec.

Forgive me if I am disturbing you for things that are perhaps useless; but if it is do-able, you will do it and if not, not. In either case I shall be content. This is what it is about. There remains with the committee from the charitable donation received from London for the first fire 7 or 8 thousand livres being held by the distributors. I am convinced that a word from Monsieur the Governor would result in their being remitted to those whom he judges appropriate. If it is possible, could Your Excellency speak to him on behalf of our Hospital, letting him know that we still owe 7 thousand livres on the money we had to borrow in order to rebuild and that we lack many necessary things, especially linen. There is a great deal of good we could do if we had anything. Every day poor people come who are truly in need. We do not have any more room to accommodate them, and it is with a heavy heart that I turn them away, but I have to do so. I have been most fortunate in what we have received from these funds: we have had in three instalments almost 20 thousand livres, but it takes so much for such large buildings. Had I known where I could get as much without stealing it, I could quickly have erected a building that would accommodate close to two hundred, but I have nothing. God in his goodness will have to be content with my good will.

I have the honour of being …

1770, 18 June. To Mr. Carleton, the Governor General.

Sir, I marvel that Divine Providence inspired you to show your charity to our Hospital in its need by sending twenty-five quarter-pounds of lard. For it, I offer you my most humble thanks. I would have never dared ask anything of you since I know that you have to give much to various poor people whose need is great. All of us in this house will offer our unworthy prayers to the Lord for your preservation, the success of your undertakings, and a good voyage.

I have the honour of being …

1770, 21 September. Monsieur Maury.

Sir, I had the honour of receiving your letter dated the 4th of April 1770 along with the list of your accounts in duplicate, one of which was referred to and settled by Monsieur the Abbé de L'Isle-Dieu. I am sending back to you one of them signed by my Sister Councillors and myself; the other I am keeping for my use should occasion arise.

There was quite a furore here when I received your letters relating that the interest on Canadian papers converted into bills had been reduced to two and a half per cent. No one in this country could believe it. In fact, we had been confused with those who did great wrong to the King of France, and all the communities of this country were victims of it, as well as many honourable people who were ruined. The innocent suffer for the guilty.

I am quite delighted that Monsieur Goguette has remitted to you the yield from the bill of exchange drawn in the name of Mademoiselle Lanoue. I am sending you what Madame the Widow Lobinois made over to us according to the model that you sent me.

I shall be quite delighted if you are able to collect what Madame Péan owes for Madame Laronde. We advanced hard cash for this lady to care for her during six and a half months of illness, to feed her, and to give her honourable burial, as was right. She told us that Madame Péan had from her 8,000 gold livres in hand and 41,000 livres in bills of exchange. The money was due to us nine years ago this past April. It is money of which we have had need during that time and of which we have been deprived for caring for her. She has left here a Gentleman with a family who is not in a comfortable situation and could use the money; the other two heirs are in France and, I believe, there is one in Mississippi.

I thank you for the news of Monsieur the Abbé de L'Isle-Dieu. He has done the impossible for our community. He has rendered us services that only he was capable of and that we shall never forget. We are most concerned for his preservation, which we ask of God daily.

We were very much moved by the loss that the Seminary of Saint-Sulpice suffered in Father Couturier. All of the Priests of the Seminary here have felt it greatly. We here shall not forget him in our unworthy prayers.

My children have a capital fund on the Hôtel de Ville with arrears for thirty years. A number of times I have sent the necessary papers to realize it. In 1752 or '53, Monsieur de L'Isle-Dieu told me that they had only to send their powers of attorney and they could collect 1,800 livres in arrears. They did not send them and it remained there. All these papers have remained either with the heirs of Monsieur de Paris or those of Monsieur Savary. Could you please find out, Sir, whether it is possible to recover them. The amount must be 2,400 livres.

I am asking you to pay Father Mongolfier a bill of exchange for 2,000 livres that I drew on you. I do not think that he will press you for it.

I am also asking you to find out from the Seminary of Saint-Sulpice about some church furnishings that we have there, for which I am enclosing a memorandum. Could you see how they are; and if you can find some opportunity without running any risk, even though it should be expensive, could you have them sent to me? I should be most obliged.

I have the honour of being ...

MEMORANDUM OF THE EFFECTS that the General Hospital of Montreal has at the Seminary of Saint-Sulpice in Paris and which are, I believe, being kept by Monsieur Joubert. They were given to the said Hospital by the late Father Normant, Superior of the Seminary of Saint-Sulpice in Montreal.

Namely:

  50 pounds of white wax
  two batiste albs trimmed with lace
  two ribbon cinctures
  one chalice with paten
  two silver cruets with plate
  one silver gilt monstrance
  one silver thurible with boat
  six hatched silver candlesticks with crucifix
  two of the same for acolytes

1770, 22 September. To Monsieur the Abbé de L'Isle-Dieu.

Sir, my very dear Father, your remembrances are infinitely dear to me and I believe that you should take pride in them as much as you can. They are sincere – for 23 years you have not ceased to give proof of that. Like me, this whole community is pervaded by a gratitude that my pen is not capable of expressing. We do not cease to offer the Lord our unworthy prayers that He may deign to supplement our weakness. He has shown so much goodness and mercy to us that I dare to believe that our desires will be granted.

We are 18 Sisters here, all unwell, who are directing a house where there are 170 people to feed and nearly all of them to support. There is very little income, most of which is derived from our work that has fallen in worth by two-thirds since we have been under the English. We are always on the verge of lack, and yet we lack no more, at least not for the necessities. I marvel each day at Divine Providence that desires to make use of such poor subjects to do a little good.

I hope that God will preserve you – I pray every day that He will do so – and all my Sisters assure you of their most humble respects and commend themselves to your prayers and Masses.

I have the honour of being with very deep respect …

Sir, my very dear Father, I forgot to tell you how delighted we are with the care and organizing activities of Monsieur Maury. I believe that you procured for us the very best in Paris. I pray God that He will preserve him.

1770, 22 September. Monsieur Feltz.

Sir, I had the honour of receiving your letters. In the first you say that you had not received mine and you thought I had forgotten you. No, Sir, I will never forget friends from whom I have received innumerable kindnesses and so many benefits, and I admit to you that your absence and that of your Wife weigh upon me daily. We speak often of you both. I am most delighted with the satisfaction which Monsieur Doire has expressed to you. I believe that his dear mother is quite content. He lost his godmother, Madame Latour, in the month of January. She left quite a lot to her heirs. Poor Fleurimont[19] will not be able to enjoy it for long. He is suffering from an illness of the chest and will hardly, I think, live till the end of the year. He is living in a new house that he had built on the land of Monsieur Silvain, which adjoined yours. It belonged to La Brocquery who sold it to him.

Mademoiselle Nouchette has married a Monsieur Augustin Chaboyer. He is the one who got married in Detroit, whose wife died childless two or three years ago.

---

19   Pierre-Philippe de Noyelles, Sieur de Fleurimont.

He is a good lad who knows how to work. It is said that he has 24 thousand livres. Fear of the English makes us give them to the first who asks for them.

I am sending you a letter for Madame de Lignery. Please be so kind as to tell her of the death of her daughter, Madame Macailye [Mackay], before giving it to her. She died on the 13th of this month, and Madame de Cuisy the younger[20] died at the beginning of April. The former died after suffering for seven or eight months from an inflammation of the lungs; the latter after four months of whooping cough. Poor [Ignace] Gamelin is still in the saddest sort of state. He is deaf, mute, and almost blind. Almost all of his body is paralysed. My sister and Lajemmerais have been dragging him about during most of the day; and a man, with another from here, have been doing so every night for nearly six months. For almost two years he has been in this condition. Madame Benac[21] gave birth yesterday in her seventh month to a daughter who died just after being baptised. I believe she injured herself helping with her father.

Monsieur Landriault always helps our Hospital. He has a number of good houses in the city and is very wise and careful. I thank you for the trouble you went to to get the payment from Madame Laronde.

Some news is that Madame Céloron[22] has become a Grey Nun. She has worn the habit for six months now. She possesses an uncommon virtue.

Our good King of France will retain everything in the end. I would not regret it if we could return to him, as some people would sometimes have us believe.

All our Sisters and the Ladies whom you know assure both you and Madame Feltz of their respects.

1770, 23 September. To Madame de Lignery.

Madame, I wish I had some happy news for you; but on the contrary, I have something very sad to report, the death of your dear daughter, Madame Macailye [Mackay], on the 13th of this month at noon. Our consolation is that she bore all with an heroic patience, that she received all the sacraments, and that it was she herself who asked for Extreme Unction, after which she still wished to make a general confession. Her husband and his brother did everything they could to see that she lacked for nothing, either in a spiritual or a temporal way. They, as well as Monsieur de Lignery, are in a distress that I cannot depict for you. Her husband and brother

---

20   Born Madeleine de Joncaire, wife of Louis-Gordien d'Ailleboust de Cuisy, died 10 April 1770.

21   Her niece, Louise Gamelin, the wife of Joseph Porlier Benac.

22   Born Catherine Eurry de La Pérelle, the widow of Pierre-Joseph de Céloron, Sieur de Blainville, Knight of Saint Louis. She was 47 years old when she entered the religious life. She was the last sister professed by Mother d'Youville and, coincidentally, like the foundress she was a widow.

are leaving shortly for London to organize their affairs. The two children[23] are in the care of their uncle, so do not be worried about them. They are totally loveable. But to return to our dear departed. It was in February, I believe, that she, scarcely in good health, gave birth to a boy of about two months. She had been suffering since that time and declined rapidly from mid-April. Her husband sometimes took her about in an open carriage so that she could get some fresh air. Madame de Bayouville did not leave her side from that time, and from May until August she was at Laprairie where she died. She always needed women to watch over her at night, and she found them here. I sent her the elderly Champigny, who is living here, to care for her at Laprairie. She has not yet returned. Monsieur Macailye [Mackay] begged me to leave her with him for a few days, which I gladly did. He gave her beautiful gown to the church of Laprairie.

We have also lost Madame de Cuisy[24] after four months of sickness that began with whooping cough and degenerated into an inflammation of the lungs. She had an edifying death. She has left behind two daughters who are not pretty, but who are quite intelligent. She asked her husband and her father-in-law and mother to have them brought up here when they are a little older. If I live, I shall take them in.

Since I last wrote to you I have no idea where Madame Lamilitier is or what has become of her. For a while she was at Madame de Joncaire's. The latter is just as you left her; on the whole, she is doing well. As for Monsieur Lamilitier, I am told that he is with Normant, the seigneur of Arpentigny, waiting for the inheritance from his grandmother.

Monsieur Chaber [Daniel de Joncaire, Sieur de Chabert et de Clausone] is much better; his wife is pregnant. They have left their last daughter with the Sisters of Pointe-aux-Trembles. Madame Sainte-Radegonde had sent her to me on New Year's Day covered with scabs, which she had had for four years. I got her healed and kept her until the beginning of August. Then her father asked for her, as did her grandmother, Madame la Morandière,[25] who has become Madame Contrecoeur.

I received your letter of the month of September and immediately passed on that of Monsieur Lacoste. He told me that he had written to you and sent you a power of attorney for you to be paid.

Mademoiselle Lanoue is doing well this year. She sends you and her brother all good wishes. Please also give him mine. There is no way for him to be happy with what the King has caused him to lose, nor can we.

---

23   Jean, born in Montreal, 10 June 1765, and Marie-Anne Françoise, born in London, England, in 1767.

24   Born Madeleine de Joncaire, wife of Louis-Gordien d'Ailleboust de Cuisy.

25   Born Marguerite Hingue de Puygibault, widow of Etienne Rocbert de la Morandière, she married Charles-Claude-Pierre Pécaudy de Contrecoeur in Montreal, 9 September 1768.

All our Sisters and the Ladies of your acquaintance assure you of their respects and offer you their condolences. Every good thing from me to your dear children, both the boys and the girls, when you write to them. My children send you their respects and also to Monsieur and Madame d'Hauterive, whom I would also ask to receive mine. If you hear anything from Monsieur Sabrevois and Monsieur and Madame Sermonville, please give them the same. If you are writing to me, please address your letters to Monsieur Maury.

I am delighted that Mademoiselle St-Michel is doing well – so much the better for her. I had not heard anything of her since she arrived in France. She wrote me in December. I have written her three times since, but I shall not do so again. The Deschambault family has been hurt by her indifference. Madame de Longueuil[26] married Monsieur Grande [the Honourable William Grant] on the 9th of September. She left with him on the 10th to live with him in Quebec City. Longueuil, who left here at the end of November, is leaving this week to join her. Monsieur Deschambault has bought the château of Vaudreuil for 18,500 livres and plans to restore it. Monsieur Duplessis is as usual and Mademoiselle Nanette is up and down. They complain much about not receiving any letters from their brother and sister. They write every year and this year have sent these letters with Monsieur Deschambault. Monsieur de Longueuil married Madame de Bonne.[27] Monsieur and Madame de Beaujeu and her daughters and a little boy she has had since are at Ile aux Noix. Mademoiselle Nouchette[28] has married Augustin Chaboyer. Madame Latour died. Fleurimont had a large inheritance of between 24 and 26 thousand from her, but he is very ill with what appears to be an inflammation of the lungs. If you hear from Madame de Noyelle or Monsieur and Madame Lacolombière,[29] please give them my greetings.

1770, 24 September. Father Villard, Superior of Foreign Missions.

Sir, even though I have not had the honour of receiving any letters from you this year, please allow me to assure you of my most humble respects. The Sisters of the Hôtel Dieu have been so kind as to let me know they have had news from you and that they were instructed to pass on your compliments, for which I thank you

---

26 Marie-Anne-Catherine Fleury d'Eschambault, widow of Charles-Jacques Le Moyne, third Baron de Longueuil.

27 Joseph-Dominique-Emmanuel Le Moyne de Longueuil married Louise Prud'homme, widow of Louis de Bonne, Knight of Saint Louis, who was killed during the siege of Quebec City in 1760.

28 Daughter of the late Joseph Nouchet and Catherine Foucault. She was living at the General Hospital where the marriage contract was signed.

29 Antoine de La Corne, Sieur de La Colombière, mainly known by the latter name, had married Marguerite Petit de Livilliers, daughter of Madeleine Gaultier de Varennes.

kindly. All our Sisters assure you of their most humble respects. They commend themselves to your prayers and Masses, as do I who am most respectfully yours …

1770, 24 September. Monsieur Héry.

I had the honour of receiving your letter dated the 2nd of April. It brings us ever new gratification. It was necessary to read your letter to the whole Community gathered together so that they could hear news of your whole family who will always be most dear to us through attachment and gratitude. No, Sir, this house will never forget your generosity. It is inscribed in so many of our records that those who come after us will know the good you have done for us. Everyday we commend you and your family to the Eternal Father. All of us and all our Ladies assure Madame Héry of our regards. I am eager to hear about Charlot. Is he studying or has he gone into business? Has Lisette grown up to be as pretty as ever? In spirit I often travel to your home, along with Sister Despins who is not in the best of health. Poor Gamelin is still in the saddest sort of condition. I do not know how my sister and poor Lajemmerais are bearing it, yet they are doing what they have to. Madame Benac gave birth on the 21st to a daughter who died just after being baptised. She has been very ill, but she is a little better today.

I have the honour of being …

Permit me to ask you, Sir, if you would be so good as to offer to the Charly heirs to whom our Hospital owes the debt of Monsieur Aliesse for Mademoiselle Lanoue – that is to say, what it owes to Madame Portneuf – half of a deed for 5,000 livres, or 2,500 livres.

Carried forward . . . . 2,500 livres
In August 1761, Mademoiselle Lanoue was ordered
to pay 5 years' interest, amounting to . . . . 625 livres
From 1761 until 1774, that is, 13 years,
Monsieur Aliesse is obliged to pay . . . . 1,625 livres
                                     4,750 livres

Monsieur Aliesse owes Madame Portneuf . . . . 3,554 livres   16 sols
And I wish to have them paid from our funds in Paris . . . . 1,195 livres   4 sols.

It will be easy for me to organize matters here with Madame Portneuf and I should be very happy to have the satisfaction of paying this amount. You know everything that the King of France has caused us to lose. Here we have nothing to do, no more work as in the old days. There are many more poor whom we very much would like to help, but the means are lacking. Had we not been relieved by the charitable donations from London, as indeed we were, having had in three years close to 18,000 livres, we would never have been able to revive ourselves after our fire. We have rebuilt as good as it was before, but there are no pictures in the church, not even a sign that there will ever be any. It will be a long time before we have as much linen as we need for the poor and for ourselves. Blessed be God that everything will work out as He wills.

From the 16th of October, 1770. I forgot to tell you that the Charly heirs must deduct a receipt of 350 livres that Madame Lanoue gave to Madame Francheville in 1763, and a like sum credited to the account of the Poulain heirs in 1762. That deducted, the bill of exchange I am sending will be for only 845 livres, 4 sols. I also forgot to tell you that Madame Céloron has become a Grey Nun. She has worn the habit for six months now. She is not young but she is good.

1771, September. To Madame Ligneris, by Madame Beaujeu, with copy.

Madame, I am very much surprised that you have not received my letters from last year. I had enclosed the last with that to Monsieur Feltz so that he could let you know beforehand of the death of Madame Macailye [Mackay]. If the cost of sending letters were not so great, I would send you the copy. I know that Monsieur de Ligneris also wrote to you.

You will have heard that the Messieurs Macailye went to London in June. It is said that their affairs are in a very bad state and that they owe much. Nevertheless, your son-in-law told me that he hoped to arrange things and that he had something to sell that would settle the debt. He did not reckon at that time on being able to go to France and he imagined that he would be coming back here during the course of the winter. His two children are quite lovely. He left them with his sister-in-law who is taking good care of them and bringing them up well. The boy is going to the French school. Monsieur de Ligneris would like to get Nanette to go to the Sisters' in Laprairie. She could eat with him and provide some company. But he is going to have difficulty; she is very much attached to her aunt and to Madame Bayouville, whom she calls "Balais". I told you last year of the death of Madame de Cuisy.[30] I am letting you know this year of her husband's marriage to the elder Chêneville daughter at the beginning of May. She seems to love the little ones very much.

It is my sad duty to tell you of the death of Madame de Joncaire[31] at the end of June and of that of Monsieur Chabert (Daniel de Joncaire, Sieur de Chabert et de

---

30   Louis-Gordien Dailleboust de Cuisy married Marie-Josette Chenneville on 15 April 1771.

31   Madeleine Le Gay, wife of Louis-Thomas de Joncaire, died at Repentigny, 22 June 1771.

Clausone) in Detroit at about the same time. Madame de Joncaire had been ill for about 6 weeks. Father Petit, the parish priest since the death of Father Dayebour (the Abbé Philippe D'ailleboust des Musseaux), was there and paid her frequent visits. She seemed to be happy to see him. She received all the sacraments. Ten or twelve days before her death, a fire broke out in her attic. She lost almost all her furniture and a good deal of wheat that was in the attic. She made her will. I have heard that she left Madame Lamilitier all her personal effects and furniture, not counting what she had given her before. Madame Lamilitier had been at York for almost a year, but she came back quite quickly. Monsieur Labbé is to be paid the note owing to him, and the rest will go to Monsieur Chabert.

Mademoiselle Lanoue is doing well. She sends untold greetings to her brother. Both she and I kiss your dear children, both the boys and the girls. Please pass on my greetings to Monsieur and Madame d'Hauterive. All our Sisters and the Ladies whom you know assure you of their respects. I commend to your prayers my niece Bleury[32] who died at the end of October 1770. Her brother, a priest at our Seminary, is mortally ill of dropsy.

The last of Monsieur St Luc's daughters, who married St Georges, also died.

I have the honour …

1771, 21 September. To Monsieur the Abbé de L'Isle-Dieu.

Sir, my very dear Father, I at last had the honour of receiving on the 15th of the present month your letter dated the 15th of April. I was troubled and greatly worried about its failure to arrive, but at last it has pleased God to relieve me by letting me hear from you yourself that you are doing quite well. I thank Him for it and implore Him to preserve you for many more years. All our Sisters and all those who are in this Hospital do likewise. We ask of the wholly good God to pour down upon you His blessings both in this world and in the world to come. I also received the letter of Monsieur Maury and his accounts, which are quite fair. Oh well, I am going to sign them and have them signed by the officers. I hope that he will disentangle the account that belongs to me. I am sending him some new burdens. I am not worried about what I owe him because I hope he will lose nothing on the advances he has made us. I am afraid that he is going to have to advance us something again this year. I was unable to avoid drawing 1,917 livres, 3 sols on him. He charged me the 265 livres he received from you. If Madame Péan pays and he collects something on the papers I sent him, he will be able to pay me back. Blessed be God! Divine Providence

---

32   Marie-Renée Gamelin-Maugras, daughter of her sister Clémence. She had married Jean Sabrevois de Bleury. Her brother, Pierre-Mathieu Gamelin-Maugras, a Sulpician, died on 12 November 1771.

provides for everything; all my trust is in It. Do not forget us in your prayers and Masses.

I have the honour …

1771, 23 September. Monsieur the Superior of Saint-Sulpice.

Our loss of Monsieur the Abbé Couturier and the pain that we felt have not been without consolation since he has been so worthily replaced. Let me dare to ask you, Father, to remember him through the kindnesses with which he so willingly honoured our house. I ask this blessing of you as well as that of your believing me to be with very deep respect,

Father …

1771, 21 September. Monsieur Maury.

Sir, on the 15th of the present month I received your letter dated the 15th of April along with your accounts. I am returning to you the copy signed by the officers. I see that I owe you 998 livres, 2 sols, 8 deniers. I am much obliged to you for the kindness you have shown in making us these advances. Unfortunately, I am afraid that you will have to advance us some more for this year. Before I received your letter, necessity caused me to draw 1,917 livres, 3 sols on you: a draft to Monsieur Cuisy in the amount of 1,200 livres and two to Madame the Widow Gamelin for 1,335 livres together. The latter 1,335 livres were postdated by two weeks. Then there was for the month of January 1772 a draft to Monsieur Jacquelin, merchant of La Rochelle, in the amount of 582 livres, 3 sols. I fear that I am overburdening you; if I had got your letter earlier, I would have tried to expend less.

As you will see, I am sending you a donation that Madame the Widow Duplessis-Faber made to the Hospital. Her lady daughters have drawn it on Monsieur Doutrolo who is their agent. I am sending you his address so that you can find out whether the mother does not have something, as do the children. Indeed, I think that the children ought to be supporting the mother. If there is something, would you please collect it. For five and a half years she and her eldest daughter have been living at the expense of the Hospital.

I should be most obliged to you if you can have Madame Péan pay me. We are in great need. Madame Laronde's son is having his business affairs conducted by Monsieur Porlier, a merchant of this city, who sought me out. I gave him your address and he will send you a power of attorney and other papers if it is necessary. Concerning what you have been so good as to inform me about my children's interest, I hope that you will be able to arrange this matter. I am delighted with the news you have given me about what our dear Father and the founder of our Hospital, Father Le Normant, left in the Seminary of Saint-Sulpice for our church. Father Mongolfier remembered that Monsieur Joubert had given us some money that had to be paid to us, although he did not recall the amount. Nothing is lost with him. As for the remainder, if there are risks in sending it on, it would be better to wait; yet, do not miss an opportunity if one arises, even if it costs something. I was greatly delighted to receive Monsieur the Abbé de L'Isle-Dieu's letter. Every year I fear to hear that he is no longer with us. He is a friend such as it is not easy to find. For 24 years he has given us ever new proof of that. I should never end were I to recount in detail all the services of the greatest moment that he has rendered us.

I see from your accounts that Brother Joseph Dellerme is still alive. Given the age he claimed to be when we took over the Hospital, he must be 90 years old. I should greatly appreciate it if you were to go to see him and let me know which house he is in.[33]

Let me know what a painting of Saint Joseph in a gilded frame … feet high by … feet wide would cost. In it the Child Jesus would be stroking Saint Joseph with his workbench and carpenter's tools in the background and a cross above his figure. A gentleman from London who is here at present has given me to hope that it could be done for 3 or 4 louis. There are paintings that are done here, but they are poorly done and very expensive.

1771, 23 September. Monsieur Carleton
[Sir Guy Carleton, Governor of Canada].

Sir, your absence and the fear that we might have lost you makes the news of your return even more agreeable. I hope that the beneficence that you have shown to the Canadians will accompany you on your return. I am asking it particularly for our house and for the foundling children whom we have taken in since we have been under English rule. I am claiming your protection in the name of His Britannic Majesty to obtain some aid for these little unfortunates. I fear that I shall be obliged to give up this good work for lack of means to maintain it. You should be able to guess, Sir, how much cruelty that would occasion for persons who wish to bury their shame with their children. This thought is enough to make an impression on a compassionate and charitable heart. I hope that you will not refuse me this blessing. I dare also to implore you to concern yourself with helping us, if it be possible, with transporting some goods, which I shall specify below for you, that are now with Monsieur Joubert, the Director and Bursar of the Seminary of Saint-Sulpice in Paris, and that were bequeathed to us

---

33   Brother Joseph Dellerme had retired to the home of a nephew in Saint-Cyprien, Agenois, France, where he died on 19 March 1772.

by the charity of Father Le Normant, the Vicar General and Superior of the Seminary of Saint-Sulpice in Montreal, and our founder, who died in '59. These goods are, namely, a silver chalice and paten, two silver cruets with tray, a silver-gilt monstrance, a silver thurible with boat, six hatched silver candlesticks with crucifix, and two candlesticks for acolytes.

I hope, Sir, that I am not seeking your aid in vain; but whether you succeed in doing so or not, I am convinced that it will not depend upon you alone. I therefore assure you in advance of all my gratitude and those sentiments with which I have the honour of being,

Sir …

I have still to discuss with you, Sir, a matter with which you are familiar: namely, that of the ill-founded claim of the Indians of Sault Saint Louis on the lands of the Seigneury of Châteauguay. I should be delighted if we could come to terms with them and the Poor be delivered from their importunities.

End of the Manuscript

Supporting Documents

Genealogy of the Du Frost Family

According to the Reform of 1669 and the Parish Registers

Prepared by Count de Palys, Vice President
of the Archaeological Society of Ille-et-Vilaine

Guyon du Frost, 1473, m. Guillemette de Brays

Jean du Frost m. Jeanne de la Roche

Pierre du Frost, 1554, m. Guyonne Rémond

Bertrand du Frost m. Gilette Caillole

Jean du Frost, Sieur du Hellan, 1617, m. Thomasse de Saint Pern

Christophe du Frost, Sieur du Hellan, 1629, m. Bertranne Le Bel

Christophe du Frost, Sieur de Breilsamin, m. Marguerite de La Forest,
Dame de la Gesmerays, 18 February 1653

Christophe du Frost, Sieur de la Gesmerays,
1661, m. Renée Gaultier de Varennes, 18 January 1701

Marguerite du Frost de Lajemmerais m. François d'Youville, 1722

From: Count de Palys, *Une Famille Bretonne au Canada – Madame d'Youville*
[A Breton Family in Canada – Madame d'Youville] (Rennes, 1894).

Baptismal Registration
of Saint Marguerite d'Youville

From: Registers of Baptisms, Marriages, and Burials of the Parish of Saint Anne, Varennes, for the year 1701

On the sixteenth day of the month of October of the year one thousand seven hundred and one Father Guillaume Bulteau delegated to this task baptized Marie Marguerite, daughter of Christophe Dufrost, Esquire, Sieur de la Jemerais Lieutenant in the Troops and of the Lady Marie Renée Gaultier de Varenne his wife, born the previous day. The godfather was Jacques René Gaultier de Varenne and the godmother Marie Marguerite Gaultier de Varenne whose signatures are appended

> Varenne
> M M Gaultier
> de la jemerais
> De St Claude, Priest, Curé

The Brothers and Sisters of Madame d'Youville all born in Varennes, Quebec

CHARLES, born 27 December 1702; ordained to the priesthood in Quebec City, 14 April 1726; died as priest of Verchères, 6 March 1750 and buried there 12 March.

MARIE-CLEMENCE, born 26 January 1704; married Pierre Gamelin-Maugras in Montreal, 16 November 1735; died in Montreal, 22 March 1768.

MARIE-LOUISE, born 13 September 1705; married Ignace Gamelin in Montreal, 31 January 1731; died in Montreal, 10 April 1789.

JOSEPH, born 29 October 1706; ordained to the priesthood in Quebec City, 21 October 1731; died as the priest of Sainte-Famille, Ile d'Orléans, 11 November 1756.

CHRISTOPHE, born 6 December 1708; died at Fourche-aux-Roseaux (now Letellier), Manitoba, 10 May 1736.

Madame d'Youville's Marriage Act

On the twelfth day of August in the year one thousand seven hundred and twenty-two, I, the undersigned, Vicar General of Monsignor the Bishop of Quebec, having granted dispensation from the three readings of the banns for reasons adduced and found acceptable by us, after having received the betrothal vows of François You, Esquire, aged twenty-two years, son of the late Pierre You, while alive Esquire and Sieur de la Découverte, Sub-lieutenant of a company of the detachment of Marine, and of the Lady Madeleine Juste, his wife of this parish, on the one part; and of the Demoiselle Marie Marguerite de la Gemeraye, aged twenty-one years, daughter of the late Christophe Dufrost, Esquire, Sieur de La Gemeraye, while alive Captain of a company of the said detachment of Marine, and of the Lady Marie Renée Gautier, his wife, also of this parish, on the other part; married them according to the rites of Holy Mother Church, in the presence of the said Lady Madeleine Juste, mother of the groom, of Thomas Joncaire, Esquire, his brother-in-law, Lieutenant in a company of the said detachment of Marine, and of Daniel Migeon, Esquire, Sieur de La Gauchetière, Lieutenant in the said detachment, also brother-in-law of the groom, of René Gautier, Esquire, Seigneur of Varennes, Lieutenant of a company of the said detachment and uncle of the bride, of Nicolas Joseph, Esquire, Sieur de Noyelle, also Lieutenant in the said detachment and cousin of the bride, and numerous other relations and friends of both parties, who have signed with me.

Francois Youville	Marie Marguerite De La Jemerais
M Just De Joncaire	Migeon de La Gauchetière
You de La Découverte	Louis[e] La Découverte
M Legay de Joncaire	Timothy Silivain
De Noyelle	Philibert
Marie Boucher widow of Varennes	La Chassaigne
Mg Gauthier, widow of Puigibault	Livilliers
Lemoine de Varennes	Noyelle
Marie Clemence Dufrost	Marguerite Livilliers
Lemoine La Chassaigne	Marie Contrecoeur Lacorne
Marguerite Puigibault	Marie Louise Largentris
La Corne Thérèse Tonty	Priat, Vicar General.

Youville-Lajemmerais Marriage Contract

11 August 1722

Marriage between
Sieur Fr. M. Hiou
de la Decouverte

and

Demoiselle Marie
Marguerite Dufro
de la Gemmerais

2849
Exped.

BEFORE us etc. were present François Magdelaine Hiou, Sieur de la Decouverte, son of the late Pierre Hiou Esquire, Sieur de la Decouverte, while alive officer of the Marine Detachment, and of Demoiselle Magdelaine Juste, his wife, father and mother of the groom of the parish of this city. The said Lady his mother, on the one part, was in attendance, as were Sieur Thimothée Sylvian, physician and surgeon of this city, and Dame Marie Renée Gaultier, his wife, previously authorized by him, and the Widow of the late Christophe Dufro Esquire, Sieur de la Gemerais, while alive Captain of a Company of the Marine Detachment in this country, the said Lady being Guardian of the Children by her marriage to the said late de La Gemerais, and standing in this capacity for Demoiselle Marie Marguerite Dufro de la Gemerais, daughter of the said late Sieur de La Gemerais and the said Dame Marie Renée Gaultier, present and consenting for the other part, As for both parties were the Right Honourable Messire Philippe de Rigaud, Marquis de Vaudreuil, holder of the Great Cross of Saint Louis, Governor and Lieutenant General of this country of New France, and Her Excellency Dame Louise Joybert, his wife; Messire Claude de Ramezay, Knight, Seigneur of La Gesse and Boisfleurant and other locales, Governor of the City and District of Montreal, and Dame Loüise Denys, his wife; Messire Jean Bouillet Esquire, Seigneur of La Chassaigne and the King's Lieutenant in the said district, and Dame Jeanne Le Moyne, his wife; Messire Charles le Moyne, Baron de Longueuil, Governor of Trois Rivières, and Dame Elisabeth Souart, his wife; these consenting to the oath and agreement of their relations, as well as other friends listed hereafter:

Baptismal registration of Marguerite d'Youville. From the parish registers of Varennes, Quebec.

Marriage act of the father and mother of Marguerite d'Youville.
From the parish registers of Varennes, Quebec.

Namely, on the part of the said Sieur François Magdelaine Hiou and of the said Dame Juste his mother and Guardian: Thomas De Joncaire, Lieutenant of a company of the Marine Detachment in this country, and Dame Marie Magdelaine Le Gué, his wife; Daniel Migeon Esquire, Sieur de la Gogetiere, Lieutenant of a Company of the said Detachment and Aide Major of the troops, Philippe Hiou and Demoiselle Marie Loüise Hiou, brother-in-law and brother and sister of the said Sieur François Magdaleine Hiou;

And on the part of the said Sieur Sylvain and the said Lady his wife and of the said Demoiselle Marie Marguerite Dufrau: Dame Magdelaine Gaultier, Widow of the late Charles Petit, Esquire, Sieur de Livilliers, while alive Captain of a Company of the Marine Detachment; René Gaultier, Esquire, Seigneur de Varenne, Lieutenant in the said detachment, and Dame Marie Jeanne Le Moyne of Sainte Heleine; Marie Marguerite Gautier, widow of the late Sieur Louis de Puygibaux, Esquire, Company Lieutenant in the said detachment and uncle of the said Demoiselle Marie Marguerite Dufro; and Demoiselle Marie Clemence and Loüise Dufro and Christophe Dufro, children of Cristophe Dufro, her sisters and brother; Sieur Nicolas Joseph Denoyel, Sub-Lieutenant in the Marine, and Dame Charlote Petit de Livilliers, his wife; Demoiselle Marie Marguerite de Livilliers and Marie Barbe de Puygibaux, her cousins; Jean Louis de la Corne Esquire, Seigneur de Chapte, Knight of the Military Order of Saint Louis, Captain and Major of the troops in this country; and Constant le Marchand, Esquire, Sieur de Lignery, Knight of Saint Louis and Captain in the said Detachment; as well as …

THOSE WHO HAVE VOLUNTARILY agreed to and recognized the articles and Conventions of Marriage, hereafter stated, namely, the said Sieur Silvain and the Lady His Wife who have promised in accordance with the opinion of the relatives and friends cited above to Give in Name and in Law in Marriage the said Demoiselle Marie Marguerite Dufro present of her own will and consent to the said Sieur François Magdelaine Hiou who legally takes the said Demoiselle Dufro in the said Name of Marriage for his wife and Lawful Spouse, and the said Marriage to be solemnized and celebrated in and with the Permission of our Holy Mother, the Roman Catholic and Apostolic Church, as soon as possible, and that it be made known to and approved by their relatives and friends according to the rights of each of the said future spouses that are to be shared in common and all the goods, furnishings, and immoveable property to be acquired from the day of their Wedding and Nuptial Benediction in accordance with the Custom of Paris to which the future Spouses have submitted themselves for the Execution, Regulation, and Governance of the said community and of the other Clauses of the present Contract, even though they should transfer their place of residence or make acquisition or have goods in countries whose customs are contrary to the dispositions of the Custom of Paris, which contrary customs the parties have expressly derogated and renounced by these presents; And notwithstanding, the said future Spouses will be bound by debts and mortgages incurred by the one or the other And created before their marriage; But if one of them does not know of the incurred debts or mortgages, they shall be acquitted of the payment, and it shall be held against the property of the One who incurred them, without the other or his or her property being bound.

Declared by the said Dame Marie Magdelaine Juste, Mother of the said Sieur the future Husband that his property and rights consist of that which came and fell due to him on the death of the late said Sieur Pierre Hiou, of which the distribution has not yet been made and which remains undivided between him and his brother and sisters, And of that which shall in the future through her death come and fall due to the said future Husband, She promised and is obligated by these presents to give, furnish, and deliver to the said future Spouses within the year following the day of their marriage and at the requisition of the said future Husband the sum of four thousand livres, And it was agreed that there shall enter into the future said union the sum of three thousand livres from the properties of whatever kind they may be of the said Sieur the future Husband And that the remainder of the above-mentioned properties shall remain his own and belong to his own stock, blood family, and line of descent. And that the properties of the said Demoiselle the future Wife that have both fallen and shall fall to her shall remain her own and belong likewise to her blood family and line of descent. In support of which future Marriage the said Demoiselle the future Wife will have as dowry the sum of six thousand livres to be paid once as a preference dowry or as a customary dowry according to her choice And for her children the which dowry, whether preference or customary, whichever shall be chosen, the said Demoiselle the future Wife and her children shall receive when the dowry shall be effected without being bound to ask for it in Law And for surety of which she shall hold a mortgage from this day on all the present and future properties of the said Sieur the future Husband.

The Survivor of the said future Spouses shall have and take beforehand as preference legacy outside of and not to be confused with the sharing of the properties of the said Union up to the sum of one thousand livres in moveable goods following the taking of the Inventory that will be made of them without addition, or the sum in cash money according to the choice of the said Survivor, along with the clothes and linen clothing and the weapons, luggage, and horses in regard to the future Husband, and the rings and jewels in regard to the future Wife, with the furnished bed valued at two hundred livres for the said Survivor.

And in case of the dissolution of the said Union the said Demoiselle the future wife and her children shall have the right to accept or renounce it, And in the case of renouncing it She will take back everything that she brought to it whether it came and fell to it by gift, inheritance, or otherwise, along with the dowry and the above-mentioned preference legacy without being bound by any debts or mortgages of the said Union Even if she had heard that she was obligated or had been condemned to pay them, in which case She will be acquitted and indemnified of them by and with the properties of the said Sieur the future Husband and for which indemnity She will hold her mortgage from this day.

Should it occur that certain properties belonging to One or the Other of the said future Spouses be sold or alienated the moneys coming from the said Sales or Alienations shall be used to obtain other real property or revenues of the same Kind for the party to whom the alienated real properties belonged, And in case of the dissolution of the said Union the said reinvestment shall be an action of reprisal to obtain the same Kind for the party from whom the said Real Properties came and shall be added to those of the same party's blood family and line of descent And the mortgage for them shall be held from this day.

FOR THUS promising and obligating and rendering, this was DONE and happened in the said Ville Marie In the House of the said Sieur and Dame Silvain In the year One Thousand Seven Hundred and twenty-two on the eleventh of August in the afternoon in the presence of Sieur Cristophe Hilarion du Laurent, Practitioner at Law, and Pierre Jacques Paumeraux, Merchant, residing in the said Ville Marie, who having Read, HAVE SIGNED.

De Ramezay
Francois Youville De la Decouverte
Denis De Ramezay
Marie Marguerite Delajemmerais
Lachassaigne
Vaudreuil   L Joibert de Vaudreuil
Moyne Lachassaigne
M Just   De Joncaire   Silivain
Migeon De Lagauchetiere   Le Gay de Joncaire
V Pierre You de La Decouverte   Mr Gautier
Louis[e] Ladecouverte   Devarenne
Marie Boucher, Widow Varenne
Magd Gautier, Widow de Puigibault
Lemoine de Varenne

De Noyelle   Livilliers Noyelle   Lacorne
Marie Clemence Dufraut   de Ligneris
Marie Loüise Lajemmerais   Marguerite Livilliers
Marguerite Puigibault
Paumereau   Du Laurent (with initials)
P. Raimbault[34]

Madame d'Youville's Six Children

TAKEN from the Registers of the Baptisms, Marriages, and Burials performed in the Parish of Montreal, dedicated to the Holy Name of Mary, on the Island and in the County and District of Montreal, Province of Quebec, for the year one thousand seven hundred and twenty-three.

On the twenty-first day of May, one thousand seven hundred and twenty-three, was baptized Francois Timothée, born today, the son of Francois Madelene You, Esquire, and Demoiselle Marguerite Du Frot, his wife. The godfather was Timothée Silvain, Esquire; the godmother, Dame Madeleine Just. The father was absent and could not sign.

Timothy Silivain
M. Just de la Découverte
Priat, Vicar

François Timothée died on 17 August 1723.

THE TWENTY-SECOND day of September in the Year one thousand seven hundred and twenty-four was baptized François, born the previous day, son of Monsieur François Hiou de la Découverte and of Demoiselle Marie Marguerite Du Fraut de La Jemeray, his Wife. The godfather was Monsieur Philippe Hiou De Ladecouverte, the godmother Marie Clemence Du Frot Lajemeray, witnesses to this proceeding, In Accordance with the Ordinance

Philippe You Ladecouverte
Marie Clemanse Dufraust
G. P. Du Lescoat, Priest

François, Abbé Youville, priest of Saint-Ours, died 10 April 1778 in Montreal.

---

34   See AJM, Répertoire des contrats de mariage [Catalogue of Marriage Contracts]. – Register of Pierre Raimbault the Elder, No. 2849.

THIS THIRD DAY of September of the year one thousand seven hundred and twenty-five, was Baptized Marie Magdeleine Ursule, born the same day, daughter of Monsieur Francois Hiouville de la Découverte and of Demoiselle Marie Marguerite de la Jemmerai, His wife. The godfather was Monsieur De Jonquer, Esquire, Lieutenant of the Troops, and the godmother was Dame Marie Renée Silvain, who have signed as witnesses to this proceeding.

In Accordance with the Ordinance

De Joncaire
Marie Rene Gautier
G. P. du Lescoat, Priest

Magdeleine-Ursule died 26 August 1726.

THE SIXTEENTH DAY of December of the Year one thousand seven hundred and twenty-six was baptized by me, the priest undersigned, Louise, born today, the daughter of Sieur François You, Esquire, Sieur de la Découverte, and of Dame Marguerite de La Gemerays, his wife. The godfather was Sieur Daniel Migeon, Esquire, Sieur de La Gauchetiere, Captain of a company of the Marine detachment; and the godmother, Demoiselle Louise You de la Découverte, who have all signed with me.

Fr Youville
Migeon Delagauchetière
Louise Ladecouverte
F. C. Chaumaux, Priest

Louise was buried in Pointe-Claire, 1 March 1727.

THE NINETEENTH DAY of July of the year one thousand seven hundred and twenty-nine was baptized Charle Magdelene, born the previous day in the evening, the son of Francois Dyouville Ladecouverte and of Dame Marguerite Dufrau Lagemeraye, his wife. The godfather was Sarle Philibert, Esquire, Sub-lieutenant in the troops of this country, and the godmother Dame Magdelene Le Guay de Jonkaire.

Francoi Dyouville
S Philiber
Magdeleine Legay de Joncair
M. Gasnault, Priest

Charles-Madeleine, Abbé Dufrost, died 7 March 1790 at Boucherville, where he was parish priest. He was the Vicar General of the Diocese of Quebec from 1775 until his death in 1790.

THE TWENTY-SIXTH DAY of February, one thousand seven hundred thirty-one, I, a priest of the Seminary of Ville Marie, baptized a boy born this day to the marriage of the deceased Francois Youville de la Déouverte and Damoiselle Marguerite Dufrost de la Jemeraye of this city. He was named Ignace. His godfather was Monsieur Ignace Gamelin, merchant of this city, and the godmother Mari Anne Sylvain, who said she did not know how to sign.

> Ignace Gamelin
> J Bouffandeau, Priest

> Ignace died 17 July 1731.

Burial Act of François d'Youville, Husband of Madame d'Youville

THE FIFTH DAY of the month of July of the year one thousand seven hundred and thirty was buried in the church the body of François Madeleine d'Youville, Esquire, Sieur de la Decouverte, aged about thirty years, who died the previous day; present were Monsieur Navetier, Priest, and Chanvieux, Clerk, who signed with us.

> Chauvieux   Navetier, Priest
> A. Déat, Priest

Inventory of the Estate of François d'Youville

24 April 1731

> INVENTORY of the Properties of the Estate of the Sieur Youville La Decouverte and his Lady Wife

> THE YEAR One Thousand Seven Hundred and Thirty-One, The twenty-fourth of April, as requested by Dame Marie Marguerite Dufro de La Gemmerais, widow of the late Sieur Youville de la Descouverte, while alive a merchant in this city, Residing in Her house situated on the Market Square of this city Both in Her name owing to the Union of Properties that existed

between the said deceased her husband and Herself, and as the Guardian of the minor children of the said deceased and Herself, and subject to the Right of Her accepting the said Union if she should judge it fitting or renouncing it. In the presence of Sieur Philippe You de la Descouverte, paternal uncle of the said minors, of Sieur Thimothé Silvain, the King's Physician and husband of Dame Marie René Gautier, grandmother of the said minors, And Sieur Jean Francois Malhiot, Merchant Burgess of the City, Their substitute Guardian by the Act of Guardianship made at the Bench of the Royal Jurisdiction of Montreal on the Fifth of This month, the said Minors as competent to speak for themselves and to receive the inheritance of the said deceased their Father, for the Preservation of the Properties and Rights of the said Parties In their names and of all others to whom it may pertain, by the Royal Notary undersigned of the said jurisdiction, There was made a Good and Faithful Inventory and Description of each and all of the Properties, furniture, utensils, linen, clothing, And money, bills, deeds, instructions, And other things left after the demise of the said deceased And that were held in common Between Them and the said widow on the day of his Demise, Shown and Made Known To the said Notary by the said Lady Widow and according to Her Oath made and given to the said notary of Montreal And Made Known each and all of the said Properties without hiding or concealing any of them under Pain of the ordinance, Below listed are the properties Appraised and Valued by Maître Nicolas Marchand, Bailiff of this Jurisdiction, Appraiser and Auctioneer, Who appraised and valued Them with the entire Stock Included, with respect to the present time, in sums of Money, as follows in the presence of Sieurs Charles Benoist and Joseph Le Cours, Legal Practitioners, who have signed with the said Parties, Having read

Marguerite Lajemmerais Widow Youville   Malhiot
Ladecouverte   Silvain   Charles Benoist
Raimbault the Younger
Royal Notary (with initials)

Firstly, in a large, high room looking out onto the said Market Square there was a bed with green serge curtains decorated with ribbons and with rods, rings and hooks Valued at ninety livres,
item . . . . 90 L.
A curtained [*en Courty*] Featherbed with a woollen mattress covered in cotton, a straw mattress, a bolster, a counterpane in bad condition valued together at
. . . . 72 L.

A cot Valued at six Livres,

  item . . . .   6 L.

Item, an armchair covered in old blue cloth, And old Upholstery stuffed with Hay and a little Wool Valued at ten livres,

  item . . . .   60 L.

Six wooden chairs upholstered in old Brocade stuffed with hay and wool Valued at ten Livres each,

  item . . . .   60 L.

An old folding Table of Pine wood val. At forty sols,

  item . . . .   2 L.

An old tapestry Carpet Valued at three Livres,

  item . . . .   3 L.

A Five-piece Tapestry in Hungarian Embroidery. Valued at sixty-five Livres,

  item . . . .   65.

A Small mirror with gilded frame Valued at twelve Livres,

  item . . . .   12.

A basket with two large, glass flagons, of which one is broken Valued at three livres,

  item . . . .   3.

A Canister Containing ten glass flagons Valued at 15 Livres,

  item . . . .   15.

A Casket covered in Wallpaper Valued at four Livres,

  item . . . .   4.

A small Keg Valued at twenty sols,

  item . . . .   1.

In the first room entered upstairs, where we made our oral report

An iron Stove scratched on the surface with its Pipe in four metal sections The whole Valued at one hundred and thirty Livres,

  item . . . .   130 L.

A very old Bergame tapestry mended about ten years ago, Valued at seven Livres ten sols,

  item 7.10

Eight old caned wooden chairs Valued at 10 sols each,

  item . . . .   4.

A small bed with a mattress of old Wool covered in Montbéliard cloth Valued at sixteen Livres,

  item . . . .   16.

A Cover of Toulouse wool Valued at ten Livres,

    item ....   10.

Item an old Quilt of different pieces of India fabric lined with an old cloth quilting

Valued at six Livres

    ....   6.

Two Trestles of Pine wood Valued at twenty sols,

    item ....   1.

A small, old Sideboard of Pine wood with its metal fittings

Valued at six Livres,

    item ....   6.

A trunk covered in black leather and lined with cloth On the inside

Valued at fifteen livres,

    item ....   15.

A small mirror with a red frame Valued at forty sols,

    item ....   2.

A small fire Shovel Valued at thirty sols,

    item 1.10

Two pasteboard Screens in very bad condition Valued together at five sols,

    item 05

A Bundle containing the Bed of one of the said Minors in which there is a Featherbed covered in coarse cloth with a small Cover of double-stitched Rouen cloth Valued at fourteen Livres,

    item ....   14.

A Knife-holder Containing Six Table Knives with Porcelain handles

Valued at ten Livres,

    item ....   10.

Another Knife-holder containing six knives in foul condition with tin handles

Valued at thirty sols,

    item 1.10

A faïence pot with tin cover Valued at thirty sols,

    item 1.10

Eight small flagons and Bottles, two of which are cracked,

Valued all together at fifty sols,

    item 2.10

An earthenware jug with broken Handle Valued at twenty-five sols,

    item 1. 5

A small iron hammer Valued at fifteen sols,

    item 15

Nine Saucers and seven faïence cups Valued together at four Livres,

    item . . . .   4 L.

Three drinking glasses And three flasks Valued all together at six Livres,

    item . . . .   6 .

A candleholder And a salt-cellar in silver-plated Brass Valued at four livres ten sols

    . . . .   4.10

A tin sugar bowl Valued at three Livres,

    item . . . .   3 .

A folio Book of the Lives of the Saints Val. At ten livres,

    item . . . .   10 .

In a Small kitchen at the side of the Yard

Twelve plates And four flat bowls in faïence Valued all together at twelve Livres,

    item . . . .   12 .

Two Copper Cauldrons with copper-plated [*coffelon* = *coppelon?*] covers Valued together at thirteen Livres,

    item . . . .   13 .

Three irons for smoothing Linen Valued all together at three Livres ten sols,

    item 3.10

An old Warming-pan filled with holes, Valued at thirty sols,

    item 1.10

A small, worn-out Meat-pie Plate with its Cover Valued at three Livres,

    item . . . .   3 .

A strainer And a Sausage Mould in tin Valued at ten sols,

    item 0.10

A candleholder And another with handle, all in brass Valued together at Five Livres,

    item . . . .   5 .

A small iron grill Valued at twenty sols,

    item . . . .   1 .

A medium-sized Frying Pan Valued at three Livres ten sols,

    item 3.10

A medium-sized Copper Saucepan Valued at fifty sols,

    item 2.10

Coffer belonging to the furniture of Madame d'Youville. The base, in Louis XIII style, was made especially for the coffer. After having founded her Community, she used it as a kind of safe. The "miraculous coins" were placed there. Preserved in Montreal.

The present Mother House of the Institute of the Sisters of Charity of the General Hospital of Montreal, called the Grey Nuns, 1190 Guy Street, Montreal, Quebec, Canada.

A Roasting Spit Valued at forty sols,

    item . . . .   2.

An iron-bound Bucket for Drawing Water, with two others bound with wood, in very bad condition Valued all together at three Livres,

    item . . . .   3.

A large, nine-pound cauldron Valued at twelve Livres,

    item . . . .   12.

A Bed consisting of two Small Featherbeds, One covered in canvas and the Other in drill Valued together at Thirty-five Livres,

    item . . . .   35.

A small mattress Covered in Montbéliard cloth Valued at thirteen L.,

    item . . . .   13.

A large woollen Blanket Valued because somewhat worn at twelve Livres,

    item . . . .   12.

Five small Cushions or Feather pillows covered in drill Valued all together at seven Livres ten sols,

    item 7.10

A small Counterpane of dyed, old India cloth Valued at forty sols,

    item . . . .   2 L.

A folding table of Pine wood on a stand Valued at forty sols,

    item . . . .   2.

A small iron pot cracked And Mended with a Hoop Valued at thirty sols,

    item 1.10

A medium-sized pot with Cover Valued at Five Livres,

    item . . . .   5.

An iron Pot Ladle Valued at twenty sols,

    item . . . .   1.

An iron tripod Valued at ten sols,

    item 10

A small Pine cupboard Valued at four livres,

    item . . . .   4.

Fifty-three and a half pounds of tin Platters, Bowls, Pots and dishes, and Measuring vessels Valued at twenty sols per Pound,

    item 53.10

Noon Having struck we have postponed the Continuation of the said Inventory to two o'clock in the Afternoon of this day And have signed.

Marguerite Lajemmerais Widow Youville   Ladecouverte
Malhiot   Silvain   Marchand (initialled)
Charles Benoist   Lecour
Raimbault the Younger,
Royal Notary (initialled)

And at two o'clock in the Afternoon of the Said Day at the request of
the said Dame Youville And
In the Presence of the above named we have continued to proceed
with the said Inventory as Follows

In the attic of the said house the following were found, namely

A large cross-saw somewhat worn with its frame Valued at five livres,
          item . . . .   5 L.
A small Spinning-wheel Valued at four Livres ten sols,
          item 4.10
The wooden frame of a Capetian armchair broken in two places
Valued at six L.,
          item . . . .   6.
An old pair of boots Valued at twenty sols,
          item . . . .   1.
A horse's harness consisting of a saddle blanket, crupper [*analoire*] ,
collar furnished with chains, a band [*veton*], and rings, And two pairs
of spare bands Valued all together because of their very bad condition
at twenty-two Livres,
          item . . . .   22.
A towing chain Valued at forty sols,
          item . . . .   2 L.
A large iron tripod Valued at four Livres,
          item . . . .   4.
Two andirons without uprights Valued at four Livres,
          item . . . .   4.
A Copper Watering-can for the Garden, old, Valued at Six Livres,
          item . . . .   6.
An old Pine Folding table on a stand [*ouallé*], Valued at thirty sols,
          item 1.10
An old silk sieve Valued at forty sols,
          item . . . .   2.
Two old woollen Blankets, Six Livres for both,
          item . . . .   6.

Three old bags, somewhat worn Valued all three at forty-five sols,

    item 2.5

A mattock and a pick Valued together at three Livres,

    item . . . .   3.

A shotgun with broken stock Valued at eight Livres,

    item . . . .   8.

An old kneading-through Valued at five Livres,

    item . . . .   5.

And the said lady Widow Youville showed a covered Bowl, two goblets, ten spoons, nine forks, six coffee spoons, a bit of chain, a coffee [...], And a piece of a seal, all in Silver, weighing all together eight marks Five ounces at forty Livres per mark,

    item . . . .   414.

In the Yard there were only Twenty-five Pounds of Light Tobacco Bundled Valued at Five sols the pound,

    item 6.05

Three tubs And two basins in very bad condition falling to pieces Valued together at fifty sols,

    item 2.10

In a storeroom were found a wicker Basket for use on a sideboard, very old Valued at 20 sols,

    item . . . .   1.

Four octavo books containing Part of the History of Rome Valued at three livres for the four books,

    item . . . .   3.

Item a Pine wardrobe with two doors with its metal fittings Valued at fifteen Livres,

    item . . . .   15.

In this wardrobe were found

Four pairs of somewhat worn scented sheets Valued at twelve Livres ten sols per pair,

    item . . . .   50.

Nine worn tablecloths of scented cloth Valued together at Eighteen livres,

    item . . . .   18.

Twenty-nine napkins of scented cloth somewhat worn Valued all together at fifteen Livres

    . . . .   15.

Three embroidered tablecloths of which one is somewhat worn The three valued together at twelve Livres,

    item . . . .   12 L.

Thirteen embroidered napkins Valued at sixteen Livres,

    item . . . .   16.

About a dozen of the same quite worn, filled with holes, and badly torn Valued all together at Five Livres,

    item . . . .   5.

Twelve pillow-cases of Morlin and Paris cloth of which six are new And six have been used, the twelve valued at seven Livres ten sols,

    item 7.10

A Square [*eguirre* = *équerre*?] in clear glass or Crystal Valued at three Livres,

    item . . . .   3.

Four small clay pots And four small faïence jam Boxes Valued all together at four Livres,

    item . . . .   4.

In the said storeroom were found the linen clothing and towels for the use of the said Widow which are Not At All Valued

A wooden washstand [*flor?*] with two worn brass basins weighing three pounds Valued at five Livres,

    item . . . .   5.

Fifty pounds of Lead weights Valued all together at sixteen livres,

    item . . . .   16.

A Hood made from finished [*traitte*] cloth of four ells of organdie [*dourgan*], Valued at ten Livres,

    item . . . .   10.

A small one from one ell Valued at fifty sols,

    item 2.10

Two pairs of sleeves of finished cloth Of which one is for a child The two pairs valued at three livres,

    item . . . .   3.

Two small worn shirts of finished cloth Valued together at twenty sols,

    item . . . .   1.

Three ounces of Sewing Silk At four Livres ten sols,

    item 4.10

Seven bonnets for a little girl And three for a Boy Valued at eleven Livres ten sols,

    item 11.10

Two Pounds of Horsehair Valued together at forty sols,

    item . . . .   2.

In a trunk was found a piece of grospoint tapestry for upholstering an armchair, unfinished, And a footstool Valued all together at thirty Livres,

    item . . . .   30.

In the said trunk the clothing and arms used by the said late Sieur
Youville

NAMELY

A Sword of gilt brass with a vermeil hilt Valued at eighteen Livres,
     item . . . . 18.
Three pairs of woven stockings in bad condition Valued all together at
thirty s.,
     item 1.10
A pair of silk hose with gold embroidered edges, in bad condition
Valued at six L.
     item . . . . 6.
An old pair of faded deerskin breeches Valued at forty sols,
     item . . . . 2.
A suit coat And waistcoat of Pinchina, somewhat worn Valued at fif-
teen Livres,
     item . . . . 15.
A waistcoat of gold and silver cloth, somewhat worn Valued at forty
Livres,
     item . . . . 40 L.
A Summer suit coat with Breeches And a waistcoat of blue taffeta
trimmed with silver lace Valued all together at sixty Livres,
     item . . . . 60.
Two old hats One trimmed with gold and the Other with silver
Valued at six Livres [each]
       . . . . 12.
Four old shirts of Rouen cloth Valued at ten livres for the four
       . . . . 10.
The said trunk with its metal fittings, very old Valued at eight Livres,
     item . . . . 8.

DECLARED BY the said Lady Widow Youville that the merchandise displayed in
the said storerooms did not belong to her, but that it had been given to her to sell on
Commission for the Account of Demoiselle the Widow Soumande and Sieur
Jacques Gadois Maugé, merchants of this city, whose invoices signed by Them she
presented: That of the said Dame Soumande in the amount of Two thousand seven
hundred and fifty-nine Livres four sols eleven deniers, dated the twenty-first of this
month and signed Anne M. Chpx [Chapoux] Widow Soumande, And That of the
said Sieur Maugé in the amount of three hundred and forty-nine Livres nineteen sols
and nine deniers, dated and settled the twenty-second of this month and signed

J. Gadois Maugé. The which invoices were initialled by the said Notary in the presence of the said Lady Widow Youville, the said Sieur Malhiot, and others above named And were signed by the said Lady Widow Youville

Marguerite Lajemerais Widow Youville

Then Was Valued a large sleigh not in working order, missing its chain
Valued at fifty sols,
item 2.10

Six o'clock having struck the Inventory was ended and its continuation postponed until tomorrow the twenty-fifth of this present month at eight o'clock in the morning And signed by

Marguerite Lajemerais Widow Youville   Malhiot   Silvain
Ladecouverte   Marchand (initialled)   Charles Benoist
Le Cour   Raimbault the Younger, (initialled)

And the twenty-fifth of the said month at eight o'clock in the morning Proceeding with the Taking of the said Inventory at the Request and in the Presence of the above

An Indian Slave aged between ten and eleven years old Valued at One Hundred and Fifty Livres,
item . . . .   150 L.

Was Inventoried

A cow and her second calf, of a reddish colour Valued at Thirty livres, item 30.

And the said Sieur Marchand signed

Marchand (initialled)

Thereafter the outstanding debts owed to the said Estate were declared by the said Lady Widow Youville NAMELY

By Francois Darles fifty-five livres,
item . . . .   55.
By the wife of the agent of Sieur de Montbrun, twenty-five sols,
item 1.5

By Patenoste, farmer of Longueuil, forty sols,

    item .... 2.

By Jean Turcot, farmer of Côte Saint Michel on this Island, twenty-one S.

    item 1.1

By one named Hunault residing at present at the house of St Germain Lemayre in Lachine four Livres,

    item .... 4.

By one named Catin, a farmer of Longueuil, three Livres fourteen sols,

    item 3.14

Jacques Depaty of l'Isle-Jésus three Livres,

    item .... 3.

By Monsieur de la Gesmeray, parish priest of Repentigny, for the balance of the price of a watch,

    item .... 35.

By Philbert La Roche twenty Livres,

    item .... 20.

By Jean Brunet Bourbonnais residing at the end of the Northern side of this Island ten Livres,

    item .... 10.

By Sieur Outelas, seven Livres ten sols,

    item 7.10

And the Following Liabilities NAMELY

Namely to the Fabrique of the Church of this City for the funeral rites and interment of the said Deceased Sieur Youville The sum of One Hundred and twenty-three,

    item .... 123 L.

To the Reverend Recollet Fathers in Remuneration for Three Hundred and Sixty Low Requiem Masses that were said for the Repose of the Soul of the said deceased Sieur Youville, two hundred and seventy-three Livres fifteen sols,

    item 273.15

To Madame the Widow of the late Monsieur Bouart The sum of Six Hundred and forty-six Livres five sols by a Bond Contracted by the said late Sieur Youville to the said Lady and dated the 17th of September 1729,

    item 646.5

To Sieur Freniere Biron The sum of seven Livres,

    item .... 7.

To the Sieurs Charly, Brothers, The sum of four hundred twenty-six
Livres two sols three deniers in Two Notes contracted by the said Sieur
Youville to the said Sieurs Charly and dated the 19th of January and
the 11th of March 1730,

      item 426.2.3

To Sieur Maurice Blondeau, merchant of this city, on current account
with the said Sieur Blondeau for supplies furnished to the said late Sieur
Youville The sum of One Hundred and seventy-seven Livres ten sols,

      item 177.10

To Desermons, tailor, forty-four Livres,

      item . . . .   44.

To Sieur Descampes The sum of Two Hundred and seventy-seven
Livres ten sols in accordance with the Agreement of the said Sieur
Youville and dated the 13th of November 1725,

      item 277.10

To Sieur Damours Defreneuse, The sum of three hundred and sixty
Livres,

      item . . . .   360.

To Sieur Poulin de Francheville The sum of forty-nine Livres,

      item . . . .   49.

To Sieur Latour, a businessman in this city, the sum of thirty Livres,

      item . . . .   30.

To Sieur Guy, The sum of twelve Livres,

      item . . . .   12.

To one Pierre Gilbert, called Laframboise, one hundred and eighty
Livres,

      item . . . .   180.

To one Pierre La Porte, farmer of Boucharville [*sic*] The sum of One
Hundred Livres,

      item . . . .   100.

To Sieur Francois Roy The sum of Twelve Hundred and forty-six
Livres ten sols due to him by a bond made before the undersigned
notary and dated the fifth of June and the 14th of September 1730,

      item 1246.10

To Sieur Rochon, Keeper of the King's Stores, by an agreement of the
said Sieur Youville the sum of sixty-two Livres,

      item . . . .   62.

To the Sieur Gadois Maugé The sum of Five Hundred and twenty-
seven Livres two sols six deniers in accordance with the certificate of
the said Maugé which we have initialled,

      item . . . .   527.2 .6

And after having attended to the business until noon the Continuation of the said Inventory was postponed until two o'clock in the Afternoon of this day And Signed

Marguerite Lajemerais Widow Youville	Malhiot
Silvain Charles Benoist Le Cour	Ladecouverte
Raimbault the Younger (initialled)	
Royal Notary	

And at two o'clock in the Afternoon Proceeding with the taking of the said Inventory at the request and in the presence of the above the Following Title Papers and Instructions were Inventoried

NAMELY

The Marriage Contract of the said deceased Sieur Youville de la Descouverte with the said Demoiselle Marie Marguerite Dufro made before Maître Raimbault, Royal Notary, the 11th of August 1722 carrying stipulation of the Union And of a preference or customary Dowry of six thousand Livres And other promissory clauses and advantages contained therein. Number one

A Deed of Sale made by Sieur de Varenne to the said Sieur Youville for land of six arpents of frontage by sixty arpents back situated on l'Isle-Jésus In arrière-fief by contract made before Maître Adhemar, Notary, the 21st of April 1725 and Ratified at the bottom by Dame de Varenne, And noted that the settlement was followed by complete payment of the price of the said sale Made before the said Maître Adhemar the 29th of May 1726. Number two.

A Contract In arrière-fief for six arpents of frontage by sixty arpents back Ceded to Sieur de Varenne by the Seigneur of the Isle-Jésus having his seat on the said Island in the Rivière des Prairies in the Place where in the past was Francois Couturier, the said Contract made before Maître Le Pallieur, Royal Notary, the 27th of April 1719. And Number three.

An act of incorporation made before Maître Adhemar, Royal Notary, the 9th of June 1727 between the late Sieur Youville and the late Sieur St-George Dupres for the Business they conducted together In the Sioux Company. Number four.

A Memorandum of what it appears that the said Sieur Youville paid at Michilimackinac for the Account of the said Sieur the late Dupres signed by the said Sieur Youville, the amount being the sum of Seven Hundred and eighty-two Livres. In which Memorandum there appear three Contested articles: One for the sum of twenty Livres paid to Sieur Marsollet, another for forty-seven Livres paid to Sieur Prudhomme, And another article for thirty-two Livres for his share of the Beaver they had borrowed from the Bay. The which articles the said Lady Widow Youville declared she had contested because she had sent collated copies of the Notes relating to the said articles to the Mississippi in order to recover the Payment or to have it accounted to the Estate of the late Dupres. Even though she did not believe that this would produce any Results, she did it in good faith, And she has signed the said Memorandum. Number Five. She has presented the said Notes and they have been attached to the memorandum, having been initialled by us, the said notary.

Marguerite Lajemerais Widow Youville

A Receipt from Sieur Prudhomme from which it appears that Sieur Youville paid to the said Prudhomme The Sum of fifty-four Livres of the same amount that he had lent to the said Sieurs Youville and Dupres, the said Receipt signed L. Prudhomme and dated in Montreal the 6th of May 1729. Number Six.

A Letter Written and sent by the said deceased Dupres to the said Sieur Youville in which, among other things, he expresses his view that not being able to find Employees, he is obliged to go down to the sea for the good of their Company And that he will have with him forty-three bundles of Beavers, And the remainder of their merchandise, the said letter being dated the 20th of October 1729 at the Tamarois, and signed by St-George Dupres. Number Seven.

A Note contracted by Jean Baptiste Amiot in the presence of witnesses to credit Charles Reaume with the amount of One Hundred and Six Livres payable in Beaver at the price of Michilimackinac of the eleventh of July 1725, on the reverse is the Order of the said Reaume endorsing it to the credit of the said Sieur Youville, the said order not being dated but signed Charles Reaume. Number Eight.

And at the Present Time the said Lady Widow declared that the said late Sieur Youville had often told her that the above-mentioned Note was neither owed nor signed over to him.

Marguerite Lajemerais Widow Youville

The said Lady Widow Youville declared that the said late Sieur Youville jointly with Sieur Philippe You de la Descouverte, his elder brother, made between Themselves and in good faith in the presence of Sieur Migeon de La Gauchetiere, Captain of the Marine Troops and Guardian of Demoiselle Marie Thereze Migeon, the child of his marriage with the deceased Dame Marie Le Gay de Beaulieu, his wife and the daughter of the said Demoiselle Madeleine Jus, and in presence of Sieurs

Maurice Blondeau and Jean Francois Malhiot, merchants of this city, the Division of the Immoveable Properties left by the Estate of the deceased Dame Madeleine Jus, their mother and the widow of the late Sieur Pierre You de la Descouverte, their father, by which Division there passed to the said late Sieur Youville a Lot and House where the said Lady Widow at present resides In this city on the Market Square bounded on both Sides and in the rear by the lots and houses of the brothers Sieurs Charly, Together with two arpents in area of land near this city and facing on the road that leads to the windmill of the Charon Brothers, which land includes one arpent of Garden enclosed by upright stakes; And to the said Sieur Philippe Ladescouverte there passed by the said Division a Lot and a large, two-storey stone house on the same, fronting on Rue Saint Paul of this city and backing on the land set aside for the fortifications of this city, and bordered on one Side by Martin Curot and on the other by Charles Jourdin La Brosse, And Also one arpent in area of land adjoining the land designated above and on the other bordered by the lands of the Poor on the Southwest Side and on the rear by the Sisters of the Congregation; with the responsibility for each of the said Sieurs Youville and Ladescouverte to pay each one half of the debts of the estate of their said Father and Mother; The which Division was made without any compensation or return on either Part; there remaining only one piece of land on the northern part of this Island not included in the said Division; And signed by

Marie Marguerite Lajemerais Widow Youville

And after having attended to this business until Six o'clock, the Taking of the said Inventory was postponed until eight o'clock tomorrow morning And signed by

Marguerite Lajemerais Widow Youville	Malhiot	Silvain
Ladecouverte Charles Benoist	Le Cour	
Raimbault the Younger (initialled)		

And the twenty-sixth of the month of April of the said year at the request And in the presence of the above the Taking of the said Inventory proceeded as follows at eight o'clock in the morning.

And the said Sieur Philippe de La Descouverte Appearing, Who after having had read to him word by word by the said notary in the presence of the above parties the Declaration of the said Lady Widow Youville Concerning the Division mentioned therein of the Immoveable Properties of the said Estate, stated and declared voluntarily that the said Declaration was true; and having truly and in good faith made the said Division, approves, accepts, and ratifies It, and desires and understands by These Presents that the said Division portions out clearly and completely its

Goods and Chattels as Legally made with the responsibility borne by the said Declaration of the said Lady To Pay each half of the debts of their said inheritance without any compensation or return by division for either; And signed in the presence of the above-named.

Malhiot   Ladecouverte   Charles Benoist – Silvain – Le Cour Raimbault the Younger (initialled)

Next, the said Widow presented an Account supplied by the said Sieur Damour of the Goods and Chattels that he had supplied to the said late Sieur Youville and Pierre Le Duc undersigned for the Company held between the said Sieurs Youville and Le Duc by which it appears that there is definitely due from the said Company to Sieur Damour the sum of Three Hundred and Twenty Livres eighteen sols and two deniers, comprising for the half owed by the said Sieur Youville a sum of One Hundred and Sixty Livres nine sols and one denier, item 160.9.1d. Number Nine

The said Lady declares that the said Le Duc had told her that he had left two eight-seated, bark canoes belonging to the said Company, one in Michilimackinac and the other in Lachine with Sieur Depelleteaux, And a travelling cauldron And signed

Marguerite Lajemerais Widow Youville

And at the Present Time the said Demoiselle Widow presented a Statement of the Indian debts of the said Company made up of seven leaves And on the verso of the ninth [sic] leaf a memorandum of the merchandise of the said Company which the said Le Duc left with her and told her that he had left the said merchandise at Michilimackinac with one of his brothers, the which Memorandum with the said Statement of Debts we have initialled.

The said Lady Widow declared that the said late Sieur Youville and She had contracted a Note with the said Lady Widow LaDescouverte for Six Thousand One Hundred and Ten Livres fifteen sols and nine deniers for the balance of an Account accrued over a long time for her Supplies Dated the 9th of June 1727 And that she also knew that they would have given to the said Lady well in advance of the above-mentioned Note a Receipt for Four Thousand Livres which she believed was given for that which the said Dame Ladescouverte promised them at their marriage And signed by

Marie Marguerite Lajemerais Widow Youville

[The following paragraph is in a different hand, presumably that of Malhiot.]

And I, Malhiot, in my Capacity as Substitute Guardian of the minor children of the late Sieur Youville expressed my opposition to the said declaration Having understood that the Four Thousand Livres declared above were or could be included in the note of the Ninth of June One Thousand Seven Hundred and Twenty-seven which was stipulated as being for the Balance of all accounts up to the said day of the ninth of June One Thousand Seven Hundred and Twenty-seven.
Malhiot.

[The handwriting of Raimbault the Younger follows.]

This completes the entire Contents of the said Inventory with the agreement of the said Sieur Malhiot, the Substitute Guardian, who has left it in the power and keeping of the said Lady Widow Youville, the Guardian, with the promise to present everything when, to whom, and howsoever it shall appertain, Made This Day the twenty-sixth of April One Thousand Seven Hundred and Thirty-one, And signed by

Marguerite Lajemerais Widow Youville			Malhiot
Ladecouverte	Silvain	Le Cour	Charles Benoist
Raimbault the Younger			
Royal Notary (initialled)			

IN THE YEAR ONE THOUSAND SEVEN HUNDRED AND THIRTY-ONE on the seventh of May at two o'clock in the afternoon In the Audience Chamber before Us, Pierre Raimbault, King's Councillor and Lieutenant General of Civil and Criminal Matters on the bench of the Royal Jurisdiction of Montreal, there appeared Dame Marie Marguerite Dufro de la Gemmeray, Widow of the late Sieur Youville Ladecouverte, when alive a merchant in this city, and the Guardian of the minor children born from her marriage with the late Sieur Youville, who informed us that for the Preservation of the Properties and Rights of the said minors and of all others to which it shall appertain, She has had made an inventory of the Properties that were held in Common between Herself and the said late Sieur Youville, the said Inventory, accepted by Maître Raimbault, Royal Notary, on the twenty-fourth of April last, which she presented to us requesting Us to Conclude and Declare Finished and Dissolved the Union of Properties which had obtained between Herself and the said late Sieur Youville and to give her an Act to this effect, In View of which, in the presence of Sieur Jean François Mailliot, the Substitute Guardian, who stated that he had been present at the said inventory, an oath was sworn by the said Lady Widow Youville that what she said was true and that She affirmed that She had declared to the best of her Knowledge at the said inventory the Goods and Chattels belonging to their said Union, that she had neither concealed nor diverted any, and had omitted to have made mention therein that the furniture of the estate of the said deceased Dame Marie Juste had been divided between the Sieur Philippe Pierre You de la Descouverte and the said late Sieur Francois You in such a Manner that Notwithstanding the Compensation that the said late Sieur Francois You, her husband, had received from the said late Lady his mother, the said Sieur Philippe La Descouverte had taken the furniture that they Evaluated Between Themselves in accordance with the Condition which they were then in, except for the excess that her husband the late Sieur You may have received over and above what the said Sieur Philippe La Decouverte received, and which she believes to amount to Thirteen Hundred and some Livres; And that the outstanding Debts owed to the said Dame Juste have still to be divided between them, As well as the Deeds held by the said Sieur La Descouverte and also a Bond for Two Thousand Livres on the Hôtel de Ville of Paris which she believes to be held by Sieur Gendron or Sieur Hersan, a merchant in Paris, which is held jointly with the said Sieur La Descouverte; Of which above-stated Declaration and Affirmation WE have given her an act And in consequence have declared the said Inventory concluded And the said Union finished and dissolved, Made and done This Day and Year.

> Marguerite Lajemerais Widow Youville
> Malhiot
> P. Raimbault
> Raimbault the Younger[35]
> Registrar
> with initials

Registration of the Seizure In Esse of the Properties of the Estate of the Deceased Sieur Ladécouverte

In the year one thousand seven hundred and thirty-two, the 16th day of August in the afternoon, By virtue of certain verdicts rendered by the Bench of the Royal Jurisdiction of Montreal against Sieur Philippe You Ladécouverte and Sieur Jean Baptiste Neveu, merchant of this city, in the name and as trustee of the unclaimed estate of the late Sieur Francois You Ladécouverte, and dated from the 1st of June 1731 and the 22nd of July last and Well and duly signed and sealed followed by the writ and repeated writs dated from the 6th of June 1731, the 17th of June last, the 29th of July, and the 4th of this month and at the request of Sieur Pierre Vessière, mer-

---

35   See AJM, Pièces judiciaires [Legal Documents] – Raimbault, 7 May 1731.

chant of Quebec City at present in this city where he is residing in the house at present occupied by Maître Foucher, the King's Procurator, situated in this said city on Rue Saint Paul in the parish of Villemarie, and on the Isle-Jésus in the house of Pierre Montheau, called Desormeaux, a farmer of the said place, in pursuit of the writs and repeated writs heretofore made and bearing upon the Refusal and failure to make payment to the said Sieur Vessières by the said Sieur Philippe Ladécouverte and the said Sieur Neveu of the amount of One Thousand and Forty-one Livres and sixteen sols claimed by the said verdicts with the interest on the amount, without prejudice to other dues, rights, actions, fees, costs of distraint, and expenses, I, Nicholas Marchand, Royal Bailiff attached to the Bench of the Royal Jurisdiction of Montreal, and there residing on Rue Notre Dame in the parish of the said Villemarie, had myself expressly brought to a house situated on the Market Square of the parish of the said Villemarie. This house was one storey in height; in one room there was a casement window on the front furnished with ironwork, a frame, iron braces, sash bolts and glass panes, all in good condition; a balcony of wooden timbers; a little room within the said room giving onto the rear where there was a casement window furnished with ironwork, a frame, iron braces, and sash bolts, but no glass panes; another room where there were two casement windows on the front furnished with ironwork, frames, iron braces, sash bolts, and glass panes, everything in good condition. One of the said two rooms as well as the whole of the said house and the premises hereinafter declared are on the same level as the said Market Square; two storerooms, in one of which there is a window furnished with ironwork, a frame, iron braces, sash bolts, and glass panes most of which are broken, and two doors of which one of the said doors leads to the said Square and the other into the main house; and in the other storeroom there is a window furnished with ironwork, a frame, iron braces, sash bolts, and glass panes most of which are broken, a door leading into the main house and a room in the rear in which there is a window furnished with ironwork, a frame, iron braces, and sash bolts, but no glass panes; the said room has a door leading into the said main house and the door is furnished with ironwork, iron braces, and latches but no metal work; the cellar and store-house are on the same level; all the doors and casement windows are furnished with iron braces, sash bolts, latches and other kinds of metal work and locks in very bad condition. The said house is made of stone and roofed with boards. There is a small yard with outhouses. The said house is built on a lot facing the said Market Square and adjoining on three sides the property of Messieurs Charly. The said lot has thirty feet of frontage by its entire depth. The which house and lot belong to the said Sieur LaDécouverte, of which house I have immediately and at present seized the foundations, the land on which it stands, and the property and placed it in the hands of our Lord the King to be sold if need be for the payment of the amount of one thousand and forty-one livres and sixteen sols, without prejudice as previously said, etc., by being publicly cried the sixty times customary in Paris and subsequently auctioned and sold by decree and legal authority of the Bench of the Royal Jurisdiction of Montreal to the highest and last bidder as is the custom of the Realm and Government, for which seized house I have appointed, appoint, and establish as auctioneer St Germain Lamoureux, residing in this said city on Rue Saint Paul in the aforementioned parish, to perform his duty in regard to the matter and overseeing of the said house and to give in the end a Good and Faithful Account of this administration when and to whom it shall appertain and to be paid his expenses and reasonable wages from the thing seized; the whole done in the presence and attendance of Sieur Jourdain, called Labrosse, and of Joseph Mercier, residing in this city, witnesses, whom I have brought expressly with me and who have signed the original and the copy of the present Seizure In Esse according to the Ordinance, made and done the said day, and signed St-Germain Lamoureux, Charles Labrosse, Joseph Mercier, and Marchand, Bailiff, with initials.[36]

Will of Sieur Silvain

30 April 1749
No. 3995
Exped.

Before the Royal Notary of the city and royal jurisdiction of Montreal undersigned and the witnesses named below, all residing in that city, was present Sieur Thimothée Silvain O'Siluya [*sic* = O'Sullivan], Esquire, King's Physician in this city and dwelling in Rue Saint Jacques, who sick in body and lying in bed in his house on the ground floor, in a Room facing onto the Street, and being completely sound in Mind, Memory, and Understanding, as it appeared to the said Notary and Witnesses by his movements, words, behaviour, and other external actions, Who considering with care the inconstancy and fragility of human life and knowing that there is nothing so certain and inevitable as death nor so uncertain as the hour of its coming, and wishing to avoid this irreversible surprise and to free himself of all his temporal affairs in order to have no other care at his Death than his Salvation, has dictated and stated to the said notaries and witnesses undersigned his last will and testament as follows.

Firstly, as a Catholic Christian he has commended and commends his soul to God the Creator, Father, Son, and Holy Spirit, imploring His divine Goodness through the merits of the Passion of Our Lord Jesus Christ not to judge him according to the enormity of his Sins or the rigour of His Justice,

---

36   See AJM, Registre des audiences [Register of Hearings], vol. 13, p. 1245.

but according to the Gentleness of His Mercy and His Fatherly Goodness, imploring also the Glorious Virgin Mary, Saint Timothy, his patron, and all the Saints of Paradise to look kindly upon him for the remainder of his days and at the hour of his Death to protect him, so that he may do penance for his Sins, die in a State of Grace, and enjoy Eternal Happiness.

The said Testator desires and understands that his debts be paid and that should any wrongs be found to have been done by him, reparation be made by the Executor of the Will hereinafter named, upon whose discretion and prudence he relies for his burial and he orders that as soon as possible a thousand masses be said.

The said Testator gives and bequeaths to the poor of the parish of this City the amount of One Hundred Livres to be paid once.

The said Testator gives and bequeaths to the work and fabrique of the parish Church of Saint Anne in Varennes, the District of Montreal, the amount of three hundred livres to be paid once for the building of a stone Chapel in the said parish to be used as an altar of repose in the processions of the Blessed Sacrament and others [*marginal note*: on the south-west side], the which amount of three hundred livres the said fabrique will not, however, be able to collect until the said stone Building has been begun.

The said Testator gives and bequeaths to the Two Children of the Lady Widow Youville, the Director of the General Hospital of this City, and to Sieur Ignace Gamelin the Younger, all the books making up his Library, without any being held back, to be divided equally among them.

And whatever remains of any and all of the other moveable or immoveable Properties, acquisitions, rights, titles, legal claims, or shares that shall appertain to the said Testator at the time of his death, in whatsoever place they may be located and in whatsoever they may consist, without holding anything back, the said Testator gives and bequeaths them as follows, namely, one third to Demoiselle Marie Louise Dufro de la Gemeraye, the wife of Sieur Ignace Gamelin, businessman in this city, to be held as her own and by her own; one third to Demoiselle Marie Clemence Dufro de la Jemeraye, the wife of Sieur Pierre Gamelin Maugras, a businessman in this said city, also to be held as her own and by her own; for he makes each of them his residuary legatees to dispose of his properties as things belonging to them; And the other and last third to the said two children of Dame Marguerite Dufro de la Jemeraye, widow of the late Francois You, Esquire, Sieur de Youville, in equal parts, whom he makes his residuary legatees to do with and dispose of his Properties as seems good to them; notwithstanding, the said Testator reserves in favour of the said Lady Widow Youville during her lifetime the use of the Properties that shall come by Inheritance to the said children as their part and portion after her death; and he orders that the personal property that will be found in his said estate as the inheritance of the said two Children of the said Lady Widow Youville shall be used to acquire additional inheritance or interest on income which she can enjoy while she is alive; and if the younger of these children of the said Lady Widow Youville, or his elder brother, decides to take Holy Orders or to join some religious order, the said Testator gives and bequeaths the funds and property of the said part and portion of the two children of the said lady Widow Youville to the said Demoiselle the Wife of the said Sieur Ignace Gamelin and to the said Demoiselle the Wife of the said Sieur Pierre Gamelin Maugras to be shared equally between them and to whom the said part and portion shall likewise belong as their own and to theirs, the said Testator substituting Them in the said part and portion of the said Two Children of the said Lady Widow Youville to enjoy and dispose of it by each of them as her own property as seems Good to them, once again after the death of the said Lady Widow Youville; and of her said Two Children, they will have the Enjoyment of it after the death of their mother, although they may not sell, hire, or transfer any part of the capital of the said properties in any way whatsoever.

And as the Executor of this present will the said Testator has named Sieur Charles Douaire, a businessman in this city whom he asks to attend carefully to the matter, and relinquishes all his worldly goods into his hands, according to Custom and Use.

The said Testator revokes all other testaments and codicils that he may have made before this present one, which alone represents his intention and last will. This was thus done, dictated, and stated by the said Testator to the said Notary and Witnesses And read to him by the said Notary in the presence of the witnesses And then read again so that he said he understood and upheld it. Done in the said room on the Ground Floor facing onto the said street In the year One Thousand Seven Hundred and Forty-nine On the thirtieth of April in the morning, in the presence of Sieurs Jean Baptiste Forestier Dulongpré and Etienne Le Beau, carpenter, Witnesses, who have signed with us the said Notary, And the said Testator having stated that he was unable to sign owing to the shaking of his hands, made his Mark thus o / .

JB Forestier
Etienne Le Beaux
Danré De Blanzy
(with initials)[37]

---

37   See AJM, Greffe du notaire Danré de Blanzy [Register of the Notary Danré de Blanzy], No. 3995.

Division among the Silvain Heirs, M. Gamelin and Others

9 November 1769
No. 3351
3 copies

Before the Royal Notaries of the Province of Quebec residing in Montreal were present the undersigned: On the one part, Sieur Ignace Gamelin, businessman of this city, and Dame Marie Louise Dufros de la Jemmeraye, his Wife, whom he has duly authorized for the purpose of these presents

And on the other part, Dame Marguerite Dufros de la Jemmeraye, the Widow of Sieur Francois You, Esquire, Sieur de Youville

And also on the other part, Joseph Boucher, Esquire, Sieur de Labroquerie, and Dame Marie Clemence Gamelin Maugras, his Wife, whom he has likewise authorized for the purpose of these presents in the name and as possessing the rights ceded from their co-heirs in the estate of Dame Marie Clémence Dufros de la Jemmeraye, their mother and mother-in-law, the Widow of Sieur Pierre Gamelin Maugras, on the day of her Death by an act of division made before Maître Panet, one of the undersigned Notaries, on the Third of September, One Thousand Seven Hundred and Sixty-eight.

The Above-named acting in their role as heirs each of a Third of the Estate of the late Dame Marie Renée Gaultier de Varennes, widow by first marriage of Sieur Christophe Dufros de la Jemmeraye and by second marriage of Sieur Silvain and residual legatee of the late Sieur Silvain, According to His Will received by Maître Danré de Blanzy, Notary, on the Thirtieth of April, One Thousand Seven Hundred and Forty-nine, Which parties desiring to Enjoy and Divide the properties belonging to the Estates of the said late Sieur and Dame Silvain have voluntarily proceeded with the division among themselves of the said properties in the Following Manner.

FIRST LOT

Firstly, the said Sieur and Dame Gamelin will have and it shall pertain to them as their Lot and the other parties will cede to them and abandon Title to their share for themselves and their heirs and as having legal claim to

1º Three Hundred and Fifty livres or shillings of interest on the principal of Seven Thousand livres owed by Charles Girardin Boulanger or His Agent for the price of a lot and house sold to him by contract made before Maître Mezière, Notary, on the Twentieth of January, One Thousand Seven Hundred and Sixty-six.

2º Land-based interest of Twenty livres as valued among the parties on the Capital of Four Hundred livres owed by the Sieur Soumande Delorme acting for Francois Le Page by contract made before Maître Adhémar, Notary, on the First of September, One Thousand Seven Hundred and Forty-seven.

3º Two-thirds of the large island of Varenne measured from the part of La Roche to the lower part of the said island.

4º Another interest of fifteen livres on the Capital of three hundred livres owed by Joseph Foisy as the remainder of a Loan of four hundred livres contracted by him before Maître Foucher, Notary, on the Seventh of July, One Thousand Seven Hundred and Fifty-six.

SECOND LOT

Secondly, the said Sieur and Dame Labroquerie will have and it shall pertain to them and the other parties will cede to them and abandon Title to their share for themselves and their heirs and as having legal claim to

1º A Garden located in this city on Rue Notre Dame and ending lengthwise at Rue St Jacques and adjoined on one side by Sieur Lefebvre Duchouquet acting as agent for Monsieur Feltz and on the other side by the Cabanac heirs signed by and named in the report of the late Sieur La Brosse, carpenter, and the pictorial map dated the Twenty-second of May, One Thousand Seven Hundred and Sixty-Six.

2º The Island with huts located in the Saint Lawrence River facing Varennes.

3º The rents owed by the Tenants of Isle Lamoureux located in front of Boucherville, those for the Six Arpents of the fief of Tremblay, and those owed at Chambly.

4º Boeure Island located below the large island facing Varennes.

THIRD LOT

And the said Lady Widow Youville will have and it shall pertain to her and the other parties will cede to her and abandon Title to their share in

1º The Land and Farm located at Varennes with Six Arpents of frontage by approximately twenty-five of depth with the houses built thereon and with the Lots that make up the wooded land of five arpents of frontage by approximately forty in depth.

2º The upper part of the large island above what is called La Roche located in the said place of Varennes and making up one-sixth of the said island, along with the farmers' island which is below the one with the huts.

The rents and the rights to the levies on the sale of immoveable property owed by the tenants of the sixteen arpents of the Silvain fief belonging to Varennes, for the said properties thus to be shared, enjoyed, done with and disposed of by the said Above-named Ladies and Gentlemen as shall seem best to them.

The said Parties agree that in case of the Sale of any of the properties mentioned in the present division they mutually commit themselves to give preference for it and to offer it to each other.

In regard to the outstanding debts owed to the said Estates and previous arrears, the Parties agree to share them among themselves by Thirds to the extent that they may be recoverable.

The said Parties also agree that in case there may be any legal proceedings occasioned by the properties thus divided the Costs will be Shared Equally by thirds and the same for any debts that may be owed by the said Estates. It was also agreed that since the lot and house belonging to the Estate of the said late Sieur Silvain and that falls to the share of Sieur and Dame Gamelin will scarcely pay the interest on its Settlement in three years, the said Sieur and Dame La Broquerie and Lady Widow Youville promise to pay to the said Sieur and Dame Gamelin during the said three years from each party eighty-three livres, six sols, eight deniers. Thus promised, obligated, made and done in the said Montreal, the Year one thousand seven hundred and sixty-nine, the ninth of November, in the afternoon, and the Parties have signed with the exception of the said Sieur Gamelin who stated that he was unable to sign owing to the infirmities that had deprived him of the ability to write and who asked Sieur Christophe Gamelin La Jemmeraye, his Son, to sign for him, the reading having been done . / . The Commitment is valid

C. Gamelin Maugras Lagemerais   Labroquerie
Gamelin Maugras Labroquerie   Widow Youville
Sanguinet   Lagemrais Gamelin
P. Panet[38]

---

38   See AJM, Greffe du notaire Pierre Panet [Register of the Notary Pierre Panet], No. 3351.

The Godchildren of Madame d'Youville

Jacques-Charles JODOIN, at Varennes, 22 March 1717. She signed: M de la gemerais.

Louise LANGLOIS, at Varennes, 16 May 1719. She signed: de Lajemerais.

Jean-Baptiste MONGEAU, at Varennes, 28 May 1721. She signed: marie marguerite Dufro.

Marie-Amable VALADE, at Montreal, 31 July 1733. She signed: Vve [Widow] Youville.

Marie-Louise-Michelle GAMELIN, 29 September 1734. She signed: M M Lajemerais Ve [Widow] Youville.

Marie-Anne-Marguerite MARCHANT de LIGNERIS, at Montreal, 3 July 1745. She signed: M M Lajemmerais veuve [widow] youville.

Jean-Baptiste DAGENAY, at Montreal, 9 June 1748. She signed: M M Dufros ve [widow] Youville.

Contract for the Supplying of Stone to the House of Charity

3696

†

[This cross is
on the contract.]

Before Anthoine Adhémar, Notary and Scrivener of the Island of Montreal, residing in Villemarie, and the witnesses named at the end, there were present in their own persons, on the one part, Sieur François Charron representing himself as well as Sieur Pierre Le Ber, Jean Fredin, and others who have joined together with them to build a House of Charity near this city; And on the other part, Jean Teyssier, called Lavigne, dwelling in the said Villemarie; the which parties have in good faith made the contracts and agreements which follow, namely, that the said Teyssier promises and obligates himself to supply to the said Sieur Charron in the said name all the lime necessary to construct the buildings that they intend to have erected near this city on the lot that Monsieur Dollier, the Superior of the Seminary of this Island, is giving them, on which they have already set up a cross; the which lime the said Teyssier promises and obligates himself to bring to the said premises and to the place that shall be indicated to him to begin from the month of April next up to the end of October likewise next, on pain of all expenses, damages, and interests, without the said Teyssier having any power to sell to other persons during the said time. And on his part, the said

Sieur Charron in the said name promises and obligates himself to pay to the said Teyssier for each of the said casks of lime fifty sols and the waste from this will be evaluated by those with the requisite knowledge and the said waste or loss will be in common between them, of which they will both in good faith mutually keep account. Moreover, the said parties have agreed that the said Sieur Charron also named will have taken from the quarry of the said Teyssier, which the said Charron has stated that he has seen and visited, all the free and corner stones required for the construction of the said building, and for the work done there to pay, just as he has stated, to the named LaBabille the amount of twenty livres, the which stones the said Sieur Charron shall have transported as seems best to him; and for each stone building of one hundred feet in length and three storeys using the stone from the said quarry the said Sieur Charron will pay to the said Teyssier the amount of fifty livres as may be needed, and if the building is larger or smaller the said Teyssier will be paid proportionately; and if the said stone, free and corner stones taken from the said quarry are found not to be right to set without free and corner stones and that they can only be used to make lime, the said Teyssiers shall be bound to have them measured by two persons possessing the requisite knowledge and after the said evaluation is done the said Sieur Charron in his own name promises to deduct from the said evaluation ten sols for each measurement, the which measurements of stone and lime shall be deducted from the price of the said Casks of Lime, for he also etc. promises and obligates himself etc. and the said Sieur Charron in his own name repeats etc. Made and done in the said Villemarie in the house and residence of the said Sieur Charron, the year one thousand six hundred and ninety-two, the seventeenth day of October in the afternoon, in the presence of Joseph Deno and Jean Quenneville, witnesses dwelling in the said Villemarie, undersigned with the said Sieur Charron and the Notary; the said Teyssier stated he did not know how either to write or to sign when asked to do so after the Reading was done according to the ordinance.

G. Quenneville   Charron[39]   Deno
Adhémar (with his initials)

---

39   François Charron signed his name with only one "r". See AJM, Greffe Adhémar [Register Adhémar], No. 3696.

Hearing

Lamoureux vs. Youville

Hearing held by Monsieur the Lieutenant General, Tuesday, 17 November 1733.

BETWEEN, on the one part, Sieur St Germain Lamoureux, appointed appraiser, represented by his agent Decoste by the Writ of the said Decoste of the 3rd of October last in default of the 6th of the month by Law against the Properties of the late Ladécouverte, recognized as Claimant on the 10th, The said writ holding the Lady Widow of Francois Youville de La Découverte to be condemned to pay to the said Sieur St Germain in the said name the amount of one hundred and eighty-one livre [sic] for one year's rent on the house situated on the Market Square of this city and adjudged to Her by the verdict of the 31st of October 1732. Besides which she has to supply to the said claimant a copy of the submission made to the notary by Sieur Ignace Gamelin the Elder, to be offered by Her to him who is so moving and with expenses; AND on the other part, Dame Marguerite Dufrost de la Jemeraye, widow of the late Francois Youville de la Découverte, the defendant appearing, who stated that she did not believe that she had to deliver the money for the said rent to the said claimant, that the pledge she had given was sufficient surety for the payment that will have to be made when the judgement to do so is rendered; and to satisfy the other claim contained in the said writ she remitted in our presence to the said Sieur Decoste the copies of the judgement whereby the Sieur Gamelin was bound surety and of the resulting notice made at the Notary's Registry on the 21st of November 1732 by which she asked for an act and to be dismissed, WE HAVING HEARD THE LITIGANTS and seen the said acts of surety of the said Sieur Gamelin have issued an act for the said remission of the said acts to the said Sieur Decoste and have consequently dismissed the said defendant from the action of the said Lamoureux L.D.C.M.[40]

Hearing

Beaucour vs.
Widow Youville

Hearing held by Monsieur Jacques Joseph Guiton Monrepos, King's Counsellor, Lieutenant General, on the bench of the Royal Jurisdiction of Montreal, Friday, the 22nd of July 1746.

---

40   See AJM, Registre des Audiences [Register of Hearings], vol. 14, p. 168.

BETWEEN on the one part, Dame Gabriel Francoise Auber, wife of Messire Josué Boiberthelot de Beaucourt, Knight of the Military Order of Saint Louis and Governor of this city and district, by Him duly authorized and as holding the power of attorney of Dominique Janson Lapalme, mason, [she] appearing as claimant represented by Bailiff Dumergue according to his capacity initialled by us this day for the purposes of the writ of Bailiff Dumergue of the sixteenth of this month whereby the defendant hereinafter named is bound to leave and vacate the premises of the house that she inhabits by the 13th of August next when the year's verbal lease is ended, the said Monsieur de Beaucour desiring to occupy it at that said time and having rented and reserved it from the said Lapalme with expenses in case of contestation; AND on the other part, Demoiselle Marie Marguerite Delajemmeraye, widow of the late Sieur François Youville, the defendant appearing, who after the said Dumergue concluded the purposes of his writ, stated that she is requesting that the power of attorney of the said Lapalme be served for her so that she can respond, WE, together with the King's Procurator, having heard the litigants, order that before a judgement can be given the power of attorney of the said Lapalme be served to the said Lady Defendant so that she may summarily respond as seems best to her on the first day of the hearing, the expenses being reserved, WE COMMAND etc.

Guiton Monrepos
Danré de Blanzy[41]

Commission as Director
of the General Hospital of Montreal

Henri-Marie De Breil de Pontbriand, Bishop of Quebec; Charles, Marquis de Beauharnois, Governor and King's Lieutenant General in New France; Gilles Hocquart, Knight, Intendant of Justice, Public Order, and Finances in this Country, all Heads of the Administration of the General Hospital established in Montreal by Letters Patent of His Majesty in the month of April 1694.

From the report that has been rendered to us of the present situation of the General Hospital of Montreal, wherein there remain only Brother Jean and Brother Joseph, and from the repeated requests that have heretofore been made to us since the nineteenth of October, one thousand seven hundred and forty-five by the Brothers Hospitallers making up the Community of the said Hospital to be discharged from the overseeing and direction of the said Hospital and from the care of

---

41   See AJM, Registre des Audiences [Register of Hearings], vol. 24, p. 7.

the poor, orphans, and crippled and infirm old men maintained in the said Hospital, owing to the small number of the said Brothers, their advanced age, and their infirmities which no longer permit them to be active and assist the said poor in the manner required and consequently to fulfil the goals set by His Majesty in establishing the said Hospital, for which reason they petition us to accept their resignation from the administration of the said Hospital and to allow them to remit to us all the moveable and immoveable properties belonging to the said Hospital to be disposed of as we see fit.

WE, insofar as is or may be needful, in consequence, and in order not to allow to vanish an institution so useful for the aid to the poor people of this Colony, have accepted and do accept the resignation and cession made to Us by the said Brothers Hospitallers.

WE HAVE provisionally and with the good pleasure of His Majesty and until may otherwise be ordained CHOSEN, NAMED, AND DEPUTIZED the Lady Widow YOUVILLE as Director of the said Hospital, in which capacity to oversee the poor interned there and the goods and properties that belong to the said Hospital, to receive the income from them to be used for the food and maintenance of the poor of the said Hospital, and to make all settlements and payments to the farmers and others supplying the said properties, all in conformity with the rulings set forth in the Letters Patent of the month of April, one thousand six hundred and ninety-four. The said Dame Youville shall be bound in the said capacity as Director to keep two accounts, entering exactly on one the amount of receipts and on the other the expenditures, so as to be able to render an account to us or to whoever will be appointed by us for the management and administration, whenever and howsoever that may be. The said Dame Youville shall not sell or transfer any of the properties of the said General Hospital for any cause or for any reason whatsoever. And since the building of the said Hospital has been completely neglected and there are many repairs that have to be done to make it habitable, WE AUTHORIZE the said Dame Youville to have done those that are most urgent and that are deemed to be indispensable by a survey to be prepared in the presence of the King's Procurator of the Royal Jurisdiction of Montreal, a copy of which survey will be sent to us along with a list of the outstanding debts owed to and by the said house. And, lastly, to place the said Dame Youville in a position that will enable her to provide the care for the said Hospital that we have committed to her oversight and administration, We have ruled that she shall be fed and lodged therein along with those persons who will be associated with her, the poor of whom she is taking care, and the two Brothers Hospitallers who are left in the said house.

WE ORDER that in the presence of the King's Procurator of the Jurisdiction and of the Brothers Hospitallers, an Inventory shall be made by Maître Danré, Notary, of the moveable and immoveable properties of the said Hospital and of the lands and papers relating to the ownership of these, the which moveables, titles, and papers the said Brothers shall be bound to present; and a notarized copy of the said inventory shall be delivered to the said DAME YOUVILLE.

MADE and done by US, Heads of the direction of the said Hospital, in Quebec City, the twenty-seventh of August, one thousand seven hundred and forty-seven.

† Henry-Marie, Bishop of Quebec
Beauharnois
Hocquart[42]

Ordinance Transferring the Properties of the General Hospital of Montreal to Madame d'Youville – 1 February 1748 [43]

HENRY MARIE DUBREIL de Pontbriand, King's Councillor in his Councils, by divine permission and with the blessing of the Apostolic Holy See, Bishop of Quebec.

ROLLAND MICHEL BARRIN, Knight, Marquis de la Galissonniere, Knight of the Royal and Military Order of Saint Louis, Captain of His Majesty's Ships, Commanding General of the whole of New France and the Province of Louisiana.

GILLES HOCQUART, Knight, King's Councillor in his Councils, Intendant of Justice, Public Order, and Finances in the said Country.

ALL HEADS of the administration of the General Hospital established in Montreal by Letters Patent of His Majesty in the month of April 1694.

WE HAVING SEEN the Inventory made of the moveable and immoveable properties of the General Hospital of Montreal by Maître Danré, Notary, and dated the fourth of September last and the days following, in compliance with our Ordinance of the preceding twenty-seventh of August, DO ORDER that the effects contained in the said inventory be remitted to Dame Youville, whom we have chosen and named as Director of the said Hospital, for which effects she shall give her receipt to be attached at the end of the original Inventory so as to render account to whom and how it may pertain; and for which to become effective, there shall be remitted in conformity with our Ordinance a notarized copy of the said Inventory. WE COMMAND etc. made and done at Quebec City on the first of February 1748. / .

H. M., Bishop of Quebec
LA GALISSONIERE
HOCQUART
Countersigned and sealed. / .

For the copy: HOCQUART

---

42   ASGM, archival copy.

43   See APQ, *Registre d'Ordonnances* [Register of Ordinances], vol. 35 (1748), pp. 2-3.

Removal from Office of Madame d'Youville, 1750

Henri Marie de Breil de Pontbriand, the Marquis de La Jonquiere, Francois Bigot, All Heads of the Administration of the Hospitals in Canada.

SEEING THAT the Ruling that we issued on the twenty-seventh of August, one thousand seven hundred and forty-seven whereby Dame Youville with her companions were given only provisional charge of the administration of the General Hospital of Montreal, We, in carrying out the orders of the King, do declare that the said Ruling no longer holds; that all the moveable and immoveable properties belonging to this house will be and shall remain attached by these presents to the General Hospital of Quebec City whose Religious Hospitallers shall take them into their care as properties belonging to the poor of their Community in Conformity with the Letters Patent of their Establishment; the said Nuns are charged with carrying out, insofar as is possible, the obligations of the foundation of the General Hospital of Montreal, and especially to feed and maintain the Ill people, the old men, the cripples, and the orphans of the district of Montreal to the extent that the income of the said Nuns will allow, and for which they shall make all settlements and payments to the farmers and others supplying the said properties; all this shall be in conformity with the rulings set forth in the Letters Patent of the General Hospital of Montreal and of that of Quebec City, except that there may be some individuals who will claim certain rights to the said properties, in which case they shall have three months within which to make their representations before Monsieur the Intendant, who by these presents himself claims jurisdiction over all discussions that may arise from the said Merger, The which, to this end, shall be Read, Published, and likewise served to the known interested parties with dispatch by the King's Procurator in the jurisdictions that cover the existing properties of the said General Hospital, The which said properties shall still remain mortgaged to the creditors of the said Hospital, for whom we expressly reserve the rights over the said properties without, however, their being extended to the properties possessed at present by the General Hospital of Quebec City, Which we have declared will only be able to accept the present merger on the express condition that it will not in any way be responsible for its former debts, but only for those that are attached to it by these presents in regard to both moveable and immoveable properties, for which the said Hospital will take charge by means of an inventory to be made in the presence of the King's Procurator in the Jurisdiction of Montreal by Maître Danré, Notary; and in order to expedite the payment of the said debts, we are allowing the Nuns of the General Hospital of Quebec City to sell the building, garden, and courtyard of the General Hospital of Montreal and the furnishings that are not worth moving to Quebec City.

And since we have been given to understand that Dame Youville and her companions may not be able to find lodgings this late in the year and that the Ill people for whom she has cared up to the present cannot for this same reason be transported to Quebec City, We have allowed and do allow them to remain in the said General Hospital until the month of July next, as well as to enable the said Dame Youville during this time to prepare the accounts and complete the Inventory of Goods and Chattels and papers with which she has been charged. Made and done in Quebec City, the fifteenth of October 1750.

> † H. M., Bishop of Quebec
> La Jonquiere
> Bigot[44]

Citizens' Petition, 1751

To Our Lords, the Bishop, Governor General, and Intendant of New France

The Undersigned Governor, King's Lieutenant, Major, officers, clergy, seigneurs, businessmen, burgesses, and inhabitants of the City and District of Montreal humbly petition and have the honour to represent to you the innumerable goods that the General Hospital has procured for this district and the necessity for maintaining it there. Furthermore, this institution was created by legitimate authority and invested with all the necessary formalities.

In fact, according to the letters patent that His Majesty granted for the establishment of the General Hospital of Quebec City in 1692, it was recognized at that time, as stated in Article 28, that the said hospital would not be sufficient for the needs of the Colony. He foresaw that the number of the poor would increase as the country became more and more established, and that as a result this hospital would not be able to accommodate all of them. His Majesty also foresaw that as the lands reached farther and farther away, the poor could not be brought back there or benefit from this source of help owing to the distance at which they were from it; he therefore at that time deemed it necessary to establish a second hospital in this City.

This undertaking was all the more easily accomplished since certain charitable people offered to perform this good work and bring it to its fulfilment. The said letters patent contain the clause and the express reservation that the said INSTITUTION SHALL SERVE IN PERPETUITY WITHOUT UNDERGOING ANY CHANGE OF PLACE OR BEING USED FOR ANY OTHER PIOUS WORK. His Majesty, in order to give greater force to these letters patent, commits therein HIS WORD AS KING and promises to those persons desiring to contribute to this

---

44   ASGM, collated copy signed by Bigot.

institution that it WILL BE IN PERPETUITY FOR THE AID AND RELIEF OF THE POOR OF THE DISTRICT OF THIS CITY.

This word so truly given rallied from every side the charity of the good and faithful citizens of this city, the work began, continued, and was fulfilled as it is today. Divine Providence inspired many to give a part of their goods to found this hospital and to make it a fit place to receive the poor of this district. The intention of the founders was to provide for the needs of the poor of the region without the revenues being transferred elsewhere, for in the latter case they never would have contributed had they thought that their intention would not be carried out.

In 1694, His Majesty re-confirmed the word that he gave in 1692 that the said INSTITUTION WILL BE IN PERPETUITY IN MONTREAL AND FOR THE POOR OF MONTREAL ACCORDING TO THE INTENTION OF THE FOUNDERS, and he dispatched the letters patent confirming all these rights and the other things contained therein.

No measures more just could have been taken to assure the firm foundation of this institution. How, then, could it be imagined that it might be destroyed or moved elsewhere? It is the King who engaged the individuals to do it at their own expense. It is he who sent them the letters patent. It is IN PERPETUITY THAT HE PLEDGED HIS ROYAL WORD THAT IT SHOULD EXIST. Most certainly, nothing can be added to or taken away from that which so legitimate an authority has determined in terms so positive. To do so, would be not to take the King at his word. It would be to make useless the letters patent rendered on this matter. It would go directly against the intention and will of the founders and benefactors as approved and authorized by the King himself and which are for this reason always to be respected and are worthy of being carried out. It would be to close one's eyes to the most urgent need of a great number of the poor of this district and to harden one's heart against their most pressing needs; and, lastly, it would be to expose oneself every day to the mortal anguish of seeing perish without hope of help an infinite number of the poor of both sexes and every age for whose relief so many charitable souls have had the intention of providing by contributing to the costs of a general hospital.

The petitioners know very well, Our Lords, that the goodness and tenderness of your hearts towards the relief of the poor and their wretchedness are so great that you cannot fail to be moved by their sad condition or wish to deprive them of a refuge that the charity of the good citizens of this city has procured for them in establishing the said General Hospital, which was founded solely with this intention and on THE WORD OF THE KING THAT IT SHOULD BE IN PERPETUITY.

No one, Our Lords, is unaware of the usefulness and, indeed, necessity of the General Hospital in this district as much for aged, ill, and retired soldiers as for orphans and abandoned children. Today it serves as a refuge for fallen women and for the insane. It is a very useful place of relief in times of epidemic, for putting up convalescents and the incurable, and a room has even been set aside there to treat the shameful diseases born of lustful excesses.

In sum, Our Lords, it is a settled and established institution that has existed since 1694; and as it contains nothing against either Religion or the state, but is solely for the relief of the poor, it would seem to merit the honour of your protection to be preserved and perpetuated according to the terms of the letters patent as being useful and necessary to the colony.

It is true that there are many debts to be paid and major repairs to be made, but we trust in Divine Providence and eagerly await the charity of pious and well-intentioned souls for this good work. We may hope that in times to come the business affairs will be satisfactorily settled by the wisdom and good guidance of the ladies who are at present caring for it and who once again today offer their labours and their pains if they are deemed worthy to continue to care for the poor.

The petitioners therefore hope, Our Lords, that your hearts already being rendered sensible to so moving a goal, you will desire to take into account the interests of the poor and afflicted of their city who without the succour of a hospital in this city shall be absolutely abandoned. It is not possible, owing to the distance between the places and the infirmities of the greater number, to move them to the Hospital of Quebec City, which is already insufficient for the needs of its own poor. Even though it will come into possession of the properties of the hospital of this city, it will still not be in any position to care for them because of the small amount of revenue it be able to collect from them, experience teaching that in this country it is difficult to make a profit from properties unless one is present and puts a great deal of effort into cultivating them. Thus, in destroying the hospital of this city whose existence depends much more on the charity of pious people and the labours of those in charge of it than on any revenues, this would amount to destroying a good work existing at present without hope of being able to replace it.

All this taken into consideration, Our Lords, may it please you in view of the evidence in the present request and seeing that by the letters patent of His Majesty granted in 1692, and confirmed by those of 1694, his intention was that the institution of a General Hospital in this city be IN PERPETUITY, to honour it by your protection in maintaining its interests and, consequently, to obtain from His Majesty that the institution of the said hospital shall be maintained and preserved, and that it will continue to possess all its properties, as it has done up to the present, and thus the petitioners would ask of him by the request, conforming to the present one, that they shall have the honour of presenting to His Excellency, Monsieur Rouillé, and that it be ordered that Dame Youville and her companions shall have the administration of the said hospital in place of the Brothers Hospitallers, some of whom are deceased and others of whom have left the house, that she enjoy the rights and privileges contained in the letters patent of 1694, which shall in this respect carry the same force concerning the administration of the properties of the said hospital, along with the offers made by the said Dame Youville and her companions to give an annual accounting of its revenues and to maintain everything in good condition according to the inventory that was made and as they were charged by the said Inventory. And the petitioners will not cease from imploring Heaven for your health and prosperity.

Longeuil, Adhemar de Lantagnac, Noyan, Malhiot, Normant, vicar general, Foucher, Sonnonnine, de Lacorne, knight, De Rouville, C. N. Lamarque, Godefroy, B. Neveu, Deat, priest, Toussains Baudry, Cheneville, Benoit, officier, Joseph Gamelin, Bondy, Courraud Lalane, Lamoinodière, Contrecoeur, Hubert, Guillon, Herbin, Toussaint Pothier, Magnan, St Ange Charly, Laforce, Jacques Hervieux, W. Guillon, priest, Dufy, I. Soumande, A. Foucher, Quentin Mauroy, J. Gadoumogé, Fr. Decouagne, Brebion, J. B. Daguilhe, Louis Mesnard, Joseph Pouget, Charle Dioney, Niger, Ch. B. Laverendry, Nicolas Morein, Thieophille Barthe, M. Falcoz, priest, Duchaine, Maugrat, Frémon, Gay, priest, Gabriel Dumon, Etienne Petit, Dartigny, Sebastien Malidor, Maubasin, Decoste, Dechambault, DeCouagne, Fourier, J. LeGuillon, Charles Douillard the Younger, Miloc, P. Guillet, Saulquin H. R., Monier, Ignace Gamelin, Héry, Lacorne-Dubreuil, J. Provanché, Peigné, priest, Bouat, P. Decouagne, Hervieux, Michel Belaire, Pierre Gagnier, Moiley, Antoine Janin, J. Caulier

Petition of Madame d'Youville and Her Associates, 1751[45]

To Our Lords, the Bishop, Governor General, and Intendant of New France

Dame Youville and her companions most humbly petition you and have the honour of reminding you that by your ordinance of the month of August 1747 you provisionally charged them with the administration of the properties of the General Hospital of Montreal and with the care of the poor who were and might in future be there; moreover, so that they might conform to your orders and with the formal promise that you made to have the Court ratify their appointment, they dedicated themselves to this work and employed all their care and all their labours to re-establishing this house which was nearly abandoned and almost totally in ruins. The Lord appeared to accept their services and showed His favour by the blessing that he freely in his pure mercy poured out on their weariness and cares by procuring for them unforeseen assistance that enabled them to begin the rebuilding and, indeed, expansion of this hospital so essential to the colony. In fact, from the four poor old men in extreme

---

45   ASGM, autograph copy of Father Louis Normant, P. S. S.

misery, without linen, uncared for, and exceedingly dirty whom they found upon arriving there, the number has today increased by more than two-thirds, cleanliness reigns, and daily fare is provided, as well as all necessities. Moreover, although this house was called a general hospital, it was nevertheless scarcely so, for those who were in charge of the administration were bound to receive only men and to exclude people of the other sex; but today people of both sexes are accepted and a hall has been set side and furnished for women; even the insane and incurables find refuge there, and charity is extended to all the afflicted. Nor has there been neglect of the salvation and rescue of fallen women and girls who corrupt the youth, for more than a dozen rooms have been opened to serve as a refuge where they are nurtured and instructed. The properties in the countryside have likewise increased in profitability through their diligence, and many noticeable changes can be seen there in the repairs they have had done.

Their zeal for the service of the poor has in nowise lessened, Our Lords; they are proud of being servants of the poor and they are at present even more ardently disposed to devote their time, their labours, and their lives to maintaining this house.

Yet, by an unforeseen reversal after so happy a beginning and without to their knowledge having given any cause for dissatisfaction, they have learned in a manner that leaves no room for doubt that you are thinking, Our Lords, of removing from them the administration of the said hospital and that you are busy arranging the transfer of its properties and revenues to that of Quebec City or to some other community. However they may evaluate their merits and talents, they nevertheless take the liberty of respectfully reminding you of the unfortunate consequences that would necessarily result from such a change. In fact, a nearly irreparable wrong would be done to the poor of the district of Montreal who hold a claim upon this house as having been built expressly for them and as a place where they can be sure of finding a secure refuge in their old age. Yet, they find themselves deprived, without resources, and exposed to dying in misery, since it is most unlikely that they can be received by the hospital of Quebec City which is sixty leagues away, thus excluding the possibility of their finding an opportunity to apply for admittance or to undertake the journey.

Besides, this action directly contravenes the intentions of the founders and abolishes so holy and so necessary an institution founded by the pious generosity of the Lords and to the formation of which the charity of the faithful has contributed, and which the alms of the people of the district of Montreal have sustained and would continue to do so if it were to remain, but which will cease absolutely if its destruction is definite. They will never forget the wrong that has been done to them and will carry always in their hearts the most piercing sorrow upon seeing the sad ruins of a house that the piety of their forefathers built to receive the members of the body of Jesus Christ.

If it be allowed on behalf of the cause of religion to adduce other reasons of interest, it can be clearly seen that the Court would be involved in considerable expenditures because by moving and changing the hospital it will be necessary to add more rooms to the hospital of Quebec City, which are at present insufficient for all the poor seeking admission. Thus, to destroy on one hand in order to build on the other appears to be a superfluous expense and contrary to the good of the colony, above all when the institution is against neither religion nor the state nor the good of the people, but on the contrary is the product of religion and helps to expand it. It is the King who by his letters patent established it and destined it for the soldiers no longer able to serve him; in the end, it is a sure refuge for all the poor of the district. It would be a great pity to see such large buildings and a church built and decorated destroyed and profaned. Your religion and your piety are too well known, Our Lords, to allow one to fear that you will resolve thus.

If it is, Our Lords, your awareness of the debts that encumber this house and of the repairs that have to be made that inclines you to doubt whether it can sustain itself without extraordinary help from the Court, which the latter would not provide, the petitioners have the honour of reminding you that their trust is completely in Divine Providence, while only your protection and the consent of His Majesty are requested. They will always receive with the greatest gratitude the blessings and goods that Providence wills for them; they in nowise would importune either you or the Court for that, because they propose within three years to liquidate the debts in France of Brother Chrétien and to come to terms with his creditors for the remission they have offered and to pay as soon as possible the debts he incurred in Canada.

In order to do which, they request that they replace the Brothers Hospitallers, that they enjoy all the rights, blessings, and privileges contained in their letters patent and which shall remain the same for them in regard to the institution and administration of the said hospital; in consequence of which, they obligate themselves to give an annual account of the revenues of the said hospital and of the alms given to the poor; and if in future, for unforeseen reasons, His Majesty shall deem it appropriate to remove the administration of the said hospital from the petitioners, he will reimburse them for the improvements, repairs, and payments that they may have made from their own money and they shall replace the creditors whom they have paid.

Letters Patent of 1753

LOUIS, BY THE GRACE OF GOD King of France and of Navarre, To all to whom these present letters shall come, GREETINGS. We have been informed that by a Decision of the twenty-seventh of August, one thousand seven hundred and forty-seven, the Lord Bishop of Quebec, Our Lord Governor and Lieutenant General in New France, and the Lord Intendant of the said country, all three heads of administration of the general hospital established in Montreal by Letters Patent of the month of April, one thousand six hundred and ninety-four, had determined, for reasons contained in the said decision, to appoint the Lady Widow Youville as Director of the said hospital, as well as of the properties belonging to it, to collect the revenues and to render an account, all as described in the said decision. Since different arrangements have been proposed in regard to the said general hospital whose affairs have been found to be in considerable disorder and it has been proposed to merge it with the general hospital established in Quebec City, and since the merger has even been provisionally ordered by an ordinance of the said Lords Administrators General of the fifteenth of October, one thousand seven hundred and fifty; but since what they believed to be the determining reasons no longer obtain owing to the offers made by the said Lady Widow Youville who always held the direction of the said hospital by a special arrangement to acquit the debts of which she found herself in charge; And since by this arrangement it will be possible to keep in Montreal the assistance for which the said institution was established; It is owing to these considerations that by Decree of our Council of the twelfth of May, one thousand seven hundred and fifty-two, We, by revoking and annulling the ordinance of the said Lords Bishop, Governor General, and Intendant of the fifteenth of October, one thousand seven hundred and fifty, containing the merger of the said hospital of Montreal with the General Hospital of Quebec City, have ordered that in consequence of the offers made by the said Lady Widow Youville to acquit the debts of the said hospital of Montreal, an act or agreement shall be drawn up between them and the said Lords Administrators General, whom we have authorized to this end, to determine the amount of the said debts and the sources that will be used by the said Lady Widow Youville to acquit them, to establish the conditions under which she shall continue to direct the said hospital, and to make such other agreements as they shall deem appropriate for this matter, including the transferral of creditors' rights to the Widow Youville for what she would have paid in discharging the said hospital, and for her and hers to exercise with cause the rights to the properties of the said hospital in case, only and following her offers, she should be relieved of the directorship of the said hospital. Be it ordered by us that the said act or Agreement shall have as an objective the establishing and fixing in a stable and permanent manner the administration of the said hospital. In consequence of the said Decree, there was passed on the eighth of September of the same year, one thousand seven hundred and fifty-two, an act between, on the one part, Sieur de Pontbriand, the Bishop of Quebec, Sieur the Marquis Duquesne, the Governor and Lieutenant General, and Sieur Bigot, the Intendant in New France, all three heads of the administration of the said hospital, and on the other part, the said Lady Widow Youville, attended by Demoiselles Louise Thaumur, Catherine Demers, Catherine Rainville, Therese Laser, Agathe Veronneau, Marie Antoinette Relle, and Marie Joseph Besnard, her companions in the said direction. From the report rendered to us of the said act, We have taken cognizance of the fact that, on the one hand, the debts of the said hospital have been established at the amount of forty-eight thousand four hundred and eighty-six livres, seventeen sols, and ten deniers, including thirty-eight thousand livres that have been owing since one thousand seven hundred and forty-seven, when the said Widow Youville became director, according to the inventory made of the goods and chattels belonging to the said hospital, as well as ten thousand four hundred and eighty-six livres, seventeen sols, and ten deniers in advances made since by the said Widow and paid from her money for expenses necessary to her administration; on the other hand, since the said Widow Youville has offered to acquit the said debts, if it pleases us to confirm her in the Direction of the said hospital, either by cancelling the said amount of ten thousand four hundred and eighty-six livres, seventeen sols, and ten deniers advanced by her for the needs of the said hospital, or through the assistance that has been assured her or that she has reason to hope for from charitable and well-intentioned people, especially a sum of eight thousand livres deposited to this end with Sieur the Abbé Cousturier, Superior of the Seminary of Saint-Sulpice in Paris, and another sum of six thousand livres bequeathed for the same purpose by Sieur Bouffandeau, priest of the Seminary in Montreal. Wishing to provide for the administration of the said hospital and to secure for the said Colony the advantages that it has reason to expect, FOR THESE REASONS and others, We acting on the advice of our Council and with our certain knowledge, full power, and Royal Authority, and both after having seen in our said Council the said act of the eighth of September, one thousand seven hundred and fifty-two, with which we have concurred and do concur, and of which a copy from the said Sieur Bigot, the Intendant, is attached and countersealed with these presents, and with the advice of the said Lord Bishop of Quebec, and the said Lords Governor and Lieutenant General and Intendant, We have ordered and by these presents signed by our hand do order, will, and find pleasing to us that which follows.

Article 1

The Lady Widow Youville and her Companions shall be and shall remain responsible for the direction and administration of the said hospital of Montreal, to which end We have substituted and do substitute them for the Brothers Hospitallers who had heretofore been established there, and We desire that they enjoy the rights, privileges, exemptions, and prerogatives contained in the said letters patent of the fifteenth of April, sixteen hundred and ninety-four, relating to the said institution.

Article 2

The Lady Widow Youville shall be bound in accordance with her offer to give and remit to the said hospital the said sum of ten thousand four hundred and eighty-six livres, seventeen sols, and ten deniers that she has advanced for expenses necessary to the hospital and to use for the payment of the other debts the said two amounts of eight thousand and six thousand livres designated for that purpose, and other means of assistance that may arise shall be applied to the same end.

Article 3

In the case in which the Lady Widow Youville and her companions shall pay the said debts out of funds belonging to them, They may replace the Creditors who will have been paid by exercising the rights to the properties of the said hospital and by disposing of them in accordance with the arrangement they shall make on this matter. But the said replacement shall only be made for the part that they have paid out of their own money and not for the debts that they will be able to pay from the interest on the revenues of the hospital or the alms they may be given. Likewise, the said replacement can only come into effect in the case in which the direction of the said hospital should be removed from the Lady Widow Youville and her Companions.

Article 4

They shall likewise be reimbursed for the expenditures they have been obliged to make from their own money for the repairs to and furnishing of the said house, but not from the revenues of the hospital or the alms that may be given to them. But they shall only be able to claim the said reimbursement in the case in which the Direction of the hospital should be removed from them within the period of thirty years from the day that these presents are registered. And should such case occur after the expiration of the said thirty years, each of them will only receive a life annuity of two hundred and fifty livres per year on the properties of the said hospital.

Article 5

They shall be fed and maintained both in sickness and in health at the expense of the House, and the fruit of their labours shall be reinvested in it.

Article 6

They shall render an account every year to the said Lords Administrators General of the revenues of the said hospital from the alms they have received and from the fruit of their labours.

Article 7

They shall not transfer properties or incur loans or extraordinary expenditures without the approval of the above-mentioned heads of administration or, indeed, without the consent of an Office of Administration if in future We deem it appropriate to establish one.

Article 8

They shall provide Brother Joseph, the last surviving of the Brothers Hospitallers whom they are succeeding, with a life annuity of two hundred and fifty livres, which may in future be increased or diminished if it is deemed necessary by the heads of administration.

Article 9

Their number shall be twelve, and this number may not be increased without Our express permission which we will only grant on the advice of the Administrators General.

Article 10

They shall divide among themselves the occupations of the House under the authority of the said Lord Bishop. They shall admit into their ranks only those persons approved by him to replace those who have departed through death or otherwise.

Article 11

They shall under the same authority remove and expel without any compensation those persons in their ranks who do not behave themselves in a fitting manner. Each individual woman will be able to leave the house when and if she should so desire.

Article 12

They shall enjoy their inherited goods and properties which they may keep as their own, like secular people living in the world. But their heirs shall not inherit the moveable goods belonging to them in the hospital at the time of their death in the service of the poor, except in the case in which they have disposed of them in their favour. And in the latter case, the effects that have been furnished to them by the hospital for their furniture, clothing, and other items pertaining to their upkeep shall not be included among their moveable goods.

Article 13

They shall allow the said Lord Bishop to prescribe for them whatever rules may be necessary for their spiritual life in the said house.

THUS WE GIVE AS A MANDATE to Our well-loved and faithful Lords, de Pontbriant, Bishop of Quebec, the Marquis du Quesne, Governor and Lieutenant General in New France, and Bigot, the Intendant of the said country, and to those who in future shall succeed them, and to Our well-loved and faithful members of the Superior Council of Quebec, and to all Our other officers to see that these presents be registered and executed in every point according to their form and content, obviating any troubles or hindrances; FOR such is Our pleasure. IN witness thereof We have had Our Seal affixed to the same letters patent. Given at Versailles, the third day of the month of June, the year of Grace, one thousand seven hundred and fifty-three and of Our reign the thirty-eighth.

LOUIS
FOR THE KING
Rouillé[46]

---

46   ASGM, Lettres patentes [Letters Patent], original manuscript.

Registration of the Letters Patent

SEEING THAT in the Council the Letters Patent of His Majesty, signed by Louis, and underneath for the King by Rouillé, given at Versailles the third of June last, whereby His Majesty gives the direction and administration of the hospital of Montreal to the Lady Widow Youville and her companions, to which end His Majesty has put them in place of the Brothers Hospitallers who had previously been established there, and wills that they enjoy the rights, privileges, exemptions, and pre-rogatives contained in the Letters Patent of the twentieth of April, one thousand six hundred and ninety-four, concerning this institution; to which Letters is joined a copy of the Act passed between My Lord the Bishop of Quebec, Du Quesne, the Governor and Lieutenant General, and Bigot, the Intendant of this country, and the said Lady Widow Youville attended by her companions, containing the offers the said Lady Youville therein mentioned, the said act being dated the eighth of September, one thousand seven hundred and fifty-two, signed by Bigot for the copy. The which above-mentioned act is confirmed by His Majesty by the above-stated Letters Patent, which HAVING BEEN HEARD, the King's Procurator General calling the motion, THE COUNCIL has ordered that the said Letters Patent and Act attached thereto be registered in the Register of Measures Introduced by this Council to be executed according to their form and content. DONE at Quebec City in the said Superior Council on Monday, the first of October, one thousand seven hundred and fifty-three.

BOISSEAU[47]

First Charge of Bishop de Pontbriand to the Grey Nuns

HENRY MARIE DU BREIL DE PONTBRIAND, by Divine Permission and with the blessing of the Holy See, Bishop of Quebec, present Suffragan of the said Holy See, Honorary Canon of the Metropolitan church of Tours, Councillor of the King in His Councils, etc. TO the Ladies of Charity charged by His Majesty with the direction of the General Hospital of Montreal in consequence of the Letters Patent registered with the Superior Council of Quebec, Greetings and the Blessing of Our Lord.

WE have seen with pleasure, our very dear Sisters, all the improvements that you have made to the house that has been entrusted to your care, and our joy has greatly increased since we have learned that you are disposed to continue to work with a new

---

47   ASGM, original copy signed by Boisseau.

courage and with the same economy. We hope that the Lord will continue to shower his blessings on your labours and we implore Him to do so most urgently.

You have asked us for rules for the internal government of your house so as to prevent the abuses that slide in unawares everywhere. While we are convinced that Rules will be of no use to you for as long as you preserve the sentiments of piety and fervour with which we see you are imbued and that Charity alone will be sufficient to maintain order among you, we think nonetheless that it would be good to meet your expectations if only to give you occasion to practise that holy obedience that is the soul of every Community. We thus promise you the Rules.

While you await them, here is what we think we ought to suggest to you.

1. Until you undertake other arrangements, we approve that you follow to the letter that which is contained in the three loose leaves written by the hand of Monsieur Normant and that you have observed for a long time. We have initialled these three leaves and wish that they be copied into a special book that will serve as a register for our ordinances and regulations. The first section should carry the inscription REGULATION, the second is a space for a commitment to be signed by you, and the third should have as title, Dispositions for Proper Conduct.

2. Although you were only supposed to receive old men and the sick, we are pleased to see that your zeal extends even to women who are regarded as dangerous and who have been sent to you by those in Authority. We do feel, however, that we should warn you that you should only receive them with a Writ from Monsieur the General, or the Commandant, or from Monsieur the Intendant, Monsieur the Commissary, or Monsieur the Judge; and we hope that these Gentlemen will pay the Hospital the board that Monsieur the Intendant wished to fix, it not being just that they be fed from the goods of the poor. We even wish that you do not so overcharge yourselves with this good work that the primary object of your institute suffer from it. And being convinced that one cannot reach the heart of these women except through gentleness, we exhort you to follow your usual practice and in no way subject them to corporal penances for their past life, otherwise leaving to your discretion how you may punish them for faults committed in the house.

3. Since you think it is fitting that all those who belong to your house should be clothed uniformly, we approve the habit that you have proposed to us, and which one of your ladies presented herself to us wearing. It is a grey dress with two or three pleats, a striped cotton apron, a black kerchief, a kind of frill of batiste or muslin, and over everything a sort of coiffe [*bagnolet*] of black gauze. We consent that in accordance with the practice of a number of ladies you wear a small silver Crucifix.

4. We hope that secular people should not in anywise come into the room where you assemble for your recreation and for the work; see if you can find a place for a room to receive them when they come to visit you.

5. Even though you are permitted to go to any confessor in the city who has the faculty to hear confessions, we exhort you to make a habit of going to the one whom

our vicar general shall appoint; he will take care to send you another one every three months; you will be able to choose them yourselves by notifying the Superior.

6. You will continue to recognize Madame Youville as Superior. When the issue of a change does arise, which I believe you do not desire and would only make as a last necessity, you will follow the rules that we shall presently prescribe; but since accidents do occur even when they are least expected, we believe that it is prudent for the said Dame Youville to choose from among her companions the three eldest whom she will instruct in the temporal affairs of the house by relating to them her projects and resources and by having them read the accounts and even sign them. And since they have to be approved by the Heads of Administration, the three first should be the kind of people who are looked upon as being discreet and counsellors of the house, whom you may choose among yourselves or elect by ballot. And since the Superior is often obliged to be absent on account of business and innumerable other needs, we have asked Monsieur Normant to interview you all individually and to appoint one of you as a substitute for the Superior in case she is unable to act. We therefore wish that you make it a duty to recognize and obey her and that she shall have the right to order you to do whatever she considers to be appropriate.

7. Since by the letters patent your number is fixed at twelve, we think that you should only fill it up by receiving new members after they have dwelt in the house for two years; nor, when the number of twelve has been filled, should more than three postulants be received, and they will probably not be vested with the habit that you have chosen until they have lived in the house for one year, been examined by you, and received your consent.

Moreover, our very dear Sisters, in conformity with the Letters Patent, would you make your comments on what we have just remarked to you and ask for any clarifications that you think are necessary. This is why we have expressly reserved for ourselves the right to change, increase, or diminish. And in order to reflect thereon more at leisure, we would like you to send us immediately a copy of the Letters Patent, of the three loose leaves that we have exhorted you to follow, and of the present regulations, giving your agreement by signing at the bottom.

Given at Montreal during the course of our Visit, under our seal and signature and countersigned by our secretary, the fifteenth of June, one thousand seven hundred and fifty-five.

† H. M., Bishop of Quebec
For Bishop Briand, Canon, Secretary

Account of the Persons Lodged
in the General Hospital of Montreal
at the Time of the Fire, 18 May 1765

This list was found in the Public Archives of Canada [now National Archives of Canada] by Monsieur Lucien Brault who kindly notified me about it and sent a photocopy.

Boarders

Mme Sermonville with 60 livres income
Mme de Blainville 150 livres income
Mesdemoiselles Nouchette, mother,
    daughter-in-law, and granddaughter
Mme Le Gardeur with 300 livres
Mademoiselle St Michel
Mme Charlotte Boisclaire
Mme Celoron

Mme Forestier
The two Demoiselles Moite
Mme Hertel
Mme Volent
Mme Louviere 200 livres
Mademoiselle Cuisy
Mme Lobinois 700 livres

The others have no resources
18 Sisters

Poor People

The Widow Herault
Marie Anne Flibote
Marie Joseph La Lande
Amable La Lande
Charlotte Coté
Catherine La Garde
La Roullard
Margueritte La Fantaisie
Francoise Gagnon
Angelique Coulon
Javotte Grignon
Marie St Pierre
Roze Gagnon
Marie La Douceure
The Widow Pilaire
Marie René La Perle

Marie Flarty
Margueritte
Josephe Peltier
Marie Anne L'Esperance
Josephe Guillory
Catherine Guiette
Colombine
Mannette St Sauveur
Anasthasie Bourgeois
Marie Josephe Laviolette
Marie Josephe Lamie
Angelique Arlain
Jannette Boismenue
Archange La Lande
Angelique Le Duc
Marie Jacques

Marie Anne Roch
The woman from Saint Maurice
Baboche Sansfaçons
Jean Delorier
Bazile La Jeunesse
François Gausselin
Jacques Charbonnier
Francois SansSoucy
Francois Champagne
Jean Baptiste, a blind man
Joseph Chatillon
Cezar Panis
Francois Perinault La Marche
Bernard Bergé
Michel Chorette
Francois La Garde

Joseph Heroux
Estienne St Amour
Louis Babin, called Picard
Bazile La Becasse
Joseph Francoeur
Alexandre Bellefeuille
Gabriel La Comble
Louis St Germain
Honoré Godereault
George Anglois
Michel Lesperance
Joseph Goguet
The simpleton La Fleur
Pierre Cary
Ambroise La Sonde

Illegitimate Children

Louison – Luc – Chrisostome – Jean – Louis – Martin – Francois – Amable – Baboche – Therese – Marie Genevieve – Marie Marguerite– Marie Josephe – Marie Angelique – Magdelaine – Marie Anne –

On the verso of the document, in another hand, is the following [in English in the original]:

An account of the persons maintained in the Convent of Soeurs Grises, as likewise of the Revenue upon which they were supported copied from one given by Madame Euville Superior of the said Convent.

fyled 27 June 1765[48]

---

48   APC, Series S, vol. XI, p. 2.

Will and Testament
of the Lady Widow Youville

8 October 1757
No. 7436

Present was Dame Marie Marguerite Dufros de la Jemerays, the widow of Sieur Francois You de Youville, dwelling in the General Hospital of Montreal, who, lying in her sickbed in one of the rooms of the said hospital looking onto the highway to Lachine, and being ever of sound mind, memory, and understanding, as appeared to the undersigned notaries by her gestures, words, comportment, and other external action, considering that nothing is so certain as death or more uncertain than the hour of its coming, and fearing its unforeseen arrival without having disposed of her last will, has made, dictated, and expressed in words in the presence of others to the said notaries her will and testament as follows.

Firstly, she has commended and commends her soul to God, beseeching His Divine Majesty through the infinite merits of the passion and death of Our Lord Jesus Christ to forgive her sins and to receive her soul into His Holy Paradise, invoking to this end the Intercession of the Glorious Virgin Mary and of all the Saints of Paradise.

The said testatrix declares since her companions have taken infinite care of her children and have not even required any board of them during the various times that they lived with her, or even during the illnesses that they endured there, without anything to recompense them, and also both for the care and for the pains they took in looking after the testatrix during the seven years that she was obliged to keep to her room with a malady of the knee, the said testatrix gives and bequeaths to her said companions all the moveable furnishings, silverware, goods, debts owed to her, and cash money, and all other things generally whatsoever in the said hospital that shall be found to belong to her on the day of her death, nothing excepted, reserved, or withheld. Thus this was done, dictated, and stated by the said testatrix to the said notaries, and read and re-read to her by one of them in the presence of others, and she stated that she understood it well.

At Montreal, in the said room, in the year one thousand seven hundred and fifty-seven, the eighth of October, at four o'clock in the afternoon, and signed and upheld by

M M Lajemmeray Widow Youville
Panet
Danré De Blanzy (with initials)[49]

---

[49]   AJM, Greffe du notaire Danré de Blanzy [Register of the Notary Danré de Blanzy], No. 7436.

Last Will and Testament
of Madame Youville

24 December 1771
No. 3778
1 copy

Before the Royal Notary of the Province of Quebec residing in Montreal undersigned and the Witnesses named at the end, there was present Dame Marie
Marguerite Dufros de la Jemmeraye, widow of Sieur François Madelaine
Youville, director and administrator of property of the poor of the General
Hospital of Montreal, dwelling in the said General Hospital, who, lying on her
sickbed but sound in mind, memory, and judgement, as appeared to the said
notary and Witnesses by her speech, gestures, and comportment, considering
that nothing is so certain as death nor so uncertain as the hour of its coming,
and fearing to be taken unawares without having set in order her affairs, has
made, dictated, and stated the present Will and Testament in the manner following:

Firstly, as a True Christian the said Testatrix commends her soul to God
Almighty, beseeching by His Divine Goodness and through the infinite merits
of the Passion and Death of Our Saviour Jesus Christ to forgive her offences and
to place her in the number of His Elect, the Most Holy Virgin and all the Saints
of Paradise interceding for her to this end.

The said Testatrix wills and intends that her debts be paid and any wrongs
that she may have done be repaired by the Executor of her will hereinafter
appointed.

The said Testatrix wills and intends that her body be buried in the General
Hospital in the place and with the ceremonies that Monsieur the Superior of
the Seminary of this city shall judge fitting, and that thirty Masses be said for
the repose of her soul, which she commends especially to the prayers of the poor
of the said General Hospital and the entire Community.

The said Testatrix declares that everything that shall be found at her death in
the hospital and more particularly in her room in the way of clothing, linen,
furniture, silver, or any other effects whatsoever at her disposal or in her use shall
belong to the said hospital.

The said Testatrix gives and bequeaths to the poor of the said General
Hospital of this city the exact half of All the Moveable Property, acquisitions,
immoveable and even personal property that she shall leave on the day of her
death, without exception, under the express condition that the heirs of the said
Testatrix in their capacity as administrators of the said General Hospital shall
be bound to receive there Messieurs François and Charles Youville, priests,

her sons, when they are in need, to be fed and lodged there in a warm and lighted area, according to their state, it being understood notwithstanding that this shall be with the permission of Monsignor the Bishop, and it shall be for the said Lord Bishop or Monsieur the Superior of the Seminary of Montreal to determine alone and without appeal what he deems is fitting for their state.

As for the other half of All her Property, consisting of moveable properties, acquisitions, immoveable, and personal properties, the said Testatrix gives and bequeaths them to the said Sieurs François and Charles You de Youville, her sons, to possess legally as their own, and so that there shall be no difficulties about the division of the said properties, the said Testatrix wills and intends that after her death, the said properties shall be divided as equally as possible into two lots by experts and people possessing the requisite knowledge, who shall be appointed by the Executor of her will hereinafter named, and by the said Sieurs Youville, her sons, and that these lots shall be drawn by chance in the usual way.

The said Testatrix wills and intends that the lot that shall fall to the poor of the said General Hospital shall in case of need be sold by the Executor of her will and that the resulting funds shall be remitted to the administrator of the said Hospital, upon whose discretion the said Testatrix completely relies.

And to execute the present will and testament, the said Testatrix has chosen and appointed as the Executor of her will Monsieur Thomas Ignace Dufy Dézaunier, a businessman of this city, whom she rightly beseeches to be so kind as to take the necessary action to render her this last service and into whose hands she relinquishes all her Worldly Goods according to the Custom. Thus this was made, dictated, and stated by the said Testatrix to the said Notary and Witnesses in the said General Hospital, in the year One Thousand Seven Hundred and Seventy-one, on the fourteenth of December in the morning, In the presence of Messire Jean François Pellissier de Feligonde, priest of the Seminary of this city, forty-four years old, and Messire Claude Poncin, also a priest of the said Seminary, forty-six years old, the Witnesses, who signed with the said Testatrix and us, the said Notary, after the first and second readings, according to the custom.

M M Lajemmerais, Widow Youville
Pellissier de Feligonde, Priest
Poncin, Priest
Sanguinet, Notary
Pierre Panet, Notary[50]

---

50   AJM, Greffe du notaire Pierre Panet [Register of the Notary Pierre Panet], No. 3778, dated 14
      December 1771.

Burial Act of Marguerite d'Youville

From the Register of the Deceased Poor in the General Hospital of Montreal in Ville Marie, Register 11 beginning in 1758.

On the twenty-sixth of December, one thousand seven hundred and seventy-one, there was buried by me, the Vicar General of the Diocese of Quebec and Superior of the General Hospital of this city, in the church of the said Hospital, the body of Dame Marie Marguerite La Gemeray, Widow Youville, first Superior and Administrator of said house, deceased the twenty-third day of the present month at the age of seventy years, two months, and eight days. Also present were Messieurs De Feligonde and Poncin, priests, undersigned.

Poncin, priest
Defeligonde, priest
Montgolfier

Iconography of Marguerite d'Youville

- Portrait of Marguerite d'Youville on her bier, water-colour by Philippe Liébert, 24 December 1771. The sole authentic portrait of Marguerite d'Youville.
- A portrait painted in 1792 by the Canadian artist François Beaucourt after the water-colour by Liébert. This painting is 2 feet 5 1/2 inches (79.93 cm) high by 1 foot 11 1/2 inches (59.69 cm) wide and is preserved in the Mother House of the Grey Nuns in Montreal.
- In Jacques Viger's *Ma Saberdache* [My Sabretache], preserved in the Archives of the Seminary of Quebec City, in Notebook E, page 126, there is an unsigned wash drawing, 4 and 3/8 inches (11.4 cm) in diameter, which represents Mother d'Youville and was inspired by Beaucourt's portrait. In the index of illustrations, page XIII, Viger has written: "Portrait of Madame de Youville by Wm Berczy the Younger, Esq. – p. 126." Notebook E is dated 1843.
- In Jacques Viger's *Album* preserved in the Bibliothèque Municipale of Montreal there is a replica of the wash drawing by Berczy, but this time painted and signed Wm Berczy.
- At the beginning of the *Vie de Mme d'Youville* [Life of Madame d'Youville] by Etienne-Michel Faillon, P. S. S., published in 1852, there is an engraving signed Rebel sculpt. that reproduces Beaucourt's portrait.
- The artist Albert Ferland made a pencil drawing after Rebel's engraving as part of his *Galerie canadienne* [Canadian Gallery]. It is the best known portrait of Mother d'Youville and has been adopted by the Community of the Grey Nuns.

Other portraits of Marguerite d'Youville have no documentary value.

End Notes

i   Their marriage contract, dated 10 January 1701, can be found in AJM, register of the notary Antoine Adhémar, No. 5452. The land brought in dowry by Marie-Renée Gaultier de Varennes was increased in extent after the division of the goods of Madame de Varennes among her children, 1 July 1707. In 1688, M. de la Gesmeray was serving under orders from M. des Bergères at Fort Niagara. We find his name at the bottom of *L'état dans lequel a été laissé le fort de Niagara en 1688* (The State in which Fort Niagara was left in 1688). Governor Frontenac noted M. de la Gesmerays' exploits in his annual report of 1689. Cf. APC, C 11 A vol. 11, p. 28 ff. Cf. also De Charlevoix, S.J., *Histoire de la Nouvelle France*, vol. 2, book 13, p. 56; book 15, p. 114; book 17, p. 224. The official service record of the elder Christophe du Frost de la Gesmerays can be found in Alphabet Laffilard, p. 241, APC, D 2, 222, vol. 1, and is as follows: Marine Guardsman at Rochfort, 25 July 1683; Sub-lieutenant in Canada, 17 March 1687; Discharged Lieutenant in Canada, autumn 1690; Lieutenant in 1692, confirmed 1 March 1693; Sub-lieutenant on Ship, 5 May 1695; Captain, 15 June 1705; died, 1 June 1708; replaced, 5 May 1710.

The Letters of Nobility of M. de la Gesmerays are quoted from Pierre-Georges Roy, *Inventaire des Lettres de Noblesse, Généalogies, Erections de Comtes et Baronnies insinuées par le Conseil Souverain de la Nouvelle France* [List of the Letters of Nobility, Genealogies, Creations of Counts and Barons Introduced by the Sovereign Council of New France] (Quebec, 1920), vol. II, pp. 97-104.

The name de la Gesmerays is spelt in various ways. The father of Madame d'Youville signed Du frost de la jemerais. The Ursulines of Quebec wrote Lagemerais. Fr. de Charlevoix, S.J., consistently writes de La Gemeraye. The Letters of Nobility give dufrost de la gesmeraye. Count de Palys, the Vice President of the Archaeological Society of Ille-et-Vilaine, who published an interesting study on this family, spells it du Frost de la Gesmerays. Madame d'Youville spelled her name in various ways until her bursar in Paris asked her to spell her name in only one way since the various spellings could create numerous problems. After this, she constantly signed Lajemmerais. This is the spelling that has prevailed and which we also accept.

ii   Pierre Boucher, Sieur de Grosbois, Royal Judge, Governor of Trois Rivières, founder and seigneur of Boucherville, was baptized 1 August 1622 in the Church of Notre Dame, Mortagne, Normandy, and died 19 April 1717 in the province of Quebec, Canada. He came to Canada with his parents in 1635, was educated by the Jesuits, and travelled throughout the country for four years in the company of the missionaries. Having mastered the various Indian dialects, he was named official interpreter at the age of twenty-three. His bravery and competence earned him the post of Governor of Trois Rivières in 1653. In 1661, Governor General d'Avaugour sent him as a deputy to the Court of France to explain the needs of the colony. At the king's command he wrote a work entitled *Histoire véritable et naturelle des moeurs et productions du pays de la Nouvelle France, vulgairement dite le Canada,* [A True and Natural History of the Customs and Products of the Land of New France, commonly known as Canada], which he dedicated to Colbert on 18 October 1663 and which was printed in Paris in 1664. His personal observations make this book a valuable document. He was the first Canadian to receive Letters of Nobility (1661). To his fifteen children he left two manuscripts that have become famous in Canada: one is a plan for one's life (1668) and the other his spiritual testament, which eloquently discloses his unfailing patriotism and well-tempered soul. The archaeologist and historian Jacques Viger reports that in the old days in every Canadian family Pierre Boucher's Testament was read kneeling once a year as a kind of profession of faith and patriotism. Since 1922 Alfred Laliberté's statue of Pierre Boucher with its inscription *Père de la Patrie Canadienne* (Father of Canada) has occupied a place of honour on the façade of the Legislative Assembly in Quebec City.

iii   At baptism, she received the names Marie Marguerite, but in the various documents pertaining to her she is almost always designated by the single given name Marguerite. In the admissions register and on the list of boarders of the Ursulines of Quebec City, it is Marguerite: "9 August 1712, Mademoiselle Marguerite Lagemerais was admitted as a boarder." Her son, the Abbé Dufrost, always called her Marguerite. At the baptism of her children, in the register of the Confraternity of a Happy Death, and in the act for the division of the inheritance from her mother, the single name Marguerite is always used. In the numerous documents relating to the inheritance from her husband, except for one instance, the situation is the same. She herself signed her correspondence and daily receipts simply "Widow Youville," but on important occasions she signed "M M Lajemmerais widow Youville." We can therefore reasonably conclude that she was known by her single given name, Marguerite.

iv   The foundation of Madame de la Peltrie for the education of native women was subsequently allotted to that of poor young Canadian women. Funds from the government and from Madame de la Peltrie were almost always granted in recompense for military service, in imitation of Saint-Cyr. Still, as the author of the *Histoire des Ursulines* [History of the Ursulines] points out, it is interesting to find on this list of beneficiaries the same names that are found on the list of the Young Ladies of Saint-Cyr. In the secular realm, the most famous of the former boarders of the Ursulines of Quebec City was Louise Elisabeth Joybert de Marsan, who married the Marquis Philippe-Rigaud de Vaudreuil, Governor General of the colony from 1703 to 1725. In 1708, Madame de Maintenon, an educator *par excellence*, chose the Marquise de Vaudreuil from among so many other ladies of the court for the honoured position of sub-governess for the royal children. This choice reveals how distinguished were the Canadian elite during this period. Madame de Vaudreuil was not able to leave

Canada before 1710 because on 12 September 1709 she gave birth to a daughter in Quebec.

v   Following the custom of the time in Canada, the younger son bore a different name from the elder. The two sons of Pierre You, Sieur de La Découverte, entered the seminary in Quebec together. The following entry is in the register: "Philippe Ladécouverte, from Montreal, 12 years old, and François Ladécouverte called Youville, 11 years old, his brother, students in the sixth form." They entered the seminary in June 1712 and left in 1714. Contrary to what has been written, François d'Youville was not an officer in the troops; he was only a trader, in the sense of the word used during that period, i.e. he traded furs with the natives.

vi   Pierre You, Sieur de La Découverte, was born in 1658 in the parish of Saint-Sauveur, La Rochelle. He was the son of Pierre You, a mason and stonecutter, and Renée Turcot, the daughter of Vincent Turcot, a tow-dresser. The genealogist, the Abbé Tanguay, who did not decipher properly this name in the registers, wrote Turrot. Fr. Archange Godbout, O.F.M., who traced the genealogies and the crafts of the Yous and the Turcots, established the correct spelling. In 1894, Count de Palys wrote: "Here and there in Saintonge Yous are still to be found." Evidence of Pierre You in Canada can be traced to 1677. On 22 March 1677 in Quebec City at the residence of Monsieur de Frontenac, Robert Cavelier de La Salle granted to the Récollet Fathers "fifteen arpents of frontage by twenty deep, located on the great lake of Ontario, bordered on one side by the grant made to Sieur You, sergeant of the garrison at said fort ..." (cf. Fr. Sixte Le Tac's *Histoire du Canada* [History of Canada], p. 191). In Montreal, on 19 April 1697, Pierre You married Madeleine Just, originally from Brèves in Burgundy, the daughter of Hébert Just and Madeleine Daumont. Their marriage contract, dated 19 April 1697, can be found in AJM, register of the notary Antoine Adhémar, No. 5147. The service record of Sieur de La Découverte is in Alphabet Laffilard, p. 187, as follows: Officer in Louisiana, 1683; Sub-lieutenant in Canada, 1685; present, 1718. According to the correspondence of the Marquis de Vaudreuil, the Sieur de la Découverte was Chief Aide to the Sieur Clérin in Montreal in 1709. Cf. APC, C 11, A vol. 30, p. 310. More detailed information on the Sieur de la Découverte can be found in Albertine Ferland-Angers, *Pierre You et son fils François d'Youville* [Pierre You and His Son, François Youville] (Montreal, 1941).

vii   Prayer from the wedding Mass: "Bless, O Lord, this ring that we bless in thy name, so that she who wears it, faithfully and wholly cleaving to her spouse, may abide in peace and in thy will and may always live in mutual affection. Through Christ our Lord. Amen."

viii   The first Notre Dame Church was opened for worship in 1683. In 1723 a beautiful stone façade was placed on it, to which was added a square tower. This tower remained uncompleted and "covered as if it were a windmill" from 1725 to 1777 when it was finished by adding a steeple with two lanterns surmounted by a cross. Madame d'Youville would have known the church without its steeple. Monsieur Jacques Viger writes in *Ma Saberdache* [My Sabretache], Notebook "E": "The beautiful steeple with two lanterns that we saw pulled down on the 30th of August 1843 dated only from 1778. A capable carpenter by the name of Rangeard was its maker. The tower was 80 feet tall by 26, and the steeple, including the cross at the top, was 80 feet = 160 feet, French measure. The tower walls were four and a half feet thick. The demolition was finished on the 18th of October 1843." The present Notre Dame church dates from 1829.

ix   Cf. Sister Marie Morin, *Annales de l'Hôtel-Dieu de Ville-Marie, 1659-1725*: The second major fire of our monastery occurred 29 June 1721, p. 47. "Madame de la Découverte's was the last house in the path of the fire that was so close that the firebrands were falling from above; but she, being wiser than the others, promised God a considerable amount for the souls in Purgatory and the fire stopped right away ..."

x   The uniform of the Carignan regiment consisted of a white suit and waist-coat, a neck-piece, the lining of the coat and sleeves in black velvet, a three-cornered hat with a silver badge of rank; there were six gold buttons on the sleeves and white leather equipment and black cartridge-case, leggings, and flint holder.

xi   On 4 March 1665, Bishop de Laval issued a pastoral letter propagating devotion to the Holy Family. He established the feast throughout the diocese as a solemn feast of the first class with octave to be celebrated on the third Sunday after Easter. It was first celebrated that year, 1665, and a chapel dedicated to the Holy Family was erected in the cathedral church in Quebec City. Pope Alexander VII not only approved the Confraternity of the Holy Family, but also endowed it with many indulgences, both plenary and partial, for its living and deceased members. In Montreal, the meetings were held in the large sacristy of the parish church. The superior was elected for only one year and then became by right counsellor for two years. The Ladies of Charity visited the sick, collected money for the poor, and supervised the distribution to them of alms received. On the death of a member, two other members kept vigil beside the mortal remains, taking turns until nine o'clock at night. The Ladies of the Confraternity carrying lighted candles had to follow the body from the house to the parish church and thence to the cemetery, without candles or ceremony. The postulancy lasted from three to four months. Madame d'Youville was admitted to the Confraternity of the Holy Family in 1727. She was elected counsellor on 5 June 1731, re-elected 25 May 1732, instructor of postulants and Lady of Charity 25 May 1734, superior 17 May 1735, instructor of postulants and Lady of Charity 8 May 1736, 20 May 1737, 20 May 1738, 28 April 1739, 17 May 1740, and treasurer 2 May 1741 (from Register No. 1 of the Confraternity of the Ladies of the Holy Family preserved in the archives of Notre-Dame Parish, Montreal).

xii   On the society of Quebec City in 1721, Father de Charlevoix, S.J., remarked: "There are hardly seven thousand souls in Quebec City, but one finds a select little world there in which nothing is lacking for the formation of a pleasant society. A Governor General with a staff, nobility, officers of the troops … wealthy merchants, or those who live as though they were… circles around the wives of the Governor and the Intendant as brilliant as could be found elsewhere … and nowhere else is our language spoken more purely" (*Journal*, vol. III, p. 79). As for himself, the Marquis de Montcalm wrote: "Quebec City seemed to me a very high-toned city, and I do not think that in France there could be more than a dozen above it for society" (Thomas Chapais, *Montcalm*, chap. VI, p. 182).

xiii   Cf. Thomas Chapais, *Le Marquis de Montcalm*. In a letter of 17 January 1759, the Marquis de Montcalm wrote to the Chevalier de Lévis about a dinner of sixty-six courses. Peter Kalm, the Swedish naturalist, noted in his account of his North American journey in 1749: "The merchants dress very elegantly and extend the sumptuousness of meals to folly."

xiv   Cf. ASQ, Copy of Letters, vol. 1, p. 471: Bishop de Laval to Monsieur de Brisacier of the French Foreign Missions, 1699: "The good Monsieur Charon has contributed greatly to the success of our mission to the Tamarois by giving us one of their brothers last year. And has also provided one this year. These contributions will save the missionaries a great deal since the cost of a missionary is as much as that of an enlisted man. Our Gentlemen and I beseech you to show especial gratitude to this good servant of God who cares as much for the missions and missionaries as though he were of the company."

       Cf. on the same subject, AAQ, Bishop de Laval to Monsieur Jean-Henri Tremblay in Paris.

       Cf. APC, B vol. 29-2, p. 315: Count de Pontchartain to Sieur Charon, 30 June 1707, on his memorandum concerning the Niagara post.

       Cf. APC, B vol. 29-2, p. 234: Orders to be sent to Sieur d'Aigremont, 30 June 1707, on the subject of caring for the sick in the Detroit fort.

xv   Monsieur Tronson wrote to Monsieur Mériel, 14 April 1699: "The suggestion that Monsieur Fredin has made to you of going with him to New England seems to me to be quite out of the ordinary. I do not know whether he has found any special opening that would give him hope of converting the young French people who are in New England. However that may be, I hardly think that you should undertake this journey without careful consideration and an order from a superior." To Monsieur Dollier, he wrote: "Monsieur Fredin is a spirited man. He may have his own views and perhaps some special interest beyond that of religion. Since this proposition comes neither from the Bishop nor from the Governor, but from an individual person otherwise committed to the Hospital, it needs to be closely scrutinized."

xvi   After his trial Louis Turc de Castelveyre returned to Santo Domingo. There he proved by his virtuous life that the complicated financial situations into which he got himself were the result rather of a fiery southern temperament and a lack of experience than of real bad faith. In the city of Cap in Santo Domingo he founded a hospice for the poor which he called Providence, but he turned the financial administration over to others and contented himself with serving as a hospitaller up to his death, which occurred on 21 May 1755. Cf. L.-E. Moreau de Saint-Méry, *Description topographique, civile, politique et historique de la partie française de l'Isle de Saint-Domingue* (Philadelphia, 1797). The library of Laval University in Quebec possesses a beautiful copy of this extremely rare work. It is there that I had the privilege of reading it.

xvii   Fourche-aux-Roseaux, the present territory of the parish of Letellier in Manitoba. When La Vérendrye's expedition arrived at Grand Portage – a portage of nine miles – at the end of Lake Superior, the volunteers refused to venture further into the unknown. The explorer then settled down at Fort Kaministigoya (the site of the present city of Fort William, Ontario) and sent his young lieutenant as an advance guard. In the autumn of 1731, Christophe de Lajemmerais reached Lake Taki Kimiwen, which means in Cree "It's always raining," hence the name Lac La Pluie, or Rainy Lake, given it by the French. There on a rise that gave a vast view of the country round about, Lajemmerais built a fort that he named in honour of his uncle the explorer Fort Saint Pierre, about two miles from the present Fort Frances. In the spring of 1732, he accompanied La Vérendrye to Lac des Bois where the latter established Fort Saint Charles. On 27 May 1733, he left Fort Saint Charles as La Vérendrye's emissary to the Governor General, Monsieur de Beauharnois (APC, Col. Moreau de Saint-Méry, vol. 10, fol. 12). He brought with him a cargo of furs, an account of their discoveries, and a map of Northern Ontario that he himself had prepared. The map is the most accurate one of its time (No. 85 of the collection of maps of N. Bellin in the Bibliothèque du Dépôt des Cartes, J.-E. Roy, *Archives de France*, p. 271; a reproduction of this map can be found in A.-G. Morice, O.M.I., *Histoire de l'Église catholique dans l'Ouest canadien* [1912], vol. 1, p. 55). Having spent the winter of 1733-1734 in Montreal, he arrived at Michilimackinac (a post on the straits separating Lake Huron from Lake Michigan) on 6 July 1734 where he met up again with La Vérendrye. He parted with him again on 12 July for Lac des Bois. In the autumn of 1735, he took command of Fort Maurepas (now Fort Alexander, Manitoba), which Jean-Baptiste de la Vérendrye had just built near the mouth of the Winnipeg River. Lajemmerais passed a winter of extreme hardship there due to the lack of provisions. When his two cousins arrived at the fort at the end of February 1736, they found him so weak that they decided to bring him back to Fort Saint Charles; but as they were going up the Red River, Lajemmerais died on 10 May at

Fourche-aux-Roseaux where his cousins buried him. Born at Varennes, 6 December 1708, he was only twenty-seven years and five months old. Before his exploratory journeys, he had taken part in expeditions against the Fox Indians and the Sioux whose habits and country he was quite familiar with. He was a member of Monsieur de la Corne's company at the Miami post (APC, C 11, A vol. 13, p.173: *Estat des soldats détachés dans les postes Outaouès* [List of soldiers detailed to the Outaouais posts], 1723-1725). On 20 April 1734, the king conferred on him the commission of sub-lieutenant in recognition of his services (APC, B vol. 61). On 26 July 1936, Canada's Commission of Monuments and Historical Sites unveiled a cairn that had been erected to his memory in Letellier, Manitoba. Today, in Fort Frances, Ontario, the Grey Nuns have a hospital where they carry on the ministry of charity in the same place where the youngest brother of their foundress – a brother whom she held at the baptismal font – built the first of a series of forts that opened the Canadian West to civilization, Fort Saint Pierre.

xviii   On 2 September 1723, Governor de Vaudreuil, whose wife was a friend of the family from Varennes, applied for a medical certificate for Timothée Sylvain. He told the Minister: "It has been suggested to me that the post of physician in Montreal be filled by Sieur Timothée Sylvain, an Irishman by birth and a gentleman who has dwelt in this city for six years and whose integrity and ability are widely known through the large number of notable cures that he has effected" (APC, C 11, A, vol. 45). In 1734, however, the Intendant, Gilles Hocquart, did not share the same opinion when he wrote to the Minister on 29 October: "Sieur Sylvain who has applied for the post of the deceased Doctor Sarrazin is a charlatan whom nobody trusts" (APC, C 11, vol. 61). Monsieur Aegidius Fauteux has published in the *Bulletin de Recherches Historiques*, vol. XXIII, a study entitled "Un médecin irlandais à Montréal avant la Cession" [An Irish Doctor in Montreal before British Rule] in which he refutes with great learning Timothy Sullivan's pretensions to nobility. The Abbé Tanguay had already reproduced in his *Dictionnaire généalogique* [Genealogical Dictionary] the false documents provided by Timothy Sullivan. Monsieur Fauteux out of concern for historical truth re-established these facts. Timothée Sylvain's naturalization certificate was registered in Quebec City on 16 November 1724.

xix   With respect to the communities, the following citation shows how they were viewed at the time. It is an answer to consultations ordered by the king in regard to the vows made by the Hospitallers of Quebec City and by the Daughters of the Congregation of Ville Marie. It does not appear that the king's intention in giving them letters patent had been to make them real religious. In accord with the texts and practice of the early Church and with the *Royal Capitularies*, the freedom of the king's subjects belonged to the king and not to the Church. The king could grant or refuse the foundation of a religious community, the privilege of taking vows, etc. Once this permission was granted, the religious authority had only the right to judge whether the person presenting him- or herself for vows had the essential dispositions to find in the religious life the way to sanctification. (AAQ, Église du Canada, vol. II, p. 57, reproduced in *Rapport de l'Archiviste de la Province de Québec pour 1940-41*, p. 419.)

xx   The following is the list of sisters admitted into the community by Mother d'Youville, with the date of their religious profession and that of their demise (cited from the Register of Sisters Having Perpetual Vows of the Institute of the Grey Nuns of Montreal, vol. 1).

1.   Sister Marie-Louise Thaumur de La Source, born Montreal 9 October 1706, daughter of Dominique Thaumur de La Source and Jeanne Prud'homme, professed 31 December 1737, died 13 September 1778.

2.   Sister Catherine Cusson, born Montreal 16 February 1709, daughter of Jean Cusson and Marguerite Aubuchon, professed 31 December 1737, died 20 February 1741.

3.   Sister Marie-Catherine Demers-Dessermont, born Montreal 2 August 1698, daughter of Robert Demers-Dessermont and Madeleine Tassé, professed 31 December 1737, died 20 August 1785.

4.   Sister Catherine Rainville, born Montreal 25 January 1711, daughter of Charles de Rainville and Suzanne Cabassier, professed 24 July 1745, died 29 November 1783.

5.   Sister Thérèse Laserre-Laforme, born Montreal 25 January 1714, daughter of Guillaume Laserre-Laforme and Angélique Brosseau, professed 22 October 1746, died 13 May 1783.

6.   Sister Agathe Véronneau, born St. François du Lac 21 April 1706, daughter of Louis Véronneau and Marguerite Maugras, professed 23 August 1749, died 20 April 1764.

7.   Sister Marie-Joseph Bénard-Bourjoli, born Boucherville 11 February 1725, daughter of René Bénard-Bourjoli and Geneviève Trottier, professed 23 August 1749, died 23 January 1796.

8.   Sister Marie-Antoinette Arelle, born Longueuil 15 April 1722, daughter of François Arelle and Marie-Augustine Bouthellier, professed 23 August 1749, died 15 April 1777.

9.   Sister Thérèse-Marguerite Lemoine-Despins, born Boucherville 23 March 1722, daughter of René-Alexandre Lemoine-Despins and Marie-Renée Leboulanger, professed 30 June 1753, died 6 June 1792.

10. Sister Marie-Joseph Gosselin, born St. Pierre de Québec 4 March 1729, daughter of Gabriel Gosselin and Geneviève Crespeau, professed 11 November 1754, died 22 August 1805.

11. Sister Thérèse Beaufrère, born 29 April 1726, professed 23 August 1755, died 29 April 1769.

12. Sister Marie-Louise Lanouillier de Boisclair, born Quebec City 23 May 1731, daughter of Jean Lanouillier de Boisclair and Marguerite Du Roy, professed 13 February 1756, died 28 September 1812. Left the community 16 October 1791.

13. Sister Marianne-Claude Varambourville, born Quebec City 3 November 1733, daughter of Antoine Varambourville and Marguerite Jovert, professed 12 December 1759, died 22 May 1813. Left the community 1 January 1775.

14. Marie-Apolline Dussault, born Lévis 7 June 1735, professed 12 December 1759, died 7 June 1809.

15. Sister Marie-Geneviève Gosselin, born Quebec City 1 November 1733, daughter of Gabriel Gosselin and Geneviève Crespeau, professed 12 December 1759, died 11 October 1815.

16. Sister Thérèse-Geneviève Coutlée, born Montreal 23 November 1742, daughter of Louis Coutlée and Marie-Geneviève Labaussé, professed 24 October 1764, died 17 July 1821.

17. Sister Marie-Madeleine Pampalon, born Quebec City 21 July 1741, daughter of Jacques Pampalon and Geneviève Legris, professed 22 February 1765, died 18 May 1776.

18. Sister Barbe-Françoise Prud'homme, born 20 February 1746, professed 22 April 1766, died 20 February 1821.

19. Sister Marie-Elisabeth Bonnet, born Montreal 14 June 1750, daughter of Pierre Bonnet called Larochelle and Marguerite Metras, professed 27 October 1769, died 12 March 1824.

20. Sister Catherine-Marie de La Pérelle, widow of Pierre Céloron de Blainville, Knight of Saint Louis, born Louisbourg 14 June 1723, daughter of François Eurry de La Pérelle and Charlotte Aubert de La Chesnaye, professed 3 July 1771, died 4 November 1797.

21. Sister Suzanne-Amable Benoit, born Montreal 6 November 1751, daughter of Sieur Claude Benoit and Thérèse Baby, admitted to the noviciate 29 May 1771, professed 20 July 1773, died 17 July 1780.

xxi Cf. APQ, *Rapport de l'Archiviste, 1941-1942* [Report of the Archivist, 1941-1942]: "Aveu et Dénombrement de Montréal en 1731, par Messire Louis Normant, p. S.-S." [Oath and Enumeration of Montreal in 1731, by Father Louis Normant, P. S. S.]. Cf. E.-Z. Massicotte, "Un recensement inédit de Montréal en 1741" [An Unpublished Census of Montreal in 1741], *Mémoires de la Société Royale du Canada/Proceedings of the Royal Society of Canada*, vol. XV (May 1921).

xxii Cf. *La Revue Canadienne* [The Canadian Review], vol. 12, 1875: "Lettres de la Mère Marie-André Regnard Duplessis de Sainte-Hélène, religieuse de l'Hôtel-Dieu de Québec" [Letters of Mother Marie-André Regnard Duplessis de Sainte Hélène, Nun of the Hôtel-Dieu in Quebec City].

xxiii Cf. *L'Union Médicale du Canada* [The Medical Association of Canada], August 1944, an offprint. Dr. Nadeau was attached to the Rutland State Sanatorium, a sanatorium for tubercular patients, in Rutland, Massachusetts. A distinguished writer and historian, he was a specialist in the medical history of New France.

xxiv In this year, 1745, Sieur François-Marie Marchant de Ligneris, Knight of Saint Louis, demonstrated his high regard for Madame d'Youville by choosing her as godmother for his daughter born 3 July. The child was christened Marie-Anne-Marguerite. The godfather was François-Daniel-Constant Marchant de Ligneris, the little girl's brother. Cf. AFND.

xxv AJM, *Registre des Audiences* [Register of Hearings], vol. 24, p. 2, 22 July 1746 – Beaucours vs. Widow Youville; ibid., p. 14, 5 August 1746 – Beaucours vs. Widow Youville. These two documents are reproduced *in extenso* in the Supporting Documents.

xxvi Elisabeth de Ramezay (1707-1780), daughter of Claude de Ramezay, Governor of Montreal, and Charlotte Denys de La Ronde, married in Montreal on 1 September 1740 Louis de Chaptes de La Corne, Knight of Saint Louis, Seigneur of Terrebonne, Lieutenant in the Royal Regiment of the French Marine, Captain of the troops in the colony.

xxvii Cf. APQ, *Aveu et Dénombrement de Montréal* [Oath and Enumeration of Montreal] in 1731, by Messire Louis Normant. Paul-Alexandre D'Ailleboust d'Argenteuil, Sieur de Cuisy (1696-1782). A "trader" and businessman, he married Thérèse Le Fournier Du Vivier on 1 February 1727. She had inherited from her parents the property mentioned here.

xxviii ASGM, autograph letter of Jacques Beaudry de Lamarche, Holder of Power of Attorney for the Brothers Hospitallers of Montreal, dated, Paris, 29 April 1742.

xxix ASGM, *Inventaire des biens meubles et immeubles des Frères hospitaliers dits Frères Charon* [Inventory of Moveable and Immoveable Property of the

Brothers Hospitallers, called the Charon Brothers], prepared by Louis-Claude Danré de Blanzy, Royal Notary, from 4 to 19 September 1747.

xxx   The specialists were Nicolas Moran, carpenter; Jean-Baptiste Le Cavalier, woodworker; René Gassien, roofer; Paul Tessier, called Lavigne, mason; Antoine Durousseau [Durozeau], blacksmith; Michel-Jacques Neveu, glazier.

xxxi   To arrive at the exact date of the opening of "Jericho," it is necessary to proceed deductively. Madame d'Youville was authorized by Intendant Hocquart. Now, the last official letter of this Intendant is dated, Quebec City, 17 August 1748. Bigot arrived 28 August 1748. As Madame d'Youville only took possession of the General Hospital on 7 October 1747, the authorization must have occurred between these two dates – October 1747 and August 1748. The letter of Madame Bégon that mentions Jericho is dated 8 January 1749. She says that Madame Bouat has been at Madame d'Youville's since Saint Martin's tide, that is, since the autumn of 1748, and that Madame Bouat asserts that Madame d'Youville has already converted the prisoners.

As for how long Jericho lasted, the last mention made is in the charge, dated 15 June 1755, of Bishop de Pontbriand addressed to the Grey Nuns. He gives Madame d'Youville instructions on this matter. It seems likely that the work continued up to the time of the British conquest. Then the whole administrative system changed, and Jericho collapsed *ipso facto*. At the time of the fire in 1765, Madame d'Youville composed a list of the people living in the Hospital and she mentions neither Jericho nor any of its detainees. In his charge of 12 May 1765, Monsieur Etienne Marchand, the Vicar General of the diocese, the See being vacant, enumerates the works of Madame d'Youville that had been greatly affected by this fire, and neither does he any longer mention the prisoners.

Cf. APQ, *Rapport de l'Archiviste, 1935* [Report of the Archivist, 1935]: Correspondence of Madame Bégon. Marie-Isabelle, or Elisabeth, Rocbert de la Morandière was born in Montreal in 1696 and died in Rochefort, France, in 1755. She had married the Chevalier Claude-Michel Bégon, Captain, who died as Governor of Trois Rivières in 1748. Her sister-in-law, Catherine Bégon, married Count de la Galissonnière who became interim Governor General of the country. Madame Bégon was therefore well situated to know the little backstage scandals in politics with which she peppers her letters. Her letters, written in journal form, were addressed to her son-in-law, Honoré Michel de la Rouvillière de Villebois, who was pay commissioner in Louisiana. Madame Bégon knew Madame d'Youville quite well because she too belonged to the Confraternity of the Holy Family. The register of the Confraternity lists Madame Bégon as Counsellor in 1730 and as in charge of visiting the sick at the same time as Madame d'Youville in 1734. The interesting journal of Madame Bégon, which covers the years 1748 to 1753, was only discovered in 1935 by

Monsieur Claude de Bonnault, the corresponding member in France of the Quebec Provincial Archives.

xxxii   Cf. *Mgr de Saint-Vallier et l'Hôpital-général de Québec* – Histoire du Monastère de Notre-Dame des Anges (religieuses hospitalières de la Miséricorde de Jésus) [Mgr. de Saint-Vallier and the General Hospital of Quebec City – History of the Monastery of Our Lady of the Angels (Religious Hospitaliers of the Mercy of Jesus)] (Quebec: Ordre de Saint Augustin, 1882). Although this work is anonymous, Philéas Gagnon in his *Essai de bibliographie canadienne* [Essay in Canadian Bibliography], tome 1, page 437, attributes it to Sister Saint-Félix, born O'Reilly, then archivist of the monastery. In chapter twenty-five, on the subject of the merger of the General Hospital of Montreal with that of Quebec City, the author says (page 323): "Our annals merely mention the project of a merger between the two hospitals; but there exists no capitular act nor any writing whatsoever that might inform us about the conduct of our community in this affair."

xxxiii   Pierre de La Rue (1688-1779) in 1722 was named ruling abbot of L'Isle-Dieu, an abbey of the Premonstratensian Order under the patronage of the Holy Virgin in the Diocese of Rouen about four leagues from that city and on an island in the River Andèle, hence the name *Insula Dei* [God's Island]. In the seventeenth century this abbey was producing 3500 francs in annual revenues. A highly distinguished and virtuous churchman, the Abbé de L'Isle-Dieu was named Vicar General of Quebec under Monsignor Dosquet in 1730, and he retained this position without interruption until 1777, without, however, ever visiting Canada. He bore the official title of Vicar General of the Colonies of New France. The Abbé de L'Isle-Dieu earned the esteem and trust of everyone by his wisdom, prudence, and charity. He was always inclined towards measures of reconciliation rather than rigour. Not only did he serve the Church in Canada with a disinterested devotion for fifty years, but he also took upon himself the then considerable expense of sending correspondence across the ocean. The Abbé de L'Isle-Dieu was actively involved in settling the financial difficulties of the General Hospital of Montreal and in obtaining Letters Patent for the Community of the Grey Nuns. In spite of advanced age and illness, he continued to watch over the interests of Madame d'Youville who deeply venerated him.

xxxiv   Fr. Pierre Duchaussois, O. M. I., entitled his history of the Grey Nuns in the Mackenzie, *Femmes Héroiques* [Heroic Women] (Paris: Editions Spes, 1927). On 11 December 1927, Mgr. Andrea Cassulo, the Apostolic Legate to Canada, said in an allocution: "The Grey Nuns! For me, to name the Grey Nuns is the same as to say the brave nuns!" Cf. ASGM, *Annales* [Annals], 51st Year, No. 12, 1927. In the guest book of the Institute, the Most Reverend Father Labouré, Superior General of the Oblates of Mary Immaculate, once wrote the following praise: "May Our Lord continue to bless this holy house and to multiply its members by the hundreds. The

Oblates express their gratitude for the zeal and devotion of these *heroic women* who have made possible the evangelization of the Canadian North West" (my emphasis).

xxxv   Mother d'Youville chose as her patron saint, Saint Margaret of Antioch in Pisidia, who bears the title Megalomartyr, or "Great Martyr." The key to Mother d'Youville's choice is perhaps supplied by one of the Responses in the Office of her feast where it is said that the holy martyr triumphed over the devil in the form of a dragon through the sign of the cross. The Response reads: "While the holy martyr redoubled her prayers, a foul dragon appeared. He attacked her and swallowed her whole." – Versicle: "But thanks to the sign of the cross, she split him in two and stepped out of the monster unhurt." This is why she is said to have triumphed by the sign of the cross. Saint Margaret has always been the patron of pregnant women. In the old days in England, her feast was celebrated as a double of the first class and as a feast of obligation for women only. Cf. Dom Prosper Guéranger, Abbot of Solesmes, *L'Année liturgique* [The Liturgical Year], vol. 4, The Time after Pentecost. No doubt that because she was the patron of the foundress, the Canadian sculptor Philippe Liébert carved on the left panel of the altar of the Sacred Heart a figure in relief of Saint Margaret of Antioch.

xxxvi   On 17 August 1766, Madame d'Youville wrote to Monsieur Savarie, her agent in France: "… We always had the work for the King's stores, and especially from twelve years ago when the storekeepers noticed the profit the King was making by giving the work to us. And we were paid no more in 1760 than we were in 1738, even a little less. As for the rations, Monsieur Bigot always kept a tight hand on the purse strings and never wanted to pay us what we deserved, with the result that we bought beef at 4 livres and he was willing to give us only 3 livres, 10 sols to the livre and the Hospital had to cover the rest. You can see, Sir, how we were treated. We had to borrow the money and pay interest on it while waiting for our payments since 1757."

xxxvii In making tents, Madame d'Youville was following an honourable precedent. According to the custom of the Pharisees that obliged their members to know and practise a handicraft, Saint Paul had learned the trade of tent making and practised it during his first stay in Corinth.

xxxviii Up until 1915 descendants of Southworth lived in Williamstown, Massachusetts, in the United States. The events related here were a family tradition.

xxxix   About Father Normant, Madame d'Youville wrote to Monsieur Maury, her agent in Paris: "Our dear Father and founder of our Hospital." She does well to say "of our hospital," as though wishing to avoid any confusion. In fact, the General Hospital and the Community of the Grey Nuns were two distinct institutions. The General Hospital depended upon the king and was under the control of the heads of the colony: the governor, the bishop, and the intendant who became *ex officio* chief administrators of the General Hospital of Montreal as they did of that of Quebec City. Moreover, the Seigneurs of the island of Montreal had inserted a reversion clause into the land grant to the Hospital in case the founding hospitallers of the House of Charity should cease to be. When the Brothers Hospitallers came to an end, the Sulpicians could have let the work stop; but as their charitable activities were well known, Father Normant, the Superior of the Seminary, exerted himself to keep this hospice open. Maximilien Bibaud in the *Dictionnaire Historique* [Historical Dictionary] rightly says: "The intelligent zeal that Madame d'Youville showed in all her actions marked her out to the Sulpicians to take over the direction of the General Hospital." In fact, it was in 1737 that Madame d'Youville through divine inspiration joined together several women of good will to do works of charity in Montreal; and it was only in 1747 that she was made directress of the General Hospital. It seems that it was through the savoir faire of Father Normant that the General Hospital was kept in Montreal, and this is how what Madame d'Youville says of him above is to be understood. On the other hand, the Abbé de L'Isle-Dieu – who had had numerous consultations with Father Cousturier, the Superior General of the Sulpicians, in order to settle the Hospital's difficulties and who as Vicar General of the diocese had conducted the negotiations with the Court – without doubt did not forget the 10,486 livres that Madame d'Youville had sacrificed to save the Hospital when he wrote to her on 20 May 1753: "I hope, nevertheless, that we are about to complete this business to your satisfaction and the advantage of the poor house that owes to you its restoration and preservation."

In their veneration for Father Normant, the Grey Nuns have on occasion given him the title "Father Founder." The eminent Father Charles-I. Lecoq, P. S. S., however, does not see it this way: "For every foundation, there is only one founder or foundress; and for the Grey Nuns, it is Madame d'Youville." At the tribunal of history, even gratitude is bound not to confuse the roles assigned by Providence.

xl The name Pointe de Lévy was given to this promontory in honour of Henry de Lévy, Viceroy of New France, in 1626. After the military achievements of the Chevalier de Lévis, the spelling of the name was changed to *Lévis* under British rule. Cf. Hormisdas Magnan, *Dictionnaire Historique et géographique des Paroisses, Missions et Municipalités de la Province de Québec* [Historical and Geographical Dictionary of the Parishes, Missions, and Municipalities of the Province of Quebec] (Arthabaska, 1925).

xli Monsignor de Pontbriand died in Montreal on 8 June 1760 and was buried beneath the old Notre Dame church. When this church was demolished, his body was exhumed on 15 July 1836 and buried in the crypt of the new church. The Abbé Jean Tambareau, P. S. S., then confessor of the Grey Nuns, gave the community the skull of this holy bishop. This relic is preserved in the museum of the Mother House, Section G, no. 8. Bishop de Pontbriand himself left to the Grey Nuns in his will his ecclesiastical apparel: gloves, cinctures, mitres, etc.

xlii   The Abbé Auguste Gosselin in his *L'Église du Canada, 1760-1775* [The Church in Canada, 1760-1775], chap. XXXIV, reports what he calls the "Gamelin affair." There was a Canadian Freemason named Pierre Gamelin who was elected warden of Notre Dame parish in Montreal on 1 January 1771. Father Gosselin says that he was the brother-in-law of Madame d'Youville. Madame d'Youville's sister, Marie-Clémence, had indeed married a man named Pierre Gamelin-Maugras on 16 November 1735, but this Pierre Gamelin died on 2 July 1757 and was buried on 3 July, according to the civil register of Notre Dame parish in Montreal. Since the letter of Monsignor Briand to Pierre Gamelin is dated 14 January 1771, he cannot be the same individual. (Cf. AAQ, vol. IV, Bishops' Letters, p. 179.) According to Ægidius Fauteux, Pierre Gamelin the Freemason was the nephew of Madame d'Youville's brother-in-law. But could it be objected that it was the nephew who died in 1757? It can be replied that the act of marriage of Madame d'Youville's niece Marie-Clémence, the daughter of Pierre Gamelin-Maugras, celebrated in Montreal on 13 November 1758, calls her "the daughter of the late Pierre Gamelin." Madame d'Youville's other sister, Marie-Louise, also married a Gamelin, Ignace, who died on 9 March 1771 and was buried on 10 March. He had been an invalid for three years according to a letter from Madame d'Youville to Monsieur Feltz, dated 22 September 1770: "Poor Gamelin is still in the saddest sort of state. He is deaf, mute, and almost blind. Almost all of his body is paralysed … For two years he has been in this condition." The scandal of the Freemason churchwarden cannot therefore have been occasioned by either of Madame d'Youville's brothers-in-law. Cf. Ægidius Fauteux, *Les Carnets d'un curieux* [An Antiquary's Notebooks], in the daily *La Patrie*, 5 May 1934.

xliii   This was the Abbé Pierre Ménard. In the list of accounts for receipts and expenditures for 30 March 1761, item 6 is for 50 livres paid to the Abbé de Villars, who was the Superior of the Seminary for Foreign Missions, for "a young seminarian named M. Ménard, according to the order of Mad. de Lajemmeraye in her letter of 21 September 1761." On 12 February 1764, the Abbé de L'Isle-Dieu wrote to Madame d'Youville: "Young Monsieur Ménard is the bearer of my letter and we are sending him back to you as a priest. He was ordained last Saturday, the eve of Passion Sunday, and he seems to be in a great hurry and very desirous of returning to his native land where, I believe, he will give great satisfaction. It is a delicate subject, but as you take an interest in him, please recommend to him much prudence, caution, and discretion in regard to the government in the circumstances in which we find ourselves. It is necessary that there be not the least slur or suspicion concerning us if we wish to preserve our freedom of religion …" The Abbé Pierre Ménard was appointed parish priest of Saint Jean, Ile d'Orléans, in 1766 and remained there until 1777. He was then transferred to the parish of Chambly where he remained until his death on 28 June 1792.

xliv   Shortly after she moved into the General Hospital, Mother d'Youville had had cabins built in the Hospital's courtyard for the mentally ill. These wooden cabins were destroyed by the fire of 1765 and were not rebuilt owing to lack of means. In 1800 the government requested the community to resume the care of the insane; and upon their acceptance, the governor, Sir Robert Shore, had a stone building constructed of about 30 x 20 feet. It was aligned with the walkway of the church in front of the Hospital and consisted of eight rooms where eight mad people were generally to be kept. In the *Rapport du Comité Spécial nommé pour s'enquérir et faire rapport sur les Etablissements dans cette Province, pour la réception et la guérison des personnes dérangées dans leur esprit* ... [Report of the Special Committee to investigate and report back on the Establishments in this Province for the reception and healing of mentally deranged people ...], dated 10 February 1824, it is stated: "In Montreal there is the General Hospital or Religious House of the Grey Nuns where poor lunatics are cared for free of charge by the elder Dr. Selby. There are eight small cells of about eight feet long, 6 feet wide, and seventeen feet, ten inches high. Since 1800 eighty-four people have been admitted and confined there. Of these there are still six, while twenty-nine have died and forty-nine have been discharged as either healed or relieved" (cf. APQ). In 1831 the Community of the Grey Nuns, without sending away the insane people entrusted to their care, ceased to admit new cases because of the unhealthy state of the building, which the Provincial Legislature did not wish to have rebuilt. In 1844 two patients still remained in the care of the nuns who at that time had them transferred to the Insane Asylum of Quebec.

xlv   Mother d'Youville's room was carefully taken apart and reconstructed in the new Mother House on Guy Street. The floor, the ceiling, the window casements, and the doors with their frames were transported there as well as the furnishings so that the reconstructed room as it can be seen today in the crypt of the Mother House is truly the room of the foundress. The work of taking it apart was facilitated by the fact that nails were not used in that period, but rather pieces of wood were connected by wooden pegs that fitted into openings or slots. The furniture of her room was preserved except for the bed; the one that is seen today is a replica.

xlvi   Fr. Henri-François Gravé de la Rive, a native of Vannes in Brittany and priest of the Seminary of Foreign Missions in Paris, came to the Seminary of Quebec City on 26 July 1754. He died in Quebec City, 4 February 1802. Elected Superior of the Seminary of Quebec City on 20 August 1768, he held that office until 1774. He was afterwards re-elected three times and was Superior from 17 August 1778 to 13 August 1781, from 13 August 1787 to 14 August 1793, and from 12 August 1798 until his death on 4 February 1802. When he was not Superior, he was in charge of the bursary and direction of the greater and lesser seminaries or of lecturing on philosophy or theology. Even during the two years he spent in Montreal he was working for the Seminary since he had followed the seminarians there. It was during those two years that he was in almost daily contact with Madame d'Youville. Fr. Gravé was made Vicar General of the Diocese of Quebec in 1778. Several days after his death, *La Gazette* [The Gazette] of Quebec City published a "Biographical Note" by the Abbé Desjardins that stated, among other things, that "Passionately devoted to the good, he spent himself in doing it without ever seeking his own advantage or sparing himself. His zeal was amazing and untiring, his talents varied. He possessed to a rare degree the talent of directing consciences and to no lesser a degree that of preaching." Fr. Jérôme Demers, the Vicar General and Superior of the Seminary of Quebec City and a contemporary and friend of Fr. Gravé, wrote to Monsieur Jacques Viger: "One can state with a clear conscience that there is no exaggeration in the 'Biographical Note' about Fr. Gravé published in the Gazette of Quebec City and that everything in it is in complete conformity with the truth" (cf. ASQ, *Ma Saberdache* [My Sabretache], Notebook E, note 41, page 225).

xlvii   The chronicler of the convent of the Ursulines at Trois-Rivières wrote about the Abbé Jean-François Sabrevois de Bleury, who was the nuns' chaplain from 1793 to 1796: "Mademoiselle de la Brocquerie preserved for us a memory from her childhood. 'One day,' she said, 'I went in the company of my mother, Clémence Gamelin-Maugras de La Brocquerie, and one of my cousins who was then very young, Jean-François Sabrevois de Bleury, to visit my aunt, Madame d'Youville. At the end of our visit, Madame d'Youville, looking at the young de Bleury and lightly touching him on the shoulder, said, "You will die a priest, my little gentleman.' As we saw, the prediction came true" (cf. *Les Ursulines des Trois-Rivières depuis leur établissement jusqu'à nos jours* [The Ursulines of Trois-Rivières from their establishment up to our days] [Trois-Rivières: P. V. Ayotte, Libraire-Editeur, 1888], Vol. 1, Book 2, chapter XIX, p. 461: *Les Chapelins du Monastère* [The Monastery Chaplains]. According to Philéas Gagnon, the sister chronicler at that time was Sister Marguerite-Marie (*Essai de Bibliographie canadienne* [Essay in Canadian Bibliography], vol. 1, p. 509).

Bibliography

Autograph Manuscripts

MOTHER D'YOUVILLE:

- *Lettres* [Letters]
- *Registre des Pauvres, Pensionnaires, Religieuses, de 1747 à 1753* [Register of the Poor, Boarders, and Sisters from 1747 to 1753]
- *Livres des comptes* [Account Books]
- Livre terrier de la seigneurie de Châteauguay [Land Book for the Seigneury of Châteauguay]
- *Mémoire sur l'admission et le Renvoi des Sujets, les Œuvres et l'administration de la Communauté* [Memorandum on the Admission and Commitment of Members and on the Works and Administration of the Community]

DUFROST, the Abbé Charles-Madeleine d'Youville:

- *Mémoire pour servir à la Vie de Mde youville* [Memoir to be Used for a Life of Madame Youville]
- *La vie de madame youville fondatrice des Sœurs de la charité à montreal* [The Life of Madame Youville Foundress of the Sisters of Charity in Montreal] [This MS was published at Lévis in 1930; there is an English translation of the latter by Sister Cécile Rioux, S .G. M., entitled *Marie Marguerite d'Youville: The Mother I Loved* (Montreal: Editions du Méridien, 1991). *Translator's Note.*]
- *Lettres* [Letters]

SATTIN, the Abbé Antoine, P. S. S.:

- *Vie de Madame Veuve Youville, fondatrice et première Supérieure de l'Hôpital Général de Montréal* [Life of Madame the Widow Youville Foundress and First Superior of the General Hospital of Montreal] [This MS was published as *Vie de Madame d'Youville* in Quebec City in 1930; there is an English translation of the latter by Sister Georgianna Michaud, S .G. M., entitled

Life of Mother d'Youville: Foundress and First Superior of the Sisters of Charity or Grey Nuns (Montreal: Editions du Méridien, 1999). *Translator's Note.*]

NORMANT de FARADON, Louis, P. S. S.:

- *Engagements primitifs et Règlements* [Original Commitment and Rules]
- *Cérémonial des Vêtures et des Professions* [Ceremonial for Investitures and Professions]
- *Suppliques* [Petitions]

MONTGOLFIER, Etienne, P. S. S.:

- *Recueil de règles et de constitutions à l'usage des Filles séculières, administratrices de l'Hôpital général de Montréal* [Collection of Rules and Constitutions Used by the Secular Daughters, Administrators of the General Hospital of Montreal]

Manuscripts

- Constitutions pour les Frères hospitaliers de la Croix et de Saint Joseph, observatins de la Règle de saint Augustin [Constitutions of the Brothers Hospitallers of the Cross and of Saint Joseph, Observants of the Rule of Saint Augustine]
- Registre des Vêtures et Professions des Frères Hospitaliers dits Frères Charon [Register of Investitures and Professions of the Brothers Hospitallers, called the Charon Brothers]
- Registre de l'Admission des Pauvres and des Sépultures [Register of Admission of the Poor and of Burials]
- Registre des Sœurs Professes de l'Institut des Sœurs Grises de Montréal [Register of the Professed Sisters of the Institute of the Grey Nuns of Montreal]
- Registre des Baptêmes et des Sépultures de l'Hôpital-général de Montréal [Register of Baptisms and Burials of the General Hospital of Montreal]
- Registre de la Confrérie des Dames de la Sainte-Famille de Montréal contenant le règlement, les minutes des Assemblées du Conseil, le catalogue des membres, etc. [Register of the Confraternity of the Holy Family of Montreal, containing the Rule, the Minutes of the Council Meetings, the List of Members, etc.]
- Jacques Viger, *Ma Saberdache* [My Sabretache]

Archives

- Archives des Sœurs Grises de Montreal [Archives of the Grey Nuns of Montreal]
- Archives de la Fabrique de Notre-Dame de Montréal [Archives of the Fabrique of Notre-Dame Church, Montreal]
- Archives Judiciaires de Montréal [Legal Archives of Montreal]
- Archives de la Paroisse de Varennes – Fabrique et registres d'état civil [Archives of the Parish of Varennes – Fabrique and Civil Registers]
- Archives de la Paroisse de Sainte-Anne du Bout de l'Isle [Archives of the Parish of Saint Anne du Bout de l'Isle]
- Archives de l'Archevêché de Québec [Archives of the Archdiocese of Quebec]
- Archives du Séminaire de Québec [Archives of the Seminary of Quebec]
- Archives de la province de Québec [Archives of the Province of Quebec (now Archives Nationales du Québec – National Archives of Quebec)]
- Archives Judiciaires de Québec [Legal Archives of Quebec]
- Archives Publiques du Canada, Ottawa [Public Archives of Canada, Ottawa (now Archives Nationales du Canada – National Archives of Canada)]

Printed Sources

- ALLAIRE, Abbé J.-B.-A. *Dictionnaire Biographique du Clergé Canadien-français*. Montréal: Imprimerie de l'Ecole catholique des Sourds-Muets, 1910.
- ATHERTON, William Henry. *Montreal (1535-1914)*. Montreal: S. J. Clarke Publishing Co., 1914.
- AUDET, Francis-J. *Varennes, Notes pour servir à l'histoire de cette seigneurie*. Montréal: Les Editions des Dix, 1943.
- BARABÉ, Paul-Henri, O. M. I. *Quelques Figures de Notre Histoire*. Ottawa: Editions de l'Université, 1941.
* BARBER, Katherine, editor. *The Canadian Oxford Dictionary*. Toronto: Oxford University Press, 1998.
- BEAUPRÉ, Marie. *Jeanne Le Ber, Première recluse du Canada Français, 1662-1714*. Montréal: Editions de l'Action Canadienne-française Ltée, 1939.
- BERTRAND, Camille. *Histoire de Montréal*. 2 vols. Montréal: Librairie Beauchemin, 1935, 1942.
- BOSWORTH, The Reverend Newton. *Hochelaga Depicta: The Early History and Present State of the City and Island of Montreal*. Montreal: William Greig, 1839.
- BOUCHER DE LA BRUÈRE, Montarville. *La Naissance des Trois-Rivières*. No. 1 des Cahiers de la Société d'Histoire Régionale, Les Trois-Rivières, 1928.
- BROUILLETTE, Benôit. *Varennes, monographie géographique*. Montréal, 1944.
- *BULLETIN des Recherches historiques*. Founded at Lévis by Pierre-Georges Roy in 1895. Monthly.
- CHAPAIS, Thomas. *Cours d'Histoire du Canada*, tome 1, *1760-1791*. Québec: J.-P. Garneau, bookseller and publisher, 1919.
  - *Le Marquis de Montcalm (1712-1759)*. Québec: J.-P. Garneau, bookseller and publisher, 1911.
- CHARLEVOIX, François-Xavier de, S. J. *Histoire et Description générale de la Nouvelle-France, avec le journal historique d'un Voyage fait par ordre du Roi dans l'Amérique Septentrionale*. 3 vols. Paris: Chez Pierre-François Giffart, rue Saint-Jacques à Sainte-Thérèse, M.DCC.XLIV [1744].

---

*   An asterisk before an entry indicates that it is an addition to Madame Ferland-Angers' original Bibliography.

- CODE, J. B. *The Veil is Lifted*. St. Ambrose College, Davenport, Iowa, The Bruce Publishing Co., Milwaukee, 1932.
- COUILLARD-DESPRÉS, Abbé Azarie. *Histoire de la Famille et la Seigneurie de Saint-Ours*. 2 vols. Montréal: Imprimerie de l'Institution des Sourds-Muets, 1915-1917.
- DANIEL, François, P. S. S. *Nos Gloires Nationales ou Histoire des principales familles du Canada*. 2 vols., illustrated. Montréal: Sénécal, 1867.
- DELALANDE, J. *Le Conseil Souverain de la Nouvelle-France*. Québec: Ls-A. Proulx, 1927.
- De PALYS, Comte. *Une Famille Bretonne au Canada – Madame d'Youville*. Rennes: Librairie Générale J. Plihon et I. Hervé, 5, rue Motte-Fablet, 1894.
- DESCHAMPS, C.-E. *Liste des Municipalités dans la Province de Québec*. Lévis: Mercier & Cie, éditeurs, 1886.
- * DICKINSON, John A., and YOUNG, Brian. *A Short History of Quebec*. Second edition. Toronto: Copp Clark Pitman Ltd., 1993.
- DuBREIL de PONTBRIAND, Vicomte. *Le Dernier Evêque du Canada français, Monseigneur de Pontbriand, 1740-1760*. Paris: Honoré Champion, éditeur, 5, Quai Malaquais, 1910.
- DUCHAUSSOIS, Pierre, O. M. I. *Femmes Héroiques*. Paris: Editions Spes, 1933.
- DUFFIN, Reverend Mother Mary G., S. G. M. *A Heroine of Charity, Mother d'Youville*. New York: Benziger Brothers, 26 Park Place, 1938.
- DUPLESSIS de Sainte-Hélène, Mère Marie-André Regnard. "Lettres, adressées à Madame Hecquet, de 1718 à 1758." Published by the Abbé Hospice Verreau in *La Revue Canadienne*, tome 12, 1875.
- * ECCLES, J. W. *Canada under Louis XIV, 1663-1701*. Toronto: McClelland and Stewart, 1964.
  * *France in America*. Rev. ed. Markham, Ontario: Fitzhenry & Whiteside, 1990.
- *EDITS, Ordonnances royaux et Arrêts du Conseil d'Etat du Roi concernant le Canada*. 2 vols. Québec: P. E. Desbarats, 1803, 1806.
- ELLIOTT, Sophy L. *The Women Pioneers of North America*. Gardenvale, Quebec: Garden City Press, 1941.
- FAILLON, Etienne-Michel, P. S. S. *Vie de Mme d'Youville, fondatrice des Sœurs de la Charité de Villemarie dans l'Ile de Montréal, en Canada*. Villemarie: Chez les Sœurs de la Charité, 1852.
  – *Vie de M. Olier, fondateur du Séminaire de Saint-Sulpice*. 2 vols. Paris: Mme Vve Poussielgue-Rusand, libraire, 1853.
  – *Vie de la Sœur Bourgeoys, fondatrice de la Congrégation de Notre-Dame de Villemarie en Canada*. 2 vols. Villemarie: Chez les Sœurs de la Congrégation de Notre-Dame, 1853.

- *Vie de Mlle Mance et Histoire de l'Hôtel-Dieu de Ville Marie.* 2 vols. Villemarie: Chez les Sœurs de l'Hotel-Dieu, 1854.
- *L'Héroine chrétienne du Canada, ou Vie de Mlle Le Ber.* Villemarie: Chez les Sœurs de la Congrégation de Notre-Dame, 1860.

* FAUTEUX, Soeur Albina, S. G. M. *Love Spans the Centuries*, Volume 1, *1642-1821.* Translated by Antoinette Bezaire, S. G. M., from *L'Hôpital Général des Sœurs de la Charité, Sœurs Grises* (Montreal, 1915). Montreal: Meridian Press, 1987.
- *Vie de la Vénérable Mère d'Youville.* Montréal: Imprimerie des Sœurs Grises,
  1929.

• FAUTEUX, Ægidius. *La Famille D'Ailleboust.* Montréal: Librairie G. Ducharme, 1917.
- *Les Chevaliers de Saint-Louis en Canada.* Montréal: Les Editions des Dix, 1940.
- *Le Duel au Canada.* Montréal: Editions du Zodiaque, 1934.
- "Les Carnets d'un Curieux." 46 articles published in *La Patrie* from 16 September 1933 to 18 August 1934.
- "Un Médecin irlandais à Montréal avant la Cession." *Bulletin des Recherches Historiques*, vol. 23, nos. 10-12 (1917).

• FERLAND, Abbé J.-B.-A. *Cours d'Histoire du Canada.* 2 vols. Québec: Augustin Côté, Publisher and Printer, 1861, 1865.

• FERLAND-ANGERS, Albertine. *Pierre You et son fils François d'Youville.* Montreal: 1941.

• FILTEAU, Gérard. *La Naissance d'une Nation.* 2 vols. Montréal: Editions de l'Action Canadienne-française Ltée, 1937.

* FITTS, Sister Mary Pauline, G. N. S. H. *Hands to the Needy: Marguerite d'Youville, Apostle to the Poor.* Garden City, New York: Doubleday & Company, Inc., 1987. (Originally published 1950.)

• GARNAULT, Emile. *Le Commerce Rochelais, les Rochelais et le Canada.* La Rochelle: Typographie E. Martin, Sieur de Mareschal, 20, rue de l'Escale, 1893.

• GARNEAU, François-Xavier. *Histoire du Canada.* Fifth edition, revised by his grandson, Hector Garneau. 2 vols. Paris: Librairie Félix Alcan, 1913.

• GAUTHIER, Henri, P. S. S. *Sulpitiana.* Montréal: Au Bureau des Œuvres paroissiales de St-Jacques, 1926.

• GIROUARD, Désiré. *Lake Saint-Louis Old and New.* Montreal: Poirier & Bessette, Publishers, 1893. *Supplement*, 1900.

• GODBOUT, Père Archange, O. F. M. "Une Mystification historique." From *Culture* (1941).

- "Origine de familles canadiennes-françaises." From *L'Etat civil français*. Lille: 1925.
- GOSSELIN, Abbé Auguste. *L'Eglise du Canada depuis Mgr de Laval jusqu'à la Conquête*. Québec: Laflamme & Proulx, 1914.
  - *L'Eglise du Canada après la Conquête*. Québec: Imprimerie Laflamme, 1916.
- GOSSELIN, Abbé Amédée. *L'Instruction au Canada sous le Régime Français, 1635-1760*. Québec: Laflamme & Proulx, 1911.
- GOYAU, Georges. *Les Origines religieuses du Canada: une épopée mystique*. Paris: Bernard Grasset, MCMXXIV [1924].
  - *Histoire Religieuse* [of France]. Vol. VI of *Histoire de la Nation Française* by Gabriel Hanotaux. Paris: Librairie Plon-Nourrit et Cie, 1922.
- GRENTE, Monsignor. *Le Beau Voyage des Cardinaux français aux Etats-Unis et au Canada*. Paris: Librairie Plon, 1927.
* HAYNE, David M., and VACHON, André, eds. *Dictionary of Canadian Biography*. Toronto: University of Toronto Press, 1966-.
- HELYOT, Père Pierre. *Histoire des Ordres Monastiques, religieux et militaires et des Congrégations séculières des deux sexes jusqu'à nos jours, 1719*. Brief introduction, notes, and supplement by V. Philippon de la Madelaine. 8 vols. Guingamp: Chez B. Jollivet, imprimeur-éditeur, 1838.
- HENEKER, Dorothy A. *The Seigniorial Regime in Canada*. Quebec: Printed by Ls-A. Proulx, 1927.
- *HISTORIQUE de Notre-Dame du Perpétuel Secours de Charny*. Anonymous. Québec: L'Action Sociale Ltée, 1928.
- *HÔPITAL (L') général des Sœurs de la Charité (Sœurs Grises)*. Anonymous. 2 vols. Montréal: Imprimerie des Sœurs Grises de Montréal, 1915 and 1933. [Tome I by Sister Albina Fauteux (q.v. for translation, *Love Spans the Centuries*, Vol. I); Tome II by Sister Clémentine Drouin (translated by Sister Antoinette Bezaire as *Love Spans the Centuries*, Vol. II [Montreal: Meridian Press, 1988]).]
- HUGUENIN, Madeleine Gleason. *Portraits de femmes*. Privately printed. Montréal: Editions La Patrie, 1938.
- HUGUET LATOUR, L. A. *Annuaire de Ville Marie*. Montréal: Chapleau & Fils, éditeurs, 1878.
- JETTÉ, Madame Berthe. *Vie de la Vénérable Mère d'Youville, Suivie d'un historique de son Institut*. Montréal: Cadieux & Derome, 1900.
- JODOIN and VINCENT. *Histoire de Longueuil*. Montréal: Imprimerie Gebhart-Berthiaume, 1889.
- JUCHEREAU de Saint-Ignace, Mère Françoise. *Histoire de l'Hôtel-Dieu de Québec*. Montauban: Chez Jérôme Legier, n.d. [1751]. (See the Notes of Philéas Gagnon in *Essai de Bibliographie canadienne*, vol. II [1895], p. 237.)

- KALM, Pierre. "Voyage dans l'Amérique du Nord." *Mémoires de la Société Historique de Montréal*, Parts 7 and 8. Montréal: 1880.
- KEEFE, Sister Saint Thomas Aquinas, M. A., Grey Nun of the Sacred Heart, Philadelphia. *The Congregation of the Grey Nuns, 1737-1910*. Washington, D. C.: The Catholic University of America Press, 1942.
- KRUMPELMANN, The Reverend Cosmas, O. S. B. *In This Sign Thou Shalt Conquer*. Muenster, Saskatchewan: St. Peter's Press, n.d.
- LALANDE, Louis, S. J. *Une Vieille Seigneurie: Boucherville*. Montréal: 1891.
- LANGLOIS, Georges. *Histoire de la Population canadienne-française*. Montréal: Editions Albert Lévesque, 1934.
- LA POTHERIE, M. de Bacqueville de. *Histoire de l'Amérique Septentrionale, divisée en quatre tomes, depuis 1534 à 1701*. Paris: 1753.
- LAROCHE-HERON, C. de. *Les Servantes de Dieu en Canada*. Montréal: John Lovell Steam Presses, 1855.
- LA RONCIERE, Ch. de. *Le Père de la Louisiane, Cavelier de La Salle*. Tours: Maison Mame, 1936.
- *LA SOLIDE DÉVOTION à la Très Sainte Famille de Jésus, Marie et Joseph, avec un catéchisme qui enseigne à pratiquer leurs vertus*. Paris: Chez Florentin Lambert, rue Saint-Jacques devant Saint-Yves, M.DC.LXXV [1675].
- LAUVRIERE, Emile. *Histoire de la Louisiane française, 1673-1939*. Paris: G.-P. Maisonneuve, éditeur, 1940.
- *LES CAHIERS DES DIX*. Published annually from 1936 to 1944. Montréal: Editions des Dix.
- LE JEUNE, Père L. *Dictionnaire général du Canada*. 2 vols. Ottawa: Université d'Ottawa, 1931.
- LEMOINE, J. M. *Historical Notes on Quebec and Its Environs*. Quebec: C. Darveau, 1888.
  – *Monographies et Esquisses*. Québec: Théophile Levasseur, Editeur, n.d.
- LEPICIER, Cardinal, O. S. M. *Le Miracle, Sa nature, ses lois, ses rapports avec l'Ordre surnaturel*. French translation of the third Italian edition by Charles Grolleau. Paris: Desclée De Brouwer et Cie, éditeurs, 1936.
- LEYMARIE, A. Léo. *Exposition rétrospective des Colonies françaises de l'Amérique du Nord*. Illustrated catalogue. Paris: Société d'Editions Géographiques, Maritimes, et Coloniales, 1929.
- LORIN, Henri. *Le Comte de Frontenac*. Paris: Armand Colin & Cie, éditeur, 1895.
- MAGNAN, Hormisdas. *Dictionnaire historique et géographique des Paroisses, Missions et Municipalités de la Province de Québec*. Arthabaska: l'Imprimerie d'Arthabaska Inc., 1925.

- *MANDEMENTS, lettres pastorales et circulaires des évêques de Québec.* Published by Monsignor H. Têtu et Monsignor C. O. Gagnon. 6 vols. Québec: Imprimerie générale A. Côté & Cie, 1887-1890.
- *MANUEL DE PIÉTÉ à l'usage des Sœurs de la Charité, dites vulgairement Sœurs Grises.* Montréal: Imprimerie des Sourds-Muets, 1908.
- MARGRY, Pierre. *Mémoires et Documents, 1614-1754.* Paris: Maisonneuve, 1879.
  - *Les Pionniers Saintongeois et la Nationalité française au Canada.*
- MARION, Séraphin. *Pierre Boucher.* Québec: Ls-A. Proulx, 1927.
- MASSICOTTE, Edouard-Zotique. *Répertoire des Arrêts, Edits, Mandements, Ordonnances et Règlements, 1640-1760.* Montréal: G. Ducharme, libraire-éditeur, 1919.
  - "Les Tribunaux et les officiers de Justice à Montréal sous le régime français." *Mémoires de la Société Royale du Canada*, vol. X (1916).
  - "Un recensement inédit de Montréal 1741." *Mémoires de la Société Royale du Canada*, vol. XV (1921).
- MASSICOTTE, E.-Z. and ROY, Régis. *Armorial du Canada Français.* Montréal: Librairie Beauchemin Ltée, 1915.
- MAURAULT, Olivier, P. S. S. *La Paroisse, Histoire de l'Eglise Notre-Dame de Montréal.* Montréal and New York: Louis Carrier & Cie, 1929.
  - *Nos Messieurs.* Montréal: Les Editions du Zodiaque, 1936.
  - *Marges d'Histoire.* 3 vols. Montréal: Librairie d'Action canadienne-française Ltée, 1929.
- McCARTHEY, Justin. *Dictionnaire de l'Ancien Droit du Canada.* Québec: J. Neilson Bookseller and Printer, 1809.
* MITCHELL, Sister Estelle, SGM *The Spiritual Portrait of Saint Marguerite d'Youville.* Translated from the French *Le vrai visage de Marguerite d'Youville* by Sister Joanna Kerwin, Grey Nun of the Sacred Heart, Philadelphia, and Sister Antoinette Bezaire, Grey Nun of Montreal. N.p.: Imprimerie Quebecor Lebonfon, 1993. (Originally published as *From the Fatherhood of God to the Brotherhood of Mankind* [1977].)
- MONDOUX, Sœur. *L'Hôtel-Dieu premier hôpital de Montréal, 1642-1763.* Montréal: 1942.
- MOREAU DE SAINT MÉRY, Louis-Elie. *Description topographique, physique, civile, politique et historique de la partie française de l'Isle Saint-Domingue.* 2 vols. Philadelphia: Chez l'Auteur, at the corner of Front and Callow Hill Streets, 1797.
  - *Loix [sic] et Constitutions des Colonies françaises de l'Amérique sous le Vent.* 6 vols. Paris: Chez Quillau, No 3 rue du Fouare, et chez l'Auteur, No 12 rue Plâtrière, 1784.

- MORICE, Père A.-G., O. M. I. *Histoire de l'Eglise catholique dans l'Ouest canadien, Du lac Supérieur au Pacifique.* 3 vols. Montréal: Granger Frères, 1912.
- MORIN, L. P. *Le Vieux Montréal, 1611-1803.* Published by H. Beaugrand. Montréal: 1884.
- MORIN, Sœur Marie. "Annales de l'Hôtel-Dieu de Montréal." *Mémoires de la Société Historique de Montréal*, Part 12. Montréal: 1921.
- MORISSET, Gérard. *Coup d'Œil sur les Arts en Nouvelle-France.* Québec: 1941.
  – *Les Eglises et le Trésor de Varennes.* Québec: Medium Enr., 1943.
  – *Philippe Liébert.* Québec: Collection Champlain, 1943.
- MURPHY, Edmund Robert. *Henry de Tonty: Fur Trader of the Mississippi.* Baltimore: The John Hopkins Press, 1941.
- NADEAU, Gabriel. "La Bufothérapie sous le Régime Français, Mme d'Youville et ses crapauds." Off-print from *l'Union Médicale du Canada* (August 1944).
- NOISEUX, Grand Vicaire. *Liste Chronologique des évêques et des prêtres … de l'Amérique du Nord.* Québec: Cary & Cie, 1834.
- *NOVA FRANCIA.* Publication of the Société d'Histoire du Canada. Editorial and Administrative Offices, 1 bis, rue François Ier, Paris (1930).
- OLIER, Jean-Jacques. *Catéchisme Chrétien pour la Vie intérieure.* New edition. Paris: Séminaire Saint-Sulpice, 1925.
  – *La Journée Chrétienne.* New edition. Paris: Séminaire Saint-Sulpice, 1925.
- PICHÉ, Odessa. *Index des Municipalités et des Paroisses de la Province de Québec de 1896 à 1924.* Québec: Ministère de la Colonisation, des Mines et des Pêcheries, 1924.
- PRUD'HOMME, L'honorable Juge L.-A. "Pierre Gaultier de Varennes, sieur de La Vérendrye." *Bulletin de la Société Historique de Saint-Boniface* (1916).
- RAMSAY, The Reverend D. S. *Life of Madame d'Youville.* Montreal: Printed at The Grey Nunnery, 1895.
- *RAPPORT de l'Archiviste de la Province de Québec.* Annual publication 1921.
- *REVUE des Questions Historiques* (Septembre 1934). Paris: 32, avenue Marceau.
- ROCHEMONTEIX, Camille de, S. J. *Les Jésuites et la Nouvelle-France au XVIIe siècle.* 3 vols. Paris: Letouzey et Ané, éditeurs, 1895-1896.
- ROY, Antoine. *Les Lettres, les Sciences et les Arts au Canada sous le Régime français.* Paris: Jouve & Cie, éditeurs, 15, rue Racine, 1930.
- ROY, J.-Edmond. *Histoire de la Seigneurie de Lauzon.* 5 vols. Lévis: Mercier & Cie, Libraires-imprimeurs, 17, Côte du Passage, 1897-1904.

- ROY, Régis. "Les Intendants de la Nouvelle-France." *Mémoires de la Société Royale du Canada* (1903).
- ROZ, Firmin. *Vue générale de l'Histoire du Canada, 1534-1934.* Paris: Paul Hartmann, éditeur, 1934.
- SAINT-PIERRE, Arthur. *L'Œuvre des Congrégations religieuses de charité dans la province de Québec.* Montréal: 1930.
- *SAINT-VALLIER (Mgr de) et l'Hôpital-général de Québec, Histoire du Monastère de Notre-Dame des Anges.* Anonymous [Sœur Saint-Félix, née O'Reilly]. Québec: C. Darveau, 1882. (See Notes of Philéas Gagnon in *Essai de Bibliographie canadienne*, vol. I, p. 437.)
- TANGHE, Raymond. *Géographie Humaine de Montréal.* Montréal: Librairie d'Action canadienne-française Ltée, 1928.
- TANGUAY, Abbé Cyrien. *Dictionnaire généalogique des familles canadiennes.* 7 vols. Montréal: 1871-1890.
- TÊTU, Monsignor Henri. *Les Evêques de Québec.* Québec: Narcisse Hardy, éditeur, 1889.
- *THE CASE of the Canadians distressed by Fire at Montreal.* Montreal: 1765.
- *UNE DISCIPLE de la Croix: La Vénérable Marguerite d'Youville, Marie-Marguerite Dufrost de La Jemmerais Veuve d'Youville.* Anonymous [Sœur Sainte-Blanche, S. G. Q.]. Québec: Sœurs de la Charité, 1932.
- *URSULINES (LES) de Québec. Depuis leur établissement jusqu'à nos jours.* 4 vols. Anonymous [Mère Saint-Thomas]. Québec: 1863-1866. (See Notes of Philéas Gagnon in *Essai de Bibliographie canadienne*, vol. I, p. 508.)
- VALLEE, Arthur. *Michel Sarrazin, 1659-1735, Un Biologiste canadien.* Québec: Ls.-A. Proulx, 1927.
- VIGER, Jacques. *Ma Saberdache.* Montréal: 1843. Manuscript in the Archives of the Seminary of Quebec.
  – *Rapports sur les Chemins, Rues, Ruelles et Ponts de la Cité et paroisse de Montréal.* Montréal: John Lovell, 1841.
- WALLACE, William Stewart. *The Dictionary of Canadian Biography.* Toronto: Macmillan, 1926.

Index of Names

An Attempt at Locating on the Map of Paul Labrosse the Places Inhabited or Frequented by Madame d'Youville
By Albertine Ferland-Angers

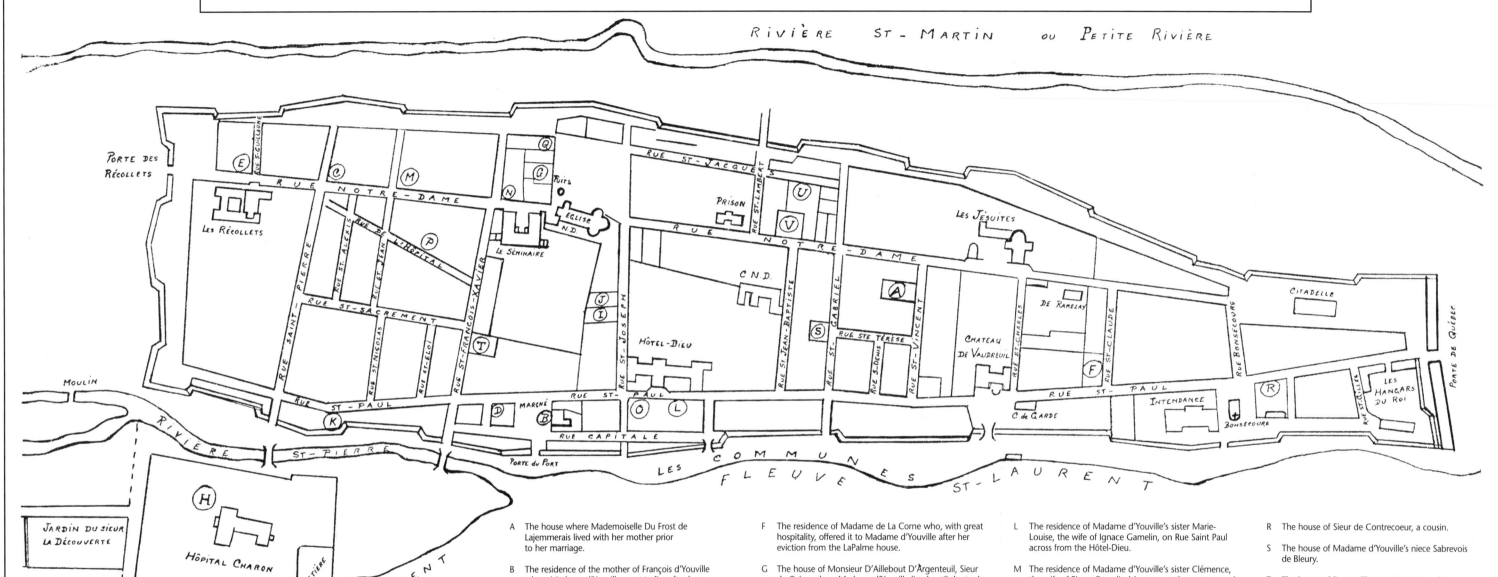

A The house where Mademoiselle Du Frost de Lajemmerais lived with her mother prior to her marriage.

B The residence of the mother of François d'Youville where Madame d'Youville went to live after her marriage. After she became a widow, she opened a small mercer's business there and remained there until the foundation of her Community.

C The house of Madame Le Verrier de Rousson where the Community of the Grey Nuns of Montreal came into being.

D The house of Monsieur Fontblanche where Madame d'Youville and her poor were given shelter after the fire of 31 January 1745.

E The house of Dominique Janson-LaPalme from which the Governor, Monsieur Josué Du Bois Berthelot de Beaucours, had Madame d'Youville evicted.

F The residence of Madame de La Corne who, with great hospitality, offered it to Madame d'Youville after her eviction from the LaPalme house.

G The house of Monsieur D'Aillebout D'Argenteuil, Sieur de Cuisy, where Madame d'Youville lived until she took over the administration of the General Hospital.

H The General Hospital of Montreal, or of the Charon Brothers, at Pointe-à-Callières.

I The place of residence of the Sieur de Varennes, the uncle and godfather of Madame d'Youville.

J The residence of the explorer Pierre Gaultier de La Vérendrye, the uncle of Madame d'Youville.

K Another house belonging to the Sieur de La Découverte on the south side of Rue Saint Paul.

L The residence of Madame d'Youville's sister Marie-Louise, the wife of Ignace Gamelin, on Rue Saint Paul across from the Hôtel-Dieu.

M The residence of Madame d'Youville's sister Clémence, the wife of Pierre Gamelin-Maugras, at the western end of Rue Notre Dame at the corner of Rue Saint Jean.

N The Elementary Schools of the Parish of Notre Dame attended by Madame d'Youville's two sons.

O The residence of Madame Louis Haincque de Puygibault, the aunt and godmother of Madame d'Youville.

P The residence of Sieur Robert de La Morandière whose wife, Marguerite Haincque de Puygibault, was Madame d'Youville's cousin.

Q The residence of Joseph De Noyelles, a cousin by marriage to Marie-Charlotte Petit de Livilliers.

R The house of Sieur de Contrecoeur, a cousin.

S The house of Madame d'Youville's niece Sabrevois de Bleury.

T The house of Doctor Thaumur Lasource whose daughter Thérèse was Madame d'Youville's first associate.

U The house of Doctor Timothée Sylvain, the second husband of Madame d'Youville's mother.

V The house of Doctor de Feltz, Madame d'Youville's physician.

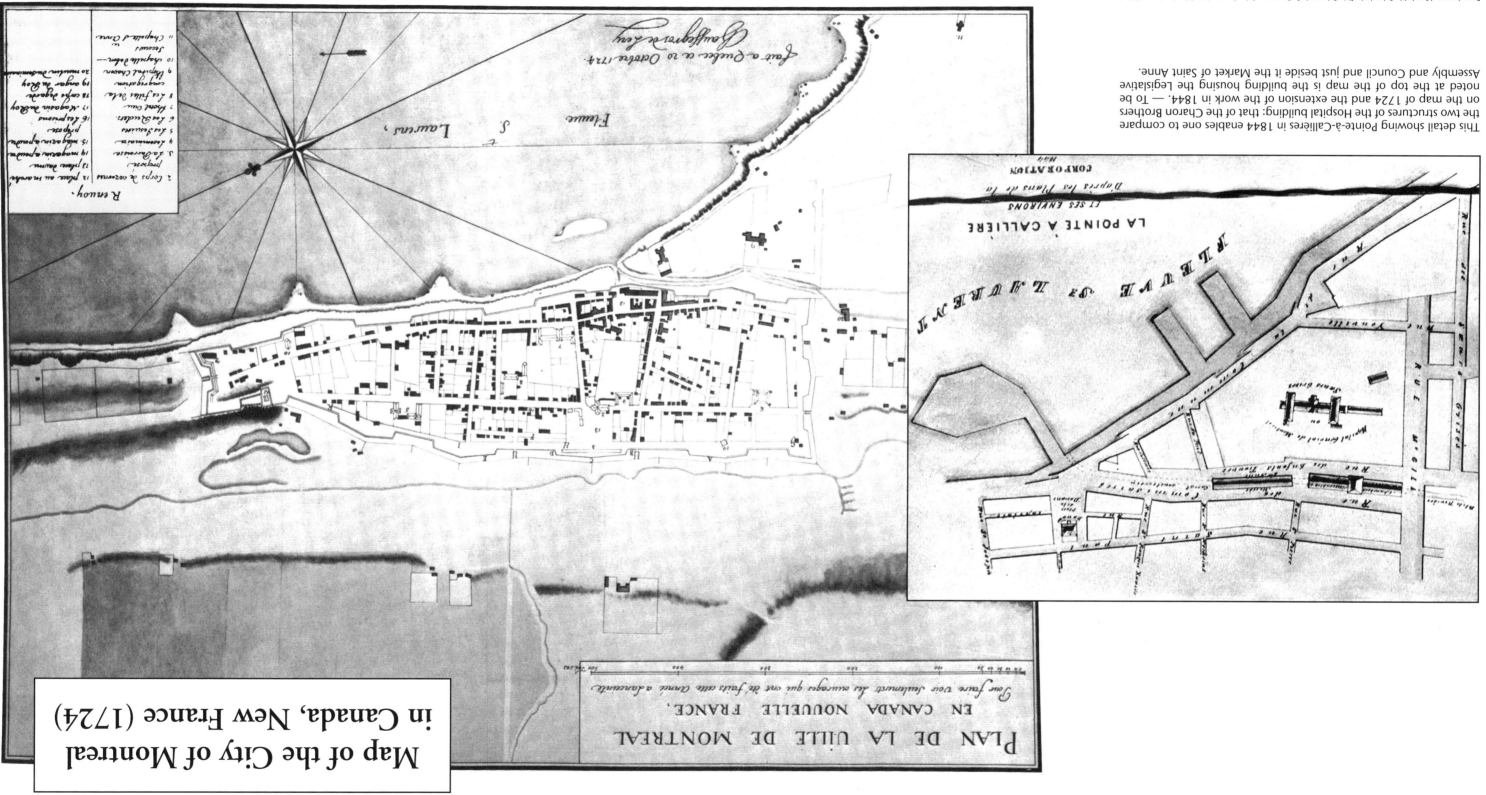

Map of the City of Montreal in Canada, New France (1724)

PLAN DE LA VILLE DE MONTREAL EN CANADA NOUVELLE FRANCE,
Pour faire voir seulement les ouvrages qui ont été faits ette année a loisir.

Fait a Quebec a 10 Octobre 1724.

This detail showing Pointe-à-Callières in 1844 enables one to compare the two structures of the Hospital building; that of the Charon Brothers on the map of 1724 and the extension of the work in 1844. — To be noted at the top of the map is the building housing the Legislative Assembly and Council and just beside it the Market of Saint Anne.

LA POINTE À CALLIERE ET SES ENVIRONS
D'après les Plans de la CORPORATION